TALKING
TO THE
ENEMY

ALSO BY SCOTT ATRAN

Cognitive Foundations of Natural History

In Gods We Trust

Plants of the Petén Itza' Maya
(with Ximena Lois and Edilberto Ucan Ek')

The Native Mind and the Cultural Construction of Nature
(with Douglas Medin)

Ba'asyir

Hambali

Kh. Sheikh Moha

Mukhlas

Amrozi

Azahari

ais

Wan Mat

Faiz Bafana

TALKING
TO THE
ENEMY

FAITH, BROTHERHOOD,
AND THE (UN)MAKING
OF TERRORISTS

SCOTT
ATRAN

An Imprint of HarperCollins Publishers

HarperCollins books may be purchased for educational, business, or sales promotional use. For information, please write: Special Markets Department, HarperCollins Publishers, 10 East 53rd Street, New York, NY 10022.

Grateful acknowledgment for permission to reproduce illustrations is made to the following: CIA, *The World Factbook*, page 6; the Jamestown Foundation/*The Jamestown Monitor*, page 20; public domain, located at the Capilla Real, Granada, Spain, page 44; Dirk Laabs, page 110; the U.S. State Department, page 175; the Spanish Ministry of the Interior, pages 177, 183, 188, 192; Manuel Marlasca/Luis Rendeles, page 192 (top left); *El Mundo*, page 192 (bottom left); Ben Aboud, al-Amrani, Akhlifa, and Achebak families, page 211; Naif Al-Mutawa, page 481. Illustrations on pages viii, 16, 26, 82, 118 147, 175, 194, 219, 243, 353, 374, 404, 408, and 490 are courtesy of the author.

FIRST EDITION

Designed by Mary Austin Speaker

Map on page 249 by Paul J. Pugliese

Library of Congress Cataloging-in-Publication Data has been applied for.

ISBN: 978-0-06-134490-9

10 11 12 13 14   OV/RRD   10 9 8 7 6 5 4 3 2 1

I dedicate this work to Vasily Arkhipov, the deputy commander of a Soviet nuclear submarine off the Cuban shore who said no to his comrades and may have saved the world.

That was on October 27, 1962, around the time my father came home from his defense job and told me at the doorstep to our house that there was "only a twenty-percent chance, son" the next day would never come.

No terrorist action today remotely poses that kind of existential threat for our world, and I hope you'll keep that in mind in reading on.

School's out at Abdelkrim Khattabi Primary in the Jamaa Mezuak neighborhood of Tetuán, Morocco. Five of the seven plotters in the Madrid train bombing who blew themselves up attended the school, as did several volunteers for martyrdom in Iraq.

CONTENTS

PART V: WAR PARTIES—GROUPS, GOD, AND GLORY

PART VI: "THE MOTHER OF ALL PROBLEMS"— PALESTINE, THE WORLD'S SYMBOLIC KNOT

PART VII: THE DIVINE DREAM AND THE COLLAPSE OF CULTURES

PREFACE

America will never be destroyed from the outside. If we falter, and
lose our freedoms, it will be because we destroyed ourselves.
—ABRAHAM LINCOLN

This work is about what almost everybody believes in but only some are willing to die for. It's about believing in something worthwhile that transcends the interests of individuals and their immediate families. It's about the nature of faith, the origins of society, and the limits of reason. It tries to answer the question, "Why do people believe in a cause, and why do some die and kill for it?"

The answer in a nutshell is that people don't simply kill and die for a cause. They kill and die for each other. This work will show how and why this has come about: in human evolution and through the history of humanity; from the jungles of Southeast Asia and the political wastelands of the Middle East, to New York, London, and Madrid.

Many creatures will fight to the death for their close kin. But only humans fight and sacrifice unto death for friends and imagined kin, for brotherhoods willing to shed blood for one another. The reasons for brotherhoods—unrelated people cooperating to their full measure of devotion—are as ancient as our uniquely reflective and autopredatory species. Different cultures ratchet up these reasons into great causes in different ways. Call it love of God or love of group, it matters little in the end. Modern civilizations spin the potter's wheel of monotheism to manufacture the greatest cause of all, humanity. All the great political isms preach devotion unto death for the sake of humanity. The salvation of humanity is a cause as stimulating as it is impossible to achieve.

Especially for young men, mortal combat in a great cause provides the ultimate adventure and glory to gain maximum esteem in the eyes of many and, most dearly, in the hearts of their peers. By identifying their devotion with the greater defense and salvation of humanity, they commit themselves to a path that allows mass killing for what they think is a massive good. The terrible history of war in the twentieth century is that more than conquest, greed, or even self-defense, all major participating nations justified killing civilian noncombatants on a massive scale to advance or preserve "civilization." Jihadism is a transnational social and political movement in the same vein.

If so many millions support jihad, why are only thousands willing to kill and die for it? We shall see that young men willing to go kill and die for jihad were campmates, school buddies, soccer pals, and the like, who become die-hard bands of brothers in a tragic and misbegotten quest to save their imagined tribal community from Crusaders, Jews, and other morally deformed, unrepentant, and therefore subhuman beings. It's in groups that they find the camaraderie of a cause, however admirable or abhorrent, and the courage and commitment that come from belonging to something larger.

Terrorists generally do not commit terrorism because they are extraordinarily vengeful or uncaring, poor or uneducated, humiliated or lacking in self-esteem, schooled as children in radical religion or brainwashed, criminally minded or suicidal, or sex-starved for virgins in heaven. Terrorists, for the most part, are not nihilists but extreme moralists—altruists fastened to a hope gone haywire.

And there is basis for real moral grievance, whether one believes exclusively in secular human rights or in the religious ethics of the house of Abraham. There's no excuse, "collateral damage" or otherwise, for the killing of innocents in Afghanistan, Iraq, Palestine, Chechnya, and elsewhere. But a divine justice that rewards the killing of innocents in the name of an eye for an eye, exalting death over life for its own believers, is the will to power of a cruel and sadistic Moloch that would leave the whole world blind.

THE SCIENCE OF UNREASON

I am an anthropologist. In the last three and a half decades, I have traveled to many places and met many kinds of people, and I have never run across anyone—believer, agnostic, or atheist—who isn't fascinated by religion. I've been with would-be martyrs and holy warriors from the Atlantic shore of Morocco to the remote forests of Indonesia, and from Gaza to Kashmir. The accounts of my experiences with aspiring killers for God and martyr wannabes and the empirical studies that come out of these encounters should make you think about terrorism in a new way: less alien and less fearsome. A scientific study of faith, like the scientific study of love, is just beginning. Applied to terrorism—one of the most compelling faith-related issues of our day and one that has largely been immune to serious scientific study because of its passion—science may someday produce downright revelation.

So it is stunning that few scientists have any idea of the progress that has been made in the study of religion. This is especially remarkable among the recent spate of so-called new atheists who believe—as Bertrand Russell (one of my heroes) and Karl Marx before them—that science has a moral duty to relieve society of the baneful burden of religion. The conceit is intellectually silly, but the politics of it isn't. In the United States, the candidacy for nearly every political high office pivots upon terrorism and how the candidate will handle its menace. Perhaps never in the history of human conflict have so few people with so few actual means and capabilities frightened so many. Even some of our best scientists and philosophers have bought into the hysteria, clamoring for the death of God and the end of faith as the cure for terrorism. It's not rejection of God but the ignorance of the meaning of God for the history of humanity and the role of faith in human thought and behavior that unsettles me. The atheism of utopian enlightenment, like the godless gulag or guillotine, can be hazardous to others.

In this work I also explore the practical consequences of understanding sacred values. Sacred values differ from the values of the marketplace and from realpolitik by incorporating moral beliefs that drive action in ways out of proportion to prospects for success. Such extreme behaviors as suicide bombings and the atrocities of the seemingly intractable political conflicts in the Middle East, Central and South Asia, and beyond are often motivated by sacred values.

These deeper cultural values that are bound up with people's identity often trump other values, particularly economic ones. But studies of populations in conflict and encounters with their leaders suggest that understanding an opponent's sacred values may offer surprising opportunities for breakthroughs to peace or at least to lessening violent competition between groups.

Through these practical considerations of how to face terrorism and to deal with seemingly intractable political conflicts, this work is also intended to provide more general insight into the origins and evolution of religion, the epidemics of war, the rise of civilizations, the creation of the concept of humanity, and the limits of reason. Whatever bit of this ambition succeeds makes the effort behind it worthwhile.

One caution: I talk to people in the languages that I've learned along the way but never formally studied. So I often write things down as I hear them. If there's a common spelling of a word or phrase in Latin characters I'll usually go with it (for example, in French-speaking countries, the English *sh* is rendered *ch*, so it's Rashid in Palestine but Rachid in Morocco), though sometimes I try to standardize (for example, Koran, instead of Quran, Qur'an; Islamiyah instead of Islamiya, Islamiyya, Islamiyyah, Islamiyyeh, Islamia; and so on).

And finally, I'm mostly used to writing dry things for scientific audiences. Should my efforts to be closer to the general reader sometimes seem too raw and personal or overly practiced because I thought there was a ring in the phrasing of an idea, I ask for your indulgence. The subject matter is more deserving.

ACKNOWLEDGMENTS

I am grateful to Isaac Ben Israel, Noam Chomsky, Baruch Fischhoff, Joseph Henrich, Lawrence Hirschfeld, Pervez Hoodbhoy, Douglas Medin, Ariel Merari, Richard Nisbett, Ara Norenzayan, Dan Sperber, and Blanka Zizka. All will no doubt recognize the strong influence that our collaborations and communications have had on what I've written. Joining Lord John Alderdice, Robert Axelrod, Richard Davis, Jeremy Ginges, Marc Sageman, and Khalil Shikaki on science projects in the field aimed at lessening threats to international peace was a particular privilege.

France's Centre National de la Recherche Scientifique and the Institut Jean Nicod at the École Normale Supérieure in Paris have given me the professional freedom to work as long and hard on any problem that I needed to. Charles Strozier and Jeremy Travis at the John Jay College of Criminal Justice gave a home to my research projects when other universities shied away from anything to do with actually talking to terrorists. The U.S. National Science Foundation, Air Force Office of Scientific Research, Office of Naval Research, and Army Research Office supported much of the scientific research that underpins the stories I tell.

My thanks also go to Andrea Fatica, Laura Reynolds, Dominick Wright, and Justin Magouirk, who coordinated the efforts of my research teams and responded with patience and diligence to often fitful demands. John Brockman prodded me into writing this work; Bob Axelrod and Lisa Chase endeavored mightily to edit out the error and confusion; and Lisa Chase and Dan Halpern at Ecco/HarperCollins helped me to realize that less can be more. Ximena Lois, our son Emiliano, my daughters Tatiana and Laura, and my brother, Harris, and our parents have worried about me as they shouldn't have had to. My hope is that ways will be found in the spirit of this work to ultimately lessen the worries of all people I care for.

Part I

THE CAUSE

In the fullness of spring, in the presence of those who never really leave us, it is the life that we honor. Lives of courage, lives of sacrifice, and the ultimate measure of selflessness—lives that were given to save others.

—BARACK OBAMA, ABRAHAM LINCOLN NATIONAL CEMETERY, ELWOOD, ILLINOIS, MAY 30, 2005

I and thousands like me have forsaken everything for what we believe.

—MOHAMMAD SIDIQUE KHAN, ELDEST OF THE JULY 7, 2005, LONDON UNDERGROUND SUICIDE BOMBERS

People . . . want to serve a cause greater than their self-interest.

—U.S. SENATOR AND THEN–REPUBLICAN PRESIDENTIAL CANDIDATE JOHN MCCAIN, VILLANOVA UNIVERSITY, PENNSYLVANIA, APRIL 15, 2008

CHAPTER 1

SULAWESI: AN ANTHROPOLOGIST AT WORK

I t was during a series of psychological studies I was running with Muslim fighters on the Indonesian Island of Sulawesi about the scope and limits of rational choice that I noticed tears welling up in the eyes of my traveling companion and bodyguard, Farhin. He had just heard of a young man who had recently been killed in a skirmish with Christian fighters, and the experiment seemed to bring the youth's death even closer to home.

"Farhin," I asked, "did you know the boy?"

"No," he said, "but he was only in the jihad a few weeks. I've been fighting since Afghanistan [the late 1980s] and I'm still not a martyr."

I tried consoling him: "But you love your wife and children."

"Yes." He nodded sadly. "God has given this, and I must have faith in the way He sets out for me."

"What way, Farhin?"

"The way of the mujahid, the holy warrior."

Farhin is one of the self-styled "Afghan Alumni" who fought the communists in Afghanistan in the 1980s. He was funneled by the future founder of Jemaah Islamiyah (JI), Abdullah Sungkar, to the Abu Sayyaf camp near the Khyber Pass to train with other Indonesian volunteers. There he also studied "Principles of Jihad" (*fiqh al-jihad*) with Palestinian scholar Abdullah Azzam, Osama

Bin Laden's mentor and originator of the concept of *al-qaeda al-sulbah* ("the strong base," or revolutionary Muslim vanguard). Later Farhin hosted future 9/11 mastermind Khaled Sheikh Mohammed in Jakarta, and in 2000 Farhin helped blow up the Philippines ambassador's residence. Although that operation was something of a dress rehearsal for the October 2002 Bali bombing that killed more than two hundred people in the deadliest single terrorist attack against the West since 9/11, Farhin declined to find suicide bombers for Bali and instead occupied himself running a training camp to battle Christians in Sulawesi.

Farhin completed my psychological experiments on the trade-offs people are willing to make in pursuit of a violent cause. The general idea is that when people consider things sacred, even if it's just bits of a wall or a few words in a language one may not even understand, then standard economic and political ways of deciding behavior in terms of costs and benefits fall apart. Farhin responded "irrationally," as most of the others had, without regard to material advantage or utility.

"Is a person a better and more deserving martyr if he kills one rather than ten of the enemy or ten rather than a hundred?" I asked.

"If his intention is pure, God must love him, numbers don't matter, even if he kills no one but himself."

"What if a rich relative were to give a lot of money to the cause in return for you canceling or just postponing a martyrdom action?"

"Is that a joke? I would throw the money in his face."

"Why?"

"Because only in fighting and dying for a cause is there nobility in life."

In the 2004 preface to *Dreams from My Father*, Barack Obama submits that post-9/11, history is challenging us again with a fractured world, and that we must squarely face the problem of terrorism.

Except that he cannot hope to understand "the stark nihilism" of the terrorists. "My powers of empathy," he laments, "my ability to reach another's heart, cannot pretend to penetrate the blank stares of those who would murder innocents with abstract, serene satisfaction."[1]

In fact, the eyes of the terrorists I've known aren't blank. They are hard but intense. Their satisfaction doesn't lie in serene anticipation of virgins in heaven. It's as visceral as blood and torn flesh. The terrorists aren't nihilists, starkly or ambiguously, but often deeply moral souls with a horribly misplaced sense of justice. Normal powers of empathy can penetrate them, because they are mostly ordinary people. And though I don't think that empathy alone will ever turn them from violence, it can help us understand what may.

I'm an anthropologist who studies what it is to be human— that's what anthropologists study—by empathizing with (without always sympathizing) then analyzing the awe-inspiring behaviors alien to our culture. Terrorism awes me as much as anything I've known, enough to pull me back from years of fieldwork in the rain forest with Maya Indians to try to understand and convey what makes humans willing to kill and die for others.

POSO, SULAWESI, AUGUST 9–10, 2005

Sulawesi is a remote isle of the Indonesian archipelago located between Borneo and New Guinea. The older name for the island is the Celebes, a Portuguese denomination that inspired in the anthropologist I would one day become a yearning to know what it would be like to be a different kind of human being from myself. Forty years ago, most of what I surmised about that distant other world came from the colonial classic, *Pagan Tribes of Borneo*, written by Charles Hose and William McDougall in 1912.[2] It kept company on my bookshelf with another favorite, T. L. Pennell's *Among the Wild Tribes of the Afghan Frontier*,[3] written three years earlier. Hose and McDougall portrayed the hunter-gatherer world of some of the Borneo and Celebes tribes as an echo from the predawn of human history: "The principal characteristics of this primitive culture," they wrote, "are the absence of houses or any fixed abode; the ignorance of agriculture, of metal-working, and of boat-making; and the nomadic hunting life, of which the blow-pipe is the principal instrument." Some of the tribes preyed on the flesh of others.

In the summer of 2005, I finally made it to the Celebes. Sulawesi had changed immensely from the preliterate society described nearly a century before, though afterimages of that predawn era remained. There were thatched and prefab houses for permanent shelter. Agriculture abounded, including the cultivation of cloves for kretek cigarettes and chocolate by way of the Maya and their Spanish conquerors. Motorized boats noisily plied the Gulf of Tomini with all manner of trade goods. People were shod in plastic and leather footwear made in China, wore Japanese watches on their wrists, and pressed cell phones from Finland to their ears. Some of the men sported American baseball caps and some of the

Map of Indonesia.

women wore the *hijab*, the Arab headscarf. The night stage was a dusty parade of Pan-like shadows, half human and half machine, flickering in the spotlights of an endless succession of motorbikes.

It was like other frontier zones between the modern and premodern worlds, where historical time is awfully compressed: along the Amazon or Congo, in the shantytowns that service the "exotic" tourist resorts that have become a big part of the world's largest business, or along the U.S.-Mexico border of the Rio Grande. In these places, modern civilization hardly developed. It mostly just happened, without the thick web of human relationships, ideas, and artifacts that make cultural life comfortable to mellow and mature. Ever new, always in decay, as Claude Lévi-Strauss—who commiserated with me that he only wanted to be a musician but having no talent became an anthropologist instead—once mused about the sad urban tropics of the New World.[4] There will be no steps worn by generations of pilgrims here.

In our shopping-mall world, exotic cultures are either charming and sensual, like that of the Tahitians, or decorative and exploitable, like that of the Pueblo Indians of the American Southwest. But the mild euphoria of West meeting Other is short-lived for someone who lingers too long. The gods of these other cultures are clichés, even for the descendants of the ancestors who worshipped them—a mix of existential angst and touchy-feely happy hermeneutics about harmony and oneness with nature and one another. The real gods, of passions and war, of weather and chaos, and the care and consolation of celestial cycles, are dust-dead or mummified in museums. Now, as the long, easy hegemony of the West over the world lurches to an end, the newly decadent and the exotic are left free as orphans. Hardly anyone cares to exploit their labor, integrate or understand them, or even notice if they were to drop off the face of the earth.

I came to Poso, a small town in Central Sulawesi that probably contains more violent Islamist groups per square meter than any other place on earth. I saw no blowpipes but many waists sporting the padang, a machete-like metal knife, and Kalashnikovs hanging over the shoulders and backs of numerous young men. Some groups still preyed on others, now killing them for their faith rather than for their meat. The groups in this little Eden of hell often call themselves "Lashkar this" or "Lashkar that," *lashkar* being a derivation of the Arabic for "army" (only when I went to Pakistan's Azad Kashmir did I find a comparable concentration of *lashkars*, as they are called there). Shortly before I arrived, two blasts in the market of the nearby Christian town of Tentene killed twenty-two people. Soon after I left, three Christian girls were beheaded on their way to school and there was another bombing. A police investigator sent me pictures of the girls' headless bodies in their skirts and blazers. I thought of my own girls and felt sick at hell's ravenous appetite. Not to be outdone, Christian militia beat and beheaded a couple of Muslims. This was after the Indonesian government executed three Christian militiamen, including a cleric, for leading a mob that massacred more than two hundred Muslims in a boarding school during a previous bout of religious war that killed more than a thousand people of both faiths. Sometimes, the *lashkars*, like bloodied sharks, would turn upon their own kind.

There's nothing peculiar to Sulawesi in all of this, save the tropical lull of its Venus flytrap beauty. The modern Balkan tribes of Europe have behaved no differently. And the greater national tribes have recently done these sorts of things on an industrial scale. Ever since the Upper Paleolithic, when our hominid forebears began forming larger groups that could dominate any threat from wild animals, people had become their own worst predators. It is the larger family, or "tribe," and not the mostly ordinary individuals in it, that increasingly has seemed to me the key to understanding the extraordinary violence of mass killing and the murder of innocents.

By "tribe" I don't mean the usual anthropological sense of a small-scale society that is organized largely on the basis of territory and kinship, especially corporate descent groups like clans and lineages. Most of the Muslims in Central Sulawesi are not tribal in this narrow sense. They are recent immigrants from different parts of Java, and some of the Christian fighters are imported from East Timor. There is an extended sense of tribe similar to philosopher Jonathan Glover's outlook in *Humanity*,[5] his very disturbing chronicle of twentieth-century atrocities. This broader idea of tribe refers to a group of interlinked communities that largely share a common cultural sense of themselves, and which imagine and believe themselves to be part of one big family and home. Today the "imagined community," as political scientist Benedict Anderson once referred to the notion of the nation,[6] extends from city neighborhoods to cyberspace.

The Jewish and Arab peoples, to give an example, are still tribal in both the narrow and the extended sense, each believing itself to be genetically linked and to share a cultural heritage. This is so despite the fact that the actual genealogical relationships invoked by Jewish Cohens (including descendants of the Hasmonean high priests), Levites, and Israelites or by Arab Adnanis (including Mohammed's tribe, the Quraish) and Qahtanis are mostly historical fictions. In the extended sense, Nazi Germany imagined itself in terms of a tribe, the fatherland, and pushed the Soviet Union away from pretensions of universal brotherhood and back to a Mother Russia, which, with the Stalin priesthood, in fact mobilized tribal passions for sacrifice in the Great Patriotic War. The United States, which originally had few tribal sentiments because of its immigrant beginnings, has become increasingly tribalized through its widening economic and political power clashes around the world. Americans increasingly fear immigration and assimilate this into the fear of terrorism to form the new tribal concept of "homeland" security. By invoking the tribe, people needn't listen to argument and are ready to rally themselves in defense of their

imagined family's honor and home against real or perceived enemies: from the hamlet wars of Jews and Arab tribes around Jerusalem to continental conflicts for the sake of America's homeland,
Russia's motherland or China's fatherland.

There are important historical differences between these
various tribal imaginings, which I will later discuss in detail. But
regardless of these differences, political scientists might interpret
all such tribal appeals as a way of "reducing transaction costs,"[7]
shortcutting the need to persuade and mobilize people. The call to
jihad in Poso is tribal, even though most of the jihadis who are here
have come to the call from elsewhere.

In 1998, a Muslim candidate was elected local governor, mark-
ing the fact that the immigrant Muslim population had surpassed
the local population that had been converted to Christianity in the
nineteenth century by missionaries from the Reformed Church of
Holland. (Muslims now number 45 percent of the total population
in Poso regency; Christians, 42 percent; and the rest are Hindu and
Buddhist.) There are various stories about how the violence began
at Christmastime in 1998, which happened that year to coincide
with Ramadan, the holy Muslim month of fasting. One oft-told
tale is that during the Muslim night prayers, some Christians were
drinking and making a ruckus in the front yard of a mosque. The
mosque's warden asked them to leave. The next day, the Christians
waylaid the warden on the street and taunted him about eating
pork for breakfast, then beat him. Next, furious Muslims attacked
Christian shops selling alcohol and also the oldest church in Poso.
Tensions rose, and one day in April 2000, Christian bands invaded
the town and attacked Muslim residents and shops, mostly with
stones, torches, and wooden staves. Retaliation begat retaliation.
Local ironsmiths began improvising homemade guns and bullets,
and by the end of the year, tens of thousands of refugees were on
the move and hundreds were dead on both sides. As word spread,
Muslims from as far away as Spain came to fight for their brethren

in the name of jihad. Despite intervals of long quiet, Poso was still the most active conflict area in Indonesia over the next decade.

In Poso, I ran psychological studies of Muslim mujahedin like Farhin on the role of sacred values in limiting rational choice, based in part on some of the initial results I had from my previous work with Palestinians. I would give each Indonesian holy warrior a questionnaire to complete. They soon began talking among themselves about what answers they should give, so I had them go off into separate places and promise not to talk. They dutifully complied. Some asked if they could consult their religious leaders about this or that question. When I said no, they accepted without protest. Except for the fact that they were mujahedin, they behaved no differently from my students.

Question A: "Would you give up a roadside bombing if it meant you could make the only pilgrimage to Mecca?" Most answered yes.

Question B: "Would you give up a suicide bombing to instead carry out a roadside bombing if it is possible?" Most answered yes.

Question C: "Could you give up a suicide bombing if it meant you could make the only pilgrimage to Mecca in your lifetime?" Most answered no.

From the perspective of the rationality that is thought to underlie standard economic or political calculations, this is not a reasonable set of responses. Rationality requires logical consistency in preferences: If A is preferred to B and B is preferred to C, then A must be preferable to C. Here, however, we have A (pilgrimage) preferred to B (roadside bombing), and B preferred to C (suicide bombing)—yet C preferred to A. I'll have more to say on the peculiarities and consequences of this sort of "moral logic" later in this book.

The nonrationality I am interested in exploring is not merely a formal or analytic one. It is also eruptive and emotional. As Farhin and I descended from Poso, we came to the former site of the first training camp in the area that Farhin set up for Jemaah Islamiyah.

The people living near the site are mostly Balinese. Farhin had rightly anticipated that no one would look for a jihadi camp in the middle of a Balinese population. If today there is a gentle people, it's the Balinese. Especially in Central Sulawesi, they have kept their good humor and grace as war swirls around them. We happened upon a Balinese wedding near the campsite. It was a colorful Hindu ceremony, elegant and delightful.

I turned to Farhin. *"Helu kthir"*—very beautiful and sweet—I said in my broken Levantine Arabic, which I had picked up many years before when I lived with the Druze people.

"Wahsh!" he rasped. (Animals!) "Look at their women; I swear by God that if I had a bomb I would use it here."

I stopped in mid-chortle, the instant I noticed the heavy-lidded look that I had seen in the eyes of killers before, in Guatemala, and would see again in Pakistan.

"Farhin, issa nahnu asadaqa?" (Now, we are friends?)

"A habibi." Yes, my beloved. He grinned as his eyes and voice lightened. *"Mundhu bada'a al-hawa yajruju min sayara."*—"After the wind left the car," which was his broken Arabic, picked up from Arabs at the Saddah training camp near the Khyber Pass in the later stages of the Soviet-Afghan war, for "Ever since the flat tire" that we had fixed while laughing at one another.

"Would you kill me for the jihad?" I asked.

"No problem," he said, this time in English, and with a laugh. Then that look again: *"Aiwah, sa'aqtruk."* (Yes, I would kill you.)

I thought I had come to the limits of my understanding of the other and could go no further. There was something in Farhin that was incalculably different from me . . . yet almost everything else about him was not.

"In all those years, after you and the others came back from Afghanistan, and before JI started up, how did you stay a part of the jihad?" I asked.

"We Afghan Alumni never stopped playing soccer together,"

he replied matter-of-factly. "That's when we were closest together in the camp"—then a megawatt smile—"except when we went on vacation, to fight the communists."

"Vacation?" I asked, puzzled because Farhin had deadpanned the word.

He smiled. "Holiday, yes, that's what we called the fighting. Training wasn't such fun."

"Fun? Do you think war is fun, Farhin?"

"War is noble in a true cause that is worth more than life. Fighting for that is a strong feeling, strong."

"And what really kept you together?" I asked again just to be sure.

"We played soccer and remained brothers—in Malaysia, when I worked on the chicken farm [of exiled Jemaah Islamiyah founder Abdullah Sungkar], then back in Java."

Maybe, then, it was something about the relation between God and soccer that was eluding me. Maybe people don't kill and die simply for a cause. They do it for friends—campmates, schoolmates, workmates, soccer buddies, bodybuilding buddies, paintball partners—action pals who share a cause. Maybe they die for dreams of jihad—of justice and glory—and devotion to a family-like group of friends and mentors who act and care for one another, of "imagined kin," like the Marines. Except that they also hope to God to die.

Then it came on me as embarrassingly obvious: It's no accident that nearly all religious and political movements express allegiance through the idiom of the family—brothers and sisters, children of God, fatherland, motherland, homeland. Nearly all major ideological movements, political or religious, require the subordination or assimilation of the real family (genetic kinship) to the larger imagined community of "brothers and sisters." Indeed, the complete subordination of biological loyalty to loyalty for the cultural cause of the Ikhwan, the "Brotherhood" of the Prophet, is the original meaning of the word *Islam*, "submission."

But what is it that binds imagined kin into a "band of brothers" ready to die for one another as are parents for their children? That gives nobility and sanctity to personal sacrifice? What is the cause that co-opts the evolutionary disposition to survive?

NATURE AND NURTURE

That afternoon I began posing "switched-at-birth" scenarios to Farhin and his brother mujahedin on whether the children of Zionist Jews raised by mujahedin families since birth would become good Muslims and mujahedin or remain Zionist Jews. Nearly all mujahedin, leaders and foot soldiers alike, answered that the children would grow up to be good Muslims and mujahedin. They usually said that everyone's *fitrah* (nature) is the same and that social surroundings and teaching make a person good or bad. This is how the alleged emir (leader) of Jemaah Islamiyah, Abu Bakr Ba'asyir, put it in an interview that I conducted with him in Cipinang prison in Jakarta:

> Environment can change people's *fitrah*—nature. Human beings have an innate propensity to *tauhid*—to believe in the one true God. If a person is raised in a Jewish environment, he'll be Jewish. But if he's raised in an Islamic environment, he'll follow his *fitrah*—nature. Human beings are born in *tauhid*, and the only religion which teaches and nurtures *tauhid* is Islam. As I said, according to Prophet Mohammed, the only things that can change a child into becoming Jewish or Christian are his parents or his environment. If he is born in an Islamic environment, he'll survive. His *fitrah* is safe. If he is born in a non-Islamic environment, his *fitrah* will be broken and he can be a Jew or a Christian. Human beings have *tauhid* since birth. However, in their life's journey they could have an epiphany to be devout Muslims. In contrast, a Muslim who fails to resist the devil's temptation can become an apostate.

American white supremacists and members of the Christian Identity movement, when asked the same question, more often give a different answer: Jews are born bad and always will be bad. It's an essentialist take on human nature, of the biologically irreversible kind, that underlies a history of racism in the West.

Shortly before the last run that day of our hypothetical scenarios, Rohan Gunaratna, a Sri Lankan who heads a program in terrorism studies out of Nanyang Technological University in Singapore, received a text message on his cell phone from an informant in another *laskar* saying that I was to be "eliminated" that evening after dark. Rohan had helped me arrange entry into Poso, running interference with the Indonesian government and some of the mujahedin commanders who occasionally "consulted" for him. "Don't worry, my friend," he said, bobbing his head left and right. "We'll get out of town before sundown. But this gives you time for a few more interviews." With a grin like a Cheshire cat's, he can sling his arms around the shoulders of killers and be calming. He'd make a good politician.

The previous day, a former mujahedin commander named Atok had warned me: "Don't go up to Poso, our people shoot whites on sight. I would have shot you dead myself last year. But killing whites or Christians is not the best way to defend Islam." I told him this change of heart was a relief, and he smiled wryly. Atok was tough as nails, but he positively melted when describing how finger-lickin' good the chicken was at the Makassar Kentucky Fried Chicken, a favorite eatery and planning spot for Sulawesi's top jihadis. Farhin and Rohan agreed that if we left at night and I sat between them in the backseat, I would be OK, and I trusted them. My guess is that one of the leaders of the Muslim charities I had been talking with didn't want me snooping around anymore. The charities, like Kompak and even the local Red Crescent (the Islamic equivalent of the Red Cross) are very much involved in the sectarian fighting and sport their own militias.

Atok, a former commander of Muslim militia in Poso: "I don't shoot whites on sight anymore."

I came into Sulawesi as a French citizen (I'm a U.S. citizen too, but mujahedin don't much like talking to Americans these days), but the text message implied that I had been Googled, which meant that whoever was after me knew that I was an American working on terrorism. Google can be a real bummer for anyone who wants to do fieldwork on the subject. I now have about twenty-four hours on the ground before someone does some Internet surfing and doesn't like what he reads about me. It's a new dimension of "fast-track anthropology" for me, academically so frustrating, but I've also learned a lot in a day.

On the wooden deck of the restaurant where I was doing my

interviews, overlooking a pastel seascape framed by low green hills, a radio was chanting sorrowful Koranic verses while two lovely young girls, their doe eyes framed by veils, fidgeted with a hi-fi belching out early Beatles. Dusk was coming and my pulse was racing. I'd started smoking kretek clove cigarettes to calm down, although I'm no smoker. Strange how the light at day's end also calms and leads to reflection, especially in this soft evening air. I found myself back with my grandmother at a Beatles concert at New York's Shea Stadium in the summer of 1965 with Ringo singing "Act Naturally," then in the spring of 1971, when she stood up in the audience and yelled at Margaret Mead during a lecture at the American Museum of Natural History: "Why don't you leave my grandson alone and let him be a doctor! Now you'll get him cooked by cannibals!"

There's a daredevil high to this sort of fieldwork, a feeling similar to what war correspondents feel, or at least those I've interacted with. Many people just pretend that dangerous and exciting things happen to them. I guess I share with some reporters not merely a dream of adventure, but an irresistible urge to live my dream and accomplish something by it, if only in witnessing what others cannot see but should.

But this line of work has its nightmarish moments. My interpreter, Huda, broke my reverie when he told me he'd been questioning a "retired" commander of Laskar Jihad, one of the first outside jihadi groups to come to Poso. "He said if a Christian would be raised by the mujahedin, the person would turn out fine, but a Jew comes from hell and is always a Jew." That was the first time in Indonesia I had gotten that response. But the real stunner came next: "And he asked me if *you* are a Jew."

"So what did you tell him?" I asked, aware what the answer would be but hoping it wouldn't.

"I told him we're all brothers in this world, so what does it matter if you're a Jew?"

As the *laskar* commander trained his gaze on me, I said in light and measured tones: "Phone the car now, in English, like you're asking for a cup of coffee." I excused myself to go to the bathroom . . . and out the back door. It was sundown, and I was silently cursing up a storm for the mess I'd gotten myself into—for the umpteenth time vowing that I'd just stay home and tend my vineyards from now on—when Farhin and Rohan pulled up and I hightailed it out of there.

We bounced through the dusk along a pothole-loving road to the Christian town of Tentene, arriving on a beautiful night: the flat silhouette of Tentene's surroundings made haunting by the sounds of night birds and tales of the *laskar*. The plan was to interview the clergyman in charge of the Central Sulawesi Christian Church, Rinaldy Damanik, a Batak from Sumatra. Farhin had fought and killed many Christians, but he now put on a shirt with flower patterns and sprinkled himself with cologne because . . . well, every red-blooded jihadi knows how wanton Christian girls are. I wondered if they would sense the bit of death that lingers about Farhin, or just his streak of the comic.

The Reverend Damanik had been arrested after the initial bout of sectarian violence in the region and taken to Jakarta. There he shared prison quarters in succession with Sayem Reda, one of Al Qaeda's master filmmakers; with Imam Samudra, the convicted operations chief of the October 2002 Bali bombings; and with Abu Bakr Ba'asyir, the emir of Jemaah Islamiyah.

Damanik told me how he managed to sneak a Koran in to Sayem Reda after prison authorities had denied him one. "He thanked me and cried," Damanik said. "He wasn't really a bad man at heart." Damanik also spent long hours with Imam Samudra, agreeing that the State was corrupt, but "I said to him that fighting corruption and abuse by killing tourists and people who had harmed no one was gravely wrong in his God's eyes and mine. Imam Samudra said to me, as a joke or maybe not, that it's a shame we didn't meet and talk first, before the Bali bombing, when together we might have come up with a better strategy to change the government."

I especially wanted to hear how the reverend and the emir got along, and also to get the former's reaction to a ridiculous tale told on the Muslim side about the *kupukupu* (butterfly) battalion of bare-breasted Christian women who would wiggle at the Muslim men and lure them to their deaths. My jaw dropped into the coffee cup when the Rev. Damanik casually asked, "Would you like to meet one of the butterflies?" It turns out that they danced their own men to war, albeit with covered breasts. They even called themselves the Butterfly Laskar. Over time, Muslims and Christians have formed a whole zoo of *laskars* that reflect one another's fantasies and fears: the *laskar labalaba* (spider army), *laskar mangoni* (bird army), the *laskar kalalaver* (bat army) that struck terror in the night.

I was even more surprised when Damanik told me how he had enjoyed the company of Ba'asyir, whom he sincerely respected. How Ba'asyir's wife regularly brought them both fruit and seemed worried about the reverend's health. Ba'asyir would confirm in the Cipinang Prison interview that the respect was mutual and strong, although he qualified the friendship that any Muslim could properly offer *kuffar* (infidels):

Yes, I was visited and was respected by him. I have a plan, if Allah allows me, to pay a visit to his house. That's what I called *muamalah dunia*—daily relations in the secular life. Because Al Koran article sixty, verse eight says that "Allah encourages us to be kind and just to the people who don't fight us in religion and don't help people who fight us." It means that we can help those who aren't against us. On these matters we can cooperate, but we also have to follow the norms of Sharia. . . . So it is generally allowed to have business with non-Muslims. We can help each other; for example, if we are sick and they help us, then, if they become sick, we should help them. When they die we should accompany their dead bodies to the grave though we can't pray for them.

Abu Bakr Ba'asyir had formally associated himself with Osama Bin Laden in 1998 (though he denied it and said the letter I had proving it so with his signature was a Mossad-CIA forgery). In 2003, Ba'asyir had been accused of plotting the assassination of then-Indonesian president Megawati Sukarnoputri and of helping to mastermind the 2002 Bali bombings. Ustaz (Teacher) Ba'asyir, as the other inmates and prison authorities reverently called him, was acquitted of both charges. I asked Ba'asyir (via an interpreter) the same sorts of questions about martyrdom and "rational choice" that I had asked would-be Palestinian martyrs and the Poso muja-hedin. For example: "Would it be possible for an act of martyrdom to be aborted if the same results can be assured by other actions, like a roadside bomb?"

Ba'asyir was the portrait of a self-assured man. He was surrounded by numerous acolytes, including convicted Jemaah Islamiyah bombers, and by prison guards who showed him deference and let him preach as he pleased from his hawk's roost. Between the white skullcap and the knee upon which rested his chin, there were sprigs of mostly salt and some pepper hair, large spectacles, and a toothy grin that

Abu Bakr Ba'asyir, alleged emir of Jemaah Islamiyah.

exuded vulpine gentility. I was booted out of the prison: "No whites now, too many coming in," I was told. So I conducted the interview over two days by text-messaging my interpreter, Taufik, who was inside with a tape recorder.

This is a parable Ba'asyir told Taufik:

If there are better ways to carry out an action and we don't have to sacrifice our lives, those ways must be chosen. Because our strength can be used for other purposes. The reason the *ulema* [learned clergy] allow this comes from a story of the Prophet Mohammed.

There was a young man who received magic training to be one of King Fir'aun's magicians. Kings in the past had magicians. [Former Indonesian president] Suharto had many. When this magician became an old man, he was asked to find a replacement. In his search, he met a priest and learned from him.

He became a better magician after learning from the priest rather than from other magicians and started to spread the word, and he received the ability to heal blind people. He healed many people, including King Fir'aun's blind minister.

Then, when this minister was able to see again, he offered to fulfill any request in his power that the magician might make. The magician replied that he hadn't healed the minister, Allah had. "He is my lord and your lord. If you want to be cured and you admit the existence of Allah, you will be cured." Then the minister went to his office.

King Fir'aun asked him, "Who has cured you?"

"The one who cured me was Allah."

"Who's Allah?"

"Allah is my God."

Fir'aun was angry and tortured the minister, who admitted that he was told this by the magician who had healed him. Then this magician was told that he would be forced to abandon his conviction and to stop his activity. But this was a matter of principle for the magician, who did not want to abandon his conviction.

Many people tried to assassinate the magician. Finally, the magician said that if King Fir'aun wants to kill him, it's easy. What Fir'aun needs to do is to gather many people in a field, put the magician in the middle, and shoot arrows into his body. But before doing that they must say, "Bismillah" [In the name of God]. When the arrows finally struck the magician, he died, but his mission to spread the word of Islam was accomplished. From this story, many *ulema* [clerics] agree to allow martyrdom actions as long as such actions will bring many benefits to the Islamic *ummat* [communities].

In The *Descent of Man*,[8] Charles Darwin wrote:

The rudest savages feel the sentiment of glory. . . . A man who was not impelled by any deep, instinctive feeling, to sacrifice his life for the good of others, yet was roused to such action by a sense of glory, would by his example excite the same wish for glory in other men, and would strengthen by his exercise the noble feeling of admiration. . . . It must not be forgotten that although a high standard of morality gives but slight or no advantage to each individual man and his children over other men of the same tribe, yet that an increase in the number of well endowed men in the advancement of the standard of morality will certainly give an immense advantage of one tribe over another tribe.

Glory is the promise to take life and surrender it in the hope of giving greater life to some group of genetically bound strangers who believe they share an imagined community under God (or under His modern secular manifestations, such as the nation and humanity). It's the willingness of at least some to give their last full measure of devotion to the imaginary that makes the imaginary real, a waking dream—and for others, a waking nightmare.

CHAPTER 2
TO BE HUMAN: WHAT IS IT?

Ah, but a man's reach should exceed his grasp,
Or what's a heaven for?

—ROBERT BROWNING, "ANDREA DEL SARTO," 1855

On a second-floor walkup off a narrow alley in Gaza's Jabali-yah refugee camp, I came to interview the family of Nabeel Masood. The neighborhood knew Nabeel as a kind and gentle boy, but he changed after the death of his two favorite cousins, who were Hamas fighters. No one remembers him wanting revenge for their deaths so much as a meaning. There had already been more than a hundred Palestinian suicide attacks before March 14, 2004, when Nabeel and his friend Mahmoud Salem from Jabaliyah, both of them eighteen, were dispatched by Muin Atallah (an officer in the Palestinian Preventive Security Service). Their mission, arranged jointly by Hamas and Fateh's Al Aqsa Martyrs Brigades, was to attack the nearby Israeli port of Ashdod. Security officials believe the two were sent to launch a 9/11-style mega-terrorist attack and blow themselves up near the port's bromine tanks.

Had they succeeded in this, the effects could have been devastating, with poisonous gases spreading to a 1.5-kilometer radius, killing thousands within minutes. As it was, they killed themselves and eleven other people. On March 22, 2004, Israel retaliated by assassinating Hamas founder and spiritual leader Sheikh Ahmed Yassin with rocket fire from a gunship as he was leaving a Gaza City mosque. Yassin's successor as leader of Hamas, pediatrician Dr. Abdel Aziz al-Rantisi, called the Ashdod bombers heroes and promised more attacks like it. An Israeli missile struck him down in Gaza on April 17, 2004.

Nabeel Masood's mother was crying softly and reading a letter when I walked in the door. She handed me the letter (written in English).

Letter of Appreciation and Admiration

Mr. and Mrs. Masood, it gives me great pleasure to inform you that your son Martyr Babeel [sic]*, has been doing well in English during the period he has spent in the 11th grade, call 3. He has passed his tests successfully. The thing I really appreciate. He was first in his class. He was distinguished not only in his hard studying, sharing, and caring, but also in his good morals and manhood. I would really like to congratulate you for his unique success in both life and the hereafter. I would like to thank from the bottom of my heart all who shared in building up Nabeel's character. You should be proud of your son's martyrdom.*

With all my respect and appreciation.

Mr. Ismael Abu-Jared

The evening before he died, he had gone to the mosque, where he sat quietly alone for hours, then visited his friends in the neighborhood and came home. I asked Nabeel's father: "Do you think the sacrifice of your son and others like him will make things better for the Palestinian people?"

"No," he said. "This hasn't brought us even one step forward."

The boy's mother only wanted back the pieces of her son's body. His father had emptied the house because it is Israel's policy to

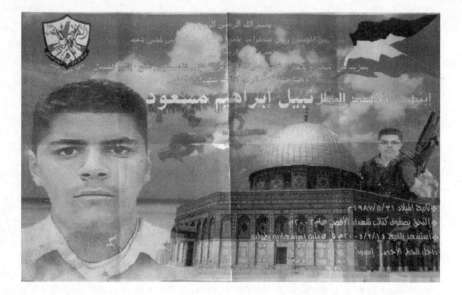

Al Aqsa Martyrs Brigade poster of Nabeel Masood, Ashdod suicide bomber.

destroy the family home of any *shaheed*, or holy warrior, although he and his wife would have done anything to stop their son if they had known. "It can't go on like this," the father lamented. "There can only be two states, one for us and one for the Israelis."

I asked if he was proud of what his son had done. He showed me a pamphlet, specially printed by Al Aqsa Martyrs Brigades and endorsed by Hamas, praising the actions of his son and the two other young men who accompanied him.

"My son loved life. Here, you take it." He pushed the pamphlet into my hands. "Burn it if you want. Is this worth a son?"

Outside in the narrow street, kids were playing fast-paced, acrobatic soccer off the high house walls, some marked with fading, ghostlike posters of the Martyr Nabeel. "What do you feel about what Nabeel did?" I asked.

"His courage will make us free!" exclaimed a boy, kicking the ball. Another boy echoed his words and gave a ferocious kick back.

Nabeel was, for one flaming moment, the hero every boy here wanted to be.

This kind of courage to kill and die is not innate. It's a path to violence that has to be cultivated and channeled to a target. The culture of violent jihad is the landscape on which the path is trodden. Fellow travelers—mostly friends and some family—walk and furrow the path together. They leave pheromone-like tracers for those who come after, letters of love for their peers and heroic posters and videos with the thrill of guns and personal power made into an eternally meaningful adventure through sacred-book-swearing devotion to a greater community and cause.

I returned to Israel on a Friday evening. Unlike Jerusalem, which is quiet on the Jewish Sabbath, Haifa atop Mount Carmel was alight. Joyful groups of high school girls were scurrying everywhere. I asked three hitchhikers who were holding hands, just as my daughters do with their friends, if anything special was up. "Yes," one girl said, very sweetly. "You're not from Haifa; you see, it's a weekend and holiday, and no school!" Hamas leaders contend that these young girls, too, merit death because they will become Israeli soldiers. The Hamas weekly, *Al Risala*, proclaimed in an editorial that "martyrs are youth at the peak of their blooming, who at a certain moment decide to turn their bodies into body parts—flowers." In a moment of naive epiphany, I felt that if this blossoming young woman could just spend a little time with one of these young men from Gaza neither would need to die. But the wall grows between them each passing day, blocking all human touch.

Then I remembered something Nabeel's father had said. I had written it down, but it hardly registered at the time: "My son didn't die just for the sake of a cause, he died also for his cousins and friends. He died for the people he loved." And my puzzling over that sentiment then became an overarching theme of study for this book.

BALTIMORE, OCTOBER 1962–NOVEMBER 1963

The day after President Kennedy's October 22, 1962, Cuban missile crisis speech, I asked my mother, as she drove me home from school, what it was all about. I remember hearing the president talk about getting ready for "danger" and "casualties" but also a "God willing" to see things turn out right. "Ask your father when he gets home," she said. I knew this time it wasn't just me in trouble.

The next morning in school we had a "duck and cover" drill: A siren went off over the school intercom and we scurried under our desks with hands over our heads to protect ourselves from the flying glass an exploding atom bomb would surely produce. A new world war, I imagined, wouldn't be much different from the one my father had been in. But because of atom bombs, I thought it would be a fast war that my family could survive inside a big steel filing cabinet with some water and an air hole. In the house we had an old copy of the *Life* magazine article, "H-Bomb Hideaway." Only $3,000!

I heard my father's car pull into the driveway. I remember very clearly—as clear as an old memory can be—my heart pounding as I asked: "Dad, is there going be an atomic war?" He looked at me with a strained but loving smile and ruffled my hair as he had when he told me that my baby brother, Harris, had been in a car accident and was in the hospital. "Only about a 20 percent chance, son." (Many years later my father told me that during the crisis he had been asked to determine whether F-4 Phantom jets armed with Sparrow missiles could knock down Soviet nuclear missiles launched from Cuba. The answer: no.)

In *Essence of Decision: Explaining the Cuban Missile Crisis*, Graham Allison and Philip Zelikow note that some interpreters of the Cuban missile crisis offer assurances to readers that "rational actors" worked predictably within an efficient "organizational behavioral paradigm" to save the day.[1] Hardly. Perusing the ExComm tapes, you do get an impression in hindsight that Jack and Bobby Kennedy were two of the only reasonable characters around. Not because they were clear about what was to be done, but because they were terribly unsure that the unassailably logical arguments for going to war were sane. If the president had listened to the generals and hawks—the ones with the best security credentials—then the Cubans, the Russians, and a great many of us would have been blown to kingdom come.[2] It was because the president and his brother cajoled an officer to delay word of the U.S. spy plane under his command having been shot at over Cuba that standard "rules of engagement" to massively retaliate weren't triggered. Unbeknownst to the Americans, Soviet submarine B-59 also happened into history, armed with nuclear torpedoes that the ship's commander, Valentin Savitsky, had targeted on a U.S. Navy vessel.[3] But chance and luck put Vasily Arkhipov, the sub's chief of staff, on board, and it was he who, in most versions told, calmed the commander and spared the world.[4]

I was ten years old, not bad at comparing things with numbers and figuring odds, and I thought the chance of us all being hit by A-bomb-driven flying glass was about the same as losing in a game of Russian roulette (which one of the Catholic boys in the neighborhood had explained to me) with a six-shooter. At that moment I remembered the same boy, Jay, also telling me about the "Immaculate Conception," in which God came into a lightbulb and threw it down to earth, where it broke all over the Virgin Mary. And I thought about God playing Russian roulette with us all, with the Jews and Catholics and Communists, with atom-bomb lightbulbs.

In the early afternoon of November 22, 1963, I happened upon Mr. Danish, our math teacher at Sudbrook Junior High School, nervously pacing out circles in the hall with a portable radio pressed hard to his ear, mumbling with eyes shut, "My God, oh my God." Mr. Danish was still at it an hour later when I passed him on my way to Mr. Feser's arts and crafts class. A few minutes into class, the school principal's voice broke in over the intercom:

"President Kennedy was shot in Dallas, Texas, today, where he died. Our prayers go the president's family, to our new president Lyndon Johnson, and to our country. School will be closed for the remainder of the day. Please all stand in a moment of silence."

A boy named Keith, who was standing across the worktable from me, made a funny face to his friend, Mike Beser, who giggled. Mr. Feser, wild with emotion, kicked Mike and dragged him into the hall. Poor Mike had giggled at the wrong time. But with that incident I became especially interested in Mike's father, Jake Beser, who worked with my father at the Westinghouse Defense Center in Baltimore.

I knew that Jake Beser was the only person to fly both atomic bombing missions against Japan. Ever since the events of the previous year, I had become obsessed with how to save my family and friends from atom bombs, and the president's assassination only made it more urgent to seek a solution. I asked my father how Mr. Beser could have done what he did. Was he the only one who liked it so much the first time that he did it again? My brother Dean would later interview Jake about this for a class project, and Jake's response was much the same as my father's: "We were still fighting Japan. They were throwing kamikazes at us and seemed willing to die to their last man. We were expecting to go to Japan as part of the invasion force. We thought more of us and more of them would likely die than in any previous campaign of the war. Then the bombs were dropped and it was all over. We came home instead of going on to fight and maybe die." (I wish I had asked my brother for a copy of that interview, but he died in a plane crash that forever made me wary of happiness.)

My father told me many years later that Jake confided to him while they were driving somewhere together that he only got to fly the A-bomb missions because he had been "chasing a skirt," but my father said he slept through the details of how Jake's pursuit of the girl landed him in the *Enola Gay* over Hiroshima. Jake apparently also had walloped General Curtis LeMay after he told Jake: "If I'd known you were a kike, I wouldn't have let you go [on the A-bomb mission]." The general never pressed charges, but Jake was the only one on the crew who wasn't decorated or promoted. After the Kennedy tapes were released to the public, people learned that LeMay, an unfunny version of the General Jack D. Ripper character in *Doctor Strangelove*, had been pressing the president to preemptively strike Cuba and perhaps even Russia during the Cuban missile crisis. Kennedy had recommended, instead, that those around him pause to read *The Guns of August*, by Barbara Tuchman, about the lead-up to World War I through a rapid chain of events that no one at the time had the patience or prescience to think through and avoid. There were some 20 million deaths in World War I, slightly fewer than half of them civilian, versus 72 million in World War II, with about two-thirds civilian deaths. Projecting the trend of casualties in major wars over the last two centuries (a mathematical trend known as a "power-law distribution"),[5] one might expect major wars to decline in frequency by about a factor of three but deaths from those wars to increase by a factor of ten (and to be overwhelmingly civilian).

"Maybe without Jake I wouldn't be here. Or you," I remember my father saying. I asked my father why America, or God, didn't first show Japan how bad the bomb could be, and not have to prove it by melting the eyeballs of so many thousands of people. (I don't recall a satisfactory answer, and to this day I still haven't heard one from anybody.) That's when I painted in Halloween colors and Gothic script the words: "God exists, or if he doesn't, we're in trouble."[6]

Some of my fellow nonreligious scientists believe that science is better able than religion to constitute or justify a moral system that regulates selfishness and makes social life possible. In fact, there doesn't seem to be the slightest bit of historical or experimental evidence to support such faith in science (though science shows that institutionalized religious belief is not necessary to regulate selfishness or make social life possible). Neither do I think scientists are particularly well suited to provide moral guidance to society. As Noam Chomsky put it in response to my criticism of "new atheists" who claim to replace faith-based morality with science-based morality: "On the ordinary problems of human life, science tells us very little, and scientists as people are surely no guide. In fact they are often the worst guide, because they often tend to focus, laser-like, on their professional interests and know very little about the world."[7]

Of course, very good scientists seek to discover profound relationships that may underlie seemingly unconnected ideas and facts. What science can do is study religion and faith, just as it studies stars and stones or bodies and brains. Science can break down the components of religion and faith into simpler parts in order to make broader and deeper connections between them and other parts of animal and human nature. For now, though, the science of religion and faith—"faith" here including belief in jihad—is still pretty slight.

"Is it not that God and society are one and the same?" French sociologist Émile Durkheim famously conjectured.[8] By instilling tribal trust and common cause, imagined kinship and faith beyond reason, religions enable strangers to cooperate in a manner that gives them an advantage in competition with other groups. In so doing, religions sanctify and incite fear (which is the father of cruelty) but also hope (which is the friend of happiness). Between the Hecatomb and Humanity, religion's polar products, the destinies of civilizations continue to evolve.

THE CAUSE

Humans and other primates have two preoccupations in life: health and social relations. Actually, they're often the same: socialize to survive. But unlike our hairy distant kin, humans are also obses-sively cause-seeking animals. So much so that we can't help believ-ing that the world was created for the cause seekers, or at least for the collectivity that seeks to show through sacrifice how much it cares. This belief that our world was intended for the committed community is what I call the Cause. It is a mystical thing, a product of our biological evolution and history that gives spiritual purpose to our lives. How and why this illusion came to drive humanity and make itself real in the creation of cultures and the religious rise of civilizations is the deep background that frames this work.

So what's the foreground about? It's about attempting to demys-tify terrorism, lessen our fears, and reduce the dangers of violent overreaction by talking with people in the field—especially terror-ists, but also ordinary folk who know them, support them, and can easily become them—and then using science to probe deeper into how they think, feel, and behave. These are tales and studies in the wild about how and why people come naturally to die and kill for the Cause—people almost never kill and die just for the Cause, but also for each other: for their group, whose cause makes their imagined family of genetic strangers—their brotherhood, father-land, motherland, homeland, totem, or tribe.

A SOCIAL CREATURE, EVEN "I"

It's only in the last few years that my thinking has deeply changed on what drives major differences, such as willingness to die and kill for a cause, between animal and human behavior. I once thought that individual cognition and personal aptitudes, together with the influence of broad socioeconomic factors like markets, media, and means of production, determined most human behavior. Now I see that friendship and other aspects of small-group dynamics, such as raising families or playing on a team together, trump most every-thing else in moving people through life. But I also see religion, and quasi-religious nationalist or internationalist devotion such as patriotism and love of humanity, as framing and mobilizing that movement with purpose and direction.

This change of mind was a long time coming. American culture, as most people who travel know, is exceptionally individualistic in one sense, but also inordinately fond of groups, at least in competition: in sports, in business, and even in the scholarly academy. Personally, I'm not comfortable with collective movements or fashions of any sort. I don't like crowds, parades, political rallies, or spectator sports (except when my children are involved), and I'm even uncomfortable when people talk about winning or working as a team. Maybe that part of my social brain is just missing, like my memory for lyrics.

Whenever I would see military marches, I'd think that members of our species didn't deserve their big brains, which waste so much cognitive power on the mindless refinement of swarming and herding. "Is that what it is to be human?" I'd wonder. "Regimented apes with guns?" At Columbia College in New York City at the end of the 1960s, the campus and the society around were feverish with social movement. I was keen on revolution then—we had a committee with professors, students, and cafeteria workers all set to change the world, Mao-style—and I was more than happy to raise my hand in favor of banning fraternities and ROTC (a college elective that focuses on military knowledge and preparation and that is unfortunately still banned at Columbia).[9] But I couldn't get into the shrill swing of demonstrations against capitalists (mostly parents and other people with money) and pigs (police), or any of the crazy collective actions to promote "worker-student solidarity." It wasn't that I realized that skill with a skillet didn't qualify someone to pass judgment on how quantum mechanics or the *Iliad* should be taught. I just didn't like being a groupie.

But I think I've come to understand that without groups, and without sincere love of them by some, our species probably wouldn't have survived. Neither would civilizations and their achievements have come about, for better or worse. A person alone can analyze history but can't make it without others.

Two lines of evidence, which converge in this book, convinced me of the importance of group dynamics in determining personal identity and behavior. The first comes from my own fieldwork and psychological studies with a certain sector of mujahedin, or Muslim holy warriors, and their supporters—particularly suicide bombers, their friends and families. The second line of evidence that people are preeminently social actors rather than individual performers comes from my reading of evolutionary biology and human history.

Where do these two lines of evidence come together? In the fact that jihad fights with the most primitive and elementary forms of human cooperation, tribal kinship and friendship, in the cause of the most advanced and sophisticated form of cultural cooperation ever created: the moral salvation of humanity. To understand the path to violent jihad is to understand how universal and elementary processes of human group formation have played out in history and have come to this point.

Like *crusade*, the word *jihad* has many nuanced and even contrary connotations. Thinkers I respect tell me that I shouldn't use the word *jihad* because it's a notion that, in the sense of an inner struggle for rightness and truth, applies to a vastly greater number of peaceful people than to terrorists, and that is true. In Rwanda, for example, jihad is taught as "the struggle to heal," and people in that most Christian of African countries have been converting in droves to Islam because many Muslim leaders and families there are widely seen, rightly, as having saved thousands of non-Muslims from being massacred while churches, governments, and the United Nations turned their backs during the genocide of the 1990s.[10] But the terrorism that I will talk about is called jihad by the perpetrators themselves, the jihadis. Of that there is no doubt. We'll see that the idea of violent jihad itself covers a range of commitments.

At one end, there's the strictly nationalist (*wataniyah*) jihad of Hamas, which rejects any aid or association involving Al Qaeda and its ilk in the struggle for a faith-based nation. At the other end, there's a new wave of Qaeda wannabes, like the young train bombers of Madrid: the *takfiri*, Muslims who would "excommunicate" fellow Muslims as lackeys of the infidel and de facto apostates, and so justify killing them, along with the infidels, to save the Muslim community from conquest and corruption.

Anthropologically and psychologically, terrorists usually are not remarkably different from the rest of the population. There are a few cruel kooks and some very bright individuals who go in for violent jihad, but most terrorists fall in between. Small-group dynamics can trump individual personality to produce horrific behavior in ordinary people, not only in terrorists, but in those who fight them.

Although there are few similarities in personality profiles across jihadi groups, some general demographic and social tendencies exist: in age (usually early twenties), where they grew up and where they hang out (neighborhood is often key), in schooling (mostly nonreligious and often science oriented), in socioeconomic status (middle-class and married, though increasingly marginalized), in family relationships (friends tend to marry one another's sisters and cousins). If you want to track a group, look to where one of its members eats or hangs out, in the neighborhood or on the Internet, and you'll likely find the other members.

It is possible to empathize with jihadi warriors and believers without needing to sympathize or share their conviction. This makes field study with them possible. The main goal of such study isn't to get you to feel or justify their sentiments, but to enable you to better appreciate the origins, character, and implications of these. If appreciation of them is faulty, then efforts to do something about them are likelier to fail.

THE DIVINE ANIMAL

Now to the second line of evidence on us being social animals, with a peculiar kind of self-realizing imagination. More than half a million years ago, the Neanderthal and human branches of evolution began to split from our common ancestor, *Homo erectus* (or perhaps *Homo ergaster*). Neanderthal, like *erectus* before, spread out of Africa and across Eurasia. But our ancestors, who acquired fully human structures of brain and body about 200,000 years ago, remained stuck in the savanna grasslands and scrub of eastern then southern Africa. Recent archaeological and DNA analyses suggest that our species may have tottered on the verge of extinction as recently as 70,000 years ago, dwindling to fewer than two thousand souls.[11] Then, in a geological blink of the eye, they became us, traipsing about on the moon and billions strong.

How did it all happen? No real evidence has emerged from science for any dramatic change in the general anatomy of the human body and brain or in basic capacities for physical endurance and perception. The key to this astounding and bewildering development, it appears, is mushrooming cultural cooperation and creativity within groups, in order to better compete against other groups.

The story of humanity has been the religious rise of civilizations, however secular in appearance the recent chapters of the story appear. The formation of large-scale cooperative societies is an evolutionary problem, because evolutionary theories of reciprocity based on kin relations or quid pro quo (scratch my back and I'll scratch yours) cannot account for the fact that people frequently cooperate with strangers of unknown reputation whom they will never meet again and whose loyalties they cannot control.[12]

But religious beliefs and obligations can reinforce cooperative norms by conferring on them sacredness, and with supernatural punishment or divine retribution for breaking with those cooperative norms. Supernaturals are the unimpeachable authors of what is sacred in society. Sacred assumptions—like "God is merciful to believers" or "This land is holy"—are beyond reason or fact. Unlike secular social contracts, they cannot be fully expressed and analyzed because they include inscrutable propositions that are immune to logic or empirical evidence—like "God is all-seeing and all-powerful," sentient but bodiless, or "good deeds will be rewarded in a heavenly paradise," which no one can ever disprove.[13] Sociologists and anthropologists argue that sacred beliefs and values authenticate society as having existence beyond the mere aggregation of its individuals and institutions.[14]

Tribal humans began merging into multitribal chiefdoms and multiethnic states lorded over by moral gods. A reason for these divine beings: to make large-scale cooperation possible between anonymous strangers. Historical and cross-cultural analyses indicate that the larger a society's population, the more likely it is to have deities who are concerned with managing morality and mitigating selfishness.[15] In the Fertile Crescent, at Eurasia's epicenter, the Hebrew tribes converged to create the concepts of One God and humanity. This God was powerful enough to preserve His chosen, blessed few, even as they scattered far and wide. For a thousand years, the religious empires of Christendom and Islam battled to save the souls, and capture the fortune and manpower, of the unchosen residue of humanity.

This historical spiral toward larger human polities was nurtured and sustained by culturally tricking and tweaking various aspects of our biologically evolved cognition in order to cope with a self-generating epidemic of warfare between expanding populations. Religion, for example, is neither a naturally selected adaptation of our species nor innate in us. But we are biologically primed by evolution to be on the lookout for potential predators, and especially guard against intelligent and cunning agents like ourselves. So hair-trigger is this survival sensibility that we see enemies in clouds or hear them in the wind. It's only a short step from imagining invisible agents to believing in their supernatural existence—a step motivated by fears of death and deception, and hopes of success and salvation. I'll show evidence that this tricking and tweaking of our species' innate and universal sensibilities is what creates religion from cognition.

Imagined kinship—the rhetoric and ritual of brotherhood, motherland, family, or friends, and the like—is also a critical ingredient of nearly all religious and political success, and another example of trick and tweak. From an evolutionary standpoint, imagined kinship isn't all that different from pornography: It too involves manipulation of naturally selected proclivities for passionate ends that may be very far removed from evolutionary needs but create a cultural reality of their own. When imagined kinship combines with team spirit, amazing things are possible: like winning battles against all odds, achieving civil rights, or you and your buddies blowing yourselves—and your perceived enemies—to bits.

It is a combination of imagined kinship and religion—or more precisely religions with morally concerned supernaturals—that made large-scale human cooperation (and competition) possible, with war a main motor for realization of these large-scale social developments. In *Imagined Communities*, Benedict Anderson describes the birth of the concept of the nation as basically a reformulation of religion and the imagined kinship of ethnicity. Secularized by the European Enlightenment, the great quasi-religious isms of modern history, as political philosopher John Gray calls them[16]—colonialism, socialism, anarchism, fascism, communism, democratic liberalism—harnessed industry and science to continue on a global scale the human imperative of cooperate to compete—or kill massively to save the mass of humanity. The War Against Terror is another moment in this continuing saga of our species toward an unpredictable somewhere between All against All and One World.

Even the idea of human rights is an outgrowth of monotheism, brought down from heaven to everyone on earth (in principle) by Europe's Enlightenment. Before monotheism, human groups didn't consider other human groups to be of one kind (Greek philosophy and Buddhism contributed to this development, but didn't quite get there). Human rights—including inalienable rights of life, liberty, and the pursuit of happiness—are anything but inherently self-evident and natural in the life of our species; cannibalism, infanticide, slavery, racism, and the subordination of women are vastly more prevalent across cultures and over the course of history. It wasn't inevitable or even reasonable that conceptions of freedom and equality should emerge, much less prevail among strangers. These, when combined with faith and imagination, become legitimized by their transcendent "sacredness."

THE CRASH OF CULTURES

Traditionally, politics and religion were closely connected to ethnicity and territory, and in more recent times to nations and cultural areas (or "civilizations").[17] No longer. As French political scientist Olivier Roy astutely notes, religion and politics are becoming increasingly detached from their cultures of origin, not so much because of the movement of peoples (only about 3 percent of the world's population migrates),[18] but through the worldwide traffic of media-friendly information and ideas. Thus, contrary to those who see global conflicts along long-standing "fault lines" and a "clash of civilizations,"[19] these conflicts represent a crisis, even collapse, of traditional territorial cultures, not their resurgence.

Many made giddy by globalization—the ever faster and deeper integration of individuals, corporations, markets, nations, technologies, and knowledge—believe that a connected world inexorably shrinks differences and divisions, making everyone safer and more secure in one great big happy family. If only it were not for people's premodern parochial biases: religions, ethnicities, native languages, nations, borders, trade barriers, historical chips on the shoulder. This sentiment is especially common among scientists and the deacons of Davos, wealthy and powerful globetrotters who schmooze one another in airport VIP clubs, three-star restaurants, and five-star hotels and feel that pleasant buzz of camaraderie over wine or martinis at the end of the day. I don't reject this world; I sometimes embrace it. But my field experience and experiments in a variety of cultural settings lead me to believe that an awful lot of people on this planet respond to global connectivity very differently than does the power elite. While economic globalization has steamrolled or left aside large chunks of humankind, political globalization actively engages people of all societies and walks of life—even the global economy's driftwood: refugees, migrants, marginals, and those most frustrated in their aspirations.

For there is, together with a flat and fluid world, a more tribal, fragmented, and divisive world, as people unmoored from millennial traditions and cultures flail about in search of a social identity that is at once individual and intimate but with a greater sense of purpose and possibility of survival than the sorrow of here today, gone tomorrow. For the first time in history, ever since the collapse of the Soviet Union shattered the brief illusion of a stable, bipolar world, most of humanity is politically engaged. Many, especially the young, are increasingly independent yet interactive, in the search for respect and meaning in life, in their visions of economic advancement and environmental awareness. These youth form their identities in terms of global political cultures through exposure to the media. Even the injustices of the blistered legacies of imperialism and colonialism are now more about how the media paints the past to construct contemporary cultural identity than about the material and mental effects of things that happened.

Global political cultures arise horizontally among peers with different histories, rather than vertically as before, in traditions tried and passed in place from generation to generation. Human rights constitute one global political culture, originally centered upon the Americas and Europe, and the quest for rights is a growing part of what former U.S. national security adviser Zbigniew Brzezinski called "the global political awakening."[20] The decidedly nonsecular jihad is another political culture in this massive, media-driven transnational awakening: thoroughly modern and innovative despite its atavistic roots in the harsh purity of the Prophet's original community in the Arabian Desert. Jihad offers the group pride of great achievements for the underachieving: an englobing web of brave new hearts for an outworn world tearing at the seams. Its attraction, to youth especially, lies in its promise of moral simplicity and of a harmonious and egalitarian community whose extent is limitless, and in its call to passion and action on humanity's behalf. It is a twisting of the tenets of human rights, according to which each individual has the "natural right" of sovereignty. It claims a moral duty to annihilate any opposition to the coming of true justice and gives the righteous the prerogative to kill. The end justifies the means, and no sacrifice of individuals is too costly for progress toward the final good.

I don't know how this crisis of territorial cultures and the ensuing conflict of global political cultures will play out in the end. But my purpose here is to help find a hopeful way forward. The intention isn't to relativize violent extremism, but to understand its moral appeal as well as its usualness in the sweep of human evolution and history, so that we may better compete against it.

What's wrong with current thinking about the causes of jihad and martyrdom? What motivations are being overlooked or ignored? What else could be done to reverse the tide? A good part of this work will respond to such questions. During the Cold War, there was an attempt to figure out communism's appeal and what to do about it. About jihadism, we still hear that it caters to the destitute and depraved, craven and criminal, or those who "hate freedom."

Politicians and pundits assure us that jihadism is nihilistic and immoral, with no real program or humanity. Yet charges of nihilism against an adversary usually reflect willful ignorance regarding the adversary's moral framework. Talk to the Devil himself and understand that jihadism is not any of this, and we may more readily win the competition where it counts most, in coming generations.

Boabdil, the last Moorish king in Spain, surrenders the keys of Granada to Ferdinand and Isabella on January 2, 1492 (by Francisco Pradilla y Ortiz).

CHAPTER 3
THE MOORS OF MEZUAK

We will continue our jihad until martyrdom in the land of Tariq ibn
Ziyad [the Berber general who led Muslim forces in the conquest
of Spain in 711]. . . . You know of the Spanish crusade against
the Muslims, and that not much time has passed since the expulsion for Al Andalus and the tribunals of the Inquisition. . . . Blood
for blood! Destruction for destruction!

—MARTYR'S VIDEO FOUND IN THE DEBRIS OF THE APARTMENT
WHERE THE MADRID TRAIN BOMBERS BLEW THEMSELVES UP
WHEN CORNERED BY POLICE, APRIL 3, 2004

In the early eighth century, Muslim forces of the Umayyad
Caliphate in Damascus captured Roman Hispania from the
Visigoths, founding an emirate over the whole of what is today
Spain and Portugal. History named these Islamic conquerors of
Spain Moors, after the North African kingdom of Maure, an ally
of Rome's archrival, Carthage, in the third century B.C. The Moors
themselves never used the term. They were Arabs who led armies
of North African Berber converts. Soldiers all, they brought no
women with them and mostly married into already established
Roman, Visigoth, Jewish, and native Iberian families. From this

social mix sprang a culturally creative and technically advanced civilization that would last almost eight hundred years.

Almost immediately after the Muslim conquest, however, the Christian Reconquista of the Moorish states in the Iberian peninsula began, pursued across the centuries through innumerable battles and political intrigues. On January 2, 1492, the Catholic monarchs Ferdinand of Aragon and Isabella of Castile rode into Granada, the last bastion of rule in Muslim Spain, or Al Andalus, with Christopher Columbus at their side. The last ruler of the Kingdom of Granada, Boabdil the Unfortunate (*el zogoybi*), rode out from the magnificent red palace of the Alhambra with eight hundred of his knights to surrender the keys of the city to the Spanish sovereigns: "I saw the King of the Moors sally from the gates of said city," wrote Columbus, "and kiss the royal hands of your Highnesses."[1] Another Christian observed that:

> There was no one who did not weep abundantly with pleasure giving thanks to Our Lord for what they saw, for they could not keep back the tears; and the Moorish King and the Moors who were with him for their part could not disguise the sadness and pain they felt for the joy of the Christians, and certainly with much reason on account of their loss, for Granada is the most distinguished and chief thing in the world.[2]

Imbued with religious and nationalist fervor, Ferdinand and Isabella issued an edict in late March 1492 expelling all Muslims and Jews from the country; a few weeks later they agreed to sponsor Columbus in a quest to discover new lands for Christianity. For almost five centuries afterward, Spain had no Muslim population. But the Moors have always retained a clear sight and glorious dream of Spain from the northern Moroccan cities of Tangiers and Tetuán, just across the narrow Strait of Gibraltar.

After surrendering the keys to Granada, Boabdil rode off into exile, crossing the hill of Los Martirios (the Martyrs), and up the desolate heights that form the skirt of the Alpujarra Mountains. From a barren summit, known even today as La Cuesta de las Lágrimas (the Hill of Tears), the fallen monarch took a last look at the splendor that was Granada. It was here, too, at a place called *el último suspiro del Moro* (the last sigh of the Moor), that his sadness was turned to bile by the reproach of his mother, Ayxa: "You do well," she supposedly said, "to weep as a woman over what you could not defend as a man." King Ferdinand added insult to injury by taking Boabdil's daughter Aixa as a concubine, then casting her off; she became a nun. Commenting on Boabdil's fate, Emperor Charles V of Spain reportedly sneered: "I would rather have made this Alhambra my sepulcher than have lived without a kingdom."[3]

Nowhere does this sorrow and bitterness linger deeper than in and around Tetuán, known in Morocco as the Andalucian City[4] and the closest African metropolis to Europe. Here is where the Moors' defeated but unbowed Grenadine knights, under the command of Abdul-Hassan al-Mandari,[5] retreated, then rallied to fight off the Christian advance into North Africa. The struggle continued well after al-Mandari's death in 1511, into the mid-twentieth century, led by descendants of the Andalucian émigrés who had remodeled the city to reflect their precious Granada. Their heroic stories of triumphant resistance to Christian conquest remain an integral part of the lore of present-day Tetuán. But redemption for the loss of the Kingdom of Granada is still missing. Like any Southern boy who has dreamed of reliving Pickett's Charge at Gettysburg, only this time winning the day, the young men of Tetuán, beckoned by the Andalucian hills they see across the Strait of Gibraltar, long for bygone glory, for the days when the Moors commanded the world's respect.

The *caid*, the local police commissar in charge of Jamaa Mezuak, a tumbledown barrio in Tetuán, was firm and formal with his French:

"Le Wali a dit non et c'est non, point à la ligne." (The governor said no, and it's no, period at the end of the line.) "You can't talk to anyone else here unless you give me a letter from the minister of the Interior, *c'est tout* (that's all)." Of course, the ministry of Interior in Rabat would promise me a yes for some indefinite tomorrow, but I didn't have time to wait on its whim.

I had come back to explore the few square blocks in Mezuak that had produced five of the seven suicide bombers who plotted the 2004 Madrid train attacks and then blew themselves up. Several other young men from the same Mezuak neighborhood had gone on to fight and die as martyrs in Iraq.[6] I felt I needed to convey a better public sense of who "the enemy" was following a reaction to a briefing I gave in March 2007 for National Security Council staff at the White House. The briefing was based in part on what I had learned in Palestine and in part on information that I had gathered in Madrid and Morocco with Marc Sageman, a forensic psychiatrist and former CIA case officer who liaised with the mujahedin out of Pakistan during the later stages of the Soviet-Afghan war. The thrust of this information was that small-group dynamics—intimate interacting networks of family, friends, schoolmates, workmates, soccer buddies, and such—were key to the making of terrorists.

At the White House I spent nearly an hour showing data about neighborhood, team, and collegial relationships, arguing that even focusing on pairs of friends—offering them both soccer scholarships, job opportunities, religion and art workshops—was likely to prove far more effective in the long run than was targeting individuals. In Palestine, I found that suicide bombers will usually turn down individual scholarships if the choice is between personal gain and family and friends. I gave the example of Nabeel Masood, the high school boy from Jabaliyah refugee camp in Gaza who blew up himself and other people in the Israeli port of Ashdod in 2004. He had a scholarship to study in England, which his mother said he was proud of, but it was no match for the eternal esteem of martyr-dom in a cause shared by friends. What if he and a friend each had had scholarships; what if they'd had the chance to go to England together? Yet for some at the briefing, it seemed this rather simple message was incomprehensible.

"But don't these young people realize that the decisions they make are their personal responsibility," a young woman on Dick Cheney's staff sternly said in her most authoritative voice, "and that if they choose violence against us we're going to bomb them?"

"Bomb them?" I was truly bowled over. "Who are you going to bomb? Madrid? London? Morocco?"

Contacts in Tetuán had given me names of five young men who had gone on to Iraq, the first of whom had been identified by his DNA as a suicide bomber in Baquba. As with the Mezuak contin-gent of the Madrid bombers, two were brothers and all were soccer buddies. It turned out that the cousin of one of the Iraq-bound volunteers was married to someone from the Madrid group, which would make the Madrid deaths a family matter for the Iraq-bound friends.

And all of them, Madrid bombers and Iraq-bound martyrs alike, had lived their formative years along Mezuak's Mamoun Street. All had gone to the Abdelkrim Khattabi primary school, where icons of Mickey Mouse framed the lessons of the day. They played soccer at the schoolyard or in the field below the Dawa Tab-ligh mosque that first promoted jihad in Mezuak. They saw the larger world on Al Jazeera at Café Chicago and other nearby hang-outs, and at the Cyprus Coiffure and other barbershops, where tending hair was always a serious matter. There they earnestly debated the meaning of world events through the filter of their common experiences.

But why did just these ten, out of many hundreds who seemed no different, decide to kill and die for friends and faith? We'll see that there's as much randomness as purpose in the process of radicalization: Someone gets the jihad bug, for whatever reason, and friends follow, gathering force from sticking together, like a stone rolling downhill.

There are, of course, a few pathological jihadis. Abu Musab al-Zarqawi, founder of Al Qaeda in Iraq, was probably a crook and a killer, and one of the two main movers of the Madrid plot, the diminutive bucktoothed Chinaman (*El Chino*), as he was called, sometimes resembled the violent, coked-up Al Pacino character in the movie *Scarface*. For the most part, though, jihadis span the normal distribution of the surrounding population. The great majority cluster under the highest part of a bell-shaped curve: average in schooling, wealth, social adjustment, psychological disposition, and intelligence, with a few outliers at the tail ends.

The idea that joining jihad is a carefully calculated decision or that people are "brainwashed" or "recruited" into "cells" or "councils" by "organizations" with "infrastructures" that can be hit and destroyed is generally wrong. This (minus, perhaps, the brainwashing part) is the way most government bureaucracies, law enforcement agencies, and military organizations are structured. It's their reality, and they mirror that reality by interpreting, understanding, and acting on the world in these terms. But generally, this isn't the way most human lives are structured, including the jihadi social movement. Hierarchical armies whose minions act on their own initiative rather than following orders tend to lose wars, but the egalitarian jihad prospers because, like Google, its leadership is distributed over a social network in ways that are fairly fluid and flat.

I also went to the neighboring Spanish enclave of Ceuta at the northernmost tip of Morocco. There, the Alonso Principe barrio, where one of the Guantánamo prisoners had come from, is a faithful image of Mezuak. I wanted to talk to the young men, so I stationed myself in the plaza where children were playing soccer. The Plaza del Padre Salvador Cervos is bookended by two cafés, one devoted to fans of the Barcelona soccer team Barça, the other to aficionados of archrival Real Madrid. Young men sipped tea in a shaded corner. An endless trickle of children and adolescents flowed through the small plaza, pausing in pairs to kick the ball. A pair became a triad, someone came and two pairs formed, then the triads became a free for all. Someone's little sister, left alone, cried, "I have to go, *adios, ciao, salaam.*" "Me too." And the plaza suddenly emptied, then filled up again.

"Who's your hero? Who do you want to grow up to be like?" I asked as I had done with the boys in Mezuak.

Number one was Ronaldinho, the Brazilian-born star of the Barcelona soccer team. Osama Bin Laden came up number three. And sandwiched between the athlete and the terrorist? The Terminator. About the Terminator's subsequent career as governor of California, the children neither knew nor cared. When I queried the older teenagers, they were ready with wary and sarcastic replies. "George Bush," said one. "Rumsfeld," said another: "I want to make the world free for democracy!" All laughed.

I asked which soccer stars they liked: Barcelona's Cameroonian striker, Samuel Eto'o; or Sergio Ramos, a defender for Real Madrid. What about Zinedine Zidane? This Frenchman of Algerian origin was probably the planet's best-known soccer star. He had previously led France to the greatest of all triumphs in team sports—the World Cup Championship—and had been named outstanding player of the 2006 World Cup, where he was famously expelled in the tournament's final match for head-butting an Italian who had insulted his family.

"Zinedine who?" a boy of about twelve asked.

"Zinedine Zidane," I said, "the greatest soccer player in all the world."

I knew that would do the trick because immediately one of the young men who had been in a corner of the plaza with others eyeing my behavior the whole time walked over and scolded the children.

"Zizou, Zizou," repeated the young man, using Zidane's nickname. Even more puzzlement on the faces of the kids. "Zinedine Zidane is an artist, a great artist." One of the younger kids poked his friend next to him. "Yes, Zidane. I remember Zidane. He's good."

The young man, Malik was his name, invited me to sit with the other young men. We talked soccer a bit, and then I turned the conversation to what I hoped would become a discussion of jihad. We spoke in a babel of Spanish, Arabic, and French that everyone around understood:

"I guess Zidane just couldn't take that insult to his family, so he butted that Italian, even if it meant losing the World Cup."

"*Qué lástima* [it's a shame], yes," said Malik, "but some things are more important than all the fame and money in the world. Some things a man can't take."

"What do you mean? What things are more important? Your family? Your religion? What?" I asked.

Malik gently put a hand on the shoulder of his son, who was standing next to him. "My son is six years old. I don't want him to live the life I've had. Look around here. This is no life. The Spanish authorities treat us like we were all criminals. Our people have been here for hundreds, maybe thousands, of years, but even the Hindus get better treatment. We are always looking for work, and when we find it, the children are left to themselves, to drugs. The twelve-year-old leads the ten-year-old around, who takes the eight-year-old, who takes my son. Our women work when they can, but if they wear a headscarf, then they're out, no matter what education or experience they have."

In fact, I'd found several young women who'd shown me their professional diplomas and said this is what happened to them.

Malik continued, "We all want a better life, a home, a safe place for our children. But some people want to be on top of others, to be rich, and so there are drugs. People are understanding this now. They are starting to become *multazim*, engaged in religion.

That's when ambitions become humble, and then no one wants to exploit another, and then you can't help but feel the suffering of your people, in Palestine, in Iraq, in Afghanistan."

Suddenly he closed his eyes, clenched his fists, and sputtered: "I swear, if George Bush were here in front of my son, I would shoot him and gladly die. And if I had the means, I would strap a bomb on myself and blow up American soldiers in Iraq even if my son, whom I love more than life, were to grow up without a father. But I have no means to get there. How can we just sit and watch the children at gunpoint with their hands in the air, terrified? Have the Americans no pity on children? I know, not all Americans support George Bush's war, but he's the worst criminal in history, he wants the whole world to obey him. It's a matter of economics— the high-up Jews are behind the war against Muslims. Palestine is the Mother of All Problems. There the people are pure, fighting evil. Some Iraqis allowed the Americans to come in; now look what they have. Sometimes we say that the Iraqis who let in the Americans are *hufiyum*, they deserve what they got. We never say *hufiyum* about the Palestinians."

The others in the park nodded their heads in agreement.

The muezzin was calling the faithful to prayer, and all excused themselves. All across the Muslim world, from Morocco to the Celebes, this haunting call stirs even the spirits of infidels, especially toward evening and in the cities. The clang of daily conflicts quiets into calm, and pointless worries fade. This surface comfort facilitates a deeper and sometimes more disquieting searching of the soul, which the messengers of jihad have learned to piggyback.

"Don't go away," said Malik. "I'll be right back after prayer."

But first he took me into the Barça Café, sat me down, and ordered tea for me. Al Jazeera was reporting on Iraq. The camera fixed on a man, his eyes wild, his distorted mouth silently screaming, his legs running frantically with no direction, a little girl in his arms, blood and brains streaming from her head. It was not the Fox or CNN video game of the Iraq war, where, in Orwellian fashion, body bags had become even more sanitized "transfer boxes" that no one was ever allowed to see except for the family just before the burial.

"Some things a man can't take."

The Café Chicago on Mamoun Street, Mezuak's main thoroughfare and market street, had fallen on hard times. The old owner had died, and the manager—who also looked as though he had known far better days—groaned that the cheapskate sons who inherited the place won't pay for supplies and so he can't offer even his best customers milk for their coffee. He shuffled the empty chairs around the table, muttered something incomprehensible at the television, and moved to where a dozen or so young men were playing a board game called parche, several smoking large hashish cigarettes. Outside, the street was bustling with hawkers selling their wares, people chattering and bargaining over anything and everything, cars beeping everything else that moves to get out of the way, and donkeys hee-hawing in protest. The smell of cumin, the sight of so many women and men dressed in formless cloth, and Arabic music blaring from radios in every other shop, all indicated that this is unmistakably the Orient, albeit its westernmost edge, the Maghreb.

The Café Chicago was a monument to having nothing else to do. Inside, the mood was languorous. The parche players glanced from time to time at the big TV screen over the bar, which was always switched to Al Jazeera. Yusef, a chain-smoking cabbie, was in the café having tea with me. He knew the martyrs of Mezuak, those who blew themselves up in Madrid and those who went to blow themselves up in Iraq. He says he left for Spain around the same time El Chino did. El Chino, though, fled Morocco to escape a murder rap and began dealing drugs in Spain. Yusef just wanted to find a decent wage. He wound up an assistant cook in Andalucia, just across the Strait of Gibraltar in southern Spain.

"The only time I ever thought I was going to kill someone was in Spain," he said. "I had been working at the same place for months, and everyone just kept calling me Moro, especially when they wanted me to clean out something especially dirty or when I did something they didn't like. They laughed at me when they called me that. I was fed up with them calling me Moro, and I blew up. I started screaming and pushing people: 'Use my name! It's Yusef! Yusef, do you hear me! I have a name. I'm not an animal! I'm a person, a human being! *Racistas!* When you come to my country, to my neighborhood, I treat you well, the neighborhood treats you well. You treat us like shit!'"

After that, for about a year, Yusef said, he was in a rage: "If someone had asked me to bomb Spanish trains to make people aware of the abuse Muslims have to take, I might have done it. Yes, God knows, I might have. But there was no jihad back then, in the nineties."

"So why aren't you part of the jihad now?" I asked.

"Because now I have less rage. Because I have responsibilities, I have small children. But you know, when I talk about these things with people, with my friends, I forget this. Well, almost."

In Spain, in France, in Britain, in Germany, in Italy, in Holland, in Belgium—in Denmark even—there is traffic in information and people to weave the web of jihad in Europe. In all of these countries, second- and third-generation children of immigrants feel personal rage at the police who are hostile to them, at the majority culture that is suspicious of them, and at their inability to find decent jobs even if they have a good education. They witness the day-to-day humiliation of their elders by bureaucrats who treat them as idiot children too slow to complete the forms.

People who are humiliated generally don't take the path of violence (as studies I present later show). But those who do may seek to avenge the humiliation of others for whom they care. Marc Sageman argues that people radicalize along the path to violence when personal rage resonates with moral outrage. They act on it if their peers do. And action groups, like soccer buddies, are already primed. Can we help to offer these young people other heroes, different dreams? But just as important, can we offer them some hope to realize them? Can we offer adventures of the heart able to conquer the countless banalities and miseries of an existence that favors drudgery, flight, or ganging for a fight?

"You see, all the young people want to go to Iraq," explained Muhsein al-Chabab, a twenty-seven-year-old man who works with Mezuak's youth to keep them from drugs and violence. "In their daily lives they are thinking about it. If the governments of Muslim countries asked for volunteers, many thousands would go. It's a religious obligation to help fellow Muslims. But Muslim governments are not for Muslims; they're for themselves."

"If it's an obligation, then why don't you and the others go to Iraq or Afghanistan?" I asked.

"There's no organized network to get there. If there were, everyone would know, even the police. It's difficult to get there. It costs money, for one thing, about five thousand euros for Iraq, more for Afghanistan; it's expensive."

I had gotten much the same story from Muslim fighters in Sulawesi and Azad Kashmir, who said they would prefer to fight Americans in Iraq rather than local Christians or Hindus, but had no organized way or means to get to Iraq or Afghanistan.

"But you seem to know something about it," I pointed out, "how to get to Iraq or Afghanistan, at least what it costs."

"Yes, I know that if I really wanted to, I could go. Everyone can find a way. But you also need a lot of courage. Maybe I'm not so courageous."

"And those who went. You think they were very courageous?"

"They gave courage to one another. Friends encourage and give courage to another. It depends on your friends."

"And that's it, just having friends who also want to go?"

"No, someone else has to guide you, to give you the money and the connections."

"Then what?"

"And then I suppose you're on your way to paradise," Muhsein said with a sad smile and a shrug.

As with most forms of violent jihad in the world nowadays, the path to glory and the grave is mostly a self-organizing affair, whether in neighborhoods or chat rooms. It's not an entirely leaderless jihad, for some people more than others are ready to take the initiative to go and others to guide, but it has no formal leadership that really matters. Al Qaeda still inspires, but has no command or control over the grass roots, where much of the terrorist action now is.

On the way down to the schoolyard soccer field for my next set of interviews, I thought, *What a simple faith. Easy to remember, easy to pass on.* A guiding thread of human history, a road to glory and to misery is this insular delusion of defending one's own group prejudice as humanity's high duty. As Iranian president Mahmoud Ahmadinejad put it, "[Muslim] religious democracy is the only path toward human prosperity and it is the most advanced type of government that humans can ever have."[7]

But when does high duty to defend the group become a moral imperative to kill noncombatants? Many millions of people express sympathy with Al Qaeda or other forms of violent political expression that support terrorism, but relatively few willingly use violence. From a 2001–2007 survey of thirty-five predominantly Muslim nations (with fifty thousand interviews randomly chosen to represent about 90 percent of the Muslim world), a Gallup study projected that 7 percent of the world's 1.3 billion Muslims thought that the 9/11 attacks were "completely justified." If one includes Muslims who considered the attacks "largely justified," their ranks almost double. Adding those who deemed the attacks "somewhat justified" boosts the number to 37 percent, which implies hundreds of millions of Muslims. (Polls also imply that 20 percent of the American public has a "great deal" of prejudice against Muslims, two-thirds has "some prejudice" against them, and 6 percent of Americans think that attacks in which civilians may be victims are "completely justified.")[8]

Of these many millions who express support for violence against the out-group, however, there are only thousands willing to actually commit violence. This also appears to be the case in the European Union, where fewer than 3,000 suspects have been imprisoned for jihadi activities out of a Muslim population of perhaps 20 million. In the United States, fewer than five hundred suspects have been arrested for having anything remotely to do with Al Qaeda ideology or support for terrorism after 9/11, with fewer than one hundred cases being considered serious out of an immigrant Muslim population of more than 2 million. As we'll see later, people usually go on to such violence in small, action-oriented groups of friends and family (with friends also tending to become family as they marry one another's sisters and cousins). But first, let's try to understand where competing claims to save humanity come from.

Part II

THE RELIGIOUS RISE OF CIVILIZATIONS

Human social organization is something necessary. . . . It is absolutely necessary for man to have the cooperation of his fellow men. As long as there is no such cooperation, he cannot obtain any food or nourishment, and life cannot materialize for him. . . . Nor, lacking weapons can he defend himself. Thus he falls prey to animals and dies much before his time. Under such circumstances, the human species would vanish.

—IBN KHALDÛN, *MUQADDIMAH* (AN INTRODUCTION TO HISTORY), 1375–1378

In civilized society [man] stands at all times in need of cooperation and assistance of great multitudes, while his whole life is scarce sufficient to gain the friendship of a few persons.

—ADAM SMITH, *THE WEALTH OF NATIONS*, 1776

Sheik Ibn Taymiah—may Allah have mercy on him—said, "The interests of all Adam's children would not be realized in the present life, nor in the next, except through assembly, cooperation, and mutual assistance. Cooperation is for achieving their interests and mutual assistance is for overcoming their adversities. That is why it has been said, 'man is civilized by nature.'"

—AL QAEDA TRAINING MANUAL

CHAPTER 4
CREATION OF THE WESTERN WORLD

Evolution by natural selection has endowed our species with weak bodies, big brains, gregariousness, and greed. These basic facts of our nature have driven the human saga forward toward increasingly global commerce, war, interdependence, and innovation. None of the particulars—personalities, nations, the rise and fall of empires—were predictable or inevitable, but the general trend follows a path that looks as probable in hindsight as a gathering storm in a video run backward. At least this seems to be the case ever since the Upper Paleolithic, when humans sallied forth from their African home and off a hundred thousand years of treadmill existence.

As animals go, we are fragile and we are vulnerable. But we have large appetites, especially for calorie-dense meat and richer protein for our big brains. Yet without weapons or bands of quick-witted and reliable cooperators, we could not bring down large game or ward off stronger rival predators. If our own ancestors had been stronger, they might have survived the competition, though as Darwin surmised in *The Descent of Man* (and Ibn Khaldûn before him), they probably would not have become "the most dominant animal that has ever appeared on this earth . . . spread more widely than any other . . . and all others hav[ing] yielded before him":

[A]n animal possessing great size, strength, and ferocity, and which, like the gorilla, could defend itself from all enemies, would probably . . . have failed to become social; and this would most effectually have checked the acquirement by man of his higher mental qualities. . . . Hence it might have been an immense advantage to have sprung from some comparatively weak creature.[1]

In the smaller, more intimate world of early humans, one's social group was everything, and other groups were often far and few. In the African scrub from which our ancestors evolved, a human without its band was like a baboon without its troop or a chimp without its clan: a dead primate.[2] Among baboons, for example, adult males will rush a predator, and some may sacrifice themselves in defense of the group, where often 80 percent of young males fail to survive to maturity.[3]

Hunting game, defending against predators, and maintaining camps for the vulnerable young were the collective's primary occupations. Defection was probably mostly limited to a person shirking responsibility. But people in a small band, as in a work crew, don't have to do much to figure out who's letting them down.

For the first hundred thousand years or so, more than half of human time on the planet, *Homo sapiens* hunted game and gathered grains in small bands scattered across the sparse grasslands of eastern and southern Africa. For the most part, they probably cooperated very strongly with one another against nature, then the chief source of competition. People seem to have spent the millennia pretty monotonously. While their more solidly built Neanderthal cousins wandered the world, humans stuck to a little corner of the planet. Those who ventured to the predator-infested, desert-like fringes of greener woodlands, areas inhabited by species more powerful and agile than they, defended their own big-brained, bipedal bodies and babies against the precariousness of life on the margins.

Our species may have tottered on the verge of extinction less than 100,000 years ago.[4] Then, in an almost miraculous change of fortune about 60,000–50,000 years ago, one or a few human bands moved out of Africa for good. This beginning of human wanderlust was likely stirred by global cooling and the attendant parching of the African grasslands, which led to loss of game and grain.[5] But there is also the strong possibility, based on circumstantial evidence relating to a "cultural explosion" of human artifacts and technologies, that a mutation rewired the brain for computational efficiency. This rewiring allowed for *recursion* (embedding whole bundles of perceptions and thoughts within other bundles of perceptions and thoughts), which is an essential property of both human language (syntactic structures) and mind-reading skills (or "theory of mind"—the ability to infer other people's thoughts and perceptions: "I know that she knows that I know that he knows that . . . etc."). Language and mind reading, in turn, became critical to development of peculiarly human forms of thinking and communication, including planning and cooperation among strangers, imagining plausible versus fictitious pasts and futures, the counterfactuals of reason, and the supernaturals of religion.

A first wave followed the food along the coast of southwest Asia, managed to cross a few hundred kilometers of open sea, and wound up in Australia 50,000–45,000 years ago. A second wave went up to Central Asia, around present-day Kazakhstan, then spread eastward and westward across the great Eurasian landmass. Humans reached Europe 40,000–35,000 years ago, staying mostly clear of Neanderthals, who were—along with the woolly bison, mammoths, and other behemoths Neanderthals hunted—already a dying breed. About 20,000–15,000 years ago, humans crossed the Bering ice bridge from eastern Siberia into the Americas; others perhaps came hunting along the ice from Western Europe (as French Solutrean-style stone tools recently found on the east coast of America suggest). All of these migrations caused a set of positive feedback loops to begin, leading to increasing sophistication in social and cultural life.

By around 30,000 years ago, humans had a number of important new technologies. Spears, bows, and bolas extended the hunter's effective range and showed that humans had mastered the principle "the best armor is to keep out of range." Harpoons, fishhooks, and nets brought in water animals as dietary staples, thus providing a more abundant food supply and a hedge against starvation. Dugout boats and seaworthy rafts enabled waterborne transport, exploration, and trade. Bone needles and buttons permitted the fashioning of clothes and shelter made of hides, which provided protection from the elements and thus wider latitude in movement. Domesticated dogs helped to track game and perhaps also provided an emergency meat supply. Upper Paleolithic cultures were almost surely able to precisely time the migration of game animals and anticipate the moves of dangerous predators, and so they became efficient hunters in a wide array of situations.

Domestication of animals was stimulated by our biosocial addiction to protein products. It enabled the growth of pastoral societies that could take with them their own sources of protein into new environments, but it also helped grow settled societies now free from the need to pursue game and so better able to focus on chosen environments. Animal labor and transportation sped up genetic and cultural exchange between human populations, and an accumulation of knowledge and experiences with plants fostered their domestication.

Plant domestication, in turn, enabled huge increases in human populations: Without it the world's peoples would probably total only in the hundreds of thousands, assuming our species survived at all. Rising populations led to bigger "social brains"—more varied and productive networks of people and their creations, especially of information (through writing, roads, and trade). But rising populations also led to morally exclusive religion and all-out war, the Mother and Father of civilizations.

As work by evolutionary biologist Jared Diamond suggests,[6] the imperative to "cooperate to compete" in ever larger groups was likely kick-started and driven forward by the peculiar climatic and geographical conditions of Eurasia's vast temperate expanse, which encouraged the spread and increase of populations and the free-flowing exchange of genetic materials, artifacts, ideas, and information among them. Descendants of the humans who remained in Africa, as well as descendants of the first wave out of Africa and into Australia, by and large remained in the Stone Age until modern times, although with some development of long-range trade, technologies for fighting and farming, division of labor, and political hierarchy.

Descendants of the second wave who made it to the Americas also mostly remained in the Stone Age, except in Mesoamerica and South America's Andean plateau, where multicity states and multiethnic empires began to form. But it was the extensive belt across Eurasia—because of its relatively temperate climate, large variety of animals to domesticate, lack of geographical barriers, and wide-open channels for the lateral flow and exchange of genes and ideas—that became a cradle of civilizations, the center stage for the world's increasing economic and political interdependence, the main avenue for cultural innovation, and the cauldron of war.

Increased interactions between nomadic and sedentary societies, while stimulating cultural innovation and development, were constantly punctuated by conflict: herders desired to move freely anywhere and take whatever they needed wherever they found it; settlers wanted to protect and grow what they had in one place. Nomads disdained settled life as effete, settlers denounced nomads as barbarian. In fact, as so many historians have pointed out, without "barbarians" to jolt them, civilized societies tended to collapse rather than continue to create. Barbarians invigorated the settler populations, which, in turn, civilized the rude invaders.[7]

In war, nomads innovated on the offense, with short and powerful composite bows, light infantry, and horse cavalry.[8] They culled their flocks with quick and lethal blows, so through butchery they knew best how to kill and cut flesh. Settled societies innovated with defensive fortifications and mass armies to resist onslaught, and to gather in sufficient strength to go out to conquer.

War, or at least the threat of war, is perhaps the chief source of the historical spread and advance of social cooperation among human populations. "I couldn't help but say to [Mr. Gorbachev]," mused Ronald Reagan in 1985 when the Cold War threatened humankind with nuclear annihilation, "just think how easy his task and mine might be . . . if suddenly there was a threat to this world from another planet. [We would] find out once and for all that we really are all human beings here on this earth together." This modern expression of an age-old sentiment echoes an old proverb, common to ancient Hebrews, Arabs, and Chinese: "The enemy of my enemy is my friend." But it was the advent of the written word that tipped human history into its next phase.

FAST FORWARD

> In the beginning was the Word, and the Word was with God, and the Word was God.
> —JOHN 1:1

Human societies, the great French anthropologist Claude Lévi-Strauss observed, divide into "cold" and "hot" cultures.[9] During most of the time when humans have walked the earth, there were only preliterate "cold" societies, whose people conceived of nature and social time as eternally static or entirely cyclical. The present order was conceived as a projection of an order that has existed since mythical times. The interpretation of the origins of the world and the development of society was rendered in mythological terms. Every element of the knowable universe would be connected in kaleidoscopic fashion to every other element in memorable stories, however arbitrary or fantastic, that could be passed down orally from generation to generation. A typical mythic account of the world might "explain" how nomadic patterns of residence and seasonal movement emanated from patterns perceived in the stars; how star patterns, in turn, got their shapes from the wild animals around; and how men were made to organize themselves into larger totemic societies, dividing tasks and duties according to the "natural order."

From its beginnings among the cuneiform tablets of ancient Mesopotamia, history flamed forward across the breadth of Eurasia into civilizations and universal religions, world commerce and world war. Writing, transported on roads and imprinted on money, contracts, and laws, opened the channels of communication and exchange that make state-level societies viable.

Mutually beneficial trade and the promise of profit could foster cooperation even among former enemies and in the long run make large-scale cooperation more sustainable. But widening the scope of war greatly quickened the pace of cooperation through the strong and narrow focus of competition: Survive, and if possible, vanquish the enemy. Thus the Greek city-states, which had been constantly warring upon one another, came together for the first time as one people to fight the common Persian foe. Aeschylus's poem, "The Battle of Salamis," gives a sense of how empires and nations first form in collective imagination through war:

> Come, O ye sons of Greeks,
> Make free your country, make your children free,
> Your wives, and fanes of your ancestral gods,
> And your sires' tombs! For all we now contend![10]

After the Persians were defeated, the Greek city-states fell again to fighting among themselves. The Greeks were saved from mutual destruction only by Alexander the Great's power to unite them in a war to end the outside Persian threat once and for all. In the process, a brief but magnificent Greek Empire was forged from the Mediterranean to the Himalayas, which paved the way for regular commerce between the western and eastern ends of Eurasian civilization in goods and technology, art and architecture, and religious and natural philosophy.

Aristotle was one of the most rational and precise philosophers who ever lived, and his reason and clarity no doubt helped to form his pupil Alexander. But Alexander's passion and imagination far transcended his teacher's. Where Aristotle taught that the independent city-state was the ideal polity, Alexander merged the Greek city-states into a springboard for launching the first world empire. Where Aristotle taught preference for friends and family, Alexander forced his generals to marry into other cultures, which he considered full and equal members of the human family.

Alexander was willing to challenge the old gods and dare their lightning bolts to strike. He created the dream of a unified political world to attain some better life for all. Only, he lacked an overarching moral framework, such as monotheism, to enable his successors to solidify his achievements and advance that dream. Even earlier, Gautama Buddha taught that all people are of the same family and that the greater the harmony of their relationships with one another and the natural world, the better for our universe. But he abandoned the political will and engines, such as those that Rome would wed to monotheism, to make enduring material progress.

Along the edge of dreams between soaring hopes and the abyss, human history has been driving up a steepening grade, fueled by religion in fits of war and peace.

THE REPUBLIC OF GOD (CHRISTENDOM)

What is the other commonwealth that remains standing now that the mundane commonwealth, embodied in the Roman Empire, has fallen?
—SAINT AUGUSTINE, THE CITY OF GOD [DE CIVITATE DEI],
ON WHAT SURVIVED AND THRIVED AFTER THE VISIGOTH
SACK OF ROME IN A.D. 410

By the time of Jesus Christ, two millennia ago, four great neighboring polities spanned Eurasia's middle latitudes: the Roman Empire, the Parthian Empire centered in Persia and Mesopotamia, the Kushan Empire of Central Asia and Northern India, and the Han Empire of China and Korea. The Kushan Empire had diplomatic links with the other three, and all four were linked by a network of trade routes, known to posterity as the Silk Road. It's along the Silk Road that Eurasia's three universalist moral religions—Judaism, Zoroastrianism, and Hinduism—continued to interact, mutating from their respective territorial and tribal origins into the three proselytizing, globalizing religions that today vie for the soul of humanity—Christianity, Islam, and Buddhism.

The three globalizing religions created two new concepts in human thought: individual free choice and collective humanity. People not born into these religions could, in principle, choose to belong (or remain outside), without regard to ethnicity, tribe, or territory. The mission of these religions was to extend moral salvation to all peoples, not just to a "Chosen People" who would light the way for others.

Still, it took some time for universal religion to overcome psychologically deep-seated ethnic and tribal biases. Although Christianity had declared people of all tribes and nations to be human beings, and potentially salvable, there was still the problem of figuring out which earthly creatures were indeed human. In 1322,

Sir John Maundeville described the peoples of the known world, who became less human the farther they were from England and Christianity:

> In Ethopia, the children, when young are all yellow; and when they grow older that yellowness turns to black. . . . Afterwards men go by many isles by sea to an isle called Milk, where [there] are very cursed people; for they delight in nothing more than to fight and slay men; and they drink gladly man's blood, which they call Dieu. . . . And thence they go by sea from isle to isle, to an isle called Tracoda, the inhabitants of which are beasts, and unreasonable, and dwell in caves which they make in the earth, for they have not sense to make houses. . . . And they eat flesh of serpents, and they speak naught, but hiss, as serpents do. After that isle, men go by the Sea of Ocean, by many isles, to a great and fair isle called Nacumera, which is in circuit more than a thousand miles. And all the men and women of that isle have dog's heads; and . . . they worship an ox for their god.[11]

Christianity, which merged Hebrew tribal belief in monotheism with Greek belief in universal laws applicable to the whole of creation, originated the inclusive concept of Humanity, the idea that all cultures and civilizations fell under one transcendent set of rules. Before universal monotheism, there was no notion of humanity in the sense of all humans being of a kind, and thus no idea of saving humankind for the "good," or of a recalcitrant and residual part of humanity rejecting salvation because they were "bad" and "evil."

During its first three centuries, Christianity gradually but inexorably won the hearts and minds of the Roman Empire's majority population of slaves, women, and the educated Greek-speaking minorities through true works of charity. Sociologist Rodney Stark shows that when plague struck, Romans of every rank would leave their own diseased relatives to die without food or water, but Christians would risk their own lives to tend the non-Christian sick, and elevated compassion over hardness.[12] Christianity achieved political control of the empire in the fourth century with Constantine's conversion. But by then Christianity had already become the majority religion of the empire through social networking and natural increase of a few percent each year over the previous centuries.

The institutions of Christianity survived Rome's fall in the fifth century, as the Catholic Church emerged to stitch together the western empire's broken pieces. But Christendom began turning from charity to violence in its mission to save humanity, and Europe plunged into the Dark Ages. By the mid-eighth century, Christendom was in lethal competition with Islam, a new variant of messianic monotheism.

As the Middle Ages tailed off in Western Europe and the second millennium began, power struggles ensued between the Western Church of Latin Rome and the Eastern Church of Greek Constantinople, and between the Roman Church and the Frank and German emperors. By the tenth century, Eastern Christians routinely denounced Western Christians as poor, uncultured barbarians. Westerners condemned Easterners as preoccupied with material wealth, effeminate, devious, wicked, and cowardly (in hiring others to fight their battles). In 1054, the Pope of Rome and the Patriarch of Constantinople excommunicated each other.

The Roman Catholic will to dominate Europe and the Middle East began at the Abbaye de Cluny in France (then the building encompassing the largest indoor space in the world—like the Pentagon today). From there, in 1073, the future Pope Gregory VII started preaching a doctrine of conquest for Christ that forbade Christians to kill other Christians who agreed with Gregory, but forgave killing all other people, especially "Saracens" (Muslims) and Jews. The monks of Abbaye de Cluny took control of the papacy and launched the Crusades to unite Christendom in a great moral campaign to recapture the Holy Land from the followers of Mohammed. The First Crusade was driven also by divine promise of limitless booty and forgiveness for any imaginable cruelty toward non-Christians.

The Crusades officially began in 1095 under Pope Urban, Gregory's successor and kindred spirit. He wanted to consolidate Christendom under Roman Church rule through a military campaign that would channel Europe's self-predatory and economically ruinous feudal factions into a united mission to recapture the Holy Land from Islam. Although the First Crusade was partly justified as a response to a call from the Eastern Orthodox Byzantine Roman Empire for help against expansion of the Muslim Seljuk Turks into Anatolia, Byzantium itself was also a target of papal ambitions.

The initial crusader wave, led by Peter the Hermit, was composed of tens of thousands of Western European peasants and vagabonds who had just barely survived a horrendous decade of famine, drought, and plague.[13] Urban promptly announced that as long as those who killed and pillaged did not turn back until they either died or reached Jerusalem, God would fulfill all of their material needs and remit all of their sins in this world and the next. The first to be looted and massacred were the Jews of Germany, in Worms, Mainz, Cologne, and elsewhere.

After ferrying the crusaders across the Bosporus Straits, Byzantine Christians reported their horror at witnessing the crusading knights and peasants skewering and roasting children on spits, as the invaders advanced from Nicaea in Anatolia (where many of the victims were actually Cappadocian Christians living under Turkish rule) to Marj Uyun in the Lebanon. When the soldiers finally took Jerusalem in 1099, they celebrated their victory by burning alive all the Jews they could find, massacring Muslim women and children, and destroying most mosques and every synagogue in the Holy City.[14]

In 1204, the "Pirate Crusade" ravaged Constantinople. The treasure and riches of Byzantium shifted to Venice and other city-states in northern Italy, spurring Europe's Renaissance. The final blow to Byzantium was the Muslim conquest of Constantinople in 1453 by Ottoman Turks.

For a thousand years, between the fall of the Rome and the fall of Constantinople, Byzantium had resisted onslaught from all sides. Without this resistance, it is unlikely that Western Europe would have survived Asian invasions to reconstitute its civilization or that Arab civilization would have received the influx of Western knowledge and talent that allowed it to flourish. The political and economic organization of the Ottoman Muslim Empire was the stepchild of Byzantium, and the Orthodox Russian Empire was Byzantium's natural-born heir.

During the sixteenth century, the Spanish Inquisition treated converted Jews as the gravest mortal danger to humanity's immortal salvation, because they hid themselves like vermin from discovery and proper treatment. But it would be wrong to think that the crusading papacy was merely destructive, for at the same time it created Western civilization, uniting the fractious, feudal Germanic tribes with remnants of ruined Rome. The aim of the Crusades was not only to reclaim the Holy Land and to rescue the Eastern Christians from the Turks, but to liberate the Church from interference from secular powers, to forestall the anarchy and plunder of those same powers, and to purify the clergy from the greedy sins of concubinage and financial corruption. The overarching idea was to create an unimpeachable moral order for Europe that could eventually be extended to the rest of the world.

The innovation of the Church of Rome was the idea of spiritual unity that could permit political diversity. This allowed the Church to lure in such heathen warrior kingdoms as Hungary and Poland without demanding that they sacrifice political independence. This *Republica Christiana* was novel in world history for its internal political variety, comparative liberty, and competition. In principle, it had no problem in allowing Europe's various kingdoms and principalities to develop the material side of culture as each saw fit—trade and roads, building and monuments, civic councils and assemblies, arms and armies, ships and exploration—so long as developments did not tear apart the spiritual unity of Europe's social fabric.

The creative force of the papacy at this time, notes historian Arnold Toynbee, "was displayed, not in the 'holy wars' of the crusading Church Militant, but in a fruitful patronage of such promising institutions as the universities and the religious Orders [rediscovering the Greeks, thanks to the Arabs], and in the triumphant enlistment of the best talents of Christendom in the service of the Holy See."[15] The spirit of science and exploration began to shift back westward, but with an allowance for diversity and competition that would rapidly lead to cumulative advances and breakthroughs in knowledge and technology, warfare and commerce on a scale vastly greater than anything that had ever come before. Like the Greek city-states that first inspired Western civilization, the dynastic and territorial states of Christian Europe formed a creative brew of cultural unity and cooperation, fervent competition and variety that would eventually drive the entire world on to a new level of interaction and innovation.

GOD WITHDRAWS

Upon the establishment of vast overseas empires, beginning in the fifteenth century, kings and princes started to gain the upper hand over the Church. With the resources of these new empires and the help of the merchant class to manage and distribute these resources, the great nobles of northern Europe fanned a Protestant Reformation that challenged the moral dominion of the Catholic Church. The Reformation, which began in 1517, when Martin

Luther nailed his Ninety-five Theses to the door of the Wittenberg Castle Church, fractured Western Christendom, shaking the foundations of faith. This was barely half a century after the fall of Constantinople.

The popularization of Protestantism through the printing press compelled papal authorities to institute the Holy Inquisition to regain control by brutally forcing the genie of free and critical inquiry back into the bottle. Tortures such as breaking bodies on the rack and water-boarding (pouring water down a person's gullet until he felt he was drowning) were favorite techniques to enforce literal belief in God's word, as the Church chose to interpret it. Smart men—like Italy's Galileo, France's René Descartes, and England's Thomas Hobbes—granted that God's word is always true but only if never taken literally.

After the Peace of Westphalia in 1648, which ended the religious wars in Europe, it was resolved that every king or prince could choose the religion to follow in his own kingdom. In 1685, the "Sun King," France's Louis XIV, ruler of Europe's most powerful and populous country, declared Protestantism illegal. This did not rekindle the wars of religion, but hundreds of thousands of Protestants fled. The exodus of the French Huguenots, especially to England and Holland, coincided with the rise of scientific thinking and experiment, such as Isaac Newton's explanation of the heavens and Antony van Leeuwenhoek's discovery of microorganisms. From Holland, which published about half of Europe's books, French exiles delighted in freewheeling attacks on church and monarchy, particularly through humor and, for the first time in Christian Europe, through pornography. A ceaseless flow of tracts wound back to France calling for religious tolerance and disdain for dogma, removal of royalty from national affairs, and admiration for science, reason, and the practical achievements of industrial technology. Soon Voltaire and the French philosophes were urging the public to read Newton, chuck the Bible, and think for itself.

In the West, particularly in science-minded circles, God was on His way to becoming a sort of lazy couch potato. Having set the world in motion, He then withdrew to watch. This distant deity would become the official Supreme Being of the French Revolution and also of Thomas Jefferson's Unitarian religion. But a lazy God left a moral void that science and reason could never seem to fill, even to our day. Science, for example, is not particularly well suited to deal with people's existential anxieties—death, deception, sudden catastrophe, loneliness, or longing for love or justice—for which there is either no reasonable or no definitive solution. It cannot tell us what we ought to do, only what we can do. Our culture is still trying to come to grips with how to bridge the moral chasm between the two. Until fairly recently, much of the Muslim world had no such worry.

American and British scholars and governments to cover the area between Turkey and India, from the Caspian Sea to the Sudan, with occasional reference to all of Muslim North Africa as well. Most of the region is arid, except for Egypt's Nile Delta, the area between Mesopotamia's Tigris and Euphrates rivers, and the narrow fringe of cultivable land known as the Fertile Crescent, which skirts the northern edge of the Arabian Desert and links Egypt to Mesopotamia.

Civilization first sprang from the great irrigation projects that channeled the waters of the Euphrates and Nile into intensive agriculture. Perennial conflict ensued between these settled peasant societies and tribes of nomadic herdsmen that issued from steppes and deserts to the east and south. Nowhere was this conflict more constant and intense than along the short and narrow strip of fertile land between the mountains of Lebanon and the Sinai Desert, the biblical Armageddon at its center. Here, monotheism was born among the Hebrew hill tribes struggling to survive atop the thin rim between the Judean Desert and the Mediterranean coast, surrounded by rivals as ruthless as the Israelites themselves: Canaanites, Amorites, Perizites, Girgashites, Jebusites, Edomites, Amalekites. Uncompromising faith kept the Hebrew tribes from drowning under a continuous flow of more powerful invaders from the south (Egyptians), east (Assyrians, Babylonians), north (Hittites, Phoenicians), and west (Philistines, Greeks, Romans).

In the sixth century, Byzantium and the Sasanids of Persia vied to manage the Arab desert tribes as buffer states, granting them gold, titles, and trading privileges. In the seventh century, Mohammed united the tribes under Islam and brought Persia under Arab rule. By the eighth century, Muslim armies were rapidly eating away at Constantinople's control of the Eastern Roman Empire and gnawing at the emergent Holy Roman Empire in the West. Iberia (Spain and Portugal) soon fell to Muslim forces and the Mediterranean, once a Roman lake, became largely Arab.

Islam burst onto the world stage with a form of monotheism uncluttered with the arcane theological disputes of Christendom— like the conflict over the divine versus dual (divine and human) nature of Christ, an argument that provoked sectarian warfare and piles and piles of Christian corpses. In the House of Islam, there was greater religious tolerance of the other monotheistic faiths, Judaism and Christianity. As in Judaism, Muslim rituals were based mostly on hygiene and health. Emphasis was on civic virtues of courage, charity, and hospitality. One theological innovation was that soldiers who fell in battle to defend Islam, the holy warriors (*mujahedin*) of holy war (*jihad*), would go straight to a paradise vastly more colorful and chock full of sensual delights than Christianity's chaste and cerebral heaven.

THE RETRACTION OF REASON

There was no science in Arab culture when Islam came to it in the seventh century, and there was no science during the initial period of Islamic expansion. But by the mid-eighth century, Muslim conquerors were ordering translations of ancient Greek philosophy texts in order to make Arabic the medium for the whole of intellectual life in their dominion: from the eastern Atlantic, across North Africa and the Middle East, to the far side of the Indian Ocean. The great ninth-century translators, such as Hunyan Ibn Ishaq, expressed excitement at the task of enabling communication among philosophers, geographers, historians, mathematicians, and alchemists from as far apart as Spain and India.

Philosophers like Al Kindi exhorted the Faithful "not to be ashamed to acknowledge truth from whatever source it comes to us. . . . For him who seeks the truth, there is nothing of higher value than truth itself."[1] The mathematician Al Khwarazmi introduced Indian—or so-called Arabic—numerals into calculations. Ibn Abi Usay'bi extolled the Hippocratic Oath as the right way for medicine, rejecting astrology. In the tenth century, Muslims established the world's first medical school, in Salerno, Italy. And for the first time in history, science became international.[2]

Islamic politics in this era was dominated by the rationalist Mu'tazili, who sought to combine faith and reason in opposition to their rivals, the Ash'ari. The Mu'tazili (from *i'tazla*, meaning "withdraw") interpreted Koranic verses metaphorically, rather than literally, especially if these had anthropomorphic content. Allah's desires and powers were not concrete things outside or over and above mankind, but resided in the spirit that moved men.

The Mu'tazili called their philosophy Divine Unity and Justice (*Al-Tawhid wa al-'Adl*). Their most eminent thinker was tenth-century Chief Justice Abd al Jabbar ibn Ahmed, who argued that life is a test for beings possessing free will, or *taklif*. Delivering justice requires the ability to understand that people are responsible for good or bad choices they make in life, and legal decisions about whether choices are good or bad should be made on the basis of *ijtihad*, independent interpretation of judicial sources rather than blind tradition.

Reaction to the Mu'tazili was sparked by the tenth-century Muslim theologian Abu al-Hassan Ash'ari, who believed in radically separating Islamic from infidel philosophy. Ash'ari appeared at a time when reason could not be trusted unless it obeyed a moral code. Scientific experiments could proceed only if they served that code. This has also been a recurrent position in Western political thought until today: for example, in Nazi Germany, where biological experiments were permitted only if they demonstrated racial inequality, or in Stalinist Russia and Maoist China, where biology was forced to serve an anti-Darwinian moral code that rejected anything inherited or innate.

One of the most influential books ever written was an Ash'ari treatise, *The Incoherence of Philosophers*, because it helped to extinguish the scientific spirit in Islam. Its author, Al Ghazali (who died in 1111) emphasized *taqlid*, obedience and imitation based on authority, over choice and independent judgment. He criticized scientific philosophy as incompatible with faith and morally "incoherent." Averroës (also known as Ibn Rushd), one of the last rationalist lights in the Islam of that age, attacked Al Ghazali in a book titled *The Incoherence of Incoherence*, which was too pithy for the public and not well received.

Arab civilization was now in retreat. The empires of Islam were no longer expanding, and the defense of acquired gains became paramount for the rulers. In the West, Christian forces were pursuing the reconquest of Spain in earnest: They reached the Tagus in 1085, and Saragossa fell in 1118. In the East, also in 1118, the Seljuk Turks began their final push on southern Persia, after having overrun western Persia, Anatolia, and Syria. The Arab Abbasid Caliphate lost control over much of the former Islamic Empire and declined to a minor state under the loose grip of Turkic warlords and Mamluks, or "White Slaves," who were initially children captured from Caucasian, Eastern Slavic, and Turkic populations and then raised by the Abbasid Caliphs to become elite cavalry.

Only in the heartland of Arabia and the area stretching from the North African and Levantine littoral to Mesopotamia would Arabic language and culture hold sway, as it still does. But through Islam and the Koran, Arabic cultural mores and language would continue to influence other Muslim peoples, though in less forward-looking ways than before. Islam itself would provide all Muslim societies not only moral and ritual precepts and theological doctrines, but also (unlike Christianity) strong guidelines for government and civil and criminal law. Muslim caliphs and sultans were Caesars *and* emissaries of God.

Even as Muslim armies successfully beat back the Crusades, the Arabs' missionary drive lapsed and Islamic civilization continued to wane. On October 2, 1187, the Kurdish warrior Saladin (Salah al-Din) recaptured Palestine from the Christian Kingdom of Jerusalem. His chivalrous relationship with Richard I of England,

Statue of Saladin on his steed by the entrance to the main market of Damascus.

the "Lionheart," earned Saladin a place in Dante's Limbo as a virtuous pagan soul. Saladin's Ayyubid Sultanate ruled Egypt, Syria, Iraq, and much of the Arabian Peninsula with considerable cultural tolerance for the age. But Arab Islamic thinking was turning inward, becoming more suspicious of conflicts between faith and reason, and more conservative.

The Mongol conquest of Baghdad in 1258 by Genghis Khan's grandson, Hulagu, ranks as a pivotal moment in the decline of Arab civilization. Throughout his long and productive career, historian Bernard Lewis has forcefully argued that the Mongols did not destroy Arab civilization, because it was in advanced decay long before they appeared. Nor, Lewis writes, did they destroy Islamic civilization, which in predominantly Persianized form thrived under their rule.[3] Still, much of the accumulated knowledge of the ages was lost when Baghdad's Great Library was sacked and burned. Survivors of the pillage saw the waters of the Tigris running black from the huge quantity of ink leached from books thrown in the river. The city's hospitals, medicines, and medical manuscripts vanished into dust and ash. Mesopotamia's irrigation infrastructure and network of canals, which had spawned our species' first civilization, were wrecked.[4]

After sacking Baghdad, Hulagu began to rebuild. He encouraged technological experimentation and constructed an observatory at Maragh—although by then, leading Arab clerics perceived all Mongol activities as demonically anti-Islamic and so ruined the observatory themselves. Despite converting to Islam, the Mongols still valued Genghis Khan's Yasa code of laws over Islamic Sharia. Arab theologians denounced the Mongol embrace of Muslim faith as false and dangerous.

Ibn Taymiyah, the son of a cleric who had fled from Baghdad to Damascus in 1268, issued a religious decree (*fatwa*) against the Mongols, declaring them apostates who must be driven out and destroyed through violent rebellion. He led resistance to the Mongol invasion of Damascus in 1300, calling for holy war (*jihad*) and martyrdom (*ishtihad*) against Mongol "infidels" (*kuffar*) to save the soul of Islam from contamination (*jahiliyah*). To recover the Golden Age of Arab civilization also required opposing the Shi'a for deviating from the true and pure way (*salafiyah*) of Mohammed and his original band of followers. (Shia Islam rejects the legitimacy of the Sunni caliphs and holds that Mohammed's cousin and son-in-law, Ali, was the first of a line of the Prophet's descendants, known as Imams, possessing special spiritual powers). The Mu'tazila and even Ash'ari forms of Sufism also had to be rejected for emphasizing personal revelation and interpretation over literal truth.

Ibn Taymiyah was a Koranic literalist, accused of anthropomorphism and imprisoned in 1306 in Cairo's citadel for taking a reference to Allah's hand, foot, and face too concretely. "What can my enemies possibly do to me?" He taunted them: "My paradise is my heart. . . . For me, prison is a place of retreat; execution is my opportunity for martyrdom." Seven hundred years later, the radical Egyptian Islamist Sayyid Qutb would suffer imprisonment and execution for his verbal assault on the "Mongols" of the new age, corrupt Muslim regimes suborned by European influence and the narrow interests of secular nationalism over the entire community of believers (*ummah*). For those who instigated the assassination of Egyptian president Anwar Sadat and who came to constitute the core of Al Qaeda, Ibn Taymiyah's philosophy and Sayyid Qutb's example became the touchstones of modern jihad.

The physical and psychological impact of the Mongol invasion on the Arab Islamic Empire is somewhat comparable to the Germanic conquest of the Western Roman Empire. It took nearly a thousand years for Europe to recover, and eventually surpass, the Greco-Roman world's level of learning and knowledge.[5] Modern jihadis argue that it's about time the Muslim world finds itself again. By that they basically mean a reunification of all Islamic societies through a process of "re-Arabization," and "regrowth" into the lands of the infidel.

REAWAKENING TO THE DREAM

The first "Arab Reawakening" began in the early eighteenth century, in the terribly austere Arabian heartland, which had produced Mohammed. Like the ninth-century religious reformer Ibn Hanbal, Muhammad ibn 'Abd Al Wahab (1703–1792) preached strict obedience to the Koran and Hadith (the Prophet's sayings) and rejection of innovations that religion didn't justify. Al Wahab allied himself with Mohammed Ibn Sa'ud, the ruler of a small market town, Dir'iyya. Together, Al Wahab and Ibn Sa'ud dedicated their struggle to expand the rule of Sharia to all Arabs and then to all Muslims. The Saudi-Wahabi alliance adopted military drill and training tactics that were becoming standard in European armies, while instilling moral fervor with a literal and uncompromising interpretation of the Koran akin to the religious fervor of the ancient Hebrew tribes of the Kingdom of Judah in the seventh century B.C.

The Wahabis invaded Syria and Iraq but were eventually crushed by Egyptian and Ottoman troops who had learned the hard way from Napoléon that "God is on the side of the army with the best artillery." Shortly after World War I, however, the Saudis conquered nearly the whole of Arabia, driving out the rival Hashemites. (The British installed the defeated Hashemite princes as rulers of the newly created kingdoms of Jordan and Iraq, whose borders were drawn by a stroke of the pen—largely by Winston Churchill and T. E. "Lawrence of Arabia" Lawrence, at the Cairo Conference of 1921.)[6]

From Napoléon's invasion of Egypt in 1798 to the Franco-British-Israeli attempt to retake the Suez Canal in 1956, European power and dominance in the area surpassed even that of the thirteenth-century Mongols. The Ottomans had rescued Islam for a pincer movement by Christian powers: Russia from the north, Venice from the west, Portugal from its trading bases in India to the east. Like the samurai of Japan, the Ottomans tried to close off their society from European influence, but only succeeded in delaying the inevitable and weakening themselves.

Britain seized Aden on the Arabian peninsula in 1839, and occupied Egypt in 1882. France annexed Algeria in 1834 and secretly split Morocco with Spain in 1904. Upon the collapse of the Ottoman Empire after World War I, the League of Nations ratified Britain's right to maintain its armies in the area and to rule Transjordan and Iraq, while France received rights to Lebanon and Syria.

In 1916, Britain and France had secretly agreed to this division of the Middle East, though this was a double-cross of the Arabs, who had been promised one nation stretching from the gates of Persia to the Mediterranean as a reward for fighting the Ottoman Turks. Then, with Lord Balfour's Declaration in 1917, Britain compromised herself with yet another compact, this time with the Jews. For their help, Britain would give them a homeland in Palestine; and so Transjordan would be separated into two mandates, Jordan and Palestine. The mandates for Britain and France were to prepare their wards for democracy, though in fact this was classic colonial rule.[7] After World War II, the appetite for colonialism waned and each mandate became an independent nation. The roots of the current confessional and territorial conflicts in the region emanate from these divisions.

But we're getting ahead of ourselves, so let's back up for minute. Following the French Revolution and the invasion of Egypt by Napoléon, the Ottoman Turks began opening embassies in Europe, importing military expertise and books, and sending students to European cities and universities. In Europe the "Young Ottomans" began criticizing the regime and smuggling clandestine published materials into Turkey. In 1729, Istanbul acquired its first printing press, but thirteen years later all printing was stopped as being potentially too subversive. In the late nineteenth and early twentieth centuries came the "Young Turks": secular, liberal, and nationalist. As with the Young Ottomans, the influence of the Young Turks was often most keenly felt in the ranks of up-and-coming military officers. They saw themselves as patriots devoted to Turkish nationalism rather than to the Islamic Caliphate. They wanted to emulate European innovation so that the Ottoman state, known as the Sick Man of Europe, could renew itself and better compete on the world stage.

ISLAM AND NATIONALISM: A FAILED MARRIAGE

After the Ottoman collapse, and the dismantling in 1923 of the last Islamic Caliphate by Turkey's secularist modernizer, Mustafa Kemal Ataturk, political ambitions in the region diverged along two paths. The first political path, secular and nationalist (pan-Arab) as opposed to religious and imperial (restoration of the Muslim Caliphate), initially predominated. Christian Arabs spearheaded this attempt at an "Arab National Reawakening" modeled on European success.[8] By the 1960s it seemed to Bernard Lewis that "in our time, that stamp [of common identity impressed by Islam] is growing dim" in the Middle East and elsewhere.[9] But Western models—whether nationalism, fascism, socialism, or communism—utterly failed to bring prosperity or even security to the Middle East or elsewhere in the Muslim world during the second half of the twentieth century.

It's far from clear if greater long-term success will come about through recent American attempts to revive this general approach in Iraq and Afghanistan with a hybrid model inspired by democratic liberalism and native confessional politics, and, of course, our insatiable need for "black gold" and "strategic depth." Already by 1942, the United States had 45 percent of the world's known reserves but was depleting these reserves at a faster rate than the rest of the world. In contrast, Saudi production at the time was increasing about tenfold per year. As State Department economic adviser Herbert Feis noted: "In all of the surveys of the situation, the pencil came to an awed pause and one point and one place—the Middle East."[10] By February 1943, Roosevelt had decided that the defense of the Middle East was "vital to the defense of the United States"[11] and that the region's oil reserves should come under U.S. control for the indefinite future, given that the center of world oil production was inexorably shifting from the Gulf-Caribbean region to the Middle East and Persian Gulf. With the dawning realization (since about 1969)[12] that exponential growth in oil production would not likely continue into the twenty-first century, despite the world's largest economies and emerging markets needing it to continue, competition for Middle East oil has only become more acute.[13]

The Bush administration's initial plans for Iraq on the model of the post–World War II Marshall Plan for Germany or General MacArthur's reconstruction of Japan seemed unwise *before* the Iraq war began.[14] The United States was able to generate civil societies in Germany and Japan because both countries were ethnically homogeneous, highly nationalistic, and economically well developed. This permitted rapid political consensus and quick reconstruction of industrial infrastructure. Rather than execute the emperor of Japan as the war criminal he was, MacArthur wisely reinstated him as a benign national figurehead to facilitate this process. Iraq, however, is a colonial construction forced upon an ethnic hodgepodge in the aftermath of World War I. In 1921,

Britain arranged a "plebiscite" in order to give Iraq to Faisal Ibn Hussein, son of the King of the Hejaz (Saudi Arabia), as compensation for Faisal being kicked out of Syria by the French. In 1968, the nationalist Baath Party seized power, forsaking its earlier pan-Arabism for a fictitious unity based on descent from ancient Mesopotamia in order to keep newfound oil wealth to itself.

The emergence of liberal democracy historically requires a high degree of nationalism as a primary source of social identity. Nationalism depends on social and economic mobility across cultural boundaries, which generally comes with industrialization. Without institutions to override primary confessional loyalties, liberal democracy has not proven strong at dealing with rival claims of long-standing ethnic communities living on traditional territory in multicultural settings.

This doesn't mean that democracy can't take root in such settings, but implementing it isn't at all easy. Simply providing an institutional framework for democracy—like elections, a constitution, and courts—may be meaningless if not organically based in local society, history, and culture, just as putting the subjects of British colonies in wigs and inserting them into an English-style courtroom did not ensure that the rule of law would prevail after independence. Fostering the creation of a large and stable middle class is probably necessary, though not sufficient (the one significant finding from political science is that maintaining a stable democracy requires maintaining a large and stable middle class). Opening up economic opportunity helps, but not if the path to economic improvement is widely perceived as undermining local moral values and inciting a collapse of traditional cultures.

RELIGIOUS COMEBACK: ISLAMIC REVIVALISM

The second political path taken after the collapse of the Ottoman Empire was inspired by Wahabism, which has aimed at uprooting and expelling the interests and influence of "infidels" in Muslim lands. Many of the muftis and mullahs (and even Shi'a ayatollahs)—all former state functionaries who originally embraced European innovations in commerce, technology, education, and government—turned against what they (often rightly) perceived as neocolonial attempts to dominate implementation of those innovations in Islamic lands for mostly European, rather than Arab or Muslim, benefit. They rejected the "trickle-down" theory of modernization.

In 1928 Egypt's Hassan Al Banna founded the Muslim Brotherhood (Ikhwan al-Musulmiyah). Through extensive charitable and educational operations, it sought to enroll people into a major political opposition group. With strong ties to Wahabism but also to Sufi mysticism, the Brotherhood campaigned against political and social injustice and British imperial rule, while painting a picture of Islam that restored the broken links of tradition by connecting them to modernity. By the end of the 1940s, the Brotherhood numbered 1 million members.

It flexibly organized itself into paramilitary cells that could hide and disperse when stronger forces prevailed, but which could unite when conditions permitted political opposition. The cell structure itself was thoroughly modern, inspired by the success of fascist and communist cell organizations in Europe. This enabled the brotherhood to survive the assassination of its founder and to spread throughout the Middle East and beyond. It still commands large and even growing support (judging from recent elections in Egypt) despite numerous crackdowns over the years by various Middle Eastern governments. The Palestinian Hamas is basically a branch of the Muslim Brotherhood, formed by joining part of the Jordanian Brotherhood (in the West Bank) with part of the Egyptian Brotherhood (in Gaza) after these parts had become separated from their parent organizations by the Israeli victory in the Six-Day War.

A "purist" (*salafi*) extension of this second path to Muslim power, more virulent and violent, categorically rejects the brotherhood's willingness to compromise with other political organizations and the state. The mission of the friends and admirers of Al Qaeda is to usher in universal justice by purging Muslim society of "deviant and impure" elements, such as Shi'ism and Sufism, which had supposedly violated the spirit and letter of the sacred texts (*sunna*) and helped to bring ruination to Islamic Arab civilization. But to accomplish this task against "the near enemy" within, the Islamic community must first fight "the far enemy," who gives life support to corrupt governments that continue to crush the aspirations of all pure Muslims and prevent others from finding the true and righteous path. This far enemy, primarily the United States and its allies, are the "New Mongols."[15] Most people in the Middle East and the larger Muslim world reject this most radical and violent political path. But its rise on the world scene will likely continue to strongly influence hearts and minds and events for some time to come.

CHAPTER 6
THE TIDES OF TERROR

And Samson said, Let me die with the Philistines. And he bowed
himself with all his might; and the house fell upon the lords, and
upon all the people that were therein. So the dead which he slew
at his death were more than they which he slew in his life.

—JUDGES 16:30

Terrorism involves spectacular and often unexpected killings
in order to destabilize the social order and promote a greater
cause.[1] The tactic is probably as old as *Homo sapiens*, but its
use waxes and wanes with the tides of history. To bring in new
blood, terrorist groups routinely goad their enemies into overre-
acting, preferably by committing atrocities: Get the others to drive
in the sheep, and collect the wool. Two millennia ago, the first Jewish revolt against Roman occupation began with youths throwing
stones, and Roman commanders telling their soldiers to sheathe
their swords and defend themselves with wooden staves. The Jewish Zealots and Sicarii ("daggers") upped the ante, much as Hamas
would do later against Israelis, and Iraqi and Afghan insurgents
would do against America's coalition. They attacked Roman soldiers and their Greek underlings in self-sacrificial acts during public ceremonies, cranking up the wheels of revenge and retribution.

The Sicarii and Zealots, who claimed to be freedom fighters but whom the Romans deemed terrorists,[2] modeled their mission on Samson, who centuries before had brought down on himself a Philistine temple for love of Israel.

The Jewish revolt ended with mass suicide of perhaps hundreds of Sicarii warriors and their families at the desert fortress of Masada in A.D. 73. But that was hardly the end of the story. This "heroic" death inspired two subsequent revolts, ending with Rome expelling Jews from Judea, including many Christians who still considered themselves Jews. Judea became "Palaestina," renamed for the Philistines. The Jewish Diaspora spread a universalizing faith to the far corners of the world, eventually converting the Roman emperor Constantine and the Arab tribesman Mohammed to monotheism.

To be sure, these subsequent developments were largely unplanned and unintended consequences of the Jewish revolt. History, like evolution, is a largely contingent affair based on opportunistic responses to chance and happenstance, whatever those who believe in Revelations, Marx, or Mohammed may preach. But one constant is that faith in a divine or historically transcendent purpose is often cause enough to excuse even the murdering of innocents, because in many a cause only the committed can be fully human.

THE ANARCHISTS AND THE FIRST AMERICAN WAR ON TERROR

While, then, every part of our country thus feels an immediate and particular interest in union, all the parts combined . . . must derive from union an exemption from those broils and wars . . . which opposite foreign alliances, attachments, and intrigues would stimulate and embitter. Hence, likewise, they will avoid the necessity of those overgrown military establishments which, under any form of government, are inauspicious to liberty, and which are to be regarded as particularly hostile to republican liberty.

—GEORGE WASHINGTON, FAREWELL ADDRESS,

SEPTEMBER 17, 1796

[W]e must reject isolationism and its companion, protectionism. Retreating behind our borders would only invite danger. In the twenty-first century, security and prosperity at home depend on the expansion of liberty abroad.

—GEORGE W. BUSH, FAREWELL ADDRESS,

JANUARY 16, 2009

Between these bookends is the history of America's ambitions. The tipping point came with the first "War on Terror" around the turn of the last century. Historian David Rapoport argues, with some justification, that anarchism represents the first wave of the modern tide of terrorism.[3] Beginning in Russia around 1870, a loosely connected worldwide movement arose, egalitarian in principle and dedicated to the elimination of the power of the state and international capital. The Russian group, Narodnaya Volya ("People's Will"), conceived of violent action as "propaganda by deed" to force the czarist state to grant constitutional rights. To this end, the only feasible politics was political terrorism, using spectacular, theatrical displays to sensitize the masses. Modern suicide bombing as a political tool stems from the assassination of Czar Alexander II of Russia in 1881 by a member of Narodnaya Volya, Ignacy Hryniewiechi, who intentionally blew himself up in the attack.

The People's Will introduced the idea that terrorists should tailor attacks to maximize publicity, and encouraged science education to gain the means to enhance the dramatic power of the deed. This was also the view expressed by Sergei Nechayev and Mikhail Bakunin in the *Revolutionary Catechism* (1870), which called on those opposing "the ruling classes," especially students, to develop a new "science of destruction," for which they should be studying "mechanics, physics, chemistry, [and] perhaps medicine." In Russia, anarchists succeeded in assassinating numerous government ministers.

The anarchist movement soon spread throughout Europe and on to the Americas. Between 1894 and 1900, anarchist assassins had killed the president of France, the empress of Austria, and the king of Italy. In September 1901, anarchist Leon Czolgosz assassinated U.S. president William McKinley. The world community of nations considered anarchism to pose the greatest threat to the internal political and economic order and to international stability. The political (and to some extent social and economic) consequences from this first wave of modern terror were similar in many respects to those of the 9/11 attacks.

In his first Annual Message to Congress after McKinley's death, the new president, Theodore Roosevelt, declared the anarchist to be the incarnation of "evil" and a "foe of liberty" acting against all mankind: "The cause of his criminality is to be found in his own evil passions and in the evil conduct of those who urge him on, not in any failure by others or by the state to do justice to him or his."[4] Roosevelt made the defeat of anarchism an overriding mission of his administration: "When compared with the suppression of anarchy, every other question sinks into insignificance. The anarchist is the enemy of humanity, the enemy of all mankind; and his is a deeper degree of criminality than any other."[5]

Roosevelt didn't restrict the fight against terrorism to anarchists alone. He expanded the war on anarchy into an imperial mission to intervene in any country around the world if necessary to protect it from foreign evil and preserve it from chaos. "Chronic wrongdoing," he said, "or an impotence which results in a general loosening of the ties of civilized society, may in America, as elsewhere, ultimately require intervention by some civilized nation, and may lead the United States, however reluctantly, in flagrant cases of such wrongdoing or impotence, to the exercise of an international police power."[6]

Most tellingly, the war against anarchy and terror helped to justify the brutal repression of a native insurgency against U.S. rule in the Philippines.

Resentful of Spain's lingering colonial hold in the Americas and sensing how easy it would be to defeat that decaying imperial power, many in the United States called for war. An opportunity came when the U.S battleship *Maine* mysteriously blew up in Havana harbor in February 1898. By the end of that year, the United States had officially taken possession of Cuba, Puerto Rico, Guam, and the Philippines. Albert Beveridge, a Republican senator from Indiana, proclaimed: "God has not been preparing the English-speaking and Teutonic Peoples for a thousand years for nothing but vain contemplation. No! He has made us the master organizers of the world. . . . He has made us adept at governments that we may administer government among savage and senile peoples."[7] President McKinley declared that "there was nothing for us to do but . . . to educate the Filipinos and to Christianise them," although most Filipinos were already practicing Catholics.

In the presidential campaign of 1900, Roosevelt accused Democratic candidate William Jennings Bryan of catering to barbarism and chaos by refusing to support America's civilizing mission in the Philippines. Civilizing in the Philippines, instituted by General Arthur MacArthur (father of Douglas MacArthur), involved a scorched-earth policy reminiscent of Sherman's march to Atlanta, devastating villages, even whole regions, and torturing prisoners, a preferred method again being water-boarding.[8]

Among the natives of the Muslim south, insurgents known as *juramentados* (from the Spanish *jurar*, to take an oath) fought with simple bladed weapons against American personnel whom they considered to be unbelievers and trespassers. They swore to become martyrs to jihad, often attacking near markets to maximize mayhem and publicity from their acts, expecting to be killed, much in the manner of the Jewish Zealots nearly two millennia before. The future commander of U.S. military forces in World War I, John "Blackjack" Pershing, was an intelligence officer in Moro Province who ordered fallen *juramentados* to be wrapped in pigskin to show their communities that heaven was barred to terrorists.[9] Muslim nationalists in the area today have appropriated the term Moros. The jihadis among them consider themselves heirs of the *juramentados*, still suffering the broken vow of the Bates Treaty of 1899, in which the United States had promised the Moros, who had long been fighting the Spanish, their sovereignty.[10]

While the anarchist threat was used to justify international adventurism, state reaction to anarchism played a formative role in creating national police and intelligence. The Secret Service and later FBI, Scotland Yard, and the Russian Okhrana (forerunner to the NKVD and KGB) were born to bust anarchist conspiracies. What seemed to make anarchism such a pressing threat was the radical transformation in political, economic, communication, and transportation patterns of the age. Under popular pressures unleashed by the French Revolution, absolute monarchies were softening into constitutional monarchies and even liberal trade democracies. People and capital moved across international frontiers with an ease that in some respects is not matched even in today's era of "globalization."

In 1912, two years before the start of World War I, Imperial Russia and the Turkish Sultanate alone required passports. Only with the world trade agreements in the late 1990s were capital flows again able to recover this pre–World War I degree of freedom. The telegraph, mass daily newspapers, and railroads flourished in this period. The first "real-time" diffusion of news across the world could be arguably dated to August 27, 1883, when the Indonesian volcanic island of Krakatoa exploded and disappeared.[11] Again in

1912, the first transpacific radiotelegraph service linked San Francisco with Hawaii.

From the beginning of human history until the nineteenth century, the exercise and extension of human power depended almost exclusively upon physical forces readily available in nature: sun, water, wind, plants, animals, and minerals accessible by muscle. By the beginning of the twentieth century, the airplane, automobile, and transcontinental communication by wireless radio were beginning to shrink time and space by quantum leaps over all previous advances.

Most worrisome was the ability of anarchists to get their hands on the first weapons of mass destruction: the machine gun, invented during the American Civil War but first used with totally devastating effect in the Boer War;[12] dynamite, invented by Alfred Nobel, and its derivatives, including hand grenades and other forms of personal bombs; and chemical weapons.

Although the policies of the U.S. and European states to combat anarchism were often predicated on fighting a well-organized international terrorist network, in fact there was little international or centralized terrorist planning (and in the case of the McKinley assassination, no organized plot at all). Remarkably, it was only when the Warren Commission inquiry into the assassination of President John F. Kennedy studied previous assassination attempts against U.S. presidents did the government conclude that there really never had been an "anarchist central."

Rather, as with current jihadi operations, anarchist attacks were usually carried out by peer groups (mostly friends and sometimes kin) who self-organized in operations of relatively few people. As with jihadism, anarchist ideology and operations often parasitized preexisting local ethnic and national aspirations and organizations: for example, the Serbian "Black Hand," which plotted the assassination of Austria's Archduke Ferdinand, sparking World War I. Following the war, Bolshevism effectively co-opted militant anarchism as a world political force. The process culminated with Stalin undermining the anarchists on the Republican side during the Spanish Civil War, giving a temporary victory to fascism and impetus for another world war.

With communism's demise came the unipolar world and a vacuum for jihad's rise.

THE AL QAEDA RIPTIDE

Al Qaeda today is mostly an idea; more a violent Islamist revivalist social movement than a terrorist organization. The Al Qaeda of the media is just a small organization within this larger social movement. After the U.S.–led invasion of Afghanistan, its shattered remnants mostly fled to the Pakistan frontier, where they now spend much of their time hiding out in caves from Predator drones. But the viral movement continues to fester among immigrant youth in Europe, and to spread in places like Yemen, Somalia, the Sahel, and the World Wide Web, where explosive dreams of glory can easily outshine the inglorious drudgery of deadened hopes.

Al Qaeda's story has been told before,[13] so here I give just a brief overview. People often confuse Al Qaeda the terrorist organization with the Qaeda-inspired jihadi social movement, because for about five years, 1996–2001, Al Qaeda more or less controlled the social movement. The segment of that movement that emerged as a threat to the United States came out of Egypt. Most of the leadership and ideology of Al Qaeda hews to the philosophy of Egypt's Sayyid Qutb (1906–1966), who was hanged by Egyptian president Gamal Abdel Nasser for sedition, and from Qutb's intellectual progeny, who assassinated Anwar Sadat in 1981. Sadat's successor, Hosni Mubarak, released most of those arrested three years later.

Some of the men released, who continued to be harassed by

the Egyptian police, migrated to Afghanistan to fight in a "holy war" against the invading Soviets (1979–1989). With the end of the Soviet-Afghan War, they continued jihad. These Arab outsiders actually didn't fight in the Soviet-Afghan War except for one small battle at Jaji, which was primarily defensive: The Arabs had put their camp on the main logistical supply line, and in the spring of 1987 the Soviets tried to destroy it. The Arabs were actually more the recipients of a Soviet attack then the initiators of any action themselves. The United States, which was funneling money and supplies to the far more important groups of Afghan mujahedin, had no contact with the Arabs in Afghanistan. Neither, really, did the Afghans themselves, who resented the Arabs trying to tell them how to worship and make jihad. That's also why almost no Afghans were closely associated with Al Qaeda until after 9/11, when America bombed them into togetherness.

After the war, many of these foreigners returned to their countries. Those already deemed terrorists couldn't return and remained in Afghanistan. In 1991, Algeria and Egypt complained to Pakistan that it was harboring terrorists, so Pakistan expelled them. Some of the most militant made their way back to Algeria, which was in a civil war, or to Sudan, invited by Hassan al-Turabi, the Sorbonne-educated leader of Sudan's ruling National Islamic Front.

Although Qutb became a leader of Egypt's Muslim Brotherhood, which first proposed to reestablish the organic wholeness of the Muslim world in a political program, his later followers, including the person who eventually became Bin Laden's closest sidekick, the Egyptian pharmacologist and surgeon Ayman Zawahiri, rabidly rejected the brotherhood's willingness to compromise with the secular authority of the state, even temporarily. Zawahiri repudiated the traditional injunction to promote the consensus of the community (*jima*) and foreswear discord (*fitna*). He argued that harmony would be restored when apostates, infidels, and those who challenge territorial ascendancy by "pure Islam" (*salafi*) were destroyed.

Salafi (from *salaf*, "ancient ones" or "predecessors" in Arabic) is an emulation, an imitation of the legendary Muslim community that existed at the time of Mohammed, which Salafis believe was the only fair and just society that ever existed. A very small subset of Salafis believe that the necessary goal of creating a Salafi state in a core Arab country cannot be achieved peacefully, either through mere force of ideas—no matter how true or noble—or through democratic elections. In this worldview, to even speak of democracy is blasphemy because the imposition of God's law cannot be left as a matter of choice among mortals. The religious utopia that jihadis seek strongly resembles the secular utopias in nineteenth- and twentieth-century European thought, such as fascism's organic ethnic community or communism's classless international society.

Takfir wal Hijira (Excommunication and Withdrawal), founded in Egypt in 1971 by agricultural engineer Shukri Mustafa, first elaborated the ideology of Qutb and began to put it into practice. Mustafa called for withdrawal from Egyptian society, which he considered alienated from the Muslim community, or *kafir*. In 1977 the group carried out its first action by kidnapping a Muslim cleric (more in reaction to police harassment than intent to attack society).

Mustafa, who was captured and executed in 1978, inspired members of al-Gama'a al-Islamiyah (the Islamic Group), an umbrella organization for militant student groups formed after the leadership of the Muslim Brotherhood renounced violence in the 1970s to avoid a confrontation with the police and army. Al-Gama'a al-Islamiyah militants were inspired by Mustafa's followers, who were tortured in prison but held fast to their faith. The umbrella organization included a group that called itself Tanzim al-Jihad, or simply Al Jihad (created in 1980), of which Zawahiri became an emir, or leader. Zawahiri was never directly implicated in the 1981 assassination of Sadat, but he was imprisoned all the same. Released in 1985, Zawahiri left for Saudi Arabia and then traveled to Peshawar, Pakistan, where he treated Muslims wounded in the war against the Soviets and met Osama Bin Laden.

Zawahiri continues to urge jihadis everywhere to inflict the greatest possible damage and cause the maximum casualties on the West, no matter how much time and effort operations take, and regardless of the consequences. Unconstrained by concrete concerns for what will happen to any population that supports them, deracinated jihadis can seriously consider any manner of attack. This includes apocalyptic visions of nuclear weapons inflicting millions of casualties on the United States unless it changes its foreign policy in the Middle East and elsewhere in the Muslim world.[14] Fortunately, there's no indication that Al Qaeda ever had the capability to acquire such weapons, and it has such ability much less now than before.

Perhaps the greatest impetus to the spread of the Takfiri doctrine that allows targeting of fellow Muslims was the Algerian civil war. The violent conflict, which cost some 200,000 lives during the 1990s, began in December 1991, when the Islamic Salvation Front (FIS) was poised to win the national elections. The secular National Liberation Front (FLN), which had ruled the country since independence from France in 1962 (and still does), canceled voting after the first round. After the FIS was banned and thousands of its members arrested, Islamist guerrillas, led by returning veterans from the Soviet-Afghan War, began an armed campaign against the state.

The guerrillas formed themselves into several groups, principally the Islamic Armed Movement (MIA), based in the mountains, and the Armed Islamic Group (GIA), based in the towns. They initially targeted the army and police, but soon started attacking civilians in a calculated campaign to instill terror and provoke the government into counteratrocities that would further alienate its popular support. Zawahiri, especially, took their lesson to heart, but he needed Bin Laden's charisma and money to globalize a new mode of action.

Takfiri doctrine represents an extreme form of Salafism, and modern Salafism is historically related to Wahabism. But it is important to understand that Wahabis are not Takfiris; nor are most Salafis. Just as Calvinism rejects opposition to the (Protestant) state, so a central tenet of Wahabism is loyalty to the (Saudi) state and rejection of violence against fellow (Sunni) Muslims. Nearly all Saudis are also Salafis, as are many Egyptians. But most reject Takfiri doctrine and even deeply oppose it (much as most Christian fundamentalists reject Christian supremacist doctrine).[15] We offend millions by simply denouncing "Salafis."

The Khartoum period is critical in the development of the Al Qaeda terrorist organization and to the Takfiri theology that allows targeting of civilians and fellow Muslims. One of Sudan's "guests" was Bin Laden and the group around him, which had called itself Al Qaeda ever since the last stages of the Soviet-Afghan War. Another guest was Zawahiri, the leader of Al Jihad, an older and distinct group but one allied with Al Qaeda since its beginning. In June 1995, with Khartoum's complicity, Zawahiri's group unsuccessfully tried to kill Mubarak on his visit to Ethiopia. A few months later, Zawahiri sent two suicide bombers to blow up the Egyptian embassy in Pakistan. Although most of the 76 people killed and wounded were Muslims, and Pakistan itself was then supporting the most radical mujahedin in Afghanistan's ongoing civil war and funneling mujahedin into Kashmir to fight India, Zawahiri reasoned that any innocent loss of life or damage to Pakistan would be rewarded in paradise as a necessary sacrifice for the cause. At first Bin Laden wasn't happy about the attack, but he would soon come to embrace Zawahiri's new theory of "martyrdom" and suicide-bombing tactics.

In Khartoum, the jihadis reasoned that they had been unable to overthrow their own governments—the "near enemy," including Zawahiri's native Egypt and Bin Laden's native Saudi Arabia—because these governments were propped up by the "far enemy,"

America. The jihadis decided to redirect their efforts. Instead of going after Egypt and Saudi Arabia, they would attack America. Because of intense pressure and threats from Egypt, Saudi Arabia, and Pakistan, and international sanctions imposed by the United States, Sudan was forced to expel Zawahiri, and then Bin Laden. In August 1996, within two months of returning to Afghanistan, Bin Laden issued a fatwa declaring war on the United States.

The fatwa clearly articulated the new goals of this movement, which were to force America out of the Middle East so that the movement would then be free to overthrow the Saudi monarchy or the Egyptian regime and establish a Salafi state. The suicide bombings of U.S. embassies in East Africa in 1988 and the USS *Cole* in 2000, as well as the attacks on the World Trade Center and Pentagon in 2001, were intended to advance this goal.

But the jihadi movement today is no longer under the control of the Al Qaeda terrorist organization and is no longer primarily aimed at freeing Muslim homelands from perceived occupiers. It has become the speckled fight of small, self-organizing groups of mostly young men who dream of belonging to a revolutionary global Islamic movement that would dispense Islamic justice. For centuries, the reasoning of Islamic jurists (*ulema*) has set down rules of inter-action to cover almost any matter of trade, war, or peace between *Dar al-Islam* (The House of Islam, Land of Islam) and *Dar al-Kufar* (the House of Unbelief) or *Dar al-Harb* (the House of War). Always clearly grounded in passages from the Koran, these rules have con-tained lethal sanctions against apostates, idolaters, and those who challenge Muslim territorial dominance and the God-given right and duty to expand that dominance across the world.

Traditionally, however, there have been strong limits on using violence except when the House of Islam is under direct threat of physical attack. If there are no strong leaders and armies to defend, then it becomes a *fard al-'ayn*—a sacred duty incumbent upon every Muslim individual—to repel the infidel by any means necessary. According to Sayyid Qutb, "When they attack Dar al-Islam, it is *fard al-'ayn*, *fard* for every Muslim, woman or man, to fight."[16] As Bin Laden and Zawahiri put it in a 1998 fatwa calling for "Jihad against Crusaders and Jews":

> Ulema have throughout Islamic history unanimously agreed that the jihad is an individual duty if the enemy destroys the Muslim countries. . . . On that basis, and in compliance with Allah's order, we issue the following fatwa to all Muslims: The ruling to kill the Americans and their allies—civilians and military—is an individual duty for every Muslim who can do it in any country in which it is possible to do it, in order to liberate the al-Aqsa Mosque [Jerusalem] and the holy mosque [Mecca] from their grip, and in order that their armies move out of all the lands of Islam, defeated and unable to threaten any Muslim.[17]

No mercy, no quarter. What the jihadi movement has done in the twenty-first century is to take such reasoning two steps further. First, because there is no pure Islamic state anywhere, then the whole world must be a House of War. Again, Qutb: "A Muslim has no country except that part of the world where the *Sharia* of God is established."[18] Second, because Islam is under global attack by America and the forces of globalization, then the whole world is a global battlefield under the injunction of *fard al-'ayn*. "American Crusader interests are everywhere," reiterated Sufyan al-Azdi al-Shahri in 2010 in the name of Al Qaeda in the Arabian Peninsula: "Attack them and eliminate as many enemies as you can." As the social movement has spread to the diaspora, it has become increasingly global in scope and apocalyptic in vision. That's the bad news. But as it washes through the margins of societies, it has also become more scattered and disjointed—materially, psychologically, and philosophically. And that's probably good news.

CHAPTER 7
A PARALLEL UNIVERSE: THE 9/11 HAMBURG GROUP AND THE THREE WAVES OF JIHAD

> There were two rams, one with horns and one without. The one
> with horns butted his head against the defenseless one. In the
> next world, Allah switched the horns from one ram to the other,
> so justice could prevail.
>
> —SUBSTITUTE IMAM AT AL QUDS MOSQUE IN HAMBURG, WHERE
> THE BOMBER PILOTS OF 9/11 PRAYED, TO MARC SAGEMAN
> AND ME WHEN WE ASKED, "WHY DID THEY DO IT?"

At a quarter to nine on the morning of September 11, 2001, Mohammed Atta, along with four other young men, seized American Airlines Flight 11 and crashed the fully fueled Boeing 767 into the North Tower of New York City's World Trade Center to reignite world history. Eighteen minutes later, Marwan al-Shehi, a friendly and perceptive young man, according to all who knew him, and another foursome of helpers banked American Airlines Flight 175 into the WTC's South Tower, where Josh Rosenthal and thousands of others had just begun their workday. Josh's mother, Marilyn, who has dedicated her life to improving health care in America and abroad, went to the United Arab Emirates to meet with Marwan's family "to try to understand why two such promising young men had to die this way." She told me that Marwan's parents still refuse to believe it could have been him, or if it was, that he must have been tricked.

Around the time Josh was killed, five hijackers stormed the cockpit of American Airlines Flight 77 from Washington-Dulles to Los Angeles. One of them, Hani Hanjour, who had once lived in the United States, took the controls while passengers who were forced to the back of the plane called loved ones on their cell phones—until 9:37 Eastern time, the minute they all perished, when the aircraft slammed into the west face of the Pentagon.

Passengers aboard a fourth flight, United Airlines 93, now aware of events at the World Trade Center, didn't die without a fight. At 9:47 Jeremy Glick phoned his wife, Lyz, to say that the passengers had voted to take over the plane. He told her that he loved her, to have "a good life" and to please take care of Emmy, their twelve-month-old daughter. Besides, joked the doomed husband and father, he still had his butter knife from breakfast, so all might not be lost. Jeremy and the other passengers overwhelmed the hijackers and tried to wrestle control of the plane from pilot Ziad Jarrah. The passengers probably saved the Capitol building, the symbolic heart of America's government. An hour before the flight, Ziad had phoned his girlfriend in Germany, Aysel Senguen, to tell her three times he loved her. But Ziad's love for a girl couldn't compete with a deeper, darker love for cause and comrades.[1]

The pilots had shorn their beards to be inconspicuous among infidels. They had perfumed their bodies for paradise, but too much has been made of that and their supposed sexual hang-ups and lust for heavenly virgins. True, Atta left behind a testament saying he wanted no earthly woman to touch and defile his remains. But he was peculiar that way. In Al Qaeda at the time, most were married men and many had several children, though all four 9/11 bomber pilots were bachelors. The personality of each jihadi is different.

What gives them all fanatical focus is not some inherent personality defect but the person-changing dynamics of the group.

Three of the pilots—Atta, Shehi, and Jarrah—were close friends from student days in Hamburg, along with a fourth, Ramzi bin al-Shibh. Ramzi, so very different from the often morose and uptight Atta, was the backslapping guiding spirit embracing the group. But he would be unable to get a visa into the United States. None of the four had a particularly religious upbringing; none had attended madrassahs. Ziad went to private Christian schools in Lebanon before going to study in Germany; Marwan entered Germany on an army scholarship from the United Arab Emirates; a friend who knew Ramzi back home in Yemen says "he was religious, but not too much"; Atta's father, a Cairo attorney, said his son was anything but a religious fanatic and that Bin Laden's video praising his son's martyrdom had to be "fake" (though now the father extols jihad).

All four told other friends that the chief reason they wanted to fight for the jihad was America's support of Israel and "the World Jewish Conspiracy," centered in New York City. This was one thing that drew the amicable Ramzi toward the far less sociable Atta when they first met at Hamburg's Al Quds mosque on Steindamm Strasse in 1995, later joined there by Marwan and Ziad. (Marc Sageman's recent interviews with their friends tell of them trying so very hard to obtain a copy of the *Protocols of the Elders of Zion*, the anti-Semitic tract concocted by the czarist police to point the seething anger of Russian peasants away from the regime and at the Jews. But in Germany, such books, by law, can't be sold.)[2]

A score of other co-religionists from those college days led these four middle-class Arab adventurers to Al Qaeda. They first came to meet one another at the Technical University of Hamburg-Harburg, or at the Hamburg University of Applied Sciences near the Al Quds mosque. But it was in not in classes or in the prayer room that they radicalized one another; it was in schmooze sessions, sometimes at the mosque, but more often in dorms and cafeterias, halal butcher shops and fast-food eateries, barbershops, campus steps, and libraries.

Sageman and I visited the typically German middle-class neighborhood in Harburg, a suburb of Hamburg, where the 9/11 plotters and many of their friends lived. Germans call it a *spiesser* neighborhood, meaning prim and proper and bordering on teddy-bear kitsch. The campus of the nearby Technical University is small and the student atmosphere pleasant, especially on those sparse occasions when the sun is out. It's hardly a hotbed of radical activity.

So how did it happen?

According to the 9/11 Commission: "Although Bin Laden, [Mohammed] Atef and [Khaled Sheikh Mohammed] initially contemplated using established Al Qaeda members to execute the planes operation, the late 1999 arrival in Kandahar of four aspiring jihadis from Germany suddenly presented a more attractive alternative . . . the enormous advantage of fluency in English and familiarity with life in the West. . . . Not surprisingly, Mohammed Atta, Ramzi Bin al-Shibh, Marwan al Shehhi, and Ziad Jarrah would all become key players in the 9/11 conspiracy."[3]

These observations hint at two important features of global jihad from its inception: planning is flexible and opportunistic, and key personnel come knocking at the door to enlist in jihad rather than being drawn in or lured by others. The Hamburg group wasn't recruited or brainwashed. Like most jihadi groups, it self-radicalized and then went looking for action. It was actually a fluid, constantly evolving network of friends and fellow travelers in search of making sense of their lives and the world, who flowed in and out, depending on the changing states of their visas, studies, jobs, girlfriends and wives, problems with the authorities, and other happenings in their lives. Some left because they felt the group was becoming too radical; others came in because of their attraction to increasingly radical words and the promise of radical deeds. There was no "organization" to speak of, certainly no "cells" to begin with.

The oldest part of the group was a small circle of members of the Syrian Muslim Brotherhood who had sought refuge in Germany in the late 1980s, after the Syrian government massacred thousands of their brethren. The Hamburg circle of Syrian brothers would congregate and discuss their angry vision of Islam and the world at three mosques near the central train station in Hamburg: Al Quds (The Holy, and the name for Jerusalem), Al Nur (The Light), and Al Muhajrin (The Immigrants).

The future 9/11 plotters would go from Harburg by subway to the mosques. They'd have to pass a row of sex shops on Steinheim Strasse to get to Al Quds and Al Nur. This, we were told, disturbed their religious sensibilities (Atta's in particular; he would sometimes insist, even though his friends might balk, that they make a long detour toward Alster Lake and back around to avoid seeing the women). Most notable was Al Quds, known as the Moroccan mosque because most of its attendees stemmed from that North African country, including its fiery jihadi preacher from Tangiers, Mohammed Fazazi. (When Marc Sageman and I visited the Al Dakhla mosque in Tangiers, where Fazazi began to preach jihad, and went across the street to a café where the men go after prayer, we were struck by the rapt attention they paid to the scantily clad women on American cable television. We left when we saw that they were not happy that we registered their wonder.) On Fridays, about 150 people from Hamburg's Moroccan community of 1,500–2,000 pray at Al Quds, a small, nondescript apartment structure with a bare second-story prayer room and a third-floor halal food shop, cafeteria, barbershop (where many of the youth hang out), and a set of five outdated computers. In the upstairs parts of the mosque, in fast-food eateries down the street, in dorms and friends' apartments, conversation would turn to Israel, the Jews, America, Bosnia, Chechnya, and the Muslim plight around the world, which

April 1, 1999: A gathering of friends at the Al Quds mosque. Third from right in the back row is Ramzi bin al-Shibh; Atta is in the middle row, far right, with hands on a friend's shoulders. (Source: DDP/ AFP)

the collapse of the Soviet Union and the torn curtain of bipolar conflict had brought into the light.

Ramzi and Atta had known each other for a couple of years before Marwan arrived from Bonn in early 1998. (Marwan, who had come to Germany in 1996 to study marine engineering, may have met Ramzi at the Bonn mosque, where Ramzi went when visiting the city.) But Marwan became the cheery and calm catalyst that made the trio click. "He was friendly, always in a good mood, well educated, humorous, and sometimes a little clumsy," one of his friends said. "He never spoke negatively about others and never used a negative word. He never looked stressed."[4]

In the summer of 1998, Marwan moved in with Ramzi and Atta in an apartment in Wilhelmsburg. All three worked at a warehouse, packing computers in crates for shipping. The next winter they moved to Marienstrasse 54, near the university in Harburg. Neighbors said that the trio holed up and the apartment stank. After about a month, Marwan moved to a nearby apartment and enrolled in the university, but often stayed with the other two. Ramzi and Atta finally vacated the apartment several months later, taking a bunch of mattresses with them.

This apparently unkempt and decidedly un-*spiesser* lifestyle was more self-conscious and intellectually refined than the neighbors suspected. It was the Takfiri way. Followers of Qutb and forerunners of Al Jihad and Al Qaeda, the Takfiris made their houses available for "fellow travelers" in imitation of the lifestyle of the Prophet and his disciples. They dreamed of accomplishing jihad as the hidden "sixth pillar" of Islam, which, as my colleagues' and my surveys among militants show, trumps four of the five traditional pillars that are incumbent upon all Muslims (prayer, alms, fasting during Ramadan, the hajj pilgrimage to Mecca) and is second only to the first pillar, the profession of faith in God and his Prophet.

The Hamburg group did not arise from the community in which its members lived; it could have been almost anywhere, in any city in Europe. They were basically the only Middle Easterners in the crowd, socially distant from most of the others around their neighborhood and the mosques: Germans, Turks, and North Africans. They weren't integrated into the community but withdrew from it to live in a parallel universe of jihad and emerged from their cocoon wanting action.

It's still not clear how the Hamburg Four made it to Afghanistan. One of their friends told my colleagues that they may have first wanted to do something in the Balkans. Ramzi met with Albanians in Hamburg and asked them how he could help Muslims in the Kosovo conflict that was escalating at the time (late 1998, early 1999). The Albanians reportedly told Ramzi they needed walkie-talkies, not more volunteers. Then the Hamburg Four apparently thought about going to Chechnya. Ramzi told his American interrogators[5] that he and Marwan were approached by someone named Khalid al-Masri on a train—probably, Ramzi surmised, because they were Arabs with beards. They struck up a conversation about

Chechnya, and al-Masri allegedly told Ramzi and Marwan to get in touch with a person in Duisburg, Mohamedou Slahi, a Mauritanian jihadi who had fought against the Soviets in Afghanistan. Slahi explained that it was difficult to get into Chechnya and recommended going to Afghanistan to train for jihad before trying to go on to Chechnya. Ramzi said that Slahi instructed them in how to get visas for Pakistan and how to hook up with the Taliban to reach Afghanistan.

So Ramzi and Marwan, along with Atta and Ziad Jarrah, finally made their way to that place of third choice, where they fell into the lap of Khaled Sheikh Mohammed, whose proposal to blow up American planes had only recently been accepted by Bin Laden, but in the teeth of opposition from other leading members of Al Qaeda.[6] You can almost imagine Khaled rubbing his hands in sublime disbelief, gushing to the Qaeda chief: "Hey, boss, look what showed up, guys with passports that can get them into the belly of the beast, America!"

THE THREE WAVES OF JIHAD

In *Leaderless Jihad*, Marc Sageman argues that terrorism has advanced in three overlapping waves[7]—the first wave corresponding with Afghanistan (1988–1991), the second culminating in 9/11 (1992–2001), and the third wave dominant today (post-2001), with significantly younger, less educated, and less skilled aspiring jihadis. Evidence from our database indicates some tendencies in the predicted direction, at least for Al Qaeda.

Of the three waves, our data show that the first has the highest percentage of professionals involved in the organization. The first wave also has significantly more professional members over laborers, skilled or unskilled. The opposite trend exists in the second and third waves—where the highest percentage of members are unskilled laborers.

The educational achievement patterns among the three waves differ significantly. The first wave has a higher percentage of people with a college education (although the second wave has the highest percentage of members pursuing advanced degrees). After the success of 9/11, many would-be jihadis went looking for Bin Laden and Al Qaeda. Some paid thousands of dollars out of their own pockets to seek out Al Qaeda or to find someone who had arms training in a Qaeda camp years before, or access to a Qaeda video filmmaker. This seems to be what happened with the "Crevice" plotters, Pakistani immigrants from Britain who went back to Pakistan for guidance and hatched a plan to bomb a shopping center and a nightclub in London. But because only bits and pieces of the old Al Qaeda are left, most who go looking for Al Qaeda obtain precious little direction or sophisticated expertise. Thankfully, they are often caught trying to get to what has not existed since just after 9/11.

Before and just after 9/11, jihadis, including suicide bombers, were on average materially better off and better educated relative to their populations of origin.[8] Many had a college education or advanced technical training. A background in science (particularly engineering and medicine) was positively associated with likelihood to join jihad.[9] The Hamburg group was rather typical.

This second wave is still ongoing. The so-called medical cell involved in a failed plot to blow up targets in London and Glasgow in the summer of 2007 may be an example. Three doctors—an Iraqi, a Saudi, and an Indian—who had recently immigrated to Britain were arrested for packing gas canisters and nails into several cars and trying to blow them up. The only real damage was the severe burning of the driver of one of the vehicles, the Indian doctor's cousin, an aeronautics engineer. The clumsy nature and execution of the plot suggest that, unlike the Hamburg group, the doctors' group and other vestiges of the second wave no longer have access to the funding and planning skills of the old Al Qaeda.

Much the same goes for the botched 2009 Christmas Day airline bombing attempt by a well-to-do Nigerian engineering student and the 2010 Times Square fizzle by a disaffected American-Pakistani MBA.

Now it's a third wave of more marginalized, underemployed youth that carries the fire. This new generation is driven in large part by a media-fueled global political awakening that has stoked vivid awareness of a collective perception of injustice and camaraderie with the sufferings in Iraq, Afghanistan, Palestine, Chechnya, and elsewhere. Moral outrage and a large dose of frustration and boredom seem to impel the search for meaning and adventure. Groups of friends and family originating from the same area "back home" in North Africa, the Middle East, or Central and Southern Asia, or from similar European housing projects and marginal neighborhoods, bond into action as they surf jihadi Web sites to find direction from Al Qaeda's inspiration. Like the older waves of jihadis, however, most in this third wave show little or no prior religious education until becoming "born again" in their late teens or early adulthood.

This "new wave" pattern of increasing marginality and "born-again" religion is reflected in European and North African groups that express allegiance to Al Qaeda,[10] as well as foreign fighters who went to Iraq (41 percent from Saudi Arabia and 39 percent from North Africa) between summer 2006 and fall 2007. Many came in bunches from the same town, for example, more than 50 young volunteers from Darnah, Libya,[11] according to West Point's *Sinjar Report on Foreign Fighters in Iraq*. Consider some data given to me by Saudi Arabia's Ministry of the Interior. Between 2004 and 2006, Saudi forces killed more than 100 perpetrators of terrorist events in the kingdom. Of the remaining 60 who were captured and imprisoned, 53 were interviewed. Nearly two thirds of those in the sample said they joined jihad through friends and about a quarter said they did through family.

Compared to an earlier Saudi sample,[12] the newer wave tends to be somewhat younger (and more likely to be single), less educated and less financially well off, less ideological, and more prone to prior involvement in criminal activities unrelated to jihad, such as drugs, theft, and aggravated assault. They are much more likely to read jihadi literature in their daily lives than other forms of literature. They tend to look up to role models who stress violence in jihad, like the late Abu Musab al-Zarqawi, than to those who justify and limit violence through moral reasoning, such as the late Abdullah Azzam. A majority come to religion in their early twenties. In the older cohort there was little traditional religious education; however, the newer cohort tends to be less ideologically sophisticated and especially motivated by desire to avenge perceived injustices against Muslims. (When I asked detainees in Saudi Arabia who had volunteered for Iraq why they had, some mentioned stories of women raped, the killing of innocents, and desecrations of the Koran; all mentioned Abu Ghraib.)

We'll explore this third wave of Qaeda wannabes at the Western edge of the Muslim world through case studies of the 2004 Madrid train bombings and related North African volunteers for martyrdom in Iraq, and then we'll look at Pakistan and Afghanistan, homegrown threats to the homeland, and the problem of Palestine. But first, we'll cast an eye on the first wave as it overlaps with the second wave at the eastern edge, in the October 2002 Bali bombings and other attacks spearheaded by militants of Indonesia's Jemaah Islamiyah.

Part III

WHITHER AL QAEDA? BALI AND MADRID

I call those who carried out these actions all mujahid. They all had good intentions, that is, jihad in Allah's way. . . . They are right that America is the proper target because America fights Islam. So in terms of their objectives, they are right, and the target of their attacks was right also. . . . If they made mistakes, they are only human beings who can be wrong. Moreover, their actions could be considered self-defense . . . they didn't attack because they defended themselves.

—ABU BAKR BA'ASYIR, ALLEGED EMIR OF JEMAAH
ISLAMIYAH, CIPINANG PRISON, JAKARTA, AUGUST 11, 2005
(AUTHOR'S INTERVIEW)

CHAPTER 8
FARHIN'S WAY

At 12:15 A.M. on Saturday, November 8, 2008, in an orange grove on Nusakambangan Island off southern Java, three men convicted of plotting the October 12, 2002, Bali bombings that killed 202 people stood in front of a firing squad. Their last social act while alive was to shout words, *"Allahu Akbar"* (God is Greatest), at their executioners, who then shot them each dead through the heart. Family members of two of the men, Amrozi, forty-seven years old, and his older brother Ali Ghufron, aka Mukhlas, forty-eight, who had flown in for the execution from the family's village of Tenggulun in eastern Java, were allowed to retrieve the bodies and bathe them, and to call home to say the deed was done.

Back at Tenggulun, a crowd of 200 had gathered to await the news in front of the Al-Islam religious boarding school, founded by the dead brothers' father, to promote a *salaf* form of Islam in line with the teachings of the school's patron, Abu Bakr Ba'asyir. "May our brothers, God willing, be invited by green birds to heaven now," said one man in the crowd. Ba'asyir, once the emir of Jemaah Islamiyah, the secret organization of radical Islamists to which the brothers belonged, was also there. He had previously been jailed and sentenced to death but then was retried on a lesser

OPPOSITE: *Farhin by the site of the Kompak–Jemaah Islamiyah training camp he ran near Poso, Sulawesi.*

charge of conspiracy and released the year before. The vice-president of Indonesia, who used to visit Ba'asyir in Cipinang Prison in Jakarta, said he couldn't understand why such a pious man had been locked up at all, and besides he saw no proof that such a thing as Jemaah Islamiyah ever even existed. (The governing coalition of minority parties at the time could not afford to alienate even radical Islamist support or to do anything that might please the invaders of Muslim Iraq.)[1]

On this execution day, Ba'asyir praised the bombers as mujahedin, echoing what he had said in my interview in Jakarta's Cipinang Prison in the summer of 2005. All three plotters had expressed defiance over the bombings and repeatedly boasted of their willingness to die. Their only regret was that 38 Indonesian Muslims had perished in the attack on the holiday nightspots that killed 160 foreigners, including 88 Australians. "I don't ask for forgiveness from infidels, I only ask for forgiveness from Muslims," Mukhlas told the international media a month before he was executed.[2]

Amrozi, dubbed by the media "the smiling assassin" for his ever-present Joker-like grin, laughed and jested with his interrogators. In court, he mocked the victims, except for the Muslims, and in press conferences smiled from ear to ear as he vowed retribution on America and infidels. But his most ecstatic grin came at the moment of his verdict, death, for which he was proud.

Back home, though, people remember the sunny smile of a friendly boy who often played pranks on his teachers and classmates. The fifth of thirteen children, Amrozi had no interest in schoolwork or studying the Koran and was expelled from junior high school. Although he said his father always wanted him to be a holy warrior, the good-looking lad liked motorbikes and taking girls on the back for a whirl. He was a whiz with his hands and became the local Mr. Fix-It, repairing everything from cell phones to cars. But he seemed to have no center.

That was never the case with his older brother, Mukhlas. From an early age, when he tended goats and began studying the Koran, Mukhlas decided that his way of life would be the ascetic and religious way, the way of the goat-tenders Moses, Jesus, and Mohammed. Mukhlas would later recall that as a fifteen-year-old in hormonal turbulence:

> If it weren't for Allah's grace and direction . . . I'm sure I would have slipped. Because my classmates were a wicked lot. . . . I had to make acquaintance with adulterers and drinkers. . . . I was once locked in by my friends, locked in to be with a prostitute. I just waited. I just kept quiet. Praise be to Allah—Allah kept me safe. . . . I never neglected prayer and never touched those women.[3]

Mukhlas's prudishness and Amrozi's grin were often taken as telltale signs in the popular press of some innate psychopathic flaw. In fact, Mukhlas became a happily married man, a loving father, kind to friends and students—most of whom had nothing to do with terrorism yet admired and even adored him. But Mukhlas, it seems, had always sought glory in the good fight for God, having found it first in Afghanistan fighting the Soviets and then back in Southeast Asia for the struggle over the region's soul. Mukhlas was always a deeply moral man, and that is what drew others to his side. These included Amrozi, and another brother, Ali Imron, who would also be involved in the Bali plot though spared with a life sentence for showing remorse in court.

The last of the trio shot in the orange grove that very early Saturday morning was a younger man, born Abdul Aziz in 1971 but known as Imam Samudra. Although his working-class parents adhered to Indonesia's Islamic Union (Persatuan Islam), which followed a Saudi Wahabi line, Imam Samudra didn't take much to religious teaching or memorizing the Koran: "I was not so motivated with the Islamic schooling system. I often skipped class. . . .

Once it got to be about two o'clock in the afternoon, I would feel sleepy. It was so boring."[4]

He liked science, electronics, computers, chess, and poetry, all of which he excelled at, putting him at the top of his high school class. He knew he had ability and wanted to use it in the service of a great and good cause, as his martyred heroes had done: the assassinated African-American Muslim leader Malcolm X and the executed leader of Darul Islam, S. M. Kartosoewirjo, whose short-lived Muslim state in Samudra's home province of Serang in western Java showed, if only for a shining moment, what a brave leader could do. Darul Islam, founded in the 1940s with the aim of establishing a caliphate in Southeast Asia, was to provide Jemaah Islamiyah with many of its core members.

Opportunity seemed to knock when Samudra met Jabir, a man about ten years his senior who had studied in the famous Al-Mukmin school in central Java, established by Ba'asyir and Abdullah Sungkar, the founder of Jemaah Islamiyah. Jabir's father had fought with Kartosoewirjo, and Jabir himself had been in the Indonesian "class of 1987" sent by Sungkar and Ba'asyir to fight the Soviets in Afghanistan. So Jabir's appeal to become a mujahid struck Samudra as from the heart.

The network for sending Indonesian volunteers to train and fight as mujahedin in Afghanistan was a well-running operation that had been in place since the first group, the Class of '85. Mukhlas had gone on with the second batch, the Class of '86, and Samudra would now join Mukhlas's younger brother, Ali Imron, in the Class of '91. But by the time Samudra arrived, the fighting was mostly over: the Soviets had withdrawn more than a year before, and the communist puppet government of President Najibullah was on the verge of collapse. Although glory would have to wait for another day, the training and, above all, the social networking that cemented faith and fellowship among the self-styled Afghan Alumni would make a strong base for future terrorist actions in Southeast Asia.

*   *   *

In the summer of 2005, I went to Indonesia to interview the Bali bomb plotters. They had agreed to the interviews, and so had the authorities. But just before I landed, a new prison warden was installed and refused to allow further one-on-one interviews (though I subsequently managed to conduct the interviews through third parties). So I flew on to Sulawesi to meet Farhin bin Ahmad, Afghan Alumni Class of '87, which included Jabir, the man who brought Imam Samudra into the JI network. The Class of '86 included Hambali, the instigator of the Bali plot who is now awaiting trial for terrorism and mass murder along with 9/11 mastermind Khaled Sheikh Mohammed (KSM). In 1996, Farhin hosted Khaled for a month at his home in Jakarta and helped him to buy books and bicycles to take back to Afghan refugees. "We talked about jihad," Farhin told me, "but nothing concrete."

Farhin drove the truck with his brother and the bomb that devastated the Philippines ambassador's residence in Jakarta in 2000. Except for Farhin (who escaped) and his brother (who was caught), most of the network involved in this attack was also behind the Bali bombing two years later. In the lead-up to Bali, Imam Samudra asked Farhin if he could find him some suicide bombers. Farhin demurred. Farhin told me that although he was willing to fight as a muhajid to kill enemies of Islam (and he has killed), and though he yearns to be a martyr (of this I'm nearly certain), he says he doesn't see the sense of suicide bombing in his country if there's a risk of other Muslims being killed. Farhin set up a training camp in Sulawesi to funnel fighters into Poso.

The interview is revealing for what it says about how JI networks form, but also demonstrates that once started down the path of radicalization and jihad, not all roads lead to Hades.

Me: "Farhin, tell me how you became involved with JI."

Farhin: "A man from Darul Islam came to our home in Jakarta and asked my father if he knew someone who wanted to go to

Afghanistan to help Muslims fight communists. My father said 'Yes, here's my son.' I was twenty."

On November 30, 1957, Farhin's father, Ahmad Kandai, attempted to assassinate Indonesian president Sukarno with a hand grenade. Kandai was tried, jailed, and later released. His sons—Farhin bin Ahmad, Abdul Jabar, Mohammed Islam, and Solahudin—all became jihadis. Kandai strongly believed in Darul Islam's mission of establishing Islamic rule in Indonesia, but gave Farhin and his other children a secular education.

"On the way to Afghanistan, in 1987, I stopped off in Malaysia and met Ustaz [Teacher] Abdullah Sungkar. He helped prepare me with religious teaching about jihad and physical training—crawling over the ground, running, jumping, martial arts—but no weapons. Then I went to Karachi with a small group on a Pakistani visa. We flew on Aeroflot because it was the cheapest. We went to the Al-Ittihad al-Islami office in Karachi, then three days to Peshawar by bus. We trained for a bit in a muhajrin [refugee] camp and then on to Camp Saddah near Khyber [Pass], about five kilometers from the Afghan border. . . . For the next two years I studied and trained with the other Indonesians at Camp Saddah. Six months basic training, then six months advanced training: infantry tactics, weapons, engineering [demolition and explosives], intelligence, and map reading.

"I trained for another year and after that gave *khas* [special warfare training, a crash course for those going into battle who haven't the time for a full training course]. Nine times I got to go on holiday, to the front to fight Najibullah [the Afghan communist leader] and the Soviets, mostly Najibullah. That was our vacation and we all prayed for more of it. Our commander was Afghan; we communicated in Farsi. I also learned Arabic for the religious courses and even some English; we trained sometimes in English."

"OK, so you spent three years training and fighting in Afghanistan."

"Not just training and fighting, but also studying: about 70 percent of the time on religion, especially *Aqidah at-Tahawiyah* [Fundamentals of Islamic Creed], and about 30 percent on preparing for battle. Abdullah Azzam came to speak on *fiqh al-jihad*. He taught that we should carry out jihad wherever Muslims are colonized. In Palestine, his own country, Muslims had been badly treated by Israel, the same conditions that face Afghanistan, which was attacked by colonizers. Abdullah Azzam used to say 'we must continue jihad no matter how long the way.'"

"What did you do after the communists were defeated?" I wanted Farhin to go on.

"I went back home. But I stopped for a while in Malaysia, to work on the chicken farm that Abdullah Sungkar set up. I cleared jungle to make some money before going home and to help the organization."

"What organization?"

"The Afghan Alumni [among the Indonesians] that Ustaz had sent on to train and fight."

"Did he ever visit you in Pakistan or Afghanistan?"

"Yes, he came with Abu Bakr Ba'asyir [Sungkar's sidekick and future successor] for about a month."

"Then what? Did you go home and did you stay part of the organization? What was the organization's structure? Did it change in time?"

"I went back to Jakarta. I sold electronics [gadgets] and smoked food on the street. I carried them, no shop or stall. We had small groups of Alumni, and we met about once a week to talk about religion and to do some physical training: martial arts, swimming, but mostly [soccer]. Then, in 1993, Zulkarnaen [the first of the Afghan Alumni, Class of '85, and master trainer for the Indonesians at Saddah] came to see me. He asked me if I would be loyal to Abdullah Sungkar. Sungkar rejected Mastruki [the leader of Darul Islam], who preached the ways of the Sufi. Mastruki's way was not pure Islam."

"Did you have to swear the loyalty oath to Sungkar's faction? Did he still consider his faction part of Darul Islam?"

"The Afghan Alumni [in Indonesia] didn't have to give an oath; he trusted us. The faction was still part of DI until 1995 or 1996 when it became JI [Jemaah Islamiyah] with an organization something like al-Gama'a al-Islamiyah [the Egyptian Islamic group whose spiritual leader, the blind cleric Omar Abdel al-Rahman, is currently serving a life sentence in U.S. federal prison for conspiring to blow up New York City landmarks].[5]

"The Alumni continued to meet in small groups, discuss religion, train, and play soccer until Abdullah Sunkgar and Abu Bakr Ba'asyir returned [to Indonesia from exile in Malaysia following the fall of Indonesia's president Suharto in 1998]. Soon after, Abdullah Sungkar died, and some of the others who had come back [from Malaysia] wanted to fight in Indonesia to help Muslims. I helped in the attack on the Filipino ambassador; I drove the truck with my brother. That was August 2000. In September, I went to Poso, in Sulawesi.

"How did you wind up in Poso to fight?" I asked.

"In September 2000, Aris Munandar said I should go to Poso to set up a branch of Kompak [an Islamic charity whose office in Central Java is headed by Munandar] and a Kompak fighting group. Every charity needs an attack group to protect it. I was the head of Kompak in Poso, we had a *dawah* [missionary] team and a military team. I had to set up both. For the fighting group, I set up a training camp here [pointing to the side of the road], right there in the jungle by the sea, because it's hidden and mostly Balinese live here so no one would suspect a Muslim training camp right here."

I was surprised: "Why would a charity group need to attack?"

"Because people who fight Muslims won't allow humanitarian help for Muslims."

"What's the relationship between Jemaah Islamiyah and Kompak?"

"No formal relation, it's person-to-person," Farhin said in English. "They have the same ideas, the same mission to help Muslims, and they work together and sometimes fight together in the same cause."

"Are you a member of both JI and Kompak, Farhin?"

"I'm not an official member of anything. You don't have to be; if your heart and allegiance are with people, then you're with them."

"People who are a part of JI, friends of yours, have killed civilians," I pressed, "not in battle but in suicide bombings, including Muslims. What do you think of that? What did you think of the Bali bombing?"

"I don't know all of the conditions. Some people say the bomb was an Israeli or American bomb."

"But people you know—Imam Samudra and Mukhlas—say they did the Bali bombing and are proud of it. Samudra trained the suicide bombers. Mukhlas blessed them all."

"I know, they probably did the small blast to frighten away people from drunkenness and molesting women, but the big blast was too powerful. Somebody else may have done it."

"Samudra and Mukhlas say it's OK to kill other Muslims for their cause," I persisted.

"It's not good to kill Muslims, I don't know if they really believe that, but it's not good. I wouldn't do that. I fight only those who fight us, and I support those who fight elsewhere, in Bosnia, Chechnya, Iraq against those who fight to colonize Muslims. But I stay here."

"Where's here?"

"Here in my country where Muslims are being killed."

"Noordin Top and Azhari are continuing with suicide bombings. What do you think of it?" (Azhari Husin, a master bomb-maker, was killed in a shoot-out with Indonesian police in November 2005, and Noordin, a master motivator, was killed in September 2009.)

"Noordin is very good at convincing young men who are eager

to fight to be martyrs. He has about ten ready to go in a *thoifah moqatilah* [special fighting group]."

"Would you join such a group to become a martyr?"

"If God wills it, but not to kill Muslims or civilians who do not fight us. That's what Abdullah Azzam taught in the way of jihad at Sayyaf [the Afghan training camp]. He didn't distinguish between Muslims. All Muslims are equal."

"In all those years, did you ever meet Bin Laden or hear the name Al Qaeda?"

"I never met Bin Laden, though I heard his name first when I was at Sayyaf's camp. I only heard about Al Qaeda after the September 11 attacks. Later I saw in the newspaper that Khaled Sheikh Mohammed was arrested for the attack on America. I saw his picture with a beard. That was strange. He stayed with me at my home [in Jakarta in 1996] for about a month. He was always clean-shaven and very polite to everybody. He dressed well, in Western clothes. He talked about the need for jihad to protect Muslims, but he was mostly interested in helping refugees in Afghanistan."

ABDULLAH AZZAM'S "AL QAEDA" VERSUS BIN LADEN'S

Early in the Soviet-Afghan War, Palestinian scholar Abdullah Azzam founded Maktab al-Khadamat, the Services Office for Arab Volunteers, which provided guesthouses in the Pakistani city of Peshawar, down the road from the Khyber Pass, as well as paramilitary training camps in the border regions of Pakistan. In Peshawar, Azzam mentored Bin Laden, who had just finished college in Jeddah, bringing in the young Saudi millionaire to help run and finance the office. Azzam visited some of the training camps to teach *fiqh al-jihad*, the way of jihad.

The fourteenth-century Muslim polymath Ibn Khaldûn described *fiqh* as "knowledge of the rules of God which concern the actions of persons who own themselves bound to obey the law respecting what is required (*wajib*), forbidden (*haram*), recommended (*mandub*), disapproved (*makruh*) or merely permitted (*mubah*)." Abdullah Azzam's teachings on *fiqh al-jihad* included topics like "The Islamic Ruling with Regards to Killing Women, Children and Elderly in a Situation of War." According to Azzam:

> Islam does not [urge followers to] kill [anyone among the infidels] except the fighters, and those who supply Mushrikin [pagans] and other enemies of Islam with money or advice, because the Koran says: "And fight in the Cause of Allah those who fight you."
>
> Fighting is a two-sided process, so whoever fights or joins the fight in any way is to be fought and slain, otherwise he, or she, is to be spared. That is why there is no need to kill women, because of their weakness, unless they fight. Children and monks are not to be killed intentionally, unless they mix with the Mushrikin . . . we fire at the Mushrikin, but we do not aim at the weak.
>
> Abusing or slaying the children and the weak inherits hatred to the coming generations, and is narrated throughout history with tears and blood, generation after generation. And this is exactly what Islam is against.

Azzam coined the term *al-qaeda al-sulbah*, "the strong base," to refer to the vanguard of a new global Islamic revolution whose symbols are the rifle and the book. In April 1988, at Geneva, the Soviets agreed to pull out their last troops by February of the next year. Before the Soviet withdrawal was complete, Bin Laden joined forces with the head of Egypt's Al Jihad, Ayman Zawahiri, and others to form a new al-qaeda vanguard very different from what Azzam had in mind.[6]

Bin Laden and Zawahiri disagreed with the limits that Azzam placed on the aims and means of jihad. Azzam was reluctant to harm civilian noncombatants. He wanted to continue jihad against Zionist Jews, Christians who occupied Muslim lands, including Spain and the Soviet republics of Central Asia, and Indian Hindus in Kashmir. But he did not want to fight against Muslims, however secular.

For Zawahiri, however, waging jihad on corrupt Muslim governments was central, especially against the "apostate" Egyptian government that had allied itself with America and made peace with Israel. In November 1989, Azzam and his two sons were killed on their way to mosque services in Peshawar by a massive explosion. Azzam's son-in-law blamed Zawahiri, but most jihadis I've talked to, including Farhin, believe on no evidence that U.S. and Israeli intelligence services, or their local partners, assassinated Azzam.

In *The Looming Tower*,[7] a Pulitzer Prize–winning account of the origins of Al Qaeda, author Lawrence Wright observes:

> The pageant of martyrdom that Azzam limned before his worldwide audience created the death cult that would one day form the core of al-Qaeda. For the journalists covering the war, the Arab Afghans were a curious sideshow to the real fighting, set apart by their obsession with dying. When a fighter fell, his comrades would congratulate him and weep because they were not also slain in battle. These scenes struck other Muslims as bizarre. The Afghans were fighting for their country, not for paradise or an idealized community. For them, martyrdom was not such a priority.

The Indonesian Afghan Alumni were much closer to the Arab volunteers in this respect than to Afghans. The Afghans resent Arabs, or anyone else, telling them what they should do.

In a letter (authenticated by Indonesian intelligence) sent from Malaysia dated 10 Rabiul Akhir 1419 (August 3, 1998) and addressed to leaders of Darul Islam, Abu Bakr Ba'asyir and Abdullah Sungkar state they are acting on Bin Laden's behalf to advance "the Muslim world's global jihad to fight against America" because "the Jews and Christians will never be satisfied until you follow their way of worship."

NO LAUGHING MATTER

I thought of Farhin telling me of his desire to blow up the beautiful Balinese wedding we had witnessed together, and I weighed that against his sidestepping involvement with the suicide bombing. Abdullah Azzam had helped to instill desire for jihad and martyrdom in Farhin, but not quite Bin Laden's way. That instinctive shying away from the actual murder,[8] and laughing together over common things, may yield common ground enough to move the path to jihad away from the most extreme forms of violence. Especially if we can learn to take advantage of a recent widening of the breach within the ranks of senior Islamists and jihadis.[9]

So, apparently, thinks General Tito Karnavian, leader of the Indonesian national police strike team Antiterrorism Detachment 88, which has tracked down the big players in those JI factions devoted to international jihad. Tito knows Farhin, and has embraced him, as he has Ali Imron, the brother of the executed Bali plotters, Mukhlas and Amrozi. Tito argues along the same lines as senior Saudi and Turkish police intelligence officers that terrorism can be more of a public health issue than a criminal matter, and that treating morally motivated terrorists as common murderers and other criminals may not be the right way to go. Tito points out that Ali Imron has helped to turn more people away from violence than he imagined. But when Tito showed a slide of himself hugging Ali Imron, whose life was spared only because he expressed remorse for his role in the bombing, a top FBI official who was on hand remarked: "Maybe that works. Maybe it's the smart thing to do. But . . . can you imagine me hugging Timothy

McVeigh? They'd have me hanging by my balls from the dome of Congress!"

At least in Iraq, and now in Afghanistan, U.S. policy has started to shift toward treating terrorism as a social and public health issue rather than a strictly military and police problem. Following the debacle of prisoner abuse at Abu Ghraib by U.S. forces, General Douglas Stone took charge of detainees for the Multi-National Force under the command of General David Petraeus. Stone, a mechanical engineer by training, a rancher of Navajo and German descent who was raised partly on an Indian reservation in Arizona, released more than one fourth of the 23,000 detainees under his charge on condition that their families and tribes take responsibility for them. Only a dozen have been recaptured in suspected insurgent activity. Thousands of those still in prison have learned to read and write. Hundreds study science and math, civics and law, Arabic and English, and how to be adept at trades that will support them after release. They play soccer, visit with their families, and discuss how to interpret the Koran they can now read for themselves. But reputation, like life itself, is a complex affair that is difficult to sustain but simple to destroy. With heavy eyes, General Stone told me: "We have turned around 180 degrees to show respect for any of the detainees in our care: respect for the culture, for the religion, and for the history of the place where our compounds are. But what those few did [at Abu Ghraib] will probably be the images best remembered of this war for a hundred years from now."

At last word, Farhin was selling coconut wood from Sulawesi, tending a small plot of cacao land, and cultivating hothouse ornamental plants. His second wife had delivered their second child. He wanted to improve his Arabic and English, but remained ready to take up arms again "if Muslims are attacked." I don't know if he has managed a transmigration to a more peaceful soul or how keen he still is on martyrdom, but at least he seemed to have shied away from killing noncombatants. He even said he is willing to come to America to explain how he sees things and to try to understand what others see. When I brought up this offer, and similar proposals from other jihadis, at the White House, the State Department, the Department of Defense, the Department of Homeland Security, the Senate, the House, and the FBI, some people laughed, others seemed bemused, and most rolled their eyes. It seemed that the idea of talking to our enemies to find out why they are our enemies could only come from Planet Fruitcake.

Sungkar
 Ba'asyir
 Hambali
 Kh. Sheikh Mohammed
 Nasir Abas
 Imam Samudra

 Ali Imron
 Mukhlas
 Amrozi
 Azahari
 Top
 Dul Matin

 Yazid Sufaat
Rais
Wan Mat
 Faiz Bafana
Ismail
 Abu Rusdan

 Idris
 Tohir
 Mubarok
 Kastari
 Al Ghozi
 Umar Patek

Some key players associated with the Bali bombing.

CHAPTER 9

THE ROAD TO BALI: "FOR ALL YOU CHRISTIAN INFIDELS!"

In September 2009, Indonesian security forces killed Noordin Top, number three on the FBI's most-wanted terrorist list, just behind Osama Bin Laden and his deputy Ayman Zawahiri. Implicated in the region's worst suicide bombings, including the Jakarta Marriott and Ritz-Carlton bombings in July 2009, Noordin headed a splinter of Jemaah Islamiyah, under his own logo, "Al Qaeda for the Malaysian Archipelago." He had been on the run since the 2002 Bali bombing. Although he did not play a large role in that attack, he and fellow Malaysian and old college chum Azhari Husin soon afterward replaced Hambali (a veteran of the Soviet-Afghan war and instigator of the Bali bombing plot), Mukhlas, and Samudra as the central figures of Indonesian terrorism.

After Azhari's death in a shootout following the second Bali bombing in 2005, Noordin's reputation began to assume mythic proportions in jihadi circles. His many amazing escapes signaled to his sympathizers that God had blessed his Qaeda-style agenda for international jihad against Western interests. Noordin vowed that he would gladly embrace martyrdom and never be taken alive. In jihadi circles, his death, too, is now the stuff of legends.

Noordin's demise is the culmination of a counterterrorism campaign launched after the first Bali bombing. But success was long in coming. How was a splinter faction of JI able to survive massive manhunts to mount spectacular suicide attacks against Western targets that succeeded, despite their apparent amateurishness, lack of financial means, and decimation of operatives?

JAKARTA, AUGUST 14, 2005

Mohammed Nasir bin Abas, the former head of Jemaah Islamiyah's Mantiqi 3 command for military training and for the territories of Sulawesi, East Kalimantan (Borneo), and the southern Philippines, dabbed at his food in the Indian restaurant and shook his head. "I cannot say that Ba'asyir ordered the Bali bombings," he said. "But he did nothing to stop Hambali from planning suicide attacks with others and killing civilians, including innocent Muslims. That's one of the reasons I quit JI. I consider myself a soldier in the defense of Islam. Soldiers fight soldiers, not tourists or other people just because they have a different religion."

After attending a religious school for two years, Abas met Sungkar, whom he called "a good and charismatic preacher" and who sent him for three years' training in Afghanistan (Afghan Alumni Class of '87) to become an arms instructor and religious teacher. In 1993, when Sungkar and Ba'asyir split from Darul Islam, Abas was asked to take a loyalty oath to the new organization. He became a top JI military trainer but also gave religious instruction. Among his trainees were future Bali bomb plotters Imam Samudra and Ali Imron.

On October 12, 2002, two young suicide bombers, Iqbal and Feri, detonated their lethal charges in the Kuta tourist district of Bali, Indonesia. The terrorists who planned this act counted on Bali's image as the Western world's idea of earthly paradise, an undulating island of gentle green curves and human grace. The attack had a message for the Balinese themselves, a Hindu people of great tolerance, that their arrogant indulgence of Western lust and their own sensuality was punishable by death by the militants' wrathful god. It was also a wake-up call to counterterrorism forces caught unaware that JI even existed.

Over the previous year, Imam Samudra, the field commander of the Bali operation, had assembled five prospective martyrs from the Islamic high schools that dotted the countryside around his hometown of Serang in the coastal region of West Java. It was in West Java that the Islamic insurgent movement Darul Islam (DI) was born in 1949, the year that the Dutch left Indonesia. And it was in a Serang high school in the late 1980s where Samudra fell under the spell of Kyai Saleh As'ad, a former DI commander who had fought with the movement's leader, S. M. Kartosoewirjo, before the latter's capture and execution. Later himself on death row for the Bali bombing, Samudra, a former high school valedictorian, remained as committed as ever to Kartosoewirjo's vision of a pure Islamic state for Indonesia, the region, and eventually the world.[1]

Of the five candidate "bridegrooms," as they were called, only the poorest, Iqbal, zealously showed the devotion and discipline that Samudra required for a martyrdom action against the Western "scum" keen on defiling and destroying Islam. On his Web site istimata.com (martyrdom.com), Samudra expressed the moral outrage felt by many jihadis in justifying suicide bombings:

> For all you Christian infidels! If you say this [Bali] killing was barbarous and cruel and happened to "innocent civilians" from your countries, then you should know you do crueler things than that. Do you think 600,000 babies in Iraq [who died as a result of U.S.-led sanctions and bombings, according to Osama Bin Laden in a 1997 interview with CNN reporter Peter Arnett][2] and half a million Afghan children and their mothers are soldiers and sinful people who should have to endure thousands of tons of your bombs???!! Where are your brains and consciences??!!! The cries of babies and the screams of Muslim women. . . . We

cannot allow unjust and barbarous actions against our Muslim brothers and sisters in any corner of the world.[3]

Samudra honored Iqbal with the task of delivering and detonating the large car bomb at the Sari Club, which was always packed with foreign tourists on the weekend but discouraged entry to Indonesians. The other suicide bomber, Feri, brought into the act later, was given a suicide vest and backpack for the nightclub Paddy's, near the Sari. Paddy's allowed Indonesians and so merited a lesser measure of carnage.

At 11:07 P.M. on that Saturday night, Feri blew himself up in the middle of Paddy's crowded floor. Iqbal, who had only learned to drive a car the day before, waited outside the Sari, as he had been told, until a sizable crowd had ventured out to see what all the commotion was about. The explosion of the chemicals in four plastic filing cabinets crammed into the car could be heard fifteen miles away. In his will, Iqbal said that he hoped his martyrdom would help to restore Kartosoewirjo's Islamic state. He did not even mention JI. Imam Samudra himself never swore an oath of allegiance to any JI leader, though he had been closely involved with the most violent leadership of JI almost since the time he'd left high school for jihad training in Afghanistan in 1990.

The conventional wisdom has it that the 2002 Bali bombing was an Al Qaeda Central operation franchised out to JI, an affiliated group with a hierarchical command structure modeled after a military organization. In fact, we'll see that the Bali plot for the most part bypassed JI's organizational structure. Bali and the other major JI attacks involving suicide bombers were largely planned and executed through local networks of friends (many made in training camps), of kin, neighbors, and schoolmates who radicalized one another until all were eager and able to kill perfect strangers for an abstract cause. Terrorist networks are generally no different than the ordinary kinds of social networks that guide people's career paths. It's the terrorist career itself that is most remarkable, not the mostly normal individuals who become terrorists.

DARUL ISLAM AND THE BIRTH OF JEMAAH ISLAMIYAH

Even before independence in 1949, Indonesia's leaders had faced a daunting task in navigating among the competing interests of strong nationalist, religious, and communist factions to forge a democratic nation encompassing hundreds of ethnic groups spread across thirteen thousand islands stretching more than three thousand miles. During the armed struggle against the Dutch, the Republican forces had to contend with Kartosoewirjo, who after having proclaimed his own Islamic State of Indonesia (Negara Islam Indonesia) in rural West Java, brought into his fold other Islamic rebellions and became the united front's first Imam. He called his movement Darul Islam, referring to the original Muslim division of the world between the House of Islam (Dar al-Islam) and the House of War (Dar al-Harb). Half a century later, Darul Islam hatched JI.[4]

In the 1950s, the international stature of Sukarno, who guided Indonesia through its independence and became its first president, rose in the company of fellow leaders of the "Non-Aligned Movement," Gamal Abdel Nasser of Egypt and Marshal Tito of Yugoslavia. But at home, relations among nationalists, communists, and Muslim groups steadily deteriorated, as competition intensified over whether Indonesia should be an Islamic state or a broadly secular one. In 1959, encouraged by the armed forces, Sukarno replaced a democratic constitution with the authoritarian "guided democracy," which combined elements more in tune with Nasser's nationalism and Tito's communist rule. Three years later, Kartosoewirjo was captured and executed. In late 1965 and early 1966, after a failed coup attempt by leftist army officers associated with the Communist Party, Muslim and nationalist gangs went on an anticommunist rampage, backed and in various regions organized by the army, commanded by General Suharto, who in 1967 forced Sukarno out of power. Hundreds of thousands of people died in what was also an ethnic cleansing of Chinese.

Suharto came in the following years to downplay Indonesia's nonaligned role and became a staunch U.S. ally. With the communists out of the way, he turned to the task of preventing Muslim groups from sharing power. Muslims felt betrayed, and a considerable body of Muslim opinion remained unrepresented for decades in Suharto's Indonesia. Surprisingly, however, the government allowed Darul Islam to reassemble, with an eye to using it to get out votes. Despite this compromised aspect of its resurgence, Darul Islam in time attracted a new generation of Islamic militants, including future JI leaders Abdullah Sungkar and Abu Bakr Ba'asyir.

Like Bin Laden, Sungkar and his sidekick, Ba'asyir, descended from Arabs of the Hadramawt region of Yemen, seafarers who over the centuries established a wide network of personal and commercial relationships across southern and southeastern Asia.[5] Sungkar and Ba'asyir preached that Muslims—indeed, all mankind—must live only by Islamic law, or Sharia. As a first step toward Islamic rule, the two clerics proposed to set up *jemaah islamiyah*, small Islamic communities that would strictly obey Sharia. In 1971, Sungkar and Ba'asyir established the Al-Mukmin *pesantren*, or religious boarding school, to "nurture both comprehension of, and zeal for, jihad . . . so that graduates of *pesantren* truly become preachers and mujahedin."[6] The following year, the school moved to the village of Ngruki on the outskirts of the city of Solo, Sungkar's birthplace in Central Java.

In 1976, Sungkar and Ba'asyir officially joined Darul Islam. Sungkar was appointed "military governor of the Islamic State of Indonesia." Two years later the pair was arrested for sedition.

They were accused of using their organization, Jemaah Islamiyah, in plotting to overthrow the government. They were released from prison three years later but fled to Malaysia in 1985 after Suharto issued a warrant for their re-arrest on charges of sedition.

The fugitives soon began rebuilding their network in exile by asking their *jemaah* in Indonesia to send volunteers who would donate a portion of their salaries. From the outset, Sungkar and Ba'asyir funneled many of the volunteers to Pakistan for military training to fight the communists in Afghanistan, and eventually for jihad in Southeast Asia. Sungkar and Ba'asyir traveled extensively, to the Philippines and Singapore, and on to Pakistan and the Middle East. The contacts they made, especially in Saudi Arabia, bore fruit later, with funds to organize and train JI militants.

In 1985, Sungkar and Ba'asyir began sending volunteers from Indonesia and Malaysia for a three-year training course at Saddah camp in Pakistan near the Khyber Pass, which belonged to the smallest of the Afghan mujahedin groups and was led by Abdul Rasul Sayyaf. From the ranks of these Afghan Alumni would arise the principal network source for the Bali bombing.

The leading players in the Bali plot trained at Saddah: Zulkarnaen, who went on to become JI's military chief, belonged to the first group, the Class of '85; Mukhlas, who became the spiritual guide and overall coordinator of the plot, was part of the Class of '86; Hambali, who instigated the plot, belonged to the Class of '87. The large Class of '90 also included Mukhlas's neighbor, Mubarok, from the village of Tenggulun in East Java, as well as future Bali bomb-makers Sarjiyo and Dulmatin. Mukhlas's brother, Ali Imron, and Imam Samudra, the plot's field commander, belonged to the Class of '91. Altogether, ten of the Bali bombing participants trained in Afghanistan.

In 1993, Sungkar officially split off from Darul Islam, accusing rival leaders of Sufism and other forms of "deviance," which undermined the pure Salafi principles of Islam that supposedly had inspired victory against the Soviets. Sungkar took with him most of the Afghan Alumni he had sponsored. Sungkar called his new organization Jemaah Islamiyah.

JI's formal structure would be set down on paper three years later in the "General Guidelines of the Struggle of Jemaah Islami-yah" (*Pedoman Umum Perjuangan al-Jamaah al-Islamiyah*, or PUPJI), a manual that contains a constitution, outlines the roles of office bearers, and gives details of how meetings must be organized. The guidelines call for humiliating and terrorizing God's enemies, destroying the forces opposed to Islamic proselytizing, and clearing the way for martyrdom. The PUPJI declares that anyone who adheres to fundamental Islamic principles and is devoid of corruption, deviation (for example, Sufism), or innovation can take the *bayat* (oath of allegiance) to the emir of JI and become a JI member.

The manual is mostly a translation of the doctrine of al-Gama'a al-Islamiyah (the Egyptian Islamic Group).[7] But it also contains elements of Indonesia's military organization, particularly in regard to the ranking of personnel and responsibility for territory. The PUPJI instructs JI to conduct itself as a "secret organization," concealing its doctrine, membership, and operations from public view. The PUPJI outlines a clear hierarchical structure. An emir rules atop the JI pyramid in coordination with the Central Leadership Council (*qiyadah markaziyah*) that he appoints. Five advisory councils operate with their Arabic titles under the central leadership: *fatwa* (rulings of Islamic law), *majelis shuro* (council of experts on various issues), *hisbah* (discipline), *mantiqi* (territorial organizations), and *wakalah* (subterritorial organizations within each mantiqi).

Mantiqi 1, initially headed by Hambali, covered most of Malaysia and Singapore and was responsible for finances and economic development. Mantiqi 2 was first directed by Abu Fatih (Abdullah Anshori). Mantiqi 2 covered most of Indonesia and was charged with recruitment and major operations leading to the establishment of an Islamic state in Indonesia. After its establishment in

1997, Mantiqi 3, initially headed by Mustafa (Pranata Yudha) of the Class of '86, covered the southern Philippines, the Malaysian state of Sabah and the Indonesian province of East Kalimantan (Borneo), and the island of Sulawesi. The territories of Mantiqi 3 were configured to provide a pipeline for military training and arms supply between Indonesia and the Philippines, which would eventually come under control of Nasir Abas. Mantiqi 4, under the leadership of Abdul Rahim Ayub, covered Australia and West Papua (New Guinea). Mantiqi 4 was the least developed.

POWER SEEPS FROM THE CENTER

Abdullah Sungkar was the central figure and source of vision, inspiration, and direction for the group until he died in November 1999, and his death was a turning point for JI, leaving a leadership void that would never truly be filled. Sungkar's longtime confidant, Ba'asyir, was expected to lead the organization forward, but Ba'asyir proved to be an inadequate successor. Although a fiery preacher, he was too diffident in operational matters for the likes of Hambali, Zulkarnaen, Mukhlas, Samudra, Azhari, and Noordin Top. And Ba'asyir couldn't keep them under his control.

Although Hambali is generally credited with leading the radical group responsible for JI's first wave of high-profile bombings, it was Zulkarnaen, JI's highly secretive military chief, who initially set the course for this violent turn. When Sungkar returned from exile in Malaysia to Solo, Indonesia, following Suharto's fall, Zulkarnaen, in June 1999, assembled the Afghan Alumni in Indonesia and lambasted leaders from Mantiqi 2 for their lack of zeal in attacking Christians and other enemies with bombs.[8] He instructed one of the future Bali plotters, Amrozi, to prepare explosives for the first attacks on Indonesian soil, against Christians in Ambon. At a meeting on August 14, 2002, he also assigned Amrozi's older brother, Mukhlas, to be overall coordinator of the Bali bombing.

Mukhlas left the operational details to his field commander, Imam Samudra, who had never sworn allegiance to JI and who chose Bali as the target and picked the suicide bombers.

Mukhlas's importance to the terrorist bombing networks associated with JI also goes far beyond his operational role. He was the spiritual guide of the radical group, and remained so for its post-Bali fragments even from his prison cell on death row. A true believer who saw his role as preordained by God, he noted during his police interrogation:

> I left for jihad at the beginning of 1986 and stayed until 1989. What motivated me was that jihad is the utmost form of religious service. After I decided to go, I performed the ritual prayer. In that prayer I dreamt I met with the Prophet (may Allah bless him and give him peace) and he gave me some advice, including an encouragement for me to depart because the journey was following the journey of the prophets.

He was a star pupil and gifted teacher from Al Mukmin *pesantren* who joined Sungkar and Ba'asyir in exile in Malaysia in 1985. At Sungkar's prodding, Mukhlas soon left for Afghanistan to join Zulkarnaen and a growing number of other volunteers to train and fight communists. Another younger brother and fellow Bali plotter, Ali Imron, followed to Afghanistan a few years later and joined Samudra as one of the Afghan Alumni in the Class of '91. In 1991, Mukhlas's family established the Al Islam *pesantren*, which was modeled on Al Mukmin, and considered Ba'asyir its patron.

Ali Imron and his neighbor, another fellow Bali plotter named Mubarok, later became teachers at Al Islam. Ali Imron managed to elude authorities for a time after the Bali bombings with the help of several Al Islam students.

In 1992, Sungkar instructed Mukhlas to set up a new boarding school, Lukman Al Hakiem *pesantren*, in Johor, Malaysia, which followed the Al Mukmin curriculum with the same goal of producing militants for jihad. Sungkar moved nearby to oversee the school and to run a chicken farm, where some of the Afghan Alumni found work. Lukman Al Hakiem quickly became the nerve center of the JI exile leadership.[9] Those associated with the school include Zulkarnaen, Hambali, Samudra, and the three brothers Mukhlas, Amrozi, and Ali Imron. In the mid-1990s, Mukhlas began giving talks on religious education to an informal group of teachers and students at the nearby University of Technology, Malaysia (UTM), in Johor. Three Malaysians from the group soon came into the center of JI's orbit: Wan Win bin Wan Mat, who lectured in project management, became a Lukman board member and head of the important Johor Wakalah; Azhari Husin, a British-trained engineer and author of books on multiple regression analysis, would become JI's master bomb maker; and Noordin Top, who taught mathematics and geology, would eventually replace Mukhlas as Lukman's director.

The radicalization at Lukman Al Hakiem paid dividends in the early 2000s for Zulkarnaen, Mukhlas, and Hambali. The 2000 Philippines Ambassador's Residence bombing and the 2000 Christmas Eve bombings marked the first time that a core group of JI terrorists gathered together to plan a large-scale action. The ambassador bombing was also the first attempt by JI to create a complex Al Qaeda–style car bombing and would serve as a model for future JI bombings.

For the Christmas Eve bombings, JI operatives placed thirty-eight bombs at churches from northwestern Sumatra, across Java, to the island of Lombok, east of Bali. Although some were duds, most of the bombs exploded, killing 19 people and injuring 120. Like the ambassador bombing a couple of months earlier, the Christmas Eve bombings served as a warm-up for Bali. In particular, the coordination across multiple groups for the Christmas Eve bombings became the model for the Bali bombing, which also involved operatives from Darul Islam and Ring Banten (another radical jihadi organization that had splintered from Darul Islam).

Kin relationships were important for both the ambassador and Christmas Eve bombings. In addition to the key tie between Farhin and the ambassador bombing, three of the participants in both events—Mukhlas, Ali Imron, and Amrozi—were brothers, and all would later take part in the Bali operation. This is representative of a larger trend among jihadis across the world to rely on family and marriage for operations—an important development because as organizations such as JI become increasingly endogamous over time (as friends begin to marry one another's siblings), they become increasingly bound by a trust that is harder for counterterrorism efforts to penetrate or break.

THE PLOT THICKENS

The Bali bombing planning process started when Hambali convened a meeting of his radical advisers, Mukhlas, Wan Min bin Wan Mat, Azhari Husin, Noordin Top, and Zulkifli Marzuki in Thailand in early 2002 to discuss future bombings. At the meeting, Hambali changed the focus to soft targets, such as bars and nightclubs, and handed out assignments. Noordin and Azhari were to "apply" for funding through Al Qaeda, Mat would arrange the transfer of funds, and Mukhlas would direct the bombing.

Because so many of these men were in hiding from Malaysian and Indonesian authorities, Mukhlas decided to work through other JI operatives in Indonesia. Like Hambali, he avoided the moderate leader, Abu Fatih. Instead he chose to work through the radical Zulkarnaen.

Mukhlas then recommended Samudra to be the field commander for the bombing. At the trials following the attack, Imam Samudra was best known for screaming at spectators, covering his ears to avoid listening to his death-sentence verdict, and generally

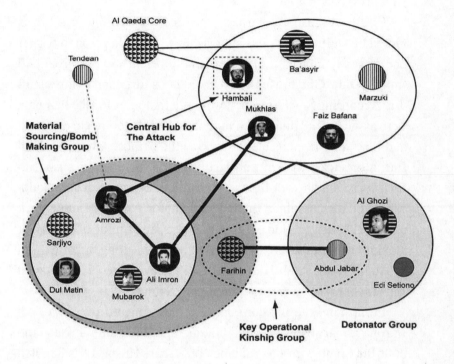

Al Qaeda Core

Tendean

Ba'asyir

Hambali

Marzuki

Mukhlas

Faiz Bafana

**Material
Sourcing/Bomb
Making Group**

**Central Hub for
The Attack**

Amrozi

Al Ghozi

Sarjiyo

Farihin

Abdul Jabar

Dul Matin

Ali Imron

Edi Setiono

Mubarok

**Key Operational
Kinship Group**

Detonator Group

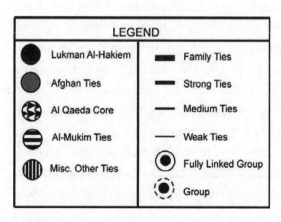

LEGEND

● Lukman Al-Hakiem	▬	Family Ties
● Afghan Ties	—	Strong Ties
✦ Al Qaeda Core	—	Medium Ties
⊖ Al-Mukim Ties	—	Weak Ties
▥ Misc. Other Ties	◉	Fully Linked Group
	◌	Group

*Philippines ambassador's
residence bombing net-
work in 2000).*

showing no remorse for his role. When asked about the Australian victims of the bombing, he responded: "Australia go to hell. The Jews and Christians go to hell. Islam will win. Islam will win. Allahu Akbar."[10]

In mid-August, Zulkarnaen convened a meeting at a house rented by Dulmatin, a Lukman teacher who would go on to trigger one of the bombs with his cell phone. Present were Amrozi, Ali Imron, Abdul Ghani, Mukhlas, Umar Patek, Idris, and Imam Samudra. According to Ali Imron, it was here that roles for the bombing were assigned and finalized: Dulmatin, Abdul Ghoni, Umar Patek, and Idris were responsible for making the bombs. Amrozi and Ali Imron procured the car and fertilizer, and arranged transportation. Idris helped with the transportation, arranged accommodations, and also obtained the U.S. dollars for Amrozi. Details such as fake IDs, destruction of serial numbers, and timing of bombs for maximum damage were discussed after the meeting. Iqbal, as well as Abdul Rauf, Andi Hidayat, Andri Octavia, Heri Hafidin, and Junaedi operated under the tutelage of Samudra.

From here, the mission planning was put into overdrive. Ali Imron, Umar Patek, Abdul Ghoni, and Dulmatin mixed and built the bomb with the guidance of Azhari Husin. Idris handled all logistical issues, Mubarok provided logistical and transportation services, and Imam Samudra directed the ongoing operation. Samudra and Ali Imron began casing areas—Denpasar, Nusa Dua, Sunar, and Kuta—provisional targets were Sari Club and Paddy's Pub on Jalan Legian. A Bali native whom Dulmatin introduced to the group named Mayskur was added to the network for a key logistics role (as "tour guide for Bali") at the last minute.

But Samudra had managed to alienate a large part of the team as a result of his abrasive, authoritarian personality. Amrozi later noted that he felt like a busboy, as he was excluded from all decisions and bomb-making activities while in Bali. Not surprisingly given his personality, Samudra was only able to convince one protégé, Iqbal, to become a suicide bomber. As a result, Dulmatin, one of the bomb-makers, was forced to recruit Feri to be the second suicide bomber. Samudra also never bothered to check whether the bombers could drive a car (they couldn't). So at the last minute, Ali Imron had to teach one of them how to drive.

Somehow amid this comedy of errors, the group was able to transport the bombs and suicide bombers to the nightclubs, and on October 12 Feri and Iqbal detonated the bombs at Paddy's Bar and the Sari Club.

AFTER BALI: THE DEVOLUTION OF JI

On August 11, 2003, the CIA, working with Thai intelligence, captured Hambali in a Muslim enclave in the ancient Thai capital of Ayutthaya, a sleepy town north of Bangkok. His arrest and subsequent transfer to Guantánamo Bay, Cuba, finally started to undo the Bali bombing network that had begun forming years before. But Azhari Husin and Noordin Top picked up the pieces to build a new, even more personalized network of family, friends, and fellow travelers in jihad.

At approximately 10:30 A.M. on September 9, 2004, a car bomb detonated outside the front gates of the Australian embassy in Jakarta, Indonesia, killing eleven people and wounding hundreds. The massive explosion created a ten-foot-deep crater, mangled the embassy's gates, and shattered windows in nearby buildings. The Australian embassy bombing was the first JI bombing led entirely by Noordin Top and Azhari Husin, without funding or direction from Hambali.

Now Noordin and Azhari were the two most wanted men in Southeast Asia. For the Australian embassy attack they had plied the traditional JI network for operatives (particularly from a handful of radical madrassahs). But many members and sympathizers began to question the wisdom of using suicide bombings to directly challenge Western interests and the Indonesian state before they had the support of the population. And these attacks, which also killed Muslims, only alienated that population.

So Azhari and Noordin were compelled to rely more heavily on fringe elements of the Muslim "charity" organization Kompak, on Darul Islam, and on Ring Banten, the DI-linked group in the Serang countryside. To a good extent, these connections were already part of the personalized networks of the principal Bali plotters, but because many other JI members refused to help out, Azhari and Noordin had to tinker in creative ways to add enough pieces and repair their networks to get the suicide bombing campaign rolling again. Their acolytes set up a training camp in West Java to train the bombers who would take part in the embassy operation. A pair of religious students, Ubeid and Urwah, assisted in setting in motion a series of relationships with anyone who could acquire explosives and make bombs.

Indonesian security forces arrested several people in the group, disrupting the planning of the embassy operation before it was implemented. JI's ability to implement the attack in the wake of these arrests attests to the resilience of its family- and school-based network. The final bombing team included Noordin, the director of operations; Azahari, the chief bomb maker and second-in-command; Rais, the field commander; and Heri Golun, Jabir, Heri Sigu Samboja, Apuy, and Achmad Hasan as team members.

The 2004 Australian embassy bombing would serve as the template for the decentralized structure that Noordin and Azhari would use to lead the 2005 Bali bombings, striking the same city as in 2002 and killing twenty people and injuring over a hundred others. But even from his Indonesian prison cell, Mukhlas would smuggle out messages to Noordin, who continued to seek out his old teacher for spiritual guidance. A corrupt prison warden smuggled in a laptop for Samudra, who used the prison's wireless connection to converse with some of the Bali 2005 plotters.

EMBERS

After the American decimation and scattering of Al Qaeda forces in Afghanistan in 2001–2002, and after the massive arrests of JI leaders and members in 2002–2003, the most violent remnants of JI lacked the financial and logistical means to carry on large-scale attacks by themselves. New trainees were now asked to pay for their own training, which meant fewer trainees. (For the Mount Ungaran training, Noordin could only find eight people ready to pay for themselves.)[11] Increasingly Azhari and Noordin looked for new sources of funding and personnel.

They sought out people to do *fa'i*, or robbing non-Muslims for a Muslim cause, because there weren't enough outside funds or members' contributions.[12] Toni Togar had turned to *fa'i* to help Noordin pay for the Marriott bombing—he robbed a bank in Medan. Imam Samudra had previously resorted to *fa'i* when he ordered his Serang group of candidate martyrs to rob a Chinese goldsmith's shop a year before the Bali bombing. But gaining experience rather than money was the aim of that exercise. (As Azhari reportedly put it, "there would always be donors," especially among wealthy Malaysians, to fund operations.)[13] With Azhari and Noordin, *fa'i* implied involvement with petty criminals, not that the new JI attack leaders themselves had any mundane, criminal ambitions. It's simply that the success of counterterrorism actions against JI and Al Qaeda required new forms of alliance and adaptation, taking advantage of new avenues of opportunity and hitherto unused niches.

The arrest of hundreds of JI members and associates after the 2002 Bali bombing, including Ba'asyir, and the increasing internal division over the suicide bombing campaign, splintered JI but did not destroy it. The traditional JI hierarchy, which had been only peripherally related to the bombing operations, lost any remaining relevance. Counterterrorism operations after Bali also fragmented the personalized networks that had been forged over the years through kinship, training camps, and schools. But the personal connections left in the pieces were sticky enough to reassemble with some new parts for three major suicide attacks: the Australian embassy in 2004, three restaurants in Bali again in 2005, and another assault in 2009 on the Jakarta Marriott and Ritz-Carlton hotels.

Even before Noordin's death in September 2009, a new coalition began to emerge between newly released prisoners and other JI-linked fugitives, families, and friends. This "cross-organizational Al Qaeda movement" (*lintas tanzim Al Qaeda*) rejected JI's provisional shift from violence to "outreach," as well as Noordin's bombing campaign that was killing Muslims and alienating the public. The new coalition was led by Dulmatin, who had fled to the southern Philippines after the first Bali bombing and then crept back to Indonesia in 2007. With the help of a founder of Ring Banten (Kang Jaja, who had enlisted the suicide bomber for the Australian embassy bombing) and Kompak's leader (Abdullah Sunata, who had been released from prison in March 2009), Dulmatin worked to set up a secure military facility that would train operatives to assassinate only those who stood in the way of establishing an Islamic state. The group followed the line of the Jordanian cleric Abu Mohammed al-Maqdisi, who preached that jihad mustn't victimize innocent Muslims and must go hand in hand with religious outreach. Al-Maqdisi had mentored the Iraq-based jihadi leader Abu Musab al-Zarqawi, but broke with him for the same reason that Dulmatin's coalition refused Noordin's tactics. Although Dulmatin and company admired Noordin and included some of his close associates (Ubeid and Urwah), they thought that he had no clue how to establish an Islamic state beyond preparing for the next attack.[14]

Fortunately, local police stumbled on the group's training facility just as it was being set up in Aceh in February 2010. In March, the national police strike team killed Dulmatin at an Internet café near Jakarta, and slew Jaja and several others in Aceh. Ubeid and some training leaders were arrested in April. Even more were killed and arrested in May, apparently still bent on a Mumbai-style rifle-and-grenade assault on President Yudhoyono and other dignitaries (scheduled for Independence Day, August 17, with some hint that the plotters might have tried stirring up things to coincide with President Obama's planned visit to Indonesia).

Today, with Hambali in American hands, with Noordin and Dulmatin dead, all eyes are understandably back on Ba'asyir, who continues to preach confrontation with the West while studiously avoiding direct support for violence. In the aftermath of the Bali plot, Ba'asyir was sentenced to three years in prison for "blessing" bombing operations, though his sentence was later reduced to eighteen months. Today, Ba'asyir is free and unbending. As he said in my interview with him before release from his well-tended quarters in Jakarta's Cipinang Prison:

> Allah's law can't be under human law. Allah's law must stand above human law. All laws must be under Islamic law. This is what the infidels fail to recognize. . . . There will be a clash between Islam and the infidels. There is no example of Islam and infidels, the right and the wrong, living together in peace. . . . They have to stop fighting Islam, but that's impossible because it is *sunnatullah* [destiny, a law of nature], as Allah has said in the Koran. They constantly will be enemies.[15]

Ba'asyir's moral acceptance of the Bali bombing, his uncompromising attitude toward all but the strictest forms of Islam, and his ruling that "Democracy is prohibited" suggests little chance of coming to terms with the committed remnants of JI. Churches in Indonesia, which Ba'asyir and others claim have no right to exist, continue to receive bomb threats.[16] The peaceful struggle must be for the goodwill of the next generation of Muslims in Indonesia

CHAPTER 10
THE JI SOCIAL CLUB

Knowledge of the interconnected networks of Afghan Alumni,
friendship, kinship, and marriage groups was very crucial to
uncovering the inner circle of Noordin.

—GENERAL TITO KARNAVIAN, HEAD OF INDONESIAN POLICE

STRIKE TEAM THAT TRACKED DOWN NOORDIN MOHAMMED

TOP (PERSONAL COMMUNICATION, DECEMBER 10, 2009)

LESS THAN MEETS THE EYE: JI AND AL QAEDA

The Bali bombing is viewed in some quarters as funded and
planned by 9/11 mastermind Khaled Sheikh Muhammed in coordination with JI CEO Hambali (who since his days in Afghanistan
fighting the communists had presumably served as the principal
liaison between Al Qaeda and the group that would form JI). At a
hearing in the U.S. military detention center at Guantánamo Bay,
Cuba, in 2007, Mohammed claimed credit for the Bali operation
as his.[1] But Nasir Abas's version of a JI hijacked by Hambali, and
President Bush's description of Hambali at the time of his capture
in 2004 as "a senior Al Qaeda leader [and] close associate of September 11 mastermind Khaled Sheikh Mohammed,"[2] would seem
to give equal importance to Hambali as an Al Qaeda operative.

In fact, Mohammed and Al Qaeda had no evident operational
input or control in the Bali plot. And in all the talk about Hambali,
Zulkarnaen's central role as the chief strategist of JI's radical militant
group is often overlooked. The almost exclusive focus on Mohammed

and Hambali may be partly an artifact of their high-profile captures, their extroverted personalities, and the tendency to overextend stories about what is in hand, or to make up stories, to fill in the gaps.

Mohammed did not join Al Qaeda until late 1998 or early 1999.[3] Only with his success in 9/11 did he rise to the top of Qaeda's heap (and to the top of the U.S. media heap, with news last fall that he would be tried for his alleged role in 9/11 in New York). Before then, Qaeda's principal connection to JI was through Abu Hafs al-Masri (Mohammed Atef), a former member of Ayman Zawahiri's Egyptian Al-Jihad and Qaeda's military leader.

Hambali's importance in JI and his links to Mohammed and Al Qaeda have also been overblown, especially in the years prior to the Bali bombing. JI's wily and furtive military leader, Zulkarnaen, had a higher position in JI and closer contacts to Al Qaeda than did Hambali in the 1990s. According to Nasir bin Abas, Zulkarnaen was always considered the head of the Afghan veterans, a source of prestige and status on a different plane than his formal position as military commander. All militant activities carried out by Afghan Alumni had to be cleared with him.[4]

THE AFGHAN ALUMNI AND THEIR ACCOMPLISHMENTS

Below is a chart that outlines the most high-profile of the Afghan Alumni and the bombings they were involved in, as well as any role they had in JI's mantiqi organization:

Bombings
Philippines Ambassador's Residence, 2000
Christmas Eve, 2000
Rizal Day, 2000 (bombings at Metro Manila in the Philippines on December 30)
Atrium Mall, 2001 (Atrium Senen shopping mall bombing in Jakarta on August 10)

*Santa Ana, 2001 (bombing of Catholic Santa Ana church
and nearby Protestant church, east of Jakarta, July 22)*
Bali 1, 2002
Jakarta Marriott. 2003
Australian Embassy, 2004
Bali 2, 2005

NAME	AFGHAN ALUMNI TRAINING CLASS (3 YEARS UNLESS NOTED)	BOMBINGS
Zulkarnaen	First Class of 1985	Bali 1
Mukhlas	Second Class of 1985	Philippines Ambassador, Christmas Eve, Singapore Plots, Bali 1
Abu Rusdan	Second Class of 1985	Hid Bali 1 bombers
Mustofa	Third Class of 1987	Sulawesi and Kalimatan mantiqi leader
Nasir bin Abas	Fifth Class of 1987	Sulawesi and Kalimatan mantiqi leader
Edy Setyono	Fifth Class of 1987	Philippines Ambassador, Christmas Eve, Atrium Mall, Santa Ana
Farhin	Fifth Class of 1987	Philippines Ambassador
Hambali	Fourth Class of 1986	Malaysia and Singapore mantiqi leader; Philippines Ambassador, Christmas Eve, Rizal, Atrium Mall, Santa Ana, Singapore Plots, Bali 1
Jabir	Sixth Class of 1991	Christmas Eve
Abdul Ghoni	Seventh Class of 1989	Christmas Eve, Bali 1
Abu Dujanah	Seventh Class of 1989	Hid Bali bombers, Met with Marriott / Australian Embassy leaders
Qotadah	Seventh Class of 1989	Marriott, Australian Embassy
Al Ghozi	Eighth Class of 1990	Philippines Ambassador, Rizal Day
Mubarok	Eighth Class of 1990	Philippines Ambassador, Christmas Eve, Bali 1

NAME	AFGHAN ALUMNI TRAINING CLASS (3 YEARS UNLESS NOTED)	BOMBINGS
Dulmatin	1990 or 1991	Philippines Ambassador, Christmas Eve, Bali 1
Faiz Bafana	No Class Information	Philippines Ambassador, Christmas Eve, Rizal Day, Atrium Mall, Santa Ana, Singapore Plots
Imam Samudra	Ninth Class of 1991	Christmas Eve, Atrium Mall, Santa Ana, Bali 1
Ali Imron	Ninth Class of 1991	Philippines Ambassador, Christmas Eve, Bali 1
Sarjiyo	Ninth Class of 1991	Philippines Ambassador, Christmas Eve, Bali 1
Asep	Did not go to Afghanistan, fought in Ambon	Atrium Mall, Santa Ana
Toni Togar	Tenth Class of 1992	Christmas Eve, Marriott
Abu Fatih	Never a Student	Mantiqi leader of most of Indonesia
Azhari Husin	Short training period in 2000	Christmas Eve, Bali 1, Marriott, Australian Embassy, Bali 2
Taufik (Dani)	Afghan training, 1994–1996	Atrium Mall, Santa Ana

There's no evidence that Hambali interacted with Mohammed at Saddah, the Afghan mujahedin training camp located in Pakistan near the Khyber Pass, though both were there (as were hundreds of others). It is possible that Hambali met Mohammed in Malaysia in 1996 when the latter visited Sungkar and Ba'asyir at Mukhlas's boarding school, Lukman Al Hakiem. But Mohammed mentions no noteworthy encounters with Hambali before 2000.

In 1997 Sungkar and Ba'asyir visited Al Qaeda leaders in Afghanistan, who had recently relocated there from Sudan. The goal at the time was to prepare the way for JI members to get training in Qaeda camps. By then Zulkarnaen, who was arguably the third-most influential member in the JI hierarchy after the two religious leaders, was back in Malaysia, occasionally lecturing at

Lukman Al Hakiem and planning the coordination of training and military activities with various jihadi organizations, including Al Qaeda in Afghanistan and the Moro Islamic Liberation Front in the Philippines. In August 1998, Sungkar and Ba'asyir called upon Darul Islam leaders and others in the region to join with them in support of Bin Laden's fatwa proclaiming "the Muslim world's global jihad."[5]

Around this time, Zulkarnaen contacted Abu Hafs al-Masri to arrange training for JI militants in Qaeda camps in Afghanistan. In early 1999, Hambali and Abu Bakr Bafana, who was treasurer for Mantiqi 3, the JI command covering the southern Philippines, Borneo, and Sulawesi, decided to go to Afghanistan to introduce the first two trainees (Zaini and Zamzulri). According to Bafana, he and Hambali were still unaware of Bin Laden's 1998 fatwa calling for jihad against American, Jewish, and Christian interests,[6] to which Sungkar and Ba'asyir's letter implicitly referred. Hambali and Bafana met very briefly with a certain "Mukhtar" in Karachi, before continuing to Kandahar. Mukhtar was a nom de guerre for Khaled Sheikh Mohammed, whom Bin Laden had just recently inducted into Al Qaeda to pursue the plot that would ultimately result in the 9/11 attacks. But at this juncture, Mohammed seems to have been no more than Abu Hafs al-Masri's point man for relaying contacts through Pakistan to Afghanistan. At the time, Ba'asyir's son, Abdul Rohim, was JI's chief contact person with Qaeda in Pakistan. Hambali's younger brother, Gun Gun, would later take over from Abdul Rohim.

Later in 1999, Hambali sent Bafana again to Afghanistan, this time explicitly to plan joint JI-Qaeda operations in line with Bin Laden's fatwa. Hambali's initial plan was to attack a U.S. warship in Singapore. He provided Bafana with videotapes of site casings, which he asked Bafana to show to Mohammed. Bafana failed to find Mohammed in Karachi and went on to Baluchistan, where he sneaked across the border to meet Abu Hafs al-Masri at Bin

Laden's camp near Kandahar. When Bafana told Abu Hafs that JI had no suicide bombers, Abu Hafs reportedly responded: "We will provide the personnel. The money we will provide. All you need to look for is the explosive, the TNT, and the transport."[7]

This is the first evidence that JI and Al Qaeda were seriously considering joint operations. As it turns out, this plan was aborted and a more far-ranging plan of action against the American and Israeli embassies and the Australian high commission in Singapore was soon in the offing. But that, too, failed to hatch, when Singapore authorities found out about the plot and closed in.

In December 1999 and January 2000, Mohammed reportedly asked Hambali to accommodate Al Qaeda operatives passing through Kuala Lumpur. The operatives included Tawfik bin Attash, who later helped bomb the USS *Cole*, and future 9/11 hijackers Nawaf al Hazmi and Khaled al Midhar. Hambali arranged for their accommodation at Yazid Sufaat's condominium in Kuala Lumpur and helped purchase airline tickets for their onward travel.[8] There is no evidence that JI was actively involved in either Qaeda action other than providing an apartment of convenience.

Sometime in mid-2000, Iman Samudra, the 2002 Bali bombing field commander, and Sufaat informed Hambali that Zacharias Moussaoui, a Frenchman of Moroccan descent, had shown up in Malaysia unannounced, sent either by Abu Hafs or Mohammed. Hambali, who was in Indonesia at the time, returned to Malaysia to discover that Moussaoui's purpose was to enroll in flight school. According to testimony entered at Moussaoui's trial in U.S. Federal District Court in Virginia in 2006:

> Hambali decried Moussaoui as very troubled, not right in the head. . . . Hambali put Moussaoui up in Yazid [Sufaat]'s condominium, which was often used to house guests. . . . Moussaoui had not come to Asia specifically to meet with Hambali, but

because Moussaoui had been sent by Abu Hafs or KSM, Hambali and his fellow guest members believed it was their obligation to assist him.[9]

Hambali, Yazid, Samudra, and Mukhlas became unsettled at Moussaoui's erratic behavior, including a bizarre request for forty tons of ammonium nitrate with no clear target in mind. Ammonium nitrate is a volatile industrial fertilizer favored as a readily available explosive by terrorists, including Timothy McVeigh, whose 1995 bombing of a federal office building in Oklahoma City registered as the deadliest terrorist event in the U.S history before 9/11. Moussaoui's JI hosts decided to buy only four tons and a plane ticket for Moussaoui. The unstable Frenchman apparently didn't even notice the amount bought and left Malaysia complaining that JI should stop reading the Koran and starting planning attacks. In the end, his JI hosts were stuck with the ammonium nitrate and the bill. When they later asked Mohammed what to do with the chemicals, he denied ever asking Moussaoui to request ammonium nitrate, let alone forty tons of it. After Moussaoui left, Mukhlas went to Pakistan to complain directly to Mohammed: "Sheikh Mohammed agreed that there was something wrong with Moussaoui," but Bin Laden liked him for some reason, and Mohammed reimbursed JI for the plane ticket and ammonium nitrate.[10]

Not until Hambali fled to Afghanistan to escape arrest for the 2000 Christmas Eve bombings in Indonesia did he and Mohammed establish a close working relationship. Over the previous eighteen months, Hambali may have been acting primarily as point man for Zulkarnaen, just as Mohammed may have been acting as point man for Qaeda military chief Abu Hafs al-Masri. The crucial and formative JI-Qaeda relationship was probably military chief to military chief. Because the highly secretive and taciturn Zulkarnaen is still at large, and Abu Hafs was killed in Afghanistan in an American air strike in November 2001, the details of the relationship between the military leaders remain unknown. There is no evidence to support the widespread urban legend that Hambali was a member of Al Qaeda's inner circle of advisers, or *shura*.

DISCIPLESHIP, KINSHIP, AND SOCIAL NETWORKS

JI's hierarchical structure had little relevance to the Bali bombing and other attacks initiated through the personalized networks associated with the Bali plotters. At the October 17, 2002, JI central command meeting shortly after the Bali bombing, there was no discussion of the bombing. Nasir Abas asked Zulkarnaen if he knew who had carried out the bombing. Zulkarnaen reportedly told Abas that it was "none of his business."[11] Mukhlas, married to Nasir Abas's sister, eventually confessed his role in the plot to his brother-in-law. But Abas was clearly out of the loop in the Bali planning. And there is no evidence that JI's then-emir Ba'asyir knew any operational details about what was going on.[12] During Ba'asyir's various trials for sedition and aiding a terrorist conspiracy, even those JI operatives who turned state's evidence either could not or refused to directly implicate Ba'asyir in the Bali plot.[13] The Bali plot and plots after spewed from a tangled web of discipleship, kinship and marriage, social networks of Afghan Alumni and other friends, and not really from any command-and-control organization. Consider:

At the dawn of the new millennium Abu Bakr Ba'asyir outlined his vision of promoting "Islamic communities" (*jemaah islamiyah*) through religious education in Islamic *pesantren* in a speech delivered to the First Indonesian Congress of Mujahedin:

> In truth, the enemies of Islam have eradicated this spirit of jihad—the love for jihad and martyrdom—from the soul of the *ummah*. The enemies of Islam know that as long as the *ummah* no longer understands jihad and the zeal for martyrdom, they

will be easily subjugated. For this reason, we must nurture both comprehension of, and zeal for, jihad, so that love for it, and for martyrdom, grow in the soul of the mujahedin: this is the most important task of Islamic social organizations in guiding and developing their members. . . . Religious boarding schools are the bulwark of Islam. . . . In order for a *pesantren* to be truly a crucible for the formation of cadres of mujahedin . . . instruction in the laws of jihad and war must also be included in the curriculum, so that graduates of *pesantren* truly become preachers and mujahedin.[14]

Sixteen of the twenty-six Bali attackers and planners either attended or were associated with one of three JI-linked radical madrassahs:[15] Al Mukmin, Lukman Al Hakiem, and Al Islam. These JI-linked radical madrassahs are both production sites and service centers for jihadis. For example, association with Lukman Al Hakiem—JI's main Malaysian madrassah, which no longer exists—increases the probability by nearly 25 percent that a jihadi will play a major role in an attack.[16] After the 2002 Bali operation, most of those who helped hide one of the bombers, Ali Imron, were associated with Al Islam, where he was a teacher.[17]

Within JI there has been a debate over whether attacks are legitimate on Indonesian soil and, if so, whether the killing of Muslims is allowed because they are *thogut*: violators of Islamic law and therefore *kafir*[18] (although *thogut* is not always equated with *kafir*, most JI people interviewed consider them as such). JI-affiliated madrassahs usually accommodate all sides of the debate. Although only a minority of their teachers and students may support both attacks on Indonesian soil and the killing of Muslims as well as foreigners for the sake of jihad, the more "moderate" majority generally wouldn't think of turning out the "radicals," much less denouncing them to police. Still, the number of madrassahs that accommodate Takfiri ideology is small. Out of some thirty thousand religious schools in Indonesia, only about fifty,[19] far less than 1 percent, preach extremist views (about the same percentage as in Pakistan, as we'll see in chapter 14), such as agreement with the statement that "it is the duty of Muslims to fight and kill non-Muslims," as we put it to the students at Al Islam in one questionnaire.[20]

The 2002 Bali operation is not unique in its reliance on school-teachers and friends from a few radical schools. Noordin's networks have also depended on these sorts of ties, which cement personal relationships and ideological commitment. For example, in the lead-up to the Australian embassy bombing, an instructor at the JI-affiliated Mahad Aly school in Solo introduced three students to Noordin. One of them, Deni, became Azhari's apprentice and took over as Noordin's chief bomb maker after Azhari was killed. Two others, Urwah and Ubeid, brought in a fourth friend from the school, Aslam (aka Parmin), to help Noordin formulate his statement of mission. The tract, titled *Sowing Jihad, Reaping Terror*, elaborated on how Bin Laden's 1998 fatwa for international jihad should be applied in Southeast Asia.

Urwah and Ubeid, together with Ubeid's brother, also helped coordinate training and logistics for the embassy bombing. Urwah and Ubeid were arrested in 2004 and released in 2007. A short while later, Ba'asyir presided over Urwah's wedding to a madrassah student. Ubeid joined the governing council of Ba'asyir's new organization, Jamaah Ansharut Tauhid. By early 2008, Urwah and Ubeid were back together connecting up with their jihadi brethren. Urwah helped Noordin enlist key participants for the hotel bombings and the abortive plot to kill President Yudhoyono, and he was killed with Noordin. (Ubeid hooked up with Dulmatin's project described in chapter 3.)[21]

The lead-up to the 2009 Jakarta hotel bombings illustrates the interplay of camaraderie and friendship, kinship and marriage, school ties and discipleship. One of the principal components of

Noordin's support network was a group from Cilacap in Central Java. In 1999, Urwah was a teacher in the JI subdivision centered on Cilacap, part of the Central Java division of Mantiqi 2. It was the job of the subdivision teacher to team up with its preacher to form study circles that focused on religious propaganda, education, and jihad. From such study groups emerged many of the JI foot soldiers who fought Christians in Ambon and Sulawesi.

Around the time that Noordin brought Urwah into his circle, just before the 2004 Australian embassy bombing, Urwah likely connected Noordin to the former *da'i* from Cilacap, Baradin (Baharudin Latif), and to Baradin's nephew, Sabit (Saeffudin Zuhri), an herbal healer who was one of the Afghan Alumni and an early member of JI. By 2005, Sabit was Noordin's point man in trying to influence an informal Islamic study group in Sumatra to blow up Western tourists. (The plot ultimately failed in November 2007, when the group's would-be suicide bomber got cold feet after Muslim women walked into the chosen target, the Café Bedudel in the West Sumatran hill city of Bukittingi.) In 2006, Noordin married his third wife, Arina, Sabit's first cousin, Baradin's daughter. In June 2009, Sabit was arrested but Baradin escaped (he was arrested in December 2009). Arina's father, who headed a JI-affiliated boarding school, had stashed explosives in his back garden with the aid of another teacher at the school. And this may have prompted Noordin to launch the hotel attacks ahead of a planned truck bombing of the Indonesian president's residence.

Four of the principal actors in the 2009 hotels plot and its planned follow-ups were part of one village family: Syaifudin Jaelani, an herbal healer and Yemeni-trained imam of a local mosque, chose the suicide bombers. Amir Ibrahim, married to Jaelani's sister, booked room 1808 in the Marriott Hotel where the suicide bombers stayed. It was he who told police about the plot against President Yudhoyono. Ibrohim, married to another of Jaelani's sisters, was the hotel florist who smuggled in the bombs.

Jaelani's older brother, Mohamad Sjahir, was a technician who had infiltrated Garuda, Indonesia's national airline.

Indonesia's counterterrorism success has relied on cracking extremist networks by grasping their social structure, and moving against likely players in that social structure. Close ties of kinship and marriage, friendship and discipleship, have made penetrating these networks very difficult, and sometimes key parts have continued to operate right under the nose of security forces. But increasing success has depended on closer scrutiny and exploitation of social connections, not in directly attacking or challenging ideas and values. Those ideas and values continue to circulate and diffuse freely, and their potential for bringing in new blood remains. The problem for the future is how to turn youth away from them, without violence or denial of liberty.

A few final observations on these networks: Although the bulk of JI considered Noordin to be outside of the JI mainstream, JI-affiliated schools, charities, and publishing houses and other religious networks provided a passive infrastructure that allowed Noordin's networks to survive and thrive. Thus, when Sabit showed up at a JI-affiliated school in Sumatra to preach violence in support of international jihad, he was not turned away, even though the schoolmaster and his superiors in JI opposed the content. They housed him and allowed him to rant as he saw fit, an errant soul but one of their own—certainly not someone they would ever denounce to the police.

There are other pieces of passive infrastructure that have helped to sustain the violent extremists. Sidney Jones of the International Crisis Group suggests that lack of modern healthcare in Indonesia has created a void filled by religious healers, like Sabit and Jaelani.[22] As with the medicine men of the Old West, these healers often move about the countryside, and their relationships have provided additional pathways and opportunities for the growth of personalized militant networks.

Finally, the suicide bombers themselves are often young men in transitional stages of life and with unsure futures. In JI-related cases, strong-willed seniors persuade younger men who seem somewhat vulnerable and marginalized that death for a cause bestows on life something sure and good. In the mold of Imam Samudra, commanding and fatherlike, Jaelani mentored a group of young men and took them to a "religious retreat" to decide who among them would become a bridegroom in paradise. He chose eighteen-year old Dani Pertama, who had just graduated high school and whose father, a poor thief, was in jail. (Jaelani also brought in a second suicide bomber, twenty-six-year-old Nana Mualana, from Samudra's home district of Banten.)

But we'll see that in other cases around the world today, it is mostly youth in transition who persuade other youth in transition that heaven is built on the foundations of hell.

CHAPTER 11
THE GREAT TRAIN BOMBING: MADRID, MARCH 11, 2004

Behold! human beings living in a cave, which has a mouth
open towards the light. . . . [B]ehind them a fire is blazing at a
distance, and between the fire and the [people] there is . . . a low
wall, like the screen which marionette players have in front of
them, over which they show puppets.

—SOCRATES, IN PLATO, *REPUBLIC*

"We need to see inside the cave," said Rogers. "We're seeing
shadows on the wall, but we don't know whether they are made
by a giant or a dwarf."

"I know what you want," said Fares. "You want to know who
makes the bombs."

"Yes," said Rogers. "But I also want to understand why he is
doing it."

—DAVID IGNATIUS, *AGENTS OF INNOCENCE: A SPY STORY*

MADRID, MARCH 7–8, 2007

At the Madrid train-bombing trial, the major defendants jabbered
and joked inside the glass cage. Strange. This was the biggest trial
for mass murder in Western Europe since World War II and the
most important trial ever for terrorism up to then. Yet there was
almost no one present from the public to watch and learn about
what the polls say is the issue the public most fears. Thus Marc
Sageman and I pretty much constituted the public (apart from a

few journalists and some family members and friends of victims and defendants).

The panel of judges sat in front of us, the defendants' cage to the right, and three long rows of lawyers were to our left. There were loads of lawyers, for the twenty-nine defendants and also for the victims. One of the victims' lawyers grilled a police agent on whether the bags that carried the bombs were sports satchels (*bolsas*), as the policeman said, or really backpacks (*mochillas*). The policeman said he wasn't 100 percent sure. "Aha!" the lawyer exclaimed, pointing out to the court that ETA (Euzkadi Ta Azka-tasuna), the Basque terrorist organization originally accused of the bombing by the Spanish government, habitually uses backpacks. (He was apparently uninformed, or uninterested in the fact that the suicide bombers of the London Underground and many other jihadis also like backpacks for bombs.)

This particular defense lawyer seemed to be just a hack for the center-right Popular Party, which lost the national election to the Socialists three days after the bombing. Now, the lawyer's job was to discredit the prosecution's case, and indirectly the Socialist party, and so help the defense. The chief judge, Juan del Olmo, whose shaved head was all that seemed to shine with any intelligence in the courtroom, sliced off the lawyer after half an hour of nonsense. "We'll solve the mystery of the *mochilla* some other time," he said. "Let's get on with the case."

The star witness for the prosecution, a former police informant called Abdelkader Farssaoui, code-named "Cartagena," immediately began to recant much of his pretrial testimony as having been coerced. He claimed the police threatened to deport him if he didn't falsely connect the dots between the plotters through drug deals—connections that he said were far fewer and more sporadic than he had originally let on. The state prosecutor, picked for this trial by routine bureaucratic rotation rather than for any special competence, plowed ahead from a prepared list of questions without looking up from her papers, almost oblivious to the fact that the witness was not cooperating at all. A bit later, another witness was called but no one in the court could understand a word she said. "Could someone get an interpreter in here?" the judge called out. An Arabic speaker was brought in but couldn't understand anything either: "I think the witness is speaking Berber," he said, referring to a language of rural Morocco. Witness excused.

One of the cage dwellers—a former bouncer, male stripper, and jewelry thief with a Mussolini-like skull and jutting jaw—flexed his pectorals and beckoned me to the glass partition, against which he'd pasted his notebook, but police waved me away. This guy was fabulously full of himself, and now that he was sort of famous, he'd written to the king of Spain. And to me, so I should be flattered. "He's got a thing for you," Marc said to me with a chuckle. He was the only one of the eighteen caged defendants who took notes, and furiously. He'd later be ejected from the court when he punched a fellow defendant for calling him a snitch, which the guy was. Mr. Muscle was accused of linking up his fellow Moroccans with an ex-con, a Spaniard who worked in a mine and pilfered explosives to sell to anybody interested, from fishermen looking to illegally blow fish out of the water to aspiring jihadis looking to blow up people. The prosecution demanded a sentence of 38,958 years for complicity in a murder of 191 people and the wounding of more than 1,800. (He'd get 10 years for trafficking in explosives.)

The Spaniard ex-con sat alone in the front row. He stared blankly for hours, gnawing the fingernails of both hands simultaneously. He said that the dynamite he traded to "the Moors" for hash and cash was supposed to be for robbing jewelry stores. Except he really couldn't explain why, when "the Moors" were carrying away the dynamite, he had called out, "And don't forget the nails and the screws!" The prosecution asked for 38,962 years for him; he got 34,715. Both sentences were bizarre, given that 40 years is the maximum that anyone in Spain may serve. The Spaniard's wife refused to look at her husband. She was also one of the accused: It was her cell phone that was used to seal the deal. But she was sitting outside the cage facing only minor charges, probably for having agreed to rat on her spouse to save herself and her brother, another ex-con who also happened to be the husband's cousin. She and her brother got off scot-free.

Most of the others in the cage were part-time petty criminals, but also would-be Soldiers of God. My eyes fixed on the one in the crowd who wore a tie. Not just any tie, but carefully matched to his other clothes, a clear statement of his exception from the common lot around him. He listened to everything stone-faced, smiling only when the state prosecutor fumbled with a witness. In pretrial testimony, his wife had described how he kicked her in the stomach while she was pregnant with twins, saying he hoped to have the same luck with their unborn as Bin Laden had with the Twin Towers. He got the twelve years the prosecution requested for having provided an apartment and video propaganda to some of the plotters.

A young man in sweats with a middleweight's gait sat giggling with another in the back row. This former track star and soccer fiend was taking out the garbage when he overheard the police radio, cried a warning to his friends, and sprinted to temporary safety as the police surrounded the apartment where the main plotters were holed up. He got 18 years instead of the 38,950 sought. His less lucky friends—a Tunisian, an Algerian, and five Moroccans who grew up in the same neighborhood—cried out, *"Mamones entren!"* (Cocksuckers, come on in!) and blew themselves to bits that went through the apartment walls into the outdoor swimming pool below.

Then there was the weaselly guy from Egypt who sat silent in the corner. He used to brag to all his fellow jihadi wannabes that Madrid was his idea. "This project took me a lot of study and a lot of patience; it took me two and a half years," he was heard to say in a wiretap but now said, My goodness I had no idea at all. He was acquitted; in fact, his alibi was that he was in Milan at the time, where Italian police had recorded him narrating the decapitation of American Nick Berg in order to excite another young Egyptian into becoming a suicide bomber.

> THE EGYPTIAN: "Kill him! Kill him! Yes, like that! Cut his throat properly. Cut his head off! If I had been there, I would have burned him to make him already feel what hell was like. Cut off his head! God is great! God is great!"
>
> YOUNG MAN: "Isn't it a sin?"
>
> THE EGYPTIAN: "It's never a sin! We hope that even their parents will come to the same end. Dogs, all of them, all of them. You simply need to be convinced when you make the decision."

But to tell the truth, this guy and most of the others look, talk, and act like a bunch of nondescript nobodies who fancied being somebodies. That's not to say that all would-be jihadis are like these knuckleheads, who make the JI radicals seem like seasoned professionals. Many surely are not. Seems it takes all kinds to make any mass movement.

"BUT I JUST DON'T UNDERSTAND, WHERE'S AL QAEDA?"

On March 7, 2007, the prosecution called to the stand the informant Abdelkader el Farssaoui, aka Cartagena, who had been the substitute imam of the Takouma mosque, where some of the plotters prayed in the Villaverde neighborhood of Madrid. Cartagena tried to warn Spanish authorities that something dangerous might be up. He was ignored:

> PROSECUTION: In the meeting when they told you that they weren't looking for mujahedin so much as martyrs, didn't you suspect from this that an attack could be committed in Spain?

CARTAGENA: Yes, I suspected, I suspected even more, I suspected that they would die in the first attack that they could carry out . . . perhaps with a [suicide] belt they would come into a place and die. And I raised my hand [when all were asked "Who is prepared" to be a martyr?], but I didn't want to be a martyr at that moment, no, no, I didn't like that, it scared me. . . .

PROSECUTION: You communicated with the police about the content of this meeting [which Cartagena called "the last supper"].

CARTAGENA: This was the first time that I realized that . . . UCIE [police] agents, something's wrong with them, something's failed, because when the supper was over I called them on Friday and they didn't like that. I told them, "it's very important," and they said that they don't work on Saturday or Sunday and so "until Monday, we're with our families. . . ." I tell them everything, and they say, "Listen, go home, don't hook up again with that group until you get the order."

The bombings in Madrid on March 11, 2004, killed nearly two hundred people and injured almost two thousand. Almost immediately José Maria Aznar, the conservative prime minister from Spain's Popular Party, declared it the work of ETA. Three days later, Spain's Socialist Party won a shock election victory over Aznar's Popular Party after voters appeared to turn on the government over its handling of the Madrid bombings, especially its continued insistence that ETA was responsible despite repeated denials from ETA and mounting evidence that the bombings were jihad-inspired. Well into the trial, about a quarter of the Spanish public continued to believe the fish story that ETA was involved, despite all evidence to the contrary.[1]

As the defendants in the Madrid train bombing trial delivered their final statements, the Paris daily *Le Monde* gave one oft-quoted expert's prevailing wisdom on how Al Qaeda managed the Madrid attack and still managed global jihad: "Al-Qaeda designates a target, in this case Spain; allied groups—here the Moroccan Fighting Islamic Group—act as facilitators and support local cells, which are then activated."[2]

"But I just don't understand," said a person in my research group, after helping to translate nearly 1,500 pages of the Spanish government's indictment against the Madrid bomb plotters, and after watching and transcribing months of videos from the trials. "Where's Al Qaeda?" Indeed.

PRELUDE TO THE PLOT

A small number of Muslim migrants in the early 1980s came to Spain from Syria, fleeing from Syrian president Hafez al-Assad's assault against the Muslim Brotherhood in his country. This violent repression culminated in the massacre of Homs in 1982, which killed at least 38,000 people and razed the city, according to President Assad's own brother. Some of these Syrian immigrants were Salafi militants seeking refuge, mostly in Madrid. They married one another's sisters or Spanish women who converted to Islam. Among those who arrived during that period were Imad Eddin Barakat Yarkas (aka Abu Dahdah), who married a Spanish actress and converted to Islam; Tayssir Alouni, who later became a journalist for Al Jazeera and interviewed Bin Laden after the 9/11 attacks; and Mustafa Setmarian Nasar (aka Abu Musa al-Suri), who became the jihadi movement's Internet guru before his capture in Pakistan in the fall of 2005.

In the early 1990s, these militant Islamists formed a support network for jihadi fighters in Bosnia and provided them with financing, shelter, sanctuary, and medical care. In 1994, they formally organized themselves, taking the name Soldiers of Allah, under the leadership of Setmarian, Yarkas, and Palestinian preacher Anwar Adnan Ahmed Saleh (Sheikh Saleh).

A year later, Setmarian went to London to edit *Al Ansar*, the newsletter of the Algerian Groupe Islamique Armé, under the leadership of Abu Qatada, a Palestinian known as Al Qaeda's spiritual leader in Europe. (After 9/11, police in Hamburg found eighteen tapes of Abu Qatada's preachings in Mohammed Atta's apartment there.)

Sheikh Saleh went to Jalalabad, Afghanistan, to establish links with Al Qaeda, particularly with Abu Zubaydah, the senior facilitator for Qaeda's operations. (Abu Zubaydah was captured in Pakistan after 9/11, water-boarded and broken, then sent to Guantánamo.) Saleh greeted and processed volunteers coming to Afghanistan for training. In 1997, Setmarian also came to Afghanistan, and took charge of various Al Qaeda training camps, often quarreling over how others handled things.

Meanwhile, in Spain, Yarkas made contact with Al Qaeda affiliates in other parts of Europe, especially in Milan, Brussels, and London. His group welcomed young jihadis returning from Bosnia, Chechnya, and Afghanistan. The militant radicalism of Yarkas's group clashed with the religious authorities in their mosques. Sheikh Moneir Mahmoud Aly al-Messery, an Egyptian Salafi who was (and still is) imam of the Saudi-funded Islamic Cultural Center, a monumental white marble building that overlooks Madrid's M-30 freeway, expelled the Yarkas group in 1995 for preaching violence. The M-30 mosque, as it's commonly known, is the center of Muslim cultural life in the Spanish capital, and the group's expulsion amounted to a de facto excommunication from the mainstream Muslim community. Later, the group would "excommunicate" Moneir in turn.

Imad Eddin Barakat Yarkas and Mustafa Setmarian Nasar.

* * *

The overt proselytism of the group around Yarkas also attracted the attention of Spanish authorities. As early as 1995, Balthasar Garzón, a judge of the National High Court, ordered surveillance and telephone wiretapping of its leaders. The police succeeded in penetrating it with the help of one of its staff officers, Maussili Kalaji. Kalaji, a Syrian, had joined the Palestinian Fateh, trained in one of its camps, then went on to spy school in the Soviet Union. For some unknown reason, he immigrated to Spain in 1981 at the age of twenty-four and was given political asylum. He became an undercover Spanish policeman and was able to foil a Hizbollah terrorist operation in Europe in November 1989, for which he was decorated. Garzón dispatched him to infiltrate Yarkas's group. Kalaji opened up a telephone shop, Ayman Telephone Systems Technology, in the Muslim neighborhood of Madrid and became part of the militant network. In a terrible irony, on March 4, 2004, a half dozen hot cell phones were brought into Ayman Telephone Systems to be unlocked. This was duly reported to the police. A week later they were used to detonate the Madrid train bombs.

This Syrian-led militant group was by no means a "sleeper cell." It was highly visible in order to attract young Muslims, radicalize them to the cause of international jihad, and send them to fight in Bosnia, Chechnya, Afghanistan, and Indonesia. It became a lightning rod for young alienated Muslims seeking a cause. Some were immigrants who had come from Morocco as teenagers and had shown personal initiative by opening up their businesses in the immigrant neighborhood of Lavapies, like Jamal Zougam, with his telephone shop on Tribulete Street, and his half brother Mohammed Chaoui, whose grocery store on the same street sold exotic fruits imported by Yarkas from Damascus. Another new adherent to the group was a Tunisian, Serhane Abdelmajid Fakhet, el Tunecino—the Tunisian—as he became known. An honors economics student who had come to Spain in 1994 for graduate study

The dreamer: Serhane Fakhet, el Tunecino (the Tunisian).

on scholarship, he would later become one of the two main instigators of the Madrid plot, and its spiritual guide.[3]

Serhane came from a fairly well-to-do family in Tunis. His father worked for the Ministry of Foreign Relations; his mother was well educated and elegant. In the Department of Economic Analysis at the Universidad Autónoma de Madrid, he specialized in European accounting procedures. The Tunisian's teachers remember him as sweet, studious, and shy. Young women who were his classmates describe him as not unattractive, but very *incomodo* (uncomfortable) around girls. He had been engaged to be married in Tunisia, but things fell through at the last minute. His friends say he never really got into nightlife in Madrid, preferring to stay home and read. The Tunisian would argue passionately over ideas, especially religion, and seemed to be hypersensitive to any perceived slights against Muslims. One professor recalled him saying: "I'm a good man, an economist, a good student. So why am I not as good as the others? Why are they better than us?"

At first, he wanted to promote Muslim-European relations. He formed a student association, but the other Arab students weren't all that interested. He tried setting up a radio station, which also fell through. Then he tried selling imported clothes from Tunisia, which didn't work out. He tried importing candies, and that failed too.

So the Tunisian began spending more and more time at the M-30 mosque, discussing the Koran with a dozen or so others who remember him with fondness. He became the accountant for the mosque's lucrative halal restaurant and also worked translating Imam Moneir's preachings. Every day, he and the others played soccer near the mosque; Sheikh Moneir, the imam, refereed. "He loved soccer," recalls a friend, "he wasn't a very good player, but he tried hard and sweated a lot."

In 1998, the Tunisian's academic scholarship ended, and his request for a renewal was refused—not for lack of smarts, but because he had basically stopped taking school studies seriously. Like many of the young, marginal North Africans in Madrid, the Tunisian started selling stolen goods on the black market in the Lavapies neighborhood of central Madrid, the old Jewish quarter. The police noticed, but did nothing. There are too many like him, they have to live, and they don't really harm anyone.

The Tunisian moved to Virgen del Coro Street near the M-30 mosque, settling in an apartment owned by Mohanndes Almallah Dabas, the tie-wearing gent who kicked his pregnant wife in the stomach. The Tunisian took in "guests" for weeks and months at a time, extolling the virtues of *takfir wal hijra*. (The phrase, to remind the reader, was first used by a movement founded in Egypt in the 1970s that preached "excommunication and withdrawal" from society, in imitation of the withdrawal of the Prophet and his companions from Mecca to Medina to gather faith and force for a renewed assault on Mecca and the world.)

Taking in fellow travelers and creating a parallel universe devoted to dreams of jihad is commonplace on the road to radicalization. There were usually around five guests in the apartment at any given time, but sometimes there were as many as ten sleeping in a room. The Tunisian would hold court, reading the writings of Bin Laden and showing videos of Muslims being killed in Bosnia, Palestine, Chechnya, and Kashmir. Some of the videos were from Abu Qutada, a friend of Almallah's brother and also of Bin Laden. One friend remembered the Tunisian booting out someone who

refused to wear gloves when handling pork and alcohol in the restaurant where the guy worked. "But he was very generous, always
lending others money. He wasn't so friendly towards Europeans,
only his own people."

At the M-30 mosque, the Tunisian got to know Amer Azizi,
a Moroccan student who attended Imam Moneir's Koran classes.
After class, discussion usually turned to politics. But apart from
discussions of Palestine, when mostly everyone became agitated,
nothing radical or violent was proposed. This soon changed.

The Tunisian went on the pilgrimage (*hajj*) to Mecca and
returned illuminated, interested only in religious matters and right-
ing the wrongs done to Muslims around the world. In October 2000,
Sheikh Saleh, one of the original members of the Yarkas group,
arranged for Azizi to train in an Al Qaeda camp in Afghanistan.
Turkish authorities arrested Azizi on his way there. He was carrying
a false passport, a compass, and religious books. Azizi said he was
just a religious student on his way to study, and the police let him go.
He returned from Afghanistan in the summer of 2001, high as a kite
on jihad. He told war stories from Afghanistan and exhorted everyone to join the mujahedin and fight in Palestine and other places.
Young people at the mosque, seeing him as an action hero, listened.

That summer, Azizi promoted a series of family picnics at the
Parque del Soto by the banks of the Navalcarnero River outside
Madrid. The regulars at these "river meetings" included Said Che-
dadi, Basel Ghalyoun, Dris Chebli, Mouhanned Almallah Dabas
and his brother Moutaz, Mustapha Maymouni, the Tunisian, and
his close friend Khalid Zeimi Pardo. The children ran around, the
women prepared the food, and the friends played soccer and discussed jihad.[4] In August, Jamal Zougam, another picnicker, went
to Tangiers to visit Mohammed Fazazi, the fiery Moroccan who
had preached at the Al Quds mosque in Hamburg where Mohammed Atta and two of the other 9/11 suicide bomber pilots had been
enraptured by Fazazi's call "to smite the head of the infidels." Zou-

gam, too, returned with righteous fire. Pardo, though, considered that they were all still merely "Salafist and not adherents of jihad."[5]

Azizi, the Tunisian, and some of the others in Sheikh Moneir's discussion group stepped up their verbal assault on those, including Muslims, who didn't follow the Takfiri way as *kuffar* (infidels), subject to *takfir* (excommunication) and execution. They considered Europe Dar al-Harb, the House of War. Imam Moneir pushed back: "Just because someone has a beard, he thinks he's a sheikh who is knowledgeable and can issue fatwas." Azizi declared that Moneir, a self-professed Salafi, "is no Moslem," and angrily stormed out of the mosque with some followers. The Tunisian was among them.

On 9/11, Judge Balthasar Garzón was convinced—wrongly it turns out—that the operation was planned in Spain when he discovered that the last tune-up meeting between Mohammed Atta and Ramzi bin al-Shibh had taken place in Spain in July 2001. He strongly suspected Yarkas and his group of being involved in this planning session and used it as an excuse to arrest the major members of this group. With the information gathered from the extensive wiretapping and Kalaji's network of informants, Garzón arrested all the core members of Yarkas's group in November 2001 in Operation Datil. (The Spanish Supreme Court later overturned Yarkas's conviction for involvement in 9/11.)

Peripheral members who were relative newcomers to the group around Yarkas escaped detection and arrest, including the Tunisian, Zougam, Maymouni, and Mouhanned Almallah Dabas. Others went into hiding. They maintained a low profile, and they were very upset at the arrest of their friends.

The incubation of the Madrid plot by the lesser-known members of Yarkas's circle began in 2002. The evidence from pretrial testimony, the trial itself, and numerous interviews with friends of the perpetrators as well as various police and intelligence agents strongly indicate that Al Qaeda had nothing to do directly with the plot at any time. No evidence has linked Yarkas or Azizi to the plot, despite frequent speculation about their supposed involvement. None of the discussions leading up to the plot mention Yarkas as a player or even as an idea man. And if Azizi, who eventually made his way to the tribal region along the Afghan-Pakistani border, had really been in the loop, then Al Qaeda would have praised him and promoted him. Ayman al-Zawahiri and others in Al Qaeda repeatedly lauded the attack, and all those involved or accused, but never mentioned Azizi. There have been other attempts to link the Madrid plot to Al Qaeda through the Moroccan Islamic Combat Group, and the Spanish state prosecutor, Olga Sanchez, remains convinced of it. There is nothing substantial in what she offers. More tellingly, there is nothing in the internal dynamics of the plot that requires, or implies, an outside driver.

Members of the group met and prayed at several neighborhood mosques in Madrid, including the Takouma mosque in Villaverde on the city's outskirts. The substitute imam, Abdelkader el Farssaoui, or Cartagena, curried favor with the men. His role was duplicitous. He harbored jihadi sympathies but he was also a police informant. Beginning in October 2002, Cartagena began informing the police Central Unit of External Information (UCIE) about the informal group of young North Africans that now called itself Al Harakat Salafiyah (the Salafi Movement), which he described as "Takfiri." The group included Zougam, Maymouni, the Tunisian, and newcomer Faisal Allouch. Cartagena testified that the group met "clandestinely, with no regularity or fixed place, by oral agreement and without any schedule, though usually on Fridays" at Allouch's apartment to chant jihadi songs and watch videos of jihadi preaching and of atrocities committed against Muslims.

Maymouni initiated the meetings, advising who in the group needed to commit which verses to memory. His role was similar to that of the deacon in American Protestant churches, who warms up the room by leading the congregation in gospel and traditional prayers. Stepping into the role of mind-shaping pastor was the Tunisian, who transported those gathered through a series of reflections on the tragedies of Muslims in Palestine, Chechnya, and elsewhere, conveyed in ways that regularly brought the group near tears. He had found his passion.

Maymouni offered the hand of his fifteen-year-old sister, who worked as a seamstress in the M-30 mosque, to the Tunisian. He married her in November 2002. Soon, by force of personality, intellect, fervor, and knowledge of the Koran, the Tunisian emerged as the group's de facto leader. After eliciting moral outrage at the barbarous actions of the enemies of Islam, he demanded actions from the group to carry out violent justice and to right perceived wrongs against Muslims. He also took individuals aside to personally discuss what each might do for the cause. According to Cartagena, although they now had "reached the conclusion that they had to undertake jihad," they really had no idea where or how do to it.

Rabei Ousmane Sayed Ahmed, "the Egyptian," now came into the picture. The Egyptian helped to convince the group that they should concentrate their desire to wage jihad closer to home, in Morocco or Spain, where they had the material resources to do something, rather than in Afghanistan or Chechnya.

Again, from Cartagena's testimony on March 7, 2007:

PROSECUTION: The written statement that you presented . . . talks of what you called the last supper or last meeting with Serhane ben Abdelmajid [the Tunisian]. . . . In this last meeting, did Serhane show any intention of committing attacks?

CARTAGENA: No, committing attacks, no, but the meeting was very extraordinary, very strange, because we had met many times with him and he hadn't done anything like he did this time. First, he asked us to disconnect our mobile phones, including taking the batteries out. We all did that, but he even went to check telephone by telephone: "Give me yours. Let's see if you took it out right. Give me yours. Give me yours." When the setting was more or less ready, he recited a bit from the Koran and said, "What we want are martyrs; we don't want troops, we don't want to prepare people to go to Afghanistan, or Chechnya, or other places of conflict. We need martyrs who are ready where they are. If one lives in France, then he's prepared for France; if one lives in Spain, then he's prepared for Spain. Who's prepared?" Everybody raised their hand, including me.

Although the Tunisian and a few friends may have had the motivation to carry out an attack, they had neither the means nor the know-how. The Tunisian continued to traffic in stolen electronic goods in Lavapies, justifying his actions with the concept of *fa'i*, which allows otherwise unlawful actions, like theft, against infidels for the good of Muslims.

Jamal Ahmidan was a short young man (a bit over 160 cm, or five four) with buck teeth and intense almond-shaped eyes that earned him the name el Chino, the Chinaman. He made sure everyone knew that bigger men would never get the better of him. The China-

man's friends say that above all he wanted respect and believed having money and being tough would gain him that. One acquaintance recalled: "He would insult people in front of their girlfriends, and you might flatten him, but then you had better be prepared for a crusade." An investigator told us: "He was a

The doer: Jamal Ahmidan, el Chino (the Chinaman).

little guy, but no matter how big you were, if the Chinaman said he would kill you, you'd believe him and shit in your pants."

He acted quickly, surprisingly, and without hesitation, with a knife, a gun, or a bomb. When he decided on something, he wouldn't let go until the deed was done—like a bulldog—whatever it was. Eventually, he would identify his own struggle for respect with that of oppressed Muslims everywhere, and he raved that he was chosen by God to be their champion and kill Jews. But he was pretty much a loner and a loose cannon until he met the Tunisian in the early fall of 2003. Together, the Chinaman and the Tunisian, the doer and the dreamer, planned and executed the most spectacular terrorist attack since 9/11.

The Chinaman was the fourth of fourteen children raised in a cement-block house on the Rue Boujmaa', just off Shaari'a Mamoun, the main market street in Jamaa Mezuak, the backdoor barrio of Tetuán, Morocco. He dropped out of high school to work with his father, but they quarreled. The Chinaman didn't like rising early and was fed up with his father always telling him to "live honestly by the sweat of your brow." He had bigger plans, and after having knifed to death someone who he said tried to steal his ring, followed in the footsteps of an older brother, who was already a successful drug trafficker.

The Chinaman told the Spanish authorities that he was an Algerian. There was a bloody civil war going on in Algeria at the time, so he knew he wouldn't be deported to Algeria. He made his way to the Spanish mainland and the capital, Madrid. Meanwhile in Morocco, he was sentenced to twenty years in absentia.

Because the Chinaman was now a wanted criminal, he could never use his real name in Spain, and that had a significant effect on him and his activities: He was confined to the underworld and always on the watch. At first, he seemed just to want to glow among the denizens of the deep. He zipped around on a motorcycle and sported fancy clothes. Then, in 1992, he met a fifteen-year-old

Christian girl named Rosa who had been on crack since she was twelve. They fell in love and he became a junkie, too.

During the Chinaman's junkie phase, his friends said he was capable of anything and really didn't care whether he got killed or not. Rosa said the big problem was tranquilizers. He'd get high on cocaine, making sure some nightclub stayed open all night for his friends, then take downers and say, "If I die, I deserve it." Once, while he and Rosa were walking to the Plaza del Dos de Mayo, the Chinaman downed a few pills. Someone he knew came up to him. He was a pest, so the Chinaman took out a knife and stabbed the guy in the stomach. The wounded man survived and dropped charges in return for a dose of smack.

The police described the Chinaman at the time as the "head of a small criminal gang dealing in heroin." Many of the small-time Moroccan dealers, junkies, and ex-cons worked for him, dealing in 5-, 10-, 20-gram doses. He was caught and sentenced to eighteen months. In jail, the Chinaman got hooked on heroin himself. But in the spring of 1995, with Rosa five or six months pregnant, he decided to kick his addiction cold turkey with the support of people at a local mosque. There he found religion, and now his mission in Lavapies was to save his fellow Muslim junkies, including the three Oulad Akcha brothers from his home barrio of Mezuak.

The Chinaman convinced Rachid and Mohammed Oulad Akcha to quit. Khalid Oulad Akcha resisted. Khalid would always remain wary of the Chinaman, though the two continued to deal together. Mohammed and Rachid became devoted to the Chinaman, willing to place their lives on the line for him. In Madrid's underworld of petty criminals, they were dubbed the Chinaman's bodyguards.

After the Chinaman kicked his drug habit, he became a serious businessman. During 1999–2000 he was dealing in Ecstasy from the Netherlands. The price of making a tablet in Holland was the equivalent of 100 pesetas (.60 euro). The selling price of a tablet on the streets of Madrid was 2,000 pesetas (12 euros). The Chinaman imported lots of 30,000 to 50,000 tablets and sold them for 465 pesetas a tablet, sometimes making the equivalent of a couple of hundred thousand dollars a deal. No longer simply small-time, the Chinaman was now a big shot in his criminal underworld. In Amsterdam, he asked some Moroccan radicals in mosques if it was permissible to sell drugs, and he was told he could sell them to "atheists" to "fuck them up," even if it killed them—*fa'i*, again. He also got a BMW 318 out of it.

Another of the Chinaman's operations was obtaining false documents for illegal immigrants, especially Chileans, according to Rosa. On March 25, 2000, police nabbed the Chinaman for this. Under the name Said Tildni, he was locked up in the Madrid Center for Internment of Foreigners. The center's chief inspector wrote of his new prisoner:

> He called the officials "Sons of a Whore" and threatened them with death once he got out of the Center. Later, in a private conversation, he claimed that he had millions coming from drugs, but that he had been chosen by Allah to benefit his people and lead them; he went on to say that, because he had no fear of dying, he was nothing less than invincible, and that his grand illusion was to march on Israel to kill Jews. In another moment of the conversation, he threatened to goad his companions into a hunger strike if his "great mission" was disturbed. It appeared that we found ourselves, if not before a religious fanatic, at least before a megalomaniac with twisted mental faculties that could imperil the peace and social stability in this Center.[6]

The Chinaman escaped from the detention center on April 4, more interested now in fighting for Islam than in making money. But where and how to fight?

According to *New York Times* reporter Andrea Elliot, who interviewed some of the Chinaman's family and friends:

One day, while traveling in Holland, he called his brothers and told them to set fire to his cars. "Life is worth nothing," Chino told his brother Mustafa. "We won't live long." (They ignored the instruction. "Mustafa likes cars," one brother explained.) . . . He began sending cash to the mother of the man he had stabbed in Tetouan. He continued to drink and do drugs. But his drunken binges sometimes ended with him crying over the stabbing and the mother of the victim. One of his Madrid friends, Abdelilah el Fadwal el Akil, recalled, "He would say that it was his fault she had lost a son, and that the least he could do was take care of her." Akil wrote to me from a Spanish prison, where he was being held as a defendant in the Madrid bombing trial.[7]

The Chinaman decided to visit his family in Morocco. He left Rosa and the baby behind and took the equivalent of 15,000 to 20,000 euros with him to take care of the charges against him. That apparently wasn't enough. He was arrested and jailed for murder, but never tried. No one, it seems, would dare testify against him.

The Chinaman's family hired one of Tetuán's better-known criminal lawyers, Mourad Elkharraz, who recounted that during the Chinaman's three years in prison in Morocco, his client went from sporting jewelry and jeans, and cursing up a storm, to what the people of Mezuak describe as "going Afghan," in emulation of the pious and heroic mujahedin who fought the Soviets in Afghanistan. That means wearing not the refined Moroccan robe, but a coarse cotton tunic and pants. It also means that one is preparing for jihad.

The Chinaman's drug-dealing buddy Abdelilah finally paid off the last 10,000 euros to get his friend out of prison, and by late July 2003, the Chinaman was back in Madrid. Rosa remembered that day well:

He called me and said, "Come down." "Where?" "To the door."
I almost died when I saw him; I was shaking. I was in love and

I still am. I mean, I know what he's done. It's very hard to say. You can't control your feelings. . . . Shit, I saw him arriving at Lavapies when he came out of prison, taking all the drug addicts to pray at the mosque. And I said, "But where are you going, Jamal?" Many times I've thought, *Was he a psychopath?* But how could he be two things, what I saw, and something different?[8]

At first, it seemed as if the Chinaman might be slipping back into his old life. He'd left the Afghan tunic behind for short-sleeved shirts and jeans again. He beat up guys who owed him drug money, but he also told his old friends, "Don't drink, don't go to bars, don't take drugs." He went back to dealing drugs with his friend Abdelilah, though he shied away from alcohol and taking drugs himself. Abdelilah was running the drug operation now, not the Chinaman. The Chinaman's heart just didn't seem to be in it anymore. "Then, like in September or October, I started hearing about Serhane, the Tunisian, and Jamal began to change," Rosa said. "He didn't touch me anymore. . . . My mother's ex-boyfriend, who was with him because he took care of his cars [the Chinaman still had plenty of money from the drug business], told me, 'Rosa, there is somebody who is eating his brain; he talks about him the whole day. Be careful, because he is telling Jamal [to get rid of] 'that Spanish girl.'"

The Afghan, Abdennabi Kounjaa', and the Kid, Asri Rifaat Anouar.

When and how the Chinaman and the Tunisian connected is unclear, but their respective social networks overlapped considerably, and there were numerous possible pathways for them to link up. One was through the many everyday interactions in the Lavapies neighborhood. The Chinaman would deal drugs in the Plaza Cabasteros and sometimes stop by the halal butcher shop owned by the family of his friend Rachid Aglif, a delinquent nicknamed "the Rabbit" (el Conejo) because of his elongated face and big front teeth. He'd walk down Tribulete Street past Jamal Zougam's phone-and-Internet shop on the way to the Alhambra restaurant, where just about everyone in the neighborhood would eat and chat on occasion, including the Tunisian. At the nearby barbershop, they'd discuss the world while their hair was cut, and make ablutions and pray there too.

The Chinaman's most loyal pals, Mohammed and Rachid Oulad Akcha, would sometimes also pray at the Alonso Cano mosque, located in a fancier neighborhood. (The mosque was just an apartment: There are many such "mosques" in European cities, with no obvious outward signs to mark them. When we talked with people on Alonso Cano Street, no one who wasn't Muslim was even aware of the mosque's existence, including people who had lived nearby for decades.) At Alonso Cano, the Tunisian, who had by now acquired a reputation in Madrid's North African community as a radical firebrand, preached the kind of things that the Oulad Akchas knew the Chinaman would appreciate. Also, in front of the Oulad Akchas' house in Villaverde, people from both the Tunisian's and the Chinaman's circles would play soccer together, and sometimes pray in the nearby mosque where Cartagena had preached (though referred to as a "substitute imam," he was actually a *da'i*, an unordained and informal preacher as the Tunisian had now become).

Two other buddies from Mezuak who would play an important part in the plot came to be tightly woven into these overlapping social networks: Abdennabi Kounjaa', who was known in Mezuak as that neighborhood's "first Afghan," and Asri Rifaat Anouar, a slight and gentle vendor of candies whom people simply called "the Kid" (el Niño). Everyone I've talked to in Mezuak says Rifaat didn't have a religious bone in his body until he hooked up with Kounjaa'. Rifaat's family seems thoroughly secular, like the Oulad Akcha family. Rifaat's sisters were known in the neighborhood as "moderns" who wore short skirts and liked *la mode* (French "fashion"). But Rifaat was drawn to the manly, bearded, brooding preacher who was Kounjaa'. Rifaat fell into jihad because he first fell for Kounjaa'. Rifaat, it appears, was gay (semen samples from a bed show Rifaat's mingled with another man's); however, there's nothing to suggest that Kounjaa', who was married, had anything more than feelings of fraternal affection and responsibility for the Kid.

As the Tunisian radicalized at makeshift mosques and soccer picnics in Madrid, so Kounjaa' radicalized at the Dawa Tabligh mosque in Mezuak (also known as al-Rohbane), and at the soccer outings nearby. He would go out to some of the less radical mosques in Mezuak and adjacent neighborhoods to distribute tracts extolling the Salafi way, calling for jihad, and denouncing the Justice and Charity movement in Morocco as a Sufi heresy, impure and un-Muslim. In Mezuak, he alone of the Madrid plotters is remembered as being intensely religious, and many who knew both the Chinaman and Kounjaa' (and being unfamiliar with the Tunisian) believe it could only have been Kounjaa' who inspired the plot and the martyrdom after. Although the Chinaman and Kounjaa' went to the same grade school and high school and lived within a few hundred meters of one another, by the time of their manhood they inhabited two different worlds, the criminal and the religious, until they joined up in Madrid.

Kounjaa' and Rifaat showed up in Madrid around 2002. Like many Moroccan immigrants, especially the illegals, Kounjaa' became a construction worker, where he hooked up with Rachid Oulad Akcha, one of the homeboys from Mezuak, and became involved in the drug trading network of the Oulad Akchas. (The Chinaman was in jail in Morocco.) One reason Rifaat came to Madrid was that he thought it would be easier to make his way to his mother's relatives in Belgium from there. Rifaat's own mother had died, and home was never the same once his father took a second wife.

Rifaat drifted closer to religion and did charity work helping out other immigrants. People liked him. Around 2003, Basel Ghalyoun, the Tunisian's friend, was apparently touched by Rifaat's sincerity and took the Kid under his wing.[9] By the time the Chinaman returned to Madrid from his prison stint in Morocco, the Mezuak homeboys had already merged socially with the Tunisian's circle. When the Tunisian and the Chinaman finally met, all became energized. Rifaat, some say, fell head over heels in love with the Chinaman. He would go on to kill and die for an unrequited passion that came to embrace the whole Muslim world.

THE CONNECTOR, THE RABBIT, AND THE THREE SPANISH STOOGES

Ahmidan's friend and suspected fellow drug peddler, Rachid Aglif, "the Rabbit," worked in the family butcher shop in Lavapies. Aglif put the Chinaman in touch with a wheeler-dealer, Rafa Zouheir, who had known Aglif since the Rabbit first came to Spain from Morocco. Zouheir, a part-time nightclub bouncer and exotic dancer, had a long string of arrests, ranging from aggravated assault and arms trafficking to car theft and narcotics. In 2001 he was arrested for robbing a jewelry store in Spain's northern province of Asturias and landed in a prison cell with a Spaniard, Antonio Toro, who had been jailed for illegal possession of hashish and explosives.

Toro introduced Zouheir to his cousin, another convict, named Emilio Trashorras, who was looking to sell explosives filched from the Conchita mines in Asturias where he and Toro sometimes worked. All three ex-cons were also informers who ratted on friends and acquaintances to help get themselves out of their frequent troubles with police.

The Connector, Rafa Zouheir; the Rabbit, Rachid Aglif; and the three Spaniards, Antonio Toro, Emilio Trashorras, and Carmen Toro-Trashorras.

In May 2003, Zouheir's handler, Victor (a captain in the judicial police, Unidad Central Operativa), told his charge to return to Asturias to contact the Spaniards about finding new customers for the explosives. In late September or early October, around the time the Chinaman connected with the Tunisian, the Chinaman let the Rabbit know that he was looking for explosives. The Rabbit turned to Zouheir, who had been hinting around at the Flowers whorehouse north of Madrid, where the two often went, that he was looking for clients to buy explosives. And so Zouheir became the plot's Connector.

On October 28, 2003, the Connector, the Rabbit, the Chinaman, and his loyal buddy, Mohammed Oulad Akcha, met at the McDonald's restaurant in the Carabanchel neighborhood of Madrid with the plot's three Spanish stooges: Emilio, his cousin

Antonio, and Carmen Toro, a department-store security agent who was Antonio's sister and Emilio's fiancée. The Spaniards called the Chinaman "Mowgli" after the darling nature boy of *The Jungle Book*, Disney's film adaptation of the Rudyard Kipling classic. Behind his back, they called him and his friends "the Moors."

The Moroccans agreed to give the Spaniards 35 kilos of hash in exchange for 200 kilos of dynamite and detonators and a bit of money. Playing with the detonators one day, the Connector almost blew off his hands as the Rabbit watched. But the hospital report didn't raise eyebrows until after the trains were bombed.

For the first delivery, Emilio instructed his courier to tell the Moors that the money "was stolen" on the bus from Asturias to Madrid. The Chinaman greeted the courier at the bus station, listened to the courier's baloney, then beat him to a bloody pulp and stripped him of everything, including his clothes. From then on, relations between the Spaniards and the Moors were civil and correct, complaisant even.

It's doubtful that the Rabbit, the Connector, or the Three Stooges knew anything about the jihadi nature of the plot they were getting into, or that they even cared to know.

In November 2003, one of the Oulad Akchas, Khalid, who was in prison in Salamanca on drug charges, called his brothers Rachid and Mohammed in Madrid. The Chinaman answered the phone.[10] Khalid suspected something dangerous afoot involving his brothers and warned the Chinaman to stay away from them. But to the Chinaman, warnings were like a red cape flashing in front of a bull.

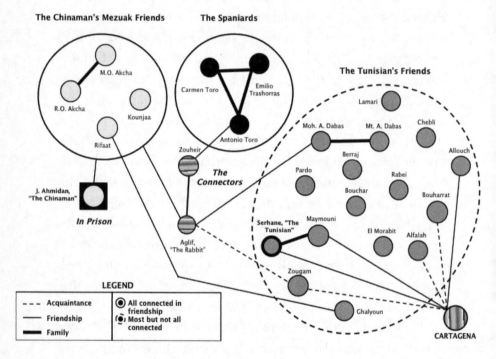

The Chinaman's Mezuak Friends

M.O. Akcha
R.O. Akcha
Kounjaa
Rifaat

J. Ahmidan, "The Chinaman"
In Prison

The Spaniards

Carmen Toro
Emilio Trashorras
Antonio Toro

Zouheir

The Connectors

Aglif, "The Rabbit"

The Tunisian's Friends

Lamari
Moh. A. Dabas
Mt. A. Dabas
Chebli
Berraj
Allouch
Pardo
Rabei
Bouchar
Bouharrat
Serhane, "The Tunisian"
Maymouni
El Morabit
Alfalah
Zougam
Ghalyoun
CARTAGENA

LEGEND

- - - Acquaintance
——— Friendship
▬▬▬ Family

◉ All connected in friendship
◉ Most but not all connected

Three main circles of friends who will become involved in the Madrid Plot (summer 2003).

CHAPTER 12
LOOKING FOR AL QAEDA

Through a series of unplanned events, two young North African immigrants bonded to plot an attack in Spain. They lived in separate worlds—religious extremism and the criminal underworld—until their paths crossed six months before the bombing. A detailed plot only began to coalesce in late December 2003, shortly after the Internet tract "Iraqi Jihad, Hopes and Risks" circulated on a Zarqawi-affiliated Web site. The tract called for "two or three attacks . . . to exploit the coming general elections in Spain in March 2004." The plot—which brought together a bunch of radical students and hangers-on, drug traffickers, small-time dealers in stolen goods, and other sorts of petty criminals—improbably succeeded precisely because it was so improbable. There was no ingenious cell structure, no hierarchy, no recruitment, no brainwashing, no coherent organization, no Al Qaeda. Yet this half-baked conspiracy, concocted in a few months, with a target likely suggested over the Internet, was the immediate cause of regime change in a major democratic society.

In June 2003, the Tunisian got as job as a real estate agent and in two months sold four apartments in Tetuán, Morocco, but was unhappy. "We have to do something for our brothers in Iraq who are being killed," the Tunisian said to his friend Khalid Pardo. "We have to do something here, break into a jewelry shop, steal money for jihad, kill a policeman." Pardo declined, saying he had a family to care for, and their friendship became strained. Another friend remembered the Tunisian saying to him in the butcher shop in Lavapies, "These infidels, we have to kill them."

At the Alhambra restaurant on Tribulete Street in Lavapies, across the street from Jamal Zougam's telephone-and-Internet shop, the Tunisian refused to allow Zougam to sit at his table. He accused Zougam of being "too soft" on the enemies of Islam. (Zougam would later be identified by eyewitnesses as having left his knapsack on one of the trains just before it exploded, and he will be sentenced to 42,992 years in prison for 191 murders.) The Tunisian similarly berated Basel Ghalyoun, another friend from the picnic outings at the Rio Navalcarnero, for being a coward (Ghalyoun will get twelve years for "belonging to a terrorist organization," as the prosecution couldn't prove an operational role in the plot). But at the time, after all was said and done, a lot was said and nothing done—until the Chinaman returned from prison and teamed up with the Tunisian in the early fall of 2003.

HATCHING THE PLOT

By late fall 2003, the Chinaman and the Tunisian were trying to raise money for the plot, tapping everyone they knew. But they still weren't sure how, where, or when to act until an Internet tract gave them the idea of blowing up something in Spain around the time of the March 2004 elections. The tract first appeared on the Zarqawi-affiliated Web site Global Islamic Media Front, which the Tunisian and the Chinaman had been logging on to systematically. The Chinaman especially identified with Abu Musab al-Zarqawi. Like the Chinaman, Zarqawi had been a violent criminal and Jew-hater who radicalized to jihad in prison. When authorities recovered the Chinaman's computer, they found it full of Zarqawi's rants and accolades to the man who claimed al-Qaeda's "mantle in Mesopotamia."

On New Year's Eve 2003, the Tunisian drove the Chinaman up to Bilbao in Spain's northern Basque country to collect drug money from a debt; they were financing their jihad in Spain. The Chinaman phoned Rosa, and in the background she overheard the Tunisian: "Leave her. She's a Christian, leave her." Rosa snapped at the Chinaman: "Is there a parrot with you?" The Chinaman snapped back: "Nobody tells me what to do." When he arrived in Bilbao, he calmly walked into a bar, whipped out a pistol, and kneecapped a fellow drug dealer who owed him money. Then the Chinaman called out after another man, who ran into the street, that he, too, had better pay up or else.

Beginning in January 2004, details of the plot were hammered out at a farmhouse outside Madrid that formerly belonged to the Tunisian's brother-in-law, who had since returned to Morocco. The brother of Rachid "the Rabbit" Aglif later testified at the trial that he and the Rabbit would bring lamb meat from their butcher shop for barbecues there and at the Navalcarnero River. But the picnics no longer included wives or children. The farmhouse and river meetings now primarily involved the Chinaman and his friends rather than the Tunisian's circle, although the Tunisian was regularly at the farmhouse leading the discussions. It seems that when push came to shove, several in the Tunisian's religious circle skirted the call for martyrdom, but the Chinaman's petty-criminal circle stood fast.

At the farmhouse, the groups coordinated efforts to acquire the weapon components and related paraphernalia: explosives, detonators, cell phones, rucksacks, and shrapnel. The Chinaman's cousin, Hamid Ahmidan, later testified that he saw members of the Chinaman's circle in the kitchen manipulating a device with cables. At Hamid's own home, after the bombing, police found 59 kilos of hashish, worth 75,000 euros, and 125,000 tablets of Ecstasy, worth 1,275,000 euros. (The prosecution asked for a sentence of twenty-three years for Hamid's complicity in the plot, which he got.)

The Chinaman frequently called Carmen Toro-Trashorras's phone to coordinate the procurement and transfer of explosives (though Carmen claimed it was really her husband, Emilio, who was using her phone to do this). Emilio worked with a combination of his contacts, small-time Spanish crooks, and the Chinaman's associates to procure and transfer the explosives. But the relationship between Emilio's circle and the Chinaman's now extended beyond business. On February 14, the Chinaman, Mohammed Oulad Akcha, and the Rabbit attended Emilio and Carmen's wedding.

The Chinaman picked up the newlyweds at the Madrid airport after their return from a honeymoon in the Canary Islands and took them directly to the farmhouse. Carmen later claimed that the Chinaman merely wanted to show the couple some property for sale. Spanish investigators later concluded that bomb preparations were going on in the house at the time. After the bombing, Carmen went free, not because the trial judges thought that she was looking for real estate while her husband was making bombs, but because—in the classic ploy of a prisoner's dilemma—by turning on her husband she could walk.

On February 28 and 29, the Chinaman, Mohammed Oulad Akcha, and Kounjaa' traveled to the Conchita mine in Asturias to pick up the explosives from Emilio. The next day, Rachid Oulad Akcha, Rifaat the Kid, and Otman El Gnaoui (who had been providing false identity papers to the Chinaman) appeared. A seventeen-year-old, nicknamed El Gitanillo (the Little Gypsy), who acted as a delivery boy for Emilio, overheard his boss telling the Chinaman, "Don't forget the nails and the screws." That and Carmen's crocodile love would get Emilio sent up for 34,715 years.

Jamal Zougam, who now seems to have jumped into the plot with both feet after some earlier hesitation over the Tunisian's willingness to kill Spanish civilians, used his business ties to acquire the phones and SIM cards needed to detonate the homemade bombs. Kaliji, the Syrian-born undercover policeman who had earlier infiltrated Yarkas's circle for Judge Garzón, provided the SIM cards and reported his suspicions, but there was no follow-up from the police or Spanish intelligence. A partial thumbprint on a SIM card led police to their first suspects only after the bombing.

The group made the bombs, filling each sport sack with ten kilos of dynamite surrounded by shrapnel of nails and screws, and connected to a cell phone–triggered detonator.

On Thursday morning, March 11, 2004, the plotters rose early and drove a stolen Renault Kangoo van to the town of Alcalá de Henares, where they boarded and exited four different trains bound for Madrid, leaving their bombs behind.

At 7:38 A.M., a train about to pull into Madrid's Atocha Station was ripped apart by three explosions, which sent hunks of human flesh smashing into the windows of nearby apartments. Sixteen seconds later, four bombs demolished another train nearing Atocha, dispersing the body parts of all kinds of people—Christian and Muslim, men and women, old and young, students and workers, and children going to daycare. Had the bombs gone off when the trains were already inside the station, thousands would probably have died in Spain's busiest terminal: Trains at that hour are filled with daily commuters, including many immigrants lured by Spain's then-booming economy.

Five kilometers away, at 7:40 A.M., another pair of bombs destroyed a train at El Pozo Station. At 7:43 a final bomb exploded at the suburban Santa Eugenia Station, killing and wounding scores more, just as the first rescue crews arrived at Atocha. About a third of the dead were immigrants from eleven countries, including a Polish man and his six-month-old daughter.

Sanae Ben Salah, thirteen, was one of three murdered Moroccans whose broken bodies were mourned at the M-30 mosque that weekend. A child of divorced parents who lived with her uncle in Alcalá de Henares, she took the morning train to school in Madrid and came around to the mosque as often as she could. She was shipped home to Morocco in a metal crate.

Around 11 A.M., police in Alcalá de Henares received a tip from someone who spotted the white Renault Kangoo by the train station. The license plate didn't match the van, the sort of detail ETA never overlooks, but no one bothered to look inside until later that afternoon. Meanwhile, Prime Minister José María Aznar, whose conservative Popular Party was up for re-election on a platform that called for muscling ETA, suspected that ETA had beaten him to the punch. Although his party was ahead of the Socialists by five points in the polls, Aznar immediately tried to convert the bombing into what seemed likely to be an election-winning crusade against the archenemy. (In 1995, only the armor on his car prevented Aznar himself from being assassinated by an ETA bomb.)

But in the van, police found a tape with Koranic verses in the cassette player, and under the seat were seven detonators like those used to denote the Goma-2 explosives identified in the trains. Koranic recitations and Goma-2 are not ETA's thing; yet that evening Aznar assured the editors of Spain's leading newspapers that all evidence pointed to the Basque separatists. He appealed to the patriotic solidarity of the editor of the Socialist-leaning daily *El País* to print the story, which *El País*[1] did. The editor of rival *El Mundo*, which supported Aznar's Popular Party, was more cautious and wanted concrete evidence before going all out for the government's tale.

Around midnight evidence started pouring in. Detectives found 10 kilos of Emilio's Goma-2 in a sports bag, surrounded by screws and nails. The explosives were connected to a detonator, which was attached by wires to a cell phone. The phone's SIM card led to two merchants who sold Zougam the hot phones and then to Zougam himself. Several survivors from one train would later identify Zougam as one of those who left a bag on board a train that morning. The dialed numbers recorded on the phone chip also led to a wider social network of North African immigrants with no known ties to ETA.

Friday afternoon the interior minister, Ángel Acebes, was still insisting that ETA was the only real suspect, although investigators on the ground knew better. Bits of evidence and assertions linking the bombing to Islamists angry at the Aznar government's support of U.S. actions in Iraq were filtering out across the Web and radio and into the streets. By evening, over a quarter of Spain's population of 40 million was in the streets demonstrating against the violence and, already for many, against what was starting to look like a government snow job to keep the illusion of ETA's involvement going until at least the election. An enraged public voted in the Socialists, who had promised to pull out of Iraq, just as the plotters had hoped.

El País, feeling used, began an unrelenting campaign against Aznar and his party for supposedly tricking the nation for political gain. Although the still-fragmentary evidence clearly pointed away from ETA, *El País* incautiously insisted that it clearly pointed toward Al Qaeda. (*El Mundo* threw earlier caution to the wind to attack the Socialists and defend the ETA thesis.) And truth, as often happens in our political world, fell into the abyss.

THE PLOTTERS BECOME MARTYRS

With the Aznar government still insisting the attack was ETA, a video soon came to light from an anonymous tip-off to a Madrid television station. The government said that a man speaking Arabic with a Moroccan accent said the attacks were revenge for Spain's "collaboration with the criminals Bush and his allies." He mentioned Iraq and Afghanistan in particular and said more blood would flow if the injustices did not end. (The Spanish government backed the U.S.-led invasion of Iraq despite polls showing 90 percent opposition to it from the Spanish public.)

"You want life and we want death," said the man in the tape, who was later identified as the Chinaman.

Immediately after the attack, the Chinaman went into hiding. He visited his brother Mohammed, who later testified that he couldn't look the Chinaman in the face. "How could you do this in a country that took you in?" Mohammed asked him.

Abdenabi Kounjaa' left behind a statement that Spanish authorities found at the house of a fellow Moroccan, Saed El Harrak, a religious friend whom Kounjaa' had first met on the job at a construction site in 2002. El Harrak says he last saw Kounjaa' on March 10, the day before the bombings, but that he was unaware of the statement: "Why would I have held on to it and not burned it if I knew what it was?" El Harrak later told the court. Part of Kounjaa's "final testament" reads: "Do not have pity on the lousy infidels because they declared war on us. They kill Muslims every day in every part of the world and all of them keep silent."

The plotters had drawn up a list of further targets and planted a bomb along the route of the high-speed train that travels between Madrid and Toledo. The cables leading to the bomb were spotted in the nick of time by personnel inspecting the tracks. The Kid's fingerprints identified him as the one who placed the bomb, but Spanish authorities told me that it was the Chinaman who likely taught the Kid what to do.[2]

On April 2, 2004, a handwritten fax in Arabic was sent to a news outlet claiming responsibility for the March 11 bombings and for placing a bomb on the high-speed train tracks in the name of "Al Qaeda in Europe." The handwriting was later identified as the Tunisian's.

Fearing an imminent attack and widespread panic, authorities cranked up their manhunt. They nabbed the Rabbit at his butcher shop. Having learned that the Kid would come by for some meat, agents told the Rabbit to put a transmitter in the bag with the food. They tracked the Kid to the subway but lost him when he threw away the bag. But through a telephone relay they caught one of the plotters' calls and staked out a second-story apartment on Calle Carmen Martín Gaite in the Madrid suburb of Leganes, where several of the plotters were hiding out.

In the middle of the night, Cartagena was hauled out from his home in southwest Spain and driven to Madrid. At around three P.M., police surrounded the redbrick apartment block in the unremarkable commuter community of Leganes. Abdelmajid Bouchar, a young Moroccan immigrant who became involved in the plot, but who was still unknown to authorities, was taking out the group's garbage when he heard a radio transmitter, saw a policewoman ringing apartment bells at the entrance to the building, and spotted her associates. He called out to his friends just before he bolted. (He managed to escape and flee the country but was caught some months later on a false passport in Eastern Europe and accused of planting bombs on the trains.)

Voices from the apartment cried out, "Allahu Akbar!" and machine-gun fire raked the street. Spain's elite Grupo Especial de Operaciones moved in to clear nearby apartments, backed by tanks and helicopters. Cartagena was told to go up to the apartment where the plotters were holed up and try to get them to surrender "or at least count them."

"Go to hell," Cartagena said he told the police, even if they separate him from his family and deport him, as he claimed they had threatened to do. In the early evening, the Chinaman called his mother in Morocco to say good-bye, she heard an explosion, and the phone went dead.

The force of the explosion propelled the body fragments of the Tunisian, the Chinaman, and his four buddies from Mezuak through the back wall into the swimming pool below. It would take several months to finally complete DNA analysis of a skull fragment from the seventh suicide. It belonged to Allekama Lamari, a known Algerian hothead.[3]

ORGANIZED ANARCHY

In hindsight, the failure of Spanish police and intelligence authorities is mind-boggling. The narcotics police were on to the Chinaman, or at least to a number of his aliases, but completely ignored the multiple clues indicating his association with jihad and with the explosives deal. The police who were trying to set up a sting for the explosives weren't at all interested in the drugs, which would have led them to the Chinaman. Cartagena's pointed warning to the police that the Tunisian just might try something spectacular for jihad was simply ignored, perhaps because Cartagena himself told them that the Tunisian had no obvious practical know-how or means for the job, but also because they just didn't want to be bothered.

There are numerous examples of the inability of the authorities to keep track of information they already had. For example, in early January 2004, the Chinaman cracked up his new BMW 530D in a multicar collision. The Madrid traffic police checked his false Belgian passport, issued in the name of Yousef Ben Saleh, the same passport and car that Madrid traffic police had checked the month before, when they had ordered the nervous owner to open his glove compartment, containing knives, a billy club, and jihadi literature. It was also the passport that Madrid traffic police checked when they ticketed the Chinaman for speeding in a Toyota Corolla with license number 9231 DCW on February 29, 2004, the day he brought a shipment of dynamite from Asturias to Madrid. And during the night of March 4, 2004, police brought in the Little Gypsy for driving the same Toyota Corolla without a license and into an accident. (Emilio Trashorras, who had sent El Gitanillo from Asturias to Madrid to pick up the Toyota, was furious that the boy had instead driven off with it to Toledo to visit an uncle.)

Starting in February 2003, Spain's antiterror brigade had "kept under surveillance a group of radical Islamists which . . . later comprised the 'commando' unit that perpetrated the March 11 attacks."[4]

But the surveillance team was dissolved in February 2004 for "lack of means" and absorbed in other security services. This and other bureaucratic missteps are appalling, given the wide reporting and awareness of intelligence failures in the lead-up to 9/11.

Perhaps to compensate for gross incompetence in tracking participants in the plot who were already known and under surveillance, Spanish authorities as well as the press insisted that the ability of the plotters to operate under the radar was clear evidence of a carefully staged plot by some Terror Central Organization, be it ETA (the favorite hypothesis of those close to rightist political circles) or Al Qaeda (the favorite hypothesis of those close to leftist political circles). Both sides stressed that the plot involved the complex coordination of dozens of participants. In fact, the plotters and the plot fell under the radar screen for precisely the opposite reason: because it was so anarchic, fluid, and improbable. Political scientists and organizational theories refer to this kind of structure as "organized anarchy,"[5] with the following four properties:

FUZZY PREFERENCES
- The network operates on the basis of ill-defined and inconsistent preferences; it discovers preference through action more than it acts on the basis of preferences. Members participate without sharing consistent goals, and decisions reflect goal ambiguity and capricious decision making.

TINKERED TECHNOLOGY
- Although the network manages to survive and carry through operations, its own processes and means are not understood by its membership. It operates on the basis of trial-and-error learning, the residue of learning from accidents or past experiences, and pragmatic inventions of necessity.

FLUID STRUCTURE THAT VARIES OVER TIME

- Participants vary in the amount of effort devoted to different domains, and their involvement varies from one time to another time. As a result, the boundaries of the network are changing and uncertain.

EMBEDDED IN LARGER SOCIAL NETWORKS RATHER THAN ISOLATED FROM THEM

- This makes it imperative to compare who opts for violence versus who doesn't within these larger networks. But police and intelligence authorities, as well as much of the press, are usually only concerned with the people directly implicated in a plot or crime and care little for understanding the wider social history and environment of their path to violence. Concentrating only on the perpetrators teaches you very little about the processes and paths of radicalization to extreme violence.

The Madrid plot was incubated by a hodgepodge of childhood friends, teenage buddies, neighborhood pals, prison cellmates, siblings, cousins, and lovers. These weren't careful, well-trained commandos. They were almost laughably incompetent, though tragically only a bit less so than Spanish law enforcement and intelligence. They got lucky, and hundreds of people were killed and wounded. If the trains had been on time, many more would have died. Fortunately, in this case, Spanish trains didn't run to a German clock.

A BIG BANG FOR FEW BUCKS

Madrid was the second most expensive jihadi terrorist attack so far this century. It cost from 52,000 to 54,000 euros (about $50,000 at the time). It was almost entirely a local operation, self-financed by work wages, collections, and mostly the Chinaman's drug activities (32,000 to 45,000 euros).[6] Although authorities were told of the drugs-for-dynamite exchange, both from informers on the drug side and informers on the dynamite side, they could not fathom that the evolutionary landscape of jihad had changed.

Today, in 2010, Spanish police and intelligence tell a different story: Jihadi networks in Spain, and in much of Europe, are very much intertwined with petty criminal networks: drug trafficking, stolen cars, credit-card fraud, and the like. This wedding of jihadi and criminal networks was not inevitable or even desirable from the jihadi side (on principle, many jihadis still shun potentially lucrative relations with common criminals). To a significant extent, the joining of jihadis and criminals was a shotgun wedding, with U.S. counterterrorism being the unwitting father of the bride holding the gun. Here's why:

To most quickly understand how 9/11 happened and to find and neutralize its planners, U.S. investigators realized early on that they had to "follow the money." September 11 was a relatively complicated affair, involving many months of planning across three or four continents. It cost money, somewhere in the range of $400,000 to $500,000.[7] Although this is a trivial amount compared to the estimated trillion or so dollars that the short-term reaction to 9/11 cost, it was enough to have left a traceable financial trail. Almost immediately, the United States compelled the world's major financial institutions to monitor money transfers that could be potentially linked to terrorist financing and to freeze the accounts of any organization—charitable or otherwise—that appeared to be involved in such transfers.

One unintended consequence of the successful implementation of this new financial regime was to force would-be terrorists to rely on local, low-cost, underground, and informal methods of financing. In addition, the elimination of Al Qaeda's training facilities in Afghanistan and the disruption of its networks for supplying expertise in logistics, bomb making, and so forth, meant that jihadis would have to find new means for executing terrorist operations. Petty criminal networks just happened to step into both of these niches: They had the informal financial wherewithal and the hands-on expertise in logistics (transport, safe houses, access to weapons) that the jihadis needed. Finally, as counterterrorism efforts continued to focus on Al Qaeda and the major jihadi organizations and operatives, many of whom continued to balk at dealing with mundane criminals, a newer wave of would-be jihadis was emerging. These were less ideological, less educated, less skilled, and so more socially compatible with petty criminals. Although lack of economic opportunity often reliably leads to criminality, it turns out that some youth who have turned to crime for lack of better opportunities really don't want to be criminals after all. Given half a chance to take up a moral cause, they can be even more altruistically prone than others are to give up their lives for their comrades and a cause.

WHERE IS AL QAEDA?

So where, indeed, is Al Qaeda? It's more up in the air than on the ground.

As in Madrid, most jihad-inspired acts of terror today are not well-planned engineering feats of military precision under clear command and control. They are opportunistic on unforeseen and contingent events: the effects of the U.S. counterterrorism financial regime in moving jihad into underground haunts shared with petty criminals; the Tunisian bonding with the Chinaman on the latter's rebound from prison; the Chinaman knowing someone who happened to know someone who happened to have been in prison with two guys who could get dynamite; having friends from the old neighborhood as confidants to bring along; police incompetence.

The weakly interlocking series of loose and flat networks of friends and family from the mosques, the neighborhoods, work, prison, and so forth gives the illusion of a deviously well structured chain whose links were carefully designed to operate as semi-autonomous cells. There was, however, no Intelligent Designer. How comes it that a plot involving nearly forty people was able to go on for months right under the noses of Spanish authorities, especially when many of the participants were known to Spanish police or intelligence and even in contact with them? The irony of it all is that if the plotters had real organization and sophisticated knowledge, they probably would have been caught before the bombings. The plot was so scattered, improbable, and whimsical that even a competent police watch wouldn't have had a light job of picking it up.

Under uncertain or constantly changing conditions, relatively fluid and flat networks that are self-organizing, decentralized, and overlapping—like terrorist or drug networks,[8] financial or black arms markets,[9] or information webs of the Google or Wikipedia kind[10]—tend to outperform relatively rigid, centralized, and hierarchical competitors. Hierarchies are structured so that the bottom layers (workers) perform day-to-day tasks and the upper layers (management) plan for the long term.[11] But in a rapidly changing world, large management structures set up for long-term maintenance of their organization's position in a predictable world often cannot compete with smaller, self-motivated, and self-correcting systems that can more readily innovate and respond when opportunities or challenges arise.

In the case of terrorist networks, the heightened burden of surviving and maintaining security under sustained attack from law enforcement and counterterrorism might be expected to put a fatal brake on efficiency and innovation. But the interlocking relations of trust and familiarity inherent in the organic bonds of friend-ship, kinship, and neighborhood make these networks highly resil-ient to local failures and to predatory attacks from the outside. Of course, criminal gangs like the Mafia and the Latin American drug cartels also have these sorts of resilient networks. Terrorist networks, though, have something more: commitment to a moral cause, which allows for greater sacrifice than is usually possible with typical reward structures based on material incentives. In the jihad, even petty criminals come to transcend any usual motives for gain. They see a way of becoming part of something grand rather than small, and willingly give up their lives for a greater cause. No criminal enterprise compares.

Well after the Madrid attack, the Chinaman's lady, Rosa, com-plained that the "Moors" in her neighborhood—a massive, run-down housing project on the edge of Madrid—"fall on their knees in front of my son telling him: 'You have to be like your father, you have to be like your father.' They see his father as a martyr."[12]

In one sense, we are greatly overestimating the threat from terrorism, by attributing it chiefly to a resurgent and power-ful Al Qaeda. In another sense, we are grossly underestimating the sources of the threat from countless neighborhoods and chat rooms around the world. These numerous but small and scattered sources do not pose a strategic threat to our existence. This reac-tion to Rosa and the Chinaman's son is perhaps the most worri-some outcome of the attack. It suggests how hard it will be to get the next generation to turn toward rather than against us. Breaking Al Qaeda is no longer the point.

CHAPTER 13
THE ORDINARINESS OF TERROR

Clockwise:
Bilal Ben Aboud,
Muncif Ben Aboud,
Adelmonim Amakchar
al-Amrani,
Hamza Akhlifa,
Younes Achebak

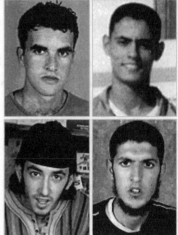

Martyrs from Mezuak.

TETUÁN, MOROCCO, MARCH 10, 2007

Marc Sageman and I left the Madrid bombing trial and traveled to the Jamaa Mezuak, that backdoor barrio of Tetuán, Morocco, from which five of the seven suicides in the Madrid train bombings came. In Mezuak, a poor but not squalid neighborhood with very little outward sign of any militant Salafi influence, and more cheerfulness than expected, there were few men in skull-caps and even fewer women who were completely veiled.

We found out about several young men who had volunteered as suicide bombers in Iraq. One of these young men had been identified by DNA analysis provided by the United States to Moroccan authorities. A main facilitator for the pipeline to Iraq seems to have been an imam at the Dawa Tabligh mosque. He was arrested along with some of the wealthy businessmen who donated charity money (*zaqat*) to him that was used to funnel the young men to Iraq.

Two policemen showed up when we went to this mosque, where many of these young men prayed. I had given the camera to Marc and the policemen started to question him. I saw some children next to the mosque and went over to talk to them in my halting Levantine Arabic. Marc would be okay—his nonchalant "who, me?" attitude was already causing the policemen to scratch their heads.

The children were, I guessed, six and eight years old. The younger one had sharp brown eyes under a baseball cap. I asked his name. "Eto'o," he said (a soccer star from Cameroon who plays on the Barcelona soccer team, Barça); the other one called himself "Ronaldinho" (a Brazilian star on the Barça team). In Tetuán and Tangiers, maybe the richest cities in Morocco, crowds of young men stand around the plazas with apparently nothing much to do; many sport Barça soccer shirts or those of archrival Real Madrid.

The older kid, Ronaldinho, said, "Eto'o is worthless." An elder standing in front of the mosque was listening and told the children not to lie to me, to show respect, as I was a visitor, a guest in the neighborhood.

A teenager came over, smiling. Nice kid. He rolled a hashish cigarette. The younger boy, Eto'o, offered it to me. I said, "I don't smoke," and the teenager reprimanded Eto'o. The teenager asked me if I wanted tea. Eto'o broke in and said, "I'll bring it, give me some money." The teenager again yelled at Eto'o.

Then Eto'o pulled on my hand: "Take me to Spain." I asked if they knew Spain. "Sure," said Ronaldinho, "we lived in Madrid." I started leading Eto'o downhill toward Marc and the police, laughing and saying, "We're going to Spain now." Eto'o said, "Good, good."

"But we'll have to swim," I told him. And he yanked his hand away and ran back up the hill.

I went back up the hill too. "Give me money to buy a bicycle," Eto'o said, his hand out. Ronaldinho chimed in, "Yes, give him the money to buy a bicycle." I said, "Sure, but I'm so tired of traveling that I need a plane of my own, so if you'll help me get a plane first, then I'll buy a bicycle." "Good, good," said Eto'o, "We take the plane (and then he swept a flat hand, palm down) and *whooooosh!*"

he expired with evident glee, "into the White House. I'm Osama Bin Laden!"

"But I thought you said you were Eto'o." I frowned in mock puzzlement.

"Mmm." Eto'o nodded, closing his eyes, scrunching up his nose, and puckering his lips as if thinking hard. "Osama is *akbar*." Osama is bigger.

Marc had somehow gotten free of the policemen, who were standing nearby and still trying to figure out what to do about us. He sauntered over to me and the children, and I told him about the conversation. "A soccer star or Osama?" Marc said. "That's maybe the big question for this whole generation." Who to be?

JAMAA MEZUAK, NOVEMBER 2008

Ali is a deeply religious man who owns the Cyprus barbershop just off Mamoun Street in the heart of Mezuak. He worries what will become of the young people in the neighborhood.

"So what made those who went and died in Madrid and Iraq choose violence?" I asked.

"They were victims, all of them, even Jamal Ahmidan [the Chinaman]. They just didn't have a true Islamic culture to make wise decisions. Most of them did some sort of smuggling. Almost everyone does some of that. For money. But that's not what took them down the path of violence. It's the false teaching: of the *Salafiyah* jihad of the *Takfiri*, of the *Khawaraj* ["outsiders," those who have gone away from the true path of the Prophet and his descendants]. They're all the same, preaching bizarre things and profiting from the ignorance of the young. In [public] school there are only two hours of Islamic teaching in a week. People need more."

"Did you know them well? The ones who died in Madrid and the ones who went to Iraq?"

"Most of them. Jamal didn't come here to cut his hair, and the

Oulad Akchas had moved out of the neighborhood, but the others came here."

"Tell me about Kounjaa'."

"Kounjaa' kept to himself. He didn't talk much. Almost never smiled. I used to give him a Jontra for twenty dirham [about two dollars]."

A client on the next stool explained: "That's the haircut of the American John Travolta."

Ali nodded. "Kounjaa' wanted to be a serious Muslim but got caught up with the wrong people," he said. "But he wasn't odd at all, just serious by nature. He had a good soul."

"That's what Rifaat's father, Ahmed, a teacher at the nearby [elementary school], also said about his son."

"He's right." Ali nodded. "Rifaat was delicate. Kounjaa' protected him and Rifaat trusted him. Both were good, caring people. I don't know how they got mixed up in Madrid. Maybe money was involved. It couldn't have had anything to do with Islam. False prophets may have lured them because they didn't have a real Islamic education."

I thought, *How often I've heard people, of whatever religion, explain religion-inspired acts they don't approve of as not coming from "real religion."* Religions survive and thrive precisely because they are inherently vague, even contradictory, and therefore forever open to interpretation.

"And what of Kounjaa's cousin, Hamza?" I asked.

"Yes, Kounjaa' was his *ibn ammat*. Married to Hamza's father's sister's daughter. Hamza liked the Jontra too. He was upset about Kounjaa'. Then he just stopped coming to get his hair cut. He let his beard grow. For about a year. His hair came down to here [the shoulders]. I knew what that meant. He was going 'Afghan,' like Kounjaa'. I talked to Hamza's brother: *Balak* [Be careful]. Then, one day, Hamza cut his hair and beard, like they all do, just before going off [to become martyrs]. The same for

Younes [Achebak] and Bilal [Ben Aboud] and Amakchar [Adel-monim al-Amrani]."

Ali stopped cutting the hair of his young client, to whom he was giving a bowl-like *coptasa* cut. "What can violence do for any of these young men? To kill innocents is not the path of the Prophet. It is the path to the gates of hell."

The *caid*, who is the local representative of the Ministry of the Interior, has a man who is his eyes and ears in each neighborhood, called the *muqqadim*. Mezuak's muqqadim came into the barbershop along with two members of the Renseignements Généraux, police intelligence. They were all dressed in black leather jackets. I silently chuckled at the sight, remembering how the tails they'd put on me the last time I visited Mezuak were easily spotted, especially in the summer when leather made them sweat like penguins in July at Coney Island. This time I had official government permission to talk to people. These guys were just checking up. The muqqadim was a nervous and wary man with hunched shoulders and arms lost in an oversize coat; with his deep-set eyes and a drooping mustache, he looked like a cross between a dachshund and bloodhound. The other two were younger and more relaxed; they smiled at me with a cool stare. So I shook hands with all of them.

"We were talking about Amakchar," I told the muqqadim. "Ali says he wasn't really part of the group."

"His father deals in sheep. He doesn't have money," the muqqadim said. "He's a simple man and ashamed of what his son did. You can meet him if you want."

"Maybe another day." I had to figure a way to meet him without the muqqadim being around, but these guys always seemed to catch up with me pretty fast.

"Amakchar was a smuggler," the muqqadim announced.

Perhaps 25,000 people cross from Tetuán into Ceuta every day, only some of them legally. Like Jamal Ahmidan, Amakchar would float contraband in tires and plastic bags between Ceuta and Tetuán along the Mediterranean coast. Sometimes people drown doing this. More often, the goods drop to the bottom of the sea. No one gets very rich this way.

I mentioned that the Chinaman tried to smuggle hashish this way after he got out of jail and before returning to Spain. But he lost the load in the water.

"Many people do this," the muqqadim said. "But smuggling is a way of life here. We don't punish people for that."

"Even drugs?" I asked.

"At least hashish. No one here thinks it's a crime. Actually, people tend to like smugglers and drug runners because these are the people who often give the most charity to the mosque and needy, and they give out the most meat in the neighborhood during the Feast of Eid."

"Sounds like the Mafia," I said.

"No, no," the muqqadim said defensively. "Here many normal, ordinary people do such things every day. And they don't tolerate violence. We don't tolerate violence." The two police intelligence officers nodded in agreement. "Violence is rare and we deal with that harshly. Heroin and cocaine are recent here. We don't like it. Violence comes with it. These drugs, we want to get rid of."

I asked the muqqadim if any of the young men who went to Iraq were captured or returned.

"No, they're all gone. After they called their parents to say they were going to become martyrs, none of their parents received word. We think they're all dead."

At the headquarters of the Direction des Affaires Générales, the administration for the Ministry of the Interior that provides the caids and muqqadims, much like the French prefectures, Amakchar's mother waylaid the muqqadim.

"I hate the name Amakchar," she said. "I'm ashamed, so ashamed of what he did. Forgive me."

"Why do you say that?" the muqqadim said consolingly. "It's not your fault."

"So you will give my other son a residency card?" she pleaded.

The muqqadim explained to me that Amakchar's younger brother is fifteen and, like every young man, will soon need a residency card.

"Of course, we'll take care of it. Just make sure the papers are in order."

I started talking to a young woman sitting in the office of the caid of the caids, the director of the Tetuán bureau of the DAG. She was a new caid, one of the first batch of female caids in Morocco, all of whom had graduated just two months before. All caids must have a doctorate or be enrolled in a doctoral program. She had a doctorate in jurisprudence. I asked her about the role of the family in these cases:

> "Of course we have to find out what's going on, but the families are often the last to know."
>
> The muqqadim agreed. "We can't blame the family. They didn't know. They never know. It's very hard on them. There's no reason to punish them."
>
> "Whose fault is it?" I asked. "How about Adelillah Fathallah?"

Fathallah was the imam of the al-Rohbane mosque. The mosque was affiliated with Dawa Tabligh, a generally nonviolent social movement that preaches and proselytizes in the name of Islam and the doing of good works—not a political movement. The mosque, under Fathallah's sway and beginning with Kounjaa', had become known in the neighborhood as the Afghan mosque. All five of the young when who went to Iraq to be martyrs regularly prayed there. Fathallah was arrested on December 26, 2006, after the last of the group had gone to Iraq and the first reports of their actions had come back. He was sentenced to six years.

"Did Fathallah's preachings convince them to go?"

"No, he didn't convince anyone to go to Iraq," the muqqadim said with surprising certainty. "He helped those who already had made up their minds to go."

At the soccer field in the local schoolyard, Ami ("Uncle") Absalam, the volunteer coach of the Mezuak soccer league, said that now that there were regular soccer practices at the schoolyard, the kids were kept busy and away from bad influences.

He thought the most important link between the Madrid plotters and the young men bound for Iraq was through Kounjaa', who was a regular guy from the neighborhood as well as a preacher of jihad who commanded respect, and who was crucially also related by marriage to one of the Iraq-bound friends.

"Hamza would play at Gharza ["the garden," a makeshift soccer field] with Kounjaa' and others," Ami Absalam told me. "I would lend him the soccer balls to play there. Hamza admired Kounjaa'. But he would also play here with Bilal at the high school."

Ami Absalam said he believed that soccer for young boys is the best antidote to violence, and so he devotes a good part of his life to helping to make soccer a passion for the boys. He receives no money for doing this day in and day out, year after year.

"I have three hundred kids here enrolled; they each pay two hundred dirham [twenty dollars] a year. If their families can't pay, I try to find the money for them. They're all basically good kids. And some of them are terrific. We have here many who could be with Real Madrid or Barça. We have lots of Zinedines."

He's a dynamo who spreads his high spirits to all those around, but suddenly his shoulders sagged. "But look at what we have to play with." He hauled up a large net bag loaded with soccer balls: all torn and frayed, and nearly deflated. "How can you learn to become great with that?"

Then he rebounded: "Just give these boys shirts and shoes and

Ami Absalam (center) and his soccer boys.

soccer balls, and they'll be all right. Some will become great players. And they won't have to go get out their tensions in other ways."

GROUPTHINK

For Americans bred on a constant diet of individualism, the group
is not where one generally looks for explanation. This, as I noted at
the beginning of the book, was certainly true for me. But science
tends to support the finding that groupthink often trumps individual volition and knowledge, whether in our society or any other.
In 1955, social psychologist Solomon Asch wanted to investigate
what human beings would do when confronted with a group that
insists that wrong is right. In his experiment, he showed groups of
seven college students the drawing of a line, and then asked each

student to identify which of several other lines matched it in length. Only one student, however, was being tested. The others were in on it with Asch and were only acting. The actors all picked the same blatantly wrong answer. Seventy-five percent of the subjects then chose the wrong line, rather than the line their own observation indicated was the correct one.

My research colleague Greg Berns, a physician and psychologist, has done brain imaging studies with his associates at Emory University using the Asch experiment. He found that subjects appeared to reach conformity by recalibrating the figure in parts of the brain dedicated to visual processing (occipital-parietal network) rather than to executive reasoning and decision making (prefrontal cortex). This suggests that people might actually picture reality differently under peer pressure. The results also indicate that to stand alone and resist conforming may be emotionally costly (for example, in being associated with increased activity in the amygdala, a "primitive" brain structure the shape and size of an almond that has long been linked with a person's emotional state).[1]

Recently, psychologists at Temple University in Philadelphia found that adolescents and young adults between ages thirteen and twenty-three were more inclined than adults were to take risks under peer influence of three or more friends. One study, dubbed the Chicken Experiment, used a driving-simulation game to see which age groups take more risks in deciding whether to run a yellow light. Results showed that "although the sample as a whole took more risks and made more risky decisions in groups than when alone, this effect was more pronounced during middle and late adolescence than during adulthood."[2] Indeed, most crimes by teens and young adults are perpetrated in packs. Sociologist Randall Collins finds that gangs and rioters (and police who try to control them) commit most of their violence when a cluster of four or more act in concert.[3]

Part of the answer to what leads a normal person to become a terrorist may lie in philosopher Hannah Arendt's notion of the "banality of evil," a phrase she used to describe the fact that mostly ordinary Germans, not sadistic lunatics, were recruited to man Nazi extermination camps.[4] In the early 1960s, psychologist Stanley Milgram tested Arendt's thesis.[5] For his experiments, Milgram recruited a number of college-educated adults, supposedly to help others learn better. When the "learner," hidden by a screen, failed to memorize arbitrary word pairs fast enough, the "helper" was instructed to administer an electric shock and to increase the voltage with each erroneous answer. (In fact, the learners were actually actors who deliberately got the answers wrong, and unbeknownst to the helpers, no electrical shock was actually being applied.) Most helpers complied with instructions to give what would have been potentially lethal shocks (labeled as 450 volts) despite the learners' screams and pleas.

Although this experiment specifically showed how situations can be staged to elicit blind obedience to authority, a more general lesson is that manipulation of context can trump individual personality and psychology to generate apparently extreme behaviors in ordinary people. In another classic experiment from more than thirty years ago, the Stanford Prison Experiment, normal college-age men were assigned to be guards or prisoners; the "guards" quickly became sadistic, engaging in what psychologist Philip Zimbardo called "pornographic and degrading abuse of the prisoners."[6] It's hard to think of a torturer as just your average Joe, but other studies indicate it's true.[7] Most of the American soldiers who humiliated detainees in Iraq's Abu Ghraib prison were probably no different.

Other research on groupthink indicates that when people are given information about the specific ability-related or morality-related behaviors that others say they will perform, these people come to believe that they also will perform such behaviors.[8]

If group cohesion is based on how much the members like the group and get along with its members, then the members are less likely to speak up against the group norms, and the group is more likely to make poor decisions. This is because like-minded individuals in a group are more concerned with their social relations than with their tasks; they are less prone to cause conflict within a group in order to maintain congeniality. When you couple this with the reality bias wherein group members believe others to be more extreme than themselves, then the whole group tends to shift to a more extreme position as people bend over backward to accommodate to what each believes is the others' more radical position. Social psychologists refer to this particular group dynamic as "extremity shift" or "outbidding," which is responsible for a "bandwagon effect,"[9] whether in the rush to support a patriotic war or the cause of martyrdom.

But there's more to group dynamics than just the weight and mass of people, their behavior, and ideas. There are also the structural relationships between group members that make the group more than the sum of its individual members. It's also the networking among members that distributes thoughts and tasks that no one part may completely control or even understand.

It's not that hard to grasp how networks transcend individual limitations of physical and mental power to get things done. Anyone who has ever worked on a team or a production line knows that. But networks also have more far-reaching properties that enable them to transcend physical constraints of space and time in surprising ways that are only now beginning to be understood by science.

Take obesity. "What does obesity have to do with terrorism?" you may reasonably ask. Well, nothing . . . and everything. Consider:

A recent medical study shows that even body weight can be strongly influenced by social networks of friends.[10] Researchers examined a densely interconnected social network of over twelve thousand people from 1970 to 2003. A person's chances of being obese increased by 57 percent if a friend became obese, 40 percent if a sibling became obese, and 37 percent if a spouse became obese. The study suggests that these trends cannot be attributed to the selective formation of social ties among people who might naturally incline to obesity. The biggest influence comes from close mutual friends, even if they live far away. The faraway friend has even more influence on your weight than do neighbors or even relatives who live with you. Although subsequent studies may show that there are other causal factors involved in these long-distance relationships, the results clearly have as much or more to do with social ties than with genes or physical proximity.

If even body weight can be significantly molded by social networks in fairly short order, and perhaps even across great distances of physical separation, think how much easier it is to motivate ideas, behaviors, and emotions among friends in neighborhoods or in chat rooms over the Internet. Indeed, studies now show that smoking, happiness, and even loneliness are also like viruses that spread best among friends. The key difference between terrorists and most other people in the world lies not in individual pathologies, personality, education, income, or in any other demographic factor, but in small-group dynamics where the relevant trait just happens to be jihad rather than, say, obesity.[11] This is what I mean by the ordinariness of terror.

It's not likely that we will ever be able to prevent terrorist attacks by trying to profile terrorists; they're not different enough from everyone else in the population to make them remarkable. Insights into homegrown jihadi attacks will come from understanding group dynamics even more than individual psychology. Small-group dynamics can trump individual personality to produce horrific behavior in ordinary people, not only in terrorists but in those who fight them. Although we can't do much about personality traits, whether biologically influenced or not, we may

Part IV

THE WILD EAST

Take up the White Man's burden—Send forth the best ye breed—
Go, bind your sons to exile
To serve your captives' need;
To wait, in heavy harness,
On fluttered folk and wild—Your new-caught sullen peoples,
Half devil and half child.

Take up the White Man's burden—
In patience to abide,
To veil the threat of terror
And check the show of pride. . . .
—RUDYARD KIPLING, 1899

CHAPTER 14
PRYING INTO PAKISTAN

I went to Pakistan in the spring of 2006 to seek out Pakistani senator Khurshid Ahmad. An economist and renowned Muslim scholar, he is also a leader of Jama'at-e-Islami, one of the Islamic world's oldest and most important revivalist movements. In a conversation in Italy, he had said to me that if the Hamas government were to accept a two-state solution, "with both Palestine and Israel having full economic, political, and military sovereignty over their pre-1967 territories, and with Palestinians allowed into Palestine and Jews into Israel, then I would recommend this solution to the entire Muslim Ummah [community]." I wanted to get that into the *New York Times*[1] and on the public record. Given prevailing stereotypes, it was a remarkable declaration by a self-proclaimed "Islamic fundamentalist" who once mentored Abdullah Azzam, cofounder of Al Qaeda, and shared a prison cell with Jama'at-e-Islami's creator Abul A'ala Maududi, who, along with the Muslim Brotherhood's Hassan al-Banna, established Islamic revivalism in the twentieth century.

I took advantage of that trip to try to learn about what was happening in that country, which I hadn't seen in thirty years. One visit to the field, nearly my last, was to the Pakistan-administered territory of Azad Kashmir. In Kashmir, as in Palestine, the British had made a mess of things when they left the Indian subcontinent in 1947, by partitioning the territory along a religious cleavage and hardening the lines of future conflict. The Hindu community had long fled or been driven out, but even the Muslim Kashmiris remembered with dread the Pathans (close cousins of Afghanistan's Pashtun tribesmen) who had ethnically cleansed the area after partition. For many Kashmiris, today's "Pathans" include the numerous Punjabis from Pakistan's heartland (the region of Punjab) who populate the plentiful jihadi groups, such as Lashkar-e-Tayibah, as well as the most feared group of all, Pakistan's Directorate for Inter-Services Intelligence (ISI).

RAWALAKOT, AZAD KASHMIR (PAKISTAN ADMINISTRATION), MAY 2006

I was cramped and cold, the mosque floor smelled of warm rot, and I did not feel safe or invisible.

"Darling, darling, you can dance with them but don't kiss them! Promise me. Promise!"

From the nearby guesthouse, she said it again. Never was I so relieved to hear what would otherwise have been a noisy intrusion into my three-in-the-morning rumination. Through the floorboards of my uncertain refuge, an abandoned Lashkar-e-Tayibah mosque, I craned to get a glimpse of her through the cracks. Ridiculous I was, lying there on my stomach with my penknife, cursing myself, again: "Another nice mess you've gotten yourself into." I had stumbled upon some recent killings while I was surveying the results of relief efforts for victims of what has become known as the Great Pakistan Earthquake of October 2005, which had devastated the region, and people who did not want the news out were out looking for me. I imagined the worst, then that angel and her overheard cell phone conversation chased away my demons.

By morning there was a plan by a group of independence-minded Kashmiri nationalists to get me out, with some of the documents I needed, to report events (which I later related in the *Bulletin of the Atomic Scientists*).[2] My only regret was that I'd miss the meeting I had arranged with Hafiz Saeed, the leader of Lashkar-e-Tayibah ("the Army of the Pure"). One of the largest militant groups in Pakistan, it was established in the late 1980s with the full support of the Pakistan ISI and financing from Bin Laden to wage jihad against India and regain the whole of Kashmir for Pakistan and Islam (although most of its militants aren't from Kashmir but from Punjab). Saeed was supposed to be under house arrest in Lahore but said over the phone that he would come up to Islamabad to talk to me about why young men "choose the path to paradise rather than surrendering their hopes." Then again, maybe it's better I didn't make it to that appointment.

In early May, seven months after the earthquake that killed more than 70,000 people and left 3 million homeless, the Pakistani army ejected most remaining foreign relief workers from the still-devastated region of Azad Kashmir, the Pakistan-controlled part of Kashmir. Then, between May 13 and 16, a series of thirty-eight throat slittings and beheadings occurred in villages of southern Azad Kashmir. The youngest victim was four months old, the oldest over seventy. The army blamed infiltrators from India. But on the morning of May 17, two men said to be armed with Sten guns and daggers accosted and followed some girls to school in the village of Sanghola. Alerted by the girls' screaming, villagers surrounded the school and captured the men.

The men claimed to be road workers, but a body search revealed ID cards of the kind carried by Pakistan's ISI. Villagers identified both as Punjabi by accent. Around noon, villagers escorted the two men, on foot, to local police at Rawalakot. Whereas most local police are Kashmiri, most army personnel at the ISI headquarters down the road from Rawalakot are Punjabi. At 11:30 P.M., six army officers, including a colonel and a brigadier, took the captured men from the police at gunpoint. The next day, Azad Kashmir's prime minister, Sardar Sikandar Hayat, declared his government "unable to protect you [people of Azad Kashmir]." Thousands demonstrated in Rawalakot, Kotli, Mirpur, and Bhimbar. The head of Azad Kashmir's ruling party and its former PM, Sardar Abdul Qayyum, said, "Elections are meaningless, the actual government will be formed by ISI." Both Hayat and Qayyum subsequently declined to participate in the July 11, 2006, elections in Azad Kashmir.

I had to cut short my sleuthing when ISI agents began following me and interrogated my hosts about any interest I might have in the *chura*, or "daggers" (meaning the recent killings) and "camps" (meaning jihadi activities). One little snake of a man, who constantly rubbed his hands like the Dickensian creep Uriah Heep and various French politicians, asked someone where I could be found late at night. That's when I went to the mosque to lie low.

While no direct evidence links ISI to the killings, many native Kashmiris I talked to and most nationalists (banned from elections because they advocate a Kashmir independent from Pakistan *and* India) believe rogue elements of the ISI were behind them. Two troubling facts credit this argument: First, there were no reports of the incidents in the mainstream Pakistani press; second, while the army initially promised the police and people of Rawalakot an investigation, they did nothing.

Kashmiris I've interviewed believe the killings were intended to further a motive shared by the ISI and the jihadi groups and certain segments of the army here; namely, to stop the peace process with India by inciting the public against India. Although Pakistan's then-president Pervez Musharraf intermittently seemed committed to a rapprochement with India, a senior army commander told me that the peace process with India was a "nonstarter, because India would only come to the negotiating table and give up Kashmir if forced to."

In February 2006, speaking to a Pugwash conference at the presidential palace, Musharraf lauded the peace process. But he was challenged from the audience by people who had witnessed almost every officially banned jihadi group operating freely in Azad Kashmir, brandishing guns from army vehicles, promising relief only to people who understood, as Lashkar-e-Tayibah's Hafiz Saeed put it, that "the earthquake is the result of the rulers' sinful policies" and God's punishment for neglecting a particular, radical view of Islam. Since this event, however, LeT and other jihadi groups have relocated away from the main roads and into more remote areas of Kotli and Trahkhil. And that's why I had an LeT mosque all to myself.

American security forces teamed with the ISI in the hunt for Osama Bin Laden are continually stunned by the Islamist sentiments of some officers. In October 2001, Musharraf sent ISI chief Lieutenant General Ahmed to Afghanistan to negotiate Bin Laden's surrender. Instead, Ahmed openly encouraged the Taliban regime to fight the Americans. Another former head of the ISI, Hamid Gul, had been openly Islamist and anti-American, and continued to enjoy influence in the ISI. He has become somewhat marginalized, but younger officers I talked to said that they were tired of getting bloodied every time America barked and the government threw some of them into the frontier provinces as a bone. "This won't go on forever," said one officer. "The army must decide." (And in 2010, things aren't all that different.)

Most worrisome is the potential for Islamists to gain control of Pakistan's nukes, which in conditions of high alert were placed under operational control of field commanders. It is almost inconceivable that the ISI was unaware of Abdul Qadeer Khan's rogue nuclear operations, carried on mostly through his family and connections with old school buddies and political cronies on whom he lavished presents, and which included transnational shipments of tons of large equipment as well as information on metallization, bomb design, manufacture, and testing from the Pakistan Atomic Energy Commission (PAEC).

Senior members of the PAEC visited Bin Laden and the Taliban in August 2001, were arrested in October 2002, then were released to stump with Lashkar-e-Tayibah.[3] Lashkar-e-Tayibah had organized a suicide attack on India's parliament in 2001 that again brought the area close to nuclear war. LeT also provided military training to a group of American citizens (known as the Virginia Paintball Group) bent on jihad and to people caught casing Australia's nuclear facilities, and went on to instigate devastating commando attacks in Mumbai in 2006 and 2008, which killed hundreds. To top it all off, the PAEC's chairman, Anwar Hussain, who was engaged in construction of a new plutonium reactor that would greatly increase Pakistan's ability to produce bombs for missile delivery, had declared, "I am proud never to have soiled my hands shaking those of Abdus Salam." Abdus Salam, who died in 1996, was Pakistan's greatest scientist, a Nobel Prize winner and humanist who belonged to the Ahmadiyeh sect, considered heretical by government decree.

"MAYBE IT'S A SHAME WE DON'T HAVE MORE EARTHQUAKES AND TSUNAMIS"

For the Kashmiri people, especially those in the hundreds of villages far from the main concentration of relief efforts in the Azad Kashmir capital of Muzaffarabad, Cubans are the real heroes. Cuba sent some three thousand doctors, providing medical care in nearly every remote corner of the devastated area, earning deep admiration. Although the Cuban hospital on the road up from the Nilam River to Rawalakot now lies deserted, there is a lesson for U.S. policy makers.

Until Barack Obama's election, U.S. relief for Indonesian victims of the December 2004 tsunami arguably was the only significant victory since 9/11 in the struggle to prevent enlistment of future terrorists for jihad, providing constructive investments of "soft power" that could generate longer-term relief from the need to use destructive and usually snowballing forms of "hard power." According to the Pew Global Attitudes Project, with the tsunami relief effort there had been improvement in favorable attitudes among Indonesians toward America and a doubling of popular support for combating terrorism (from 23 percent in 2003 to 50 percent), as Indonesians focused on dangers they faced rather than on distaste for U.S. policies. This suggests that quiet aid might best counter the growth of violent extremism.

When I brought up the example of the Cuban doctors at a briefing on the Middle East in Washington organized by the chief of naval operations, one senior officer said tongue-in-cheek: "Maybe it's a shame we don't have more earthquakes and tsunamis," but, "can you imagine the doctors in this town giving up six-figure salaries for a bunch of people with no health insurance?" and then finally, "We're just not built to help people, and maybe that should change." (At another meeting, an Air Force general said to me: "We're trained to do D's: devastate, destroy, defeat, defend. Now we're asked to go into places and do R's—recover, reform, rebuild, renew. To do that, we'd have to know how to blow apart things in just the right way so we can later come in and rebuild them. Tell me, how the hell are we gonna do that?")

AT THE THAI-MALAYSIAN BORDER, LATE NOVEMBER 2008

An Indian reporter tracked me down to ask who I thought might be behind the Mumbai attacks that had begun the day before on hotels, a hospital, a café, and a Jewish center. A previously unknown Muslim group called Deccan Mujahideen—a name suggesting origins inside India—claimed responsibility. But I told him, "This smells like Lashkar-e-Tayibah," for a number for reasons: There were multiple attack units, at least some of the attackers apparently came by sea, they probably used GPS and computers to coordinate their actions, they chose targets that would kill high-profile foreigners and Jews, and (like Al Qaeda) no demands were made, and all hostages were being killed.

Lashkar-e-Tayibah had been training people with the Taliban in Afghanistan and also on the Pakistani side of the border in the Mohmand region of the Tribal Areas near Peshawar, I told the reporter, and may have set up a hybrid operation with local sympathizers in India. They'd done a dry run from Karachi to Bombay by sea in March 2007.[4] I also told him that as long as Pakistan was unstable and unable or unwilling to control jihadi groups like LeT, the whole region could blow up.[5] India showed remarkable restraint in the attack's aftermath, as Pakistan first denied, then admitted LeT involvement and invited, then disinvited Indian representatives to help conduct the investigation. As one senior member of the U.S. National Security Council staff told me, "One of our biggest worries is that LeT will do something else and goad the Indians to take an irreversible step toward a cataclysmic confrontation." They were patient this time but likely to be less so the next time. In 2010, Hafiz Saeed was still publicly promoting anti-Indian actions with impunity.[6]

Of all the Al Qaeda affiliates operating out of Pakistan, LeT is the most ambitious and dangerous. LeT was founded in 1987 by Zafar Iqbal and Hafiz Saeed, both professors from the Lahore University of Engineering and Technology. Saeed, as smart and wily a character as they come, has advocated using weapons of mass destruction against Western interests and has made greater efforts to enlist physics students than the rural poor in his cause.

LeT was probably responsible (along with Jaish-e-Mohammed) for the attack on India's parliament in December 2001 that brought Pakistan and India to the brink of massive war (millions of soldiers were mobilized and both countries were put on nuclear alert) and also for the November 2008 attack in Mumbai that killed 164 and badly rattled India's government and people. Although primarily concerned with "liberating" Kashmir from India, LeT has been implicated in far-ranging shenanigans, including training members of the Virginia Paintball group (who wanted to fight with the Taliban and Al Qaeda in Afghanistan but were arrested before they could do anything) and the Pendennis case in Australia (a bomb plot that perhaps also involved casing nuclear facilities).

The group's public face, Jamaat-ud-Dawa, is a "charitable organization" that runs Islamic schools. But these also tend to put a greater stress on scientific and technical education than just parroting the Koran. LeT operations require sophistication that is not typically taught in Pakistani madrassahs:[7] how to blend into foreign environments; intense training and instruction on how to master electronic circuitry and chemistry for manufacturing explosives; how to interpret complex architectural plans in order to set up barricades and defenses on the fly (and so easily outmaneuver Indian security forces in their own territory); and how to commandeer and navigate ships at sea and coordinate operations across international frontiers with video, telephone, and global positioning systems (GPS) run from laptops. (In Pakistan, there may be as many as one hundred jihadi-producing madrassahs out of twenty to forty thousand, well below 1 percent of the total [comparable to what we found in Indonesia; see chapter 10]. These few mostly support the Taliban and the purist Deoband version of Islam that the Taliban practice. But the Taliban and their madrassah support are more local expressions of religious and tribal affinity than of global jihad.)

In 2002, LeT was officially banned by Pakistani president General Pervez Musharraf, under strong U.S. pressure to join the United States–led "war on terror." The ban simply prompted LeT to shift bank accounts to its "charity" outlet and move some operations and offices from the Punjab to Azad Kashmir and the Afghan border regions. (In December 2008, just after Mumbai, over a hundred Jamaat-ud-Dawa militants were arrested in the North-West Frontier Province alone.)[8] More recently, LeT has been using camps in Azad Kashmir and Pakistan's tribal areas to train for global jihad. It is present in at least seventeen countries and has operations in Bangladesh, Afghanistan, Pakistan's tribal areas, and Baluchistan, and some of its fighters have even turned up in Iraq.

Like other militant groups in Pakistan, LeT sees an anti-Muslim conspiracy among Indians, Americans, and Israelis. And so all are enemies and fair game. But unlike other jihadi groups in Pakistan, LeT doesn't attack the Pakistani army and state and still cooperates closely with the ISI. A number of retired Pakistani Army officers impressed by LeT's ideology have joined its ranks as volunteers.[9] But despite its formidable organizational infrastructure, LeT, like Jemaah Islamiyah, appears to have a fluid membership based extensively on social networks of family and friends. No evidence directly implicates LeT's spiritual guide Saeed in terrorist operations. He may be involved, but as we've seen with JI, there's no need of that for complex, coordinated attacks to be successful.

What makes LeT so much more dangerous than JI is not its organization, financing, or even global networking, but its avowed interest in obtaining access to nuclear weapons in a country where significantly many who have access to that technology have militant Islamist sympathies. In April 2004, Hafiz Saeed declared that "mass killing of nonbelievers is the only solution to international conflicts in the Muslims' favor." To which Pakistani nuclear physicist Pervez Hoodbhoy said, "I am more worried about extremists having access to nuclear materials, particularly highly enriched uranium-235 (HEU), rather than a completed weapon. Because of secrecy requirements, it is very difficult for outsiders to monitor the output of uranium enrichment or plutonium reprocessing plants."[10] Hoodbhoy, who blames the rise of jihadi activity in Pakistan in part on the Reagan administration's support for Pakistan's militant Muslim dictator Zia ul-Haq, told me: "I truly hope this is the one time the CIA is doing its job."[11]

NUCLEAR FIZZLE

Pakistan is a nuclear weapons state that is politically very unstable. It now produces fissile material at a faster rate than any other country, the number of its plutonium reactors has increased from one to three in a few years,[12] and jihadis are increasingly challenging the government and trying to attack the country's nuclear installations (which were located in the west, near areas where the Taliban now operate, to be as far as possible from the Indian border in the east).[13] The main power that keeps the country together is the army, which is still deciding who the real enemy is. Tens of millions of Pakistan's youth see no justice on the horizon and, were they to totally lose hope and radicalize, would end up a threat not just to India, but to the whole world.

But despite the increasing danger posed by conditions in Pakistan to regional and world stability, as matters now stand, material threats from nonstate terrorists in general, and religious terrorists in particular, are much more limited than our public usually assumes. A generation ago, at the height of the Cold War, the Soviet Union and the United States had tens of thousands of nuclear weapons that could annihilate much of the adversary's population in ninety minutes or so.[14] Today's terrorists do not remotely pose such a threat (nuclear scientists who give expert advice to the government on terrorist threats too often assume that it's just as easy for terrorists to make bombs as it is for trained nuclear scientists). Even our darkest present fear and the Department of Homeland Security's "worse case scenario"—the explosion of one or two 1- to 10-kiloton nuclear bombs by terrorists—pales by comparison.

I posed the following question to native Pakistanis knowledgeable about the country's nuclear industry: Suppose, for whatever reason, a group of mujahedin and their supporters wanted to be able to place a workable nuclear device (or several devices) that could be exploded in a foreign country on another continent (that could only be reached by sea or air), even if only to scare that country into changing its foreign policy. What's the best way you think they might go about doing this so that it would not really be possible to trace where the materials came from or to identify the group or country responsible?"[15]

Responses ruled out:

Manufacturing a plutonium device like the one North Korea now says it has (which can only be used in an implosion mode that is hard for those operating outside of the government to engineer because it requires highly sophisticated technology to achieve exact spherical symmetry and extremely precise timing).

Stealing a HEU device from existing stockpiles (because of sophisticated locks that render the weapon useless if tampered with).

Smuggling in a ready-made bomb by ship under the control of others.

Building a gun-type device, weighing 500–1,000 kg, would require a bit of room (at least a large apartment) and engineering four elements: a "gun" that shoots a "uranium bullet" from one end of a "rail" to a "uranium target" at the other end. Neither the bullet nor target has enough uranium-235 to generate a chain reaction, but when slammed together, they acquire critical mass sufficient for a nuclear explosion. According to respondents, Pakistan has about eighty "grapefruits," HEU (U-235) cores that could be used for an atomic weapon (in addition to weapons-grade plutonium). Respondents also indicated that Islamist sympathy within the Pakistani security forces has declined through purging, but militant Islamist support in atomic energy circles remains "at about 20 percent." They noted that to make a bomb, one might infiltrate the Pakistan Atomic Energy Commission, in particular the grapefruit-storage facilities, partially irradiate two U-238 "dummy" grapefruits, and substitute these for U-235 grapefruits.

The whole gambit would require fifteen to twenty people, handling or fabricating 1,500–2,000 parts over two to three years, and ideally, two completely independent teams (minimally related on a "need to know" basis) that would each include:

Nuclear engineers (1 designer, 1 backup)
Technical engineers (machine precision, rail, bullet, target)
Procurement team
Transportation team (perhaps redundant with procurement
    team)
Assembly team (in countryside)—keep to minimum number
Delivery, pickup truck to target in the city
Detonation, suicide bomber (more reliable than remote det-
    onation)

Experts at the U.S. Department of Homeland Security judged the outcome of this exercise plausible, except for the ability or necessity of irradiating U-238 to exactly the level of U-235.

According to physicist Richard Garwin, who helped design the world's first hydrogen bomb, the blast of a gun-type "nuclear fizzle bomb" would immediately kill hundreds of thousands of people in a densely populated area like Manhattan. As Garwin notes, "Although a country would not be destroyed by such an explosion, it could ruin itself by its reaction."[16]

It is a remarkable fact that there is almost no national public discussion or international planning for such an event. The response after a terrorist nuclear attack would be a watershed event in human history, and very likely would cause vastly greater casualties, social dislocation, and economic disruption than the attack itself.[17]

So that is the darkest fear, although no terrorist group has ever come close to acquiring a nuclear weapon on its own. From its inception, Al Qaeda has tried. In its pre-9/11-heyday endeavors to do so, amateurish and almost comical, it failed. (Bioterrorism is perhaps a more plausible fear; all it would take is someone ingesting anthrax and sitting for a spell in an airport to cause death and mayhem.) Now, Al Qaeda has too little infrastructure left to attempt much of anything. But since 2007, with the emergence of the Pakistani Taliban and its embrace of Al Qaeda to help it fight the Pakistani state, including attacks on nuclear facilities, the nuclear danger has increased beyond the threat posed by LeT. A key to defusing this new danger, as well as whatever global threat still remains from Al Qaeda, is Afghanistan.

CHAPTER 15

A QUESTION OF HONOR: WHY THE TALIBAN FIGHT AND WHAT TO DO ABOUT IT

No one loves armed missionaries, and the first lesson of nature and prudence is to repulse them as enemies.

—MAXIMILIEN ROBESPIERRE, *SUR LA GUERRE (ON WAR)*, 1792

LANDI KOTAL, KHYBER PASS, JULY 1976

"Tat, tat, tat, tat, tat, bad position, bad position," the old Afridi tribesman sputtered as he pointed an invisible rifle at the rugged and barren hills of the Khyber Pass.

"Why bad position?" I asked a Pakistani army man, a dentist who happened to be watching the exchange with delighted curiosity and who spoke fairly good English. He explained that, here, the luckless English soldiers had passed through in 1919 on their way to losing (their third and last war in) Afghanistan.

"Ah, but good position with Nadir Khan in Kabul, tat, tat, tat, tat, tat, good position," gleefully squealed the man's equally ancient tea partner, a Wazir tribesman who had joined the father of the last king of Afghanistan in sacking the capital ten years later.

The Afridi lowered his head: "No good position now. No good the fight now. Bad position."

"Why bad position now?" I asked.

The army dentist queried the two white-bearded gentlemen

and came back with a laugh: "They say it's been so calm since [Kabul was sacked in 1929] that a man has no opportunity to become a man!"

"Bad position," the Wazir nodded in sad agreement. "Bad position."

Nothing I had seen or heard while driving across Afghanistan that summer with two Mexican friends in search of a future research site (and a bit of exotic adventure, I grant) hinted that the whole region would soon be ablaze for the next thirty years. There was something I later remembered, though. A former Red Army officer—Tomalchoff, I think his name was—who managed his girlfriend's bookstore on the Île Saint-Louis in Paris had given me copies of maps he had made of the country, with markings of where gasoline could be found, and told me his old buddies had built a wide cement road across the south of Afghanistan that could support the weight of tanks. "The Russians are coming! The Russians are coming!" he exclaimed, cheerfully citing the title of a film comedy that had been popular about a decade before. But I had made nothing of it then.

First stop out of Iran and into Herat, the ancient city of Aria, whose Persian population Genghis Khan had nearly exterminated in 1221. I came looking for Alexander the Great's citadel; and I finally found it by its smell, for the palace was now the place where people came to shit. There may have been no value to cultural patrimony, but there was to cultural independence. In Herat, the population first rose up against the Soviets in 1979, killing thirty-five Russian advisers. In return, the Afghan communists, backed by the Red Army, killed nearly twenty-five thousand civilians.

Then we drove north to Mazar-e-Sharif, a city of mostly Tajiks and Uzbeks, where people with both hands missing—someone told me this was because they were repeat thieves who had been punished with amputation, but I can't confirm that—were rolling chopped raw meat between their toes and placing them on skewers over wood-coals to sell to passersby. In 2001, with help from U.S. air power and special forces, the Northern Alliance took the city, with massive killings of civilians. Because the massacres were perpetrated by allies of the U.S.-backed coalition, no one has (yet) had to pay.

In the center of the country I traveled by horse. Once in a wood I happened on a young woman who had dropped her veil to pull water from a well. I stared at her beauty. She quickly covered her face and scurried away. Suddenly she stopped, turned to me, and took the veil from her face—if ever a look could launch a thousand dreams! I whipped out a camera, but she covered her face as the shutter clicked and ran away. But that moment was burned into my memory for life.

Near the terraced, turquoise lakes of Bandi Amir, a dull thunder rumbled behind a hill. The most acrobatic horsemen I had ever seen in my life soon shot out from a whirl of dust, playing for the trophy of a headless sheep kept in constant motion. I rode on through this country of the Hazara, descendants of the Mongols, to see the Buddhas of Bamyan, beautiful giant statues carved in the cliffs fifteen hundred years ago. In 2001,

Afghan girl, July 1976.

the Taliban leader, Mullah Omar, ordered the Buddhas dynamited because they were "idols." The Sharia scholars of Cairo's Al Azhar University tried to talk him out of it, but he responded that he would decide what Sharia meant in his country. And why was the outside world so interested in stonework when his people were starving?

In Kabul, it was so hot you could fry an egg on the hood of a car, and I did. Huge Pashtun soldiers in ill-fitting, woolen Red Army surplus fatigues guarded official buildings, and stank mightily but stoically. In the park, even bigger greased-up men were wrestling for a crowd that was cheering, aside from a cluster of silent women shrouded in thick, formless cloth from head to toe except for the latticework at eye level that let them see.

On Chicken Street, cruising in a pink Cadillac with great tail-fins, a young man rolled down the window and asked what I was doing. When I told him, he said he wanted to chat about anthropology. We continued in his car, talking about Margaret Mead and Claude Lévi-Strauss, except that every time he saw a pretty Western girl he'd invite her to his village palace and offer to take her up K-2 (the second highest mountain in the world) with or without oxygen. His father was a close cousin of the deposed king, Zahir Shah. We went to his family's palace (or rather, one of them), where the entire village was at the young man's call. He had gathered together a motley collection of foreigners—a mad, rustic salon, including one Palestinian man who pressed me all day and much of the night to join him in buying a fleet of refrigerated Mercedes trucks in Germany to ferry lettuce to Saudi Arabia. "Can you imagine," he said, "a Palestinian and a Jew in such a business together? We could save the Middle East!"

It turned out that the young Afghan lord had been living in exile in Flushing, Queens, New York, but had recently been allowed back by the country's president, another cousin who had overthrown the monarchy and declared the country a republic. When the communists took power, the first thing they did was to kill the president,

Mohammed Daoud Khan, along with a slew of his relatives. I never learned what happened to that extravagant but genial young man, but I suspect he would have been better off staying in Queens.

Through Jalalabad and up toward the Khyber Pass, a curve on a high mountain road suddenly cropped up, our van turned sharply, and the front left wheel went into the void and over what seemed like a thousand-foot drop. The three of us in the van dared not move. As we fruitlessly cursed and debated what to do, a black and blurry line in the distance began to come into focus. It was a very tall Pashtun tribesman, elegant but strongly built, with green eyes full of laughter. He hopped off his horse, roped the van, pulled us to safety, brought us home as guests, and told us what he thought of our lands and his: "America good; Mexico, bandit, very good; Afghanistan top good."

Into Landi Kotal at the top of the Khyber Pass, I was shooting the breeze with the Afridi tribesman and his Wazir companion (I suspected they had become friends simply because they were old rather than because the traditional enmity between their tribes had lessened), as four young boys somehow managed to unhinge the engine block from the back of our van and were struggling to lift the thing away. The army dentist stopped them with a stern word, shooed them away, and with a smile that showed pleasure both at his thought and his command of English, threw up his hands and said, "Boys will be boys." Now, after years of almost constant war, I imagine the old Afridi and Wazir would see that such boys had indeed become "men's men."

Although reading more than a thousand years of Arab and Muslim history would show little pattern to predict the attacks of 9/11, the present predicament in Afghanistan rhymes as well with the past as the lines of a limerick.

Afghanistan is not like Iraq. And what may work well in Iraq, like propping up governments and surging with troops, may not be so wise for Afghanistan. Iraq is part of Mesopotamia, home to the world's first centralized government and civilization. Its relatively flat and open geography and great rivers have favored intensive agricultural production, urban development, and easy commerce and communication throughout history. In Mesopotamian Iraq, central governments supported by large standing armies have brought order and stability. Not so in Afghanistan or the border regions of Pakistan, which are also not like Vietnam in the 1960s and 1970s, where a strong state backed communist insurgents. They must be dealt with on their own terms.

The harsh, mountainous, landlocked country of Afghanistan is midway along the ancient Silk Road connecting China and India to the Middle East and Europe. Its critical geostrategic location has been coveted by a never-ending stream of foreign interlopers, from Alexander the Great to the generals of Soviet Russia and the United States. In 1219, Genghis Khan laid waste to the land because its people chose to resist rather than submit. He exterminated every living soul in cities like Balkh, capital of the ancient Greek province of Bactria, home to Zoroastrianism, and a center of Persian Islamic learning. With urban centers devastated, the region became an agrarian backwater under Mongol rule. In 1504, Babur, a descendant of both Genghis Khan and the Persianized Mongol Timur the Lame (Tamerlane), established the Moghul Empire in Kabul and dominated India. But by the early 1700s, the central government in Afghanistan, never strong for long, had collapsed, and much of the region was self-ruled by the Afghans, also known as the Pashtun, fiercely independent tribes who speak *aliba*, a Persian dialect.

The Pashtun, almost all of whom are Sunni Muslim, are divided into a few major tribal confederations, and numerous tribes and subtribes. In 1747, Ahmad Shah Durrani founded a regional empire based on cross-tribal alliances between the Durrani confederation, which provided the political and landowning elite that governed the country, and the larger Ghilzai confederation, which provided the fighters. This was the foundation of modern Afghanistan.

In the nineteenth century, the country became a buffer state in "the Great Game" between British India and czarist Russia's ambitions in Central Asia. The British gave up trying to occupy and rule Afghanistan after the first Anglo-Afghan War, which ended in 1842, when tribal forces slaughtered 16,500 soldiers and 12,000 dependents of a mixed British-Indian garrison, leaving a lone survivor on a stumbling pony to carry back the news. Still, the British remained determined to control Afghanistan's relations with outside powers. In 1879, they deposed the Afghan amir following his reception of a Russian mission at Kabul. But in keeping with anticolonial stirrings unleashed in the wake of World War I, the Afghans wanted to recover full independence over foreign affairs, which they did following the Third Anglo-Afghan War from 1919 to 1921. The country remained independent until 1979, when the Russians (Soviets) returned for another go at control, followed in 2001 by the American-led invasion (with Britain as the junior partner) to bring Afghanistan into the Western camp after its brief spell of independence under Taliban control.

All Pashtun trace their common descent from one Qais Abdur Rashid, through his youngest son Karlan. Folklore has it that the Afridi tribesmen of the Karlandri confederation are Rashid and Karlan's most direct descendants. Although smaller than the Durrani and Ghilzai confederations, the Karlandri confederation, which straddles the present Afghan-Pakistan border, includes the most bellicose and autonomous of the Pashtun tribes. From the time of Herodotus and Alexander, historians have described how the Afridis controlled and taxed the passage of other tribes and foreigners through the Khyber Pass. The British thought the Afridi fearsome characters and fine shots, and so paid them off handsomely, or preferentially enlisted them in the Khyber Rifles and other crack frontier units to help them keep at bay the other Karlandri tribes, most notably the Wazirs of North Waziristan and the Mehsuds of South Waziristan.

Although the Wazirs and Mehsuds were hereditary enemies who constantly fought one another, they would unite in jihad against any foreign attempt to gain a foothold in Waziristan, spurred on by local religious leaders (mullahs) and their martyr-dom-seeking students (talibs). The British army missionary, T. L. Pennell, described the situation a century ago in *Among the Wild Tribes of the Afghan Frontier*:

> Waziristan (the country of the Wazirs and Mahsuds), is severely left alone, provided the tribes do not compel attention and inter-ference by the raids into British territory; which are frequently perpetrated by their more lawless spirits. . . . [T]ribal jealousies and petty wars are inherent. . . . Hence the saying, "The Afghans of the frontier are never at peace except when they are at war!" For when some enemy from without threatens their indepen-dence, then . . . they fight shoulder to shoulder, [although] even when they are all desirous of joining some *jihad*, they remain suspicious of each other. . . . Mullahs sometimes use the power and influence they possess to rouse the tribes to concerted war-fare against the infidels. . . . The more fanatical of these Mullahs do not hesitate to incite their pupils [*taliban*] to acts of religious fanaticism, or *ghaza*, as it is called. The *ghazi* is a man who has taken an oath to kill some non-Mohammadan, preferably a European, as representing the ruling race; but, failing that, a Hindu or a Sikh. The mullah instills in him the idea that if in doing so he loses his own life, he goes at once to Paradise . . . and the gardens which are set apart for religious martyrs.[1]

After much bloodletting, the British realized that any attempt at permanent occupation or pacification of the warring tribes would only unite them, and that it would be nearly impossible to defeat their combined forces without much greater military and financial means than Britain could afford. So Britain finally settled on a policy of containment, institutionalized by Lord Curzon, Viceroy of India. Having come to India in 1899, shortly after one bad spate of Wazir and Mehsud uprisings, Curzon had established the North-West Frontier Province (NWFP) as a buffer zone, splitting the tribal areas between Afghanistan and that part of British India which is now Pakistan. "Our policy was to interfere as little as possible with the internal organization and independence of the tribes," he said, and by *control and conciliation* "endeavour to win them over" to secure the frontier.[2]

Control involved withdrawing British forces from direct administration of the frontier region, including parts of Afghanistan, "for which our Regular troops were neither recruited nor suited," Curzon noted. Some well-defended outposts would remain to protect the roads that were being built to help integrate and secure the tribes through commerce (Afghanistan still has no railroad network). But the government would most rely on "forces of tribal Militia, levies and police, recruited from the tribesmen themselves," though trained and directed by English officers. Conciliation meant subsidizing the "friendlies" to hold off the "hostiles" until they, too, realized that it was in their own self-interest to accept British bounty for abandoning their traditional "outlaw" ways, or at least raids against British territory.

After the partition of India in 1947, the successor state of Pakistan continued the policy of co-opting "friendlies" with various incentives (arms, money,

Map of Pakistan's Federally Administered Tribal Areas.

political position) to hold off the hostiles. Going a step further, the country's founder, Muhammad Ali Jinnah, decided that concentrations of regular troops from the brigade level up would be evacuated from Waziristan and the other Federally Administered Tribal Areas wedged between the NWFP and Afghanistan. He aptly called his plan Operation Curzon.[3]

THE THIRTY YEARS' WAR AND THE RISE OF THE TALIBAN

The Pashtun comprise over 40 percent of Afghanistan's population, about the same as a century ago. The Tajiks contribute almost 30 percent; the Hazara and Uzbek each just a bit less than 10 percent. But the Pashtun have long dominated the country, politically and militarily. Except for a nine-month interlude in 1929, Durranis lorded over the country until the communist takeover in 1978 that killed Mohammed Daoud Khan.

Daoud's government and its predecessor had been very wary of introducing reforms, especially concerning the status of women. They feared the kind of unrest that had unseated Amanullah, the Durrani amir who had fought the British in the third Anglo-Afghan War to gain full independence for his country in 1921. Inspired by the policies of Turkey's secular reformer Kemal Ataturk, Amanullah embarked on an ambitious modernization program, which resulted in a rebellion of Pashtun tribal and religious leaders that removed him from the throne in 1929. He was initially replaced by an ethnic Tajik, whom the Pashtuns came to view as an usurper. So the tribesmen threw their support behind one of Amanullah's generals, Zahir's father, who had been exiled by Amanullah for questioning the wisdom of the amir's policies. He sacked Kabul in 1929 with mostly Wazir and Mehsud tribal forces and became king. Despite the assassination of Zahir's father in 1933, and Daoud's coup in 1973, Afghanistan enjoyed half a century (1929–1978) of relative peace and accommodation between the central government and the tribes.

This was followed by a Thirty Years' War that began when the communist government threw caution to the wind and immediately proclaimed a secular socialist government that tried to force far-reaching land reforms and push programs to better the status of women. The tribes rebelled, the regime was about to collapse, and so the Soviets invaded Afghanistan in December 1979 to "save socialism." The radical reforms were rescinded, but the Soviet occupation generated even greater tribal resistance. The call to jihad brought in Muslim volunteers from around the world, and financial and logistical support from Pakistan, Saudi Arabia, and the United States. In 1980, U.S. National Security Adviser Zbigniew Brzezinski, swathed in a Pashtun turban and waving an AK-47 near the Khyber Pass, exhorted the mujahedin to fight "because your cause is right and God is on your side. . . . Allahu Akbar!"[4]

Pashtun traditionally identify themselves first and foremost by *qawm*, which Westerners usually translate as "clan," a subtribal identity traditionally based on kinship and residence. In the past, male members of each qawm were invariably blood-related. But the change toward a market economy has somewhat lessened the strict importance of kin relations and encouraged new qawms based on patron-client economic networks.[5] More recently, *qawm* has come to mean any segment of society bound by solidarity ties, whether by kinship and residence, occupation and patron-client relations, religious interests, or dialect. A qawm can involve a varying number of individuals, depending on context and situation. During the Soviet-Afghan War, as in the present Taliban insurgency, the notion of *qawm* became even more ambiguous and flexible to allow for strategic manipulations of identity to carry out group actions in shifting contexts.[6] But especially among the hill tribes, qawms are still heavily family-oriented and much the primary reference groups for military action.

The mujahedin fought primarily to defend their faith and community against a hostile ideology, an oppressive government, and a foreign invader: "It was a spontaneous defense of community values and a traditional way of life by individual groups initially unconnected to national or international political organizations."[7] Their tactics differed from place to place, qawm to qawm. Although few guerilla commanders were military professionals, Afghanistan under Daoud and Zahir had a conscript army in which most twenty-two-year-old males served two years. The tribes scorned professional soldiers as mercenaries, but they had supported the draft because it provided basic military know-how that helped boys become men even in peacetime. Friendships made during military service also later eased cooperation among guerrilla groups.[8]

Over the course of the war, state institutions decayed. But there were also profound changes in local communities that helped pave the way for the emergence of the Taliban after the war. The old elite of large landowners and tribal elders ceded to a new cadre of younger military hotshots from less prestigious backgrounds who began to play an important role in the administration of community life. At the same time, there was a sharp expansion of the role of the Islamic clergy (*ulema*). Clerics with an advanced madrassah education (*malawi*) and knowledge of Sharia enjoyed greater prestige than the boorish mullahs. The ulema were able to leverage this prestige into political influence that cut across tribal boundaries by networking with Pakistani political parties that funneled money and supplies to the mujahedin (some provided to them by the United States via Pakistani intelligence) and by morally restraining military commanders from arbitrary actions that benefited only themselves and their kin.[9]

Soviet forces withdrew in February 1989. But only after the Soviet Union collapsed, ending all outside assistance to a local client regime that was holding on by the skin of its teeth, did Kabul fall to the mujahedin forces, in April 1992. The mujahedin immediately took to fighting among themselves for control of the city and the countryside. A state of near-anarchy prevailed as demobilized and penniless warriors became outlaws who preyed even on women and the weak. Reacting to a series of outrages around the southern city of Kandahar, a small group of religious students (*taliban*), led by their teacher, Mullah Omar, killed the worst of the bandits in 1994 and proclaimed a new movement, the Taliban, that would unify the country by using the sword of pure virtue to cut away all vice (including the playing of music, shaving the face, and educating women). With Pakistan's aid, their power spread to other Pashtun areas. Taliban forces took Kabul in 1996 (although Mullah Omar chose to remain in Kandahar) and extended control over the whole country except the Tajik-controlled northeast by 1998.

Final victory came to the Taliban on September 9, 2001, when, with Al Qaeda's assistance, a suicide bomber posing as a journalist managed to kill Ahmad Shah Massoud, the legendary Tajik commander of the Northern Alliance known as the Lion of Panshir. Two days later, Al Qaeda attacked the United States, apparently without informing the Taliban leadership of its plans. Most probably, Bin Laden assumed that by helping the Taliban to win Afghanistan, Qaeda was free to use the country as its base from which to launch attacks. Taliban religious leaders, however, judged that Bin Laden had abused his status as a "guest" in the country and urged Mullah Omar to "invite" Bin Laden to leave.

The United States would not wait upon such customs, which were judged insincere (but wrongly so, as we'll see). With U.S. air and special forces in support, the Northern Alliance entered Kabul in November 2001. In Afghanistan, a governing coalition rapidly emerged of Afghanistan's Durrani president, Hamid Karzai, and the Tajik-led successors of the U.S.-backed Northern Alliance. The Taliban opposition in the country has come to include disaffected Durranis, Ghilzai, and factions of the Karlandri confederation (such as the Haqqani of the Zadran tribe, whose leader Jalaluddin was called "goodness personified" during the Soviet-Afghan War by Congressman Charlie Wilson,[10] and is today one of Al Qaeda's principal allies).

When U.S.-backed forces first swept through Afghanistan, many of the remaining Taliban commanders fled for sanctuary to the Pashtun border regions of Pakistan. The Americans then began bombing these sanctuaries from the air and prodding the Pakistani army to make fitful incursions into tribal areas. The result was that hitherto unaligned Pakistani Pashtun began joining forces with the Afghan Taliban and Al Qaeda. This, in turn, has enabled Al Qaeda to survive, the Afghan Taliban to regroup and take the fight back into Afghanistan, and the Pakistani Taliban to emerge as a threat to Pakistan itself.

Pakistani Taliban are mostly enlisted from factions of the Mehsud, Wazir, and other Karlandri tribes. Before 2001, many of these tribal factions were largely unresponsive to the Afghan Taliban program to homogenize and integrate tribal custom, and suppress tribal independence under a single religious administration that claimed strict adherence to Sharia (in fact, a peculiarly Pashtun version of Sharia with a heavy dose of tribal custom). But the Pashtun border tribes became outraged at the Pakistani government for sending troops into the area and allowing Americans to bomb their homelands in an effort to kill off Al Qaeda and root out the Afghan Taliban. In Pakistan today, there's no overarching Taliban organization that commands and controls the actions of its numerous tribal factions and unaffiliated adherents (often foot soldiers who fight for pay, status, and other rewards).

In the past, the Afghan Taliban tried to suppress tribal sentiments and the role of the qawms. Now, the New Taliban vie with the U.S.-backed coalition to enlist these sentiments to turn the qawms into militia. Both sides have grudgingly bowed to the fact that Pashtun politics is indeed truly local and that local politics must be mastered before grander schemes are tried. The problem is that the Taliban are better at this than we are.

A MATTER OF HONOR

A key factor helping the Taliban is the moral outrage of Pashtun tribes against those who deny them autonomy, including a right to bear arms to defend their tribal code, known as Pashtunwali. Its sacred tenets include protecting women's purity (*namus*), the right to personal revenge (*badal*), the sanctity of the guest (*melmastia*), and sanctuary (*nanawateh*). Among all Pashtun tribes, inheritance, wealth, social prestige, and political status accrue through the father's line.

This social structure means that there can be no suspicion that the male pedigree (often traceable in lineages spanning centuries) is "corrupted" by doubtful paternity. Thus, revenge for sexual misbehavior (rape, adultery, abduction) warrants killing seven members of the offending group and often the "offending" woman. Yet hospitality trumps vengeance: If a group accepts a guest, all must honor him, even if prior grounds justify revenge. That's one reason American offers of millions for betraying Osama Bin Laden continued to fail.

Afghan hill societies have withstood many would-be conquests and bouts of turmoil by keeping order with Pashtunwali in the absence of central authority and state institutions.[11] When seemingly intractable conflicts arise, like repeating cycles of revenge or problems caused by hosting guests and giving sanctuary, rival parties convene councils (*jirgas*) of elders and third parties to seek solutions through consensus.[12] Although the Taliban argue that Sharia always supersedes Pashtunwali, in fact the Taliban's idiosyncratic version of Sharia incorporates Pashtunwali's main tenets. For example, in allowing executions for murder or violations of women to be carried out by members of the aggrieved family, state punishment is confounded with personal revenge.

A common view in the West is that the blood feuds and the restriction of women "to the home or the tomb" are intrinsic to the Muslim religion or to the primitiveness of the Pashtun. But anthropologists will tell you that the constant fission and fusion of the tribes, and stringent enforcement of women's isolation from men, have more to do with the way some societies at the margins of the desert have adapted their social structures to extreme fluctuations in the availability of resources and the intense competition for them. Arabs and Kurds,[13] Pashtuns and Pathans,[14] Persian Bakhtiaris and Baluchis,[15] all share this basic social structure.

This social structure, which resembles a constantly branching tree, but where the branches become ever more entangled through marriage alliances, generates myriad ways of maneuvering for control over women, flocks, land, political allies, and other resources. When resources become scarce and competition intensifies, tribal relationships may contract and the patrilineages begin to tear apart at their branching points—and so the saying: "Me against my brother, brothers against cousins, cousins against the clan, clans against the tribe, the tribes against the world." These tribal segments, or factions, may then go on to seek out alliances of convenience even with distant and unrelated groups—hence, "the enemy of my enemy is my friend," even if the enemies of the moment are from one's own kin group and the friends are from another.[16]

A structural corollary to maintaining this flexible system of alliances is the honor-bound duty to harbor the "guest," whether friend or foe (because any foe is also a potential friend, and vice versa). As Pennell noted, "the relationship between host and guest is inviolable." He leveraged this fact to get the mullahs, who otherwise would have had his head, to tolerate his medical missionary work: "After having offered us hospitality and broken bread with us, we should be recognized as guests of the Mullah, and any opposition which he might have been contemplating against us would be seen at once by the observant Afghans around to have been laid aside in favour of the reception due to an honoured guest."[17]

Here is how anthropologist Thomas Barfield analyzed the internal Taliban debate over what to do with their Qaeda guests shortly after 9/11:

With a nuanced approach that would have done credit to any Pashtun tribal *jirga*, the assembled clerics told Omar that he must indeed protect his guest, but that because a guest should not cause his host problems, Osama should be asked to leave Afghanistan voluntarily as soon as possible. It is notable that the question Omar tabled was not one of *sharia* jurisprudence, but rather an issue of Pashtunwali. Very fittingly, the last major policy decision of the Taliban before they were driven from Afghanistan was based on good customary law standards in which religious law provided only window dressing.[18]

While Mullah Omar readily gave sanctuary to Bin Laden after his expulsion from Sudan in 1996, Qaeda's attacks on the U.S. embassies in Kenya and Tanzania in 1998 and the 2000 bombing of the USS *Cole* focused intense international hostility on the Taliban. In June 2001, Omar declared that Bin Laden had no authority to issue fatwas, confiscated the Qaeda leader's satellite phone, and put him under armed guard. The 9/11 Commission Report notes that Omar had previously "invited" Bin Laden to move to where he might be easier to control after the Qaeda leader gave an inflammatory interview on CNN in 1997. For their part, a number of jihadi leaders denounced Bin Laden's association with the "infidel" Taliban, religious deviants "created and controlled by Pakistan" and its intelligence services and thus worthy of excommunication (*takfir*).[19]

Instead of keeping pressure on the Taliban to resolve the issue in ways they could live with, the United States ridiculed their deliberation and bombed them into a closer alliance with Al Qaeda. Pakistani Pashtun then offered sanctuary to their Afghan brethren and guests.

Recently, someone who served with the U.S. Afghan mission for some years asked if I would be willing to help evaluate America's success in winning hearts and minds. The first thing I asked her was: "Do the Afghans you're in contact with accept Americans as guests, and do the Americans act as if they were guests?" A bit startled, she answered, "Of course not, we're here because we have to be." I then asked, "Do they act as if they are the hosts and masters?" She didn't respond at first, so I gave her this scenario: "Surely you must have seen or heard about accidents on the road involving a U.S. military vehicle colliding with some Afghan's donkey-drawn cart. What happened? Do the American military personnel come out of the vehicle and try to help the poor fellow?" Her answer: "Never. They leave the scene, those are the rules of the engagement; any Afghan knows where to find us to lodge a complaint or make a claim." I told her that I'd bet my bottom dollar that Al Qaeda doesn't behave that way, because they understand what it means to be a guest, and that's one good reason why they survive among the Pashtun tribes.

In the summer of 2009, U.S. Secretary of State Hillary Clinton declared: "We and our Afghan allies stand ready to welcome anyone supporting the Taliban who renounces Al Qaeda, lays down their arms, and is willing to participate in the free and open society that is enshrined in the Afghan constitution."[20] To get the tribesmen to lay down arms for a flag that many do not even know represents the country is about as farfetched as getting the National Rifle Association to support a constitutional repeal of Americans' right to bear arms. Moreover, as Marc Sageman observes, "There's no Al Qaeda in Afghanistan and no Afghans in Al Qaeda."[21] The original alliance between the Taliban and Al Qaeda was largely one of convenience between a poverty-stricken national movement and a transnational cause that brought material help. U.S. pressure on Pakistan to hit the Taliban and Al Qaeda in their current sanctuary birthed the Pakistani Taliban, who forge their own ties to Al Qaeda to undermine the Pakistani state that has attacked them. While some Taliban use the rhetoric of global jihad to inspire their ranks or enlist foreign fighters into their insurgency, they showed no inclination to hit Western interests abroad before 2010. The continued presence of Qaeda remnants in Pakistan, and Pakistani Taliban attacks on the state, including at least three attacks on nuclear facilities,[22] warrants concerted action in Pakistan, not Afghanistan. Pakistan understands this and engages unaligned Taliban against antigovernment and pro-Qaeda Taliban to meet the threat (well aware that all Taliban support insurgency against foreign troops in Afghanistan).

Here, despite U.S. pressure, Pakistan prefers a policy, seasoned by wars, of "respect for the independence and sentiment of the tribes" advised by Lord Curzon: as "we are dealing with an enemy habituated to every form and habit of guerrilla warfare, even if [military action] attended with maximum success, no permanent results can be obtained," while the Afghan frontier would be "ablaze from one end to the other [causing] an intolerable burden on finances."[23]

U.S.-sponsored "reconciliation" may be fatally flawed in demanding that Pashtun hill tribes give up the arms that have kept them independent (or that they join progovernment militia), and support a constitution that values Western-inspired rights and judicial institutions over customary canons and forms of consensus that have sustained the tribes against all enemies. U.S. presidential envoy Richard Holbrooke suggests that victory in Afghanistan is possible if those Taliban who pursue self-interest, rather than "ideology," can be co-opted with material incentives. But as veteran war correspondent Jason Burke said to me: "Today, the logical thing for the Pashtun conservatives is to stop fighting and get rich through narcotics or Western aid, the latter being much lower risk. But many won't sell out."[24] Although newer, fair-weather Taliban are deep into the drug trade, as are government allies who help to make it Afghanistan's main economy, committed veteran Taliban have tended to avoid at least internal trafficking on moral grounds (whereas producing and selling drugs for consumption by infidels is righteous).

Outsiders who do not understand local cultural and group dynamics tend to ride roughshod over values they don't grasp. To improve women's status in Pashtun lands may take time (it took women's suffrage a century in our country), and as the Soviets learned there, not by foreign programs. As we find again and again—in our research in Morocco, Palestine, Iran, Pakistan, India, and Indonesia—helping to materially improve lives will not reduce support for violence, and can even increase it, if people feel such help compromises their most cherished values. And do we really want to build up a society with so-called friendlies or reconcilables who can turn to or away from us on a dime?

WHEN LESS IS MORE

Al Qaeda is already on the ropes globally, with ever-dwindling financial and popular support and a drastically diminished ability to work with other extremists worldwide, much less command them in major operations. Its lethal agents are being systematically hunted down, while those Muslims whose souls it seeks to save are increasingly revolted by its methods.

Unfortunately, this weakening viral movement that abuses religion may have a new lease on life in Afghanistan and Pakistan because we are pushing the Taliban into its arms. By overestimating the threat from Al Qaeda in Afghanistan, we are making it a greater threat to Pakistan and the world. Afghanistan and the tribal areas of Pakistan are unlike Iraq, the ancient birthplace of central government, or 1960s Vietnam, where a strong state was backing the Communist insurgents. Afghanistan and Pakistan must be dealt with on their own terms.

We're winning against Al Qaeda in places where antiterrorism efforts are local and built on the understanding that the ties binding terror networks now are more cultural and familial than political. Take Southeast Asia. The three sets of factors that our research found to be responsible for operations prepared by Jemaah Islamiyah–affiliated extremists—friendship through fighting (Afghan Alumni), kinship and marriage, and school ties and discipleship (madrassah connections)—were also implicitly understood by local security forces and used to track and break up the terrorist networks.[25]

Similarly, security officials in the Philippines have combined intelligence from American and Australian sources with similar tracking efforts to crack down on their terrorist networks, and as a result most extremist groups are either seeking reconciliation with the government—including the deadly Moro Islamic Liberation Front on the island of Mindanao—or have devolved into kidnapping-and-extortion gangs with no ideological focus. The separatist Abu Sayyaf group, once the most feared force in the region, now has no overall spiritual or military leaders, few weapons, and only a hundred or so fighters.[26]

In the West, Al Qaeda's main focus, there hasn't been a successful attack directly commanded by Bin Laden and company since 9/11. The American invasion of Afghanistan devastated Al Qaeda's core of top personnel and its training camps. In an October 2009 appearance before the Senate Foreign Relations Committee, Sageman testified that "seventy-eight percent of all global neo-jihadi terrorist plots in the West in the past five years came from autonomous homegrown groups without any connection, direction or control from al Qaeda Core or its allies [and] refutes claims by some heads of the intelligence community that all Islamist plots in the West can be traced back to the Afghan-Pakistani border."[27] The real threat is homegrown youths who gain inspiration from Bin Laden but little else beyond an occasional self-financed spell at a degraded Qaeda-linked training facility.

The 2003 invasion of Iraq encouraged many of these local plots, including the train bombings in Madrid in 2004 and London in 2005. In their aftermaths, European law and security forces

stopped plots from coming to fruition by stepping up coordination and tracking links among local extremists, their friends, and
friends of friends, while also improving relations with young Muslim immigrants through community outreach. Morocco, Saudi
Arabia, and Turkey have taken similar steps.

Now we need to bring this perspective to Afghanistan and Pakistan—one that is smart about cultures, customs, and connections. The
present policy of focusing on troop strength and drones, trying to win
over people by improving their lives with Western-style aid programs,
only continues a long history of foreign involvement and failure.

Of course, antiterrorism measures are only as effective as the
local governments that execute them. Afghanistan's government is
corrupt, unpopular, and inept. So what do we do? There's no Taliban central to talk to (although the United States and NATO are
talking to locals who fight them, with some local successes). To be
a Taliban today means little more than to be a Pashtun tribesman
who believes that his fundamental beliefs and customary way of
life, including the right to bear arms to defend the tribal homeland
and protect its women, are threatened by foreign invaders.[28]

While most Taliban claim loyalty to Afghanistan's Mullah
Omar, this allegiance varies greatly: Pakistani Taliban leaders,
including Baitullah Mehsud, who was killed by an American drone
in August 2009, and his successor, Hakimullah Mehsud, wounded
by a drone in early 2010, rejected Mullah Omar's call to forgo suicide bombings against Pakistani civilians. Although American officials constantly pressure Pakistan to root out the Haqqani fighters,
who are perhaps the deadliest foes of NATO forces in Afghanistan, Pakistan's military considers the Haqqanis assets to influence the future shape of Afghanistan once the Americans leave.[29]
Pakistani security forces also use other branches of the Mehsud
who call themselves "Taliban" in the fight against Americans in
Afghanistan, to battle fellow Taliban who attack Pakistan.[30]

We hold the Taliban together. Without us, their deeply divided coalition could well fragment. The resurgent strength of today's Taliban depends on support by notoriously unruly Pashtun hill tribes in Pakistan's border regions unsympathetic to the original Taliban program of homogenizing tribal custom and politics under one rule. And the Taliban could well kick out Bin Laden if he became more of a headache to them than we are: Al Qaeda may have close relations to the Haqqani network of the Zadran tribe in North Waziristan and to the Shabi-Khel subtribe of the Mehsud out of South Waziristan, but Qaeda isn't so popular with many Taliban factions and forces.

We have already been through one round of cranking up forces in Afghanistan, and it backfired. Until 2004, the U.S.-led NATO coalition had a modest footprint in Afghanistan of about 20,000 troops, mainly to protect Kabul, and there were few terrorist acts such as suicide attacks and roadside bombings: fewer than ten from 2001 to 2004. During 2005, the coalition started to ratchet up troop levels in order to wipe out the last vestiges of the Taliban and to eradicate poppy crops. According to data collected by Robert Pape, suicide attacks increased by an order of magnitude—with 9 in 2005, nearly 100 in 2006, 142 in 2007, and 148 in 2008.[31] There were 739 roadside bombings in 2006, nearly 2,000 in 2007, and more than 3,200 in 2008. Unlike Iraq, nearly all suicide attacks and roadside bombings have targeted coalition forces and installations rather than the civilian population.

In August 2009, General Stanley McChrystal, the top allied commander in Afghanistan, reported that the situation had become "serious. . . . We face not only a resilient and growing insurgency; there is also a crisis of confidence among Afghans—in both their government and the international community—that undermines our credibility and emboldens the insurgents."[32] Thus a radical change in U.S. policy was needed for two reasons: "Our conventional warfare culture" has alienated the people, and there is a lack of "responsive and accountable government" to win them over. The report recommended "radically expanded coalition forces at every echelon," to gain the initiative and to protect "those critical areas where the population is most threatened." And so in 2010, additional Western forces were deployed in all major regions, including the Pashtun areas in the south and east, bringing the total to well over a hundred thousand, on par with Soviet military involvement thirty years before.

There was precious little in the McChrystal report to suggest that our continuing support of the central government would make it any less corroded. As one senior U.S. counternarcotics official put it to me in September 2009:

> My personal opinion is that Karzai's brother is a crook and is involved in constructing the framework of what Afghanistan is becoming, where there is no other economy than the drug trade. With the fox in the henhouse, the hens will never be safe. [The departments of] Defense and State have spent close to ten billion [dollars] to counter [the drug economy] in Afghanistan. If you look at just eradication, it's close to four billion. There were some years where we eradicated less than five hundred hectares per year, or more than ten million per hectare, which doesn't make sense.

Even a "good" year, like 2008, saw only 5,000 hectares eradicated out of more than 150,000 cultivated. A 3 percent risk on losing a crop deters nobody from planting poppies for huge profit.[33]

The Taliban were morally rigid and did detestable things, especially to women, but by and large they weren't corrupt. The people hardly loved the Taliban, but appreciated that they stopped widespread rape and pillage and effectively brought order to the country. The original Taliban were just as aggressive as the Communists in trying to use military force to impose a single political administration and worldview on the fractious Afghan population. But the Taliban were far less centralized, and their worldview was far less alien to the Pashtun tribes whose children, orphaned and separated from their elders by the war against the Communists and then civil war, had become the foot soldiers of the Taliban's New Order.

General McChrystal's report relied on celebrity politicos (like Anthony Cordesman) and a few experienced with Afghanistan's people (like former National Public Radio reporter Sarah Chays).[34] The five teams of the "Human Terrain System" experiment in Helmand, Paktia, and other Afghan Pashtun areas, which embedded uniformed and armed cultural anthropologists in infantry units, also provided "peripheral input" (as one team member put it to me). Nevertheless, the report was a public relations and political success. It prodded President Obama to commit thirty thousand more troops to a counterinsurgency effort against a major segment of the Afghan population, with the focus on converting a deeply unpopular and corrupt regime into a unified, centralized state for the first time in that country's history.

Unlike Al Qaeda, the Taliban are interested in *their* homeland, not ours. True, some now threaten to attack American cities in retaliation for hundreds of their family and friends recently killed by drones, such as Hakimullah Mehsud and his cousin Qari Hussain Mehsud, who trains suicide bombers for the Pakistani Taliban and claimed support for would-be Times Square bomber, Faisal Shahzad, as "revenge for the rain of drones." But other Pakistani Taliban vociferously deny any wish to attack America. Things are different now from what they were before 9/11. The Taliban know how costly keeping Qaeda can be. There's a good chance that enough of the factions in the loose and fractious Taliban coalition would decide for themselves to disinvite their troublesome guest if we contained them by maintaining pressure without trying to subdue them or hold their territory, intervening only when we see movement to help Al Qaeda or act beyond the region. A long leash on the Taliban is likely to be far more effective than a short one. And in the fight against violent extremism more generally, as far as our direct involvement goes, less just may be more.[35]

CHAPTER 16
THE TERROR SCARE: EXAGGERATING THREATS AT HOME AND ABROAD

> Man prefers to believe what he prefers to be true.
>
> —FRANCIS BACON

PINK ELEPHANTS

A woman was standing at a bus stop, wildly flailing her umbrella. A curious onlooker approached and asked, "Why do you keep waving your umbrella about?"

The woman replied with some annoyance that such an idiotic question should be asked of her: "Why, to keep the pink elephants away, of course."

"But, my dear lady," the onlooker protested, "there are no pink elephants around."

The woman, exasperated, retorted, "Precisely, because I keep them away."

The Pink Elephant Fallacy is an example of the simplest of all failures of critical thought, circular reasoning. We are told that U.S. troops fight in Iraq and Afghanistan to keep Al Qaeda from attacking the United States. Some say, "But there is no evidence that Al Qaeda now has the means or plans to attack the United States." The answer they get is: "Precisely, because our troops in Iraq and Afghanistan keep Al Qaeda away."[1]

At a town hall meeting in Shanghai with Chinese students in late 2009, President Obama reiterated George W. Bush's claim that "the greatest threat to United States security are terrorist networks like Al Qaeda,"[2] an opinion echoed in Europe.[3] But how great a threat is terrorism, really? Certainly 9/11 was a massive, murderous attack, but not one with serious effects on America's national fabric—apart from those caused by the country's fitful *reaction* to the attack, which continues to focus on wiping out the threat by means of our might rather than containing it with the help of others who manage some things better.

By itself contemporary terrorism cannot destroy our country or our allies or even seriously damage us. However, we can do grievous harm to ourselves by taking the terrorists' bait and reacting in ill-conceived, uninformed, and uncontrolled ways that inflate and so empower our enemies, alienate our friends, and frighten our own citizens into believing that they must give up basic liberties in order to survive. It is in this sense that terrorism does pose an existential threat: to our most sacred values of individual freedom and choice, to our sense of personal and collective security, and to any hope of peace of mind. Our fitful reaction also risks empowering extremist elements in less secure states, such as Iraq, Iran, Afghanistan, and Pakistan, which could end up producing a true strategic menace.

THE NEW WAVE

The cases we've looked at suggest that the growth and development of terrorist networks is largely a decentralized and evolutionary process, based on contingent adaptations to unpredictable events and improbable opportunities, more the result of localized tinkering (of fragmentary connections between semi-autonomous parts) than intelligent design (hierarchical command and control). As in any natural evolutionary process, individual variation and environmental context are the creative and critical determinants of future directions and paths. To ignore variation and context is to entirely miss the character of natural group formation and development, along with better chances for intervention and prevention of enemy attacks from the bottom up rather than from the top down.

Ever since the second U.S.-led interventions in Iraq and Afghanistan, and with the rapid spread of Internet access, we are witnessing a more egalitarian (at least among males), less educated and materially well off, and more socially marginalized wave of would-be jihadi martyrs. Those few who are willing to commit to extremist violence usually emerge in small groups of action-oriented friends. They frequently come from the same neighborhood and interact during sporting activities, such as playing soccer together or becoming camping and hiking companions who learn to take care of one another under trying conditions. Increasingly, they may first meet in a chat room, where anonymity on the Worldwide Web paradoxically helps to forge intimate emotional ties among people who might otherwise physically put one another off. They learn to live in a conceptually closed community of comrades bound to a cause, which they mistake for the real world. Although more nationally oriented militant groups, such as Hamas and Lebanese Hizbollah, have tended to resemble the earlier Al Qaeda in being generally more educated, skilled, and well-off economically than the surrounding population, they, too, are beginning to show regression to a more meager state. (Though Hizbollah, which is backed by the Iranian state and adheres to a Shi'ite tradition of a strong religious hierarchy alien to the Sunni, retains a well-organized and worldwide chain of command and control.)

In the United States, most arrests and convictions for terrorism have involved entrapment by law enforcement agents of jihadi wannabes usually far from being able to actually execute a plot. Because the path that leads to extremist violence usually involves numerous contingent and even random factors, it's far from likely that most of those arrested would have gone on to violence on their own or through their natural milieu. In 2003 the FBI arrested

Iyman Faris, an Ohio trucker who met Qaeda people in Pakistan and then wanted to destroy the Brooklyn Bridge with blowtorches, a crackpot plan as likely to succeed as selling the bridge to Warren Buffett. Another half-baked scheme involved four Muslim immigrants in the Philadelphia area who were convicted in December 2008 of plotting to storm Fort Dix in New Jersey (and perhaps also the Dover Air Force Base in Delaware) disguised as pizza deliverymen. The investigation was prompted by a clerk at a local store who informed police that he was asked by one of the men to copy a tape containing scenes of militants firing into the air and calling for jihad. It's pretty clear government informants prodded the men into making incriminating comments for wiretaps.

Less harebrained, but still far from execution, was a September 2009 plot by Najibullah Zazi, an airport bus driver, and Zarein Ahmedzay, a New York City cabbie, to bomb the New York subway. They trained in Pakistan with another accomplice to fight Americans in Afghanistan, but Qaeda operatives, including Rashid Rauf, a planner of the 2006 plot to blow up U.S.-bound planes with liquid explosives, convinced them to return home to do something, as the 2005 London Underground bombers had done. On May 1, 2010, Faisal Shahzad bungled the execution of a car bomb in Times Square. The son of a former Pakistani air force general, Shahzad became an American-educated MBA and naturalized citizen. But by summer 2009 he had lost his Connecticut home to the bank, left his job, and seemed estranged from his wife. He found solace in a militant religious rebirth, went to see family in Pakistan and "find himself" again, wanted to fight Americans in Afghanistan (his father was against it), and found jihad when a militant friend apparently steered him to Pakistani Taliban leaders. After a primer in bomb making in Waziristan, Shahzad returned to avenge America's assault on fellow Muslims and his own aspirations.

"No one wants to believe that the threat inside our country comes mainly from disaffected young men," one top FBI official told me, "and it rarely goes beyond fantasy, although if somebody did manage to do something, and we were caught with our pants down, Congress and the public would go bananas." When sleepers have been brought up in public as a "near certainty,"[4] including by former CIA director George Tenet,[5] those in the know just grit their teeth in silence.

Matters remain worse in Britain and other parts of western Europe, where even middle-class Muslim youth often feel socially marginalized and liable to seek universal meaning for frustrated personal aspirations in a violent mass movement. Consider the train bombings in Madrid (2004) and London (2005) and a foiled series of independent plots to blow up planes out of Heathrow Airport (summer 2006), to car-bomb London landmarks (summer 2007), to attack targets in Denmark and Germany (fall 2007), and to hit Barcelona's subway (winter 2008).

European governments have begun developing culturally smart outreach programs for marginalized Muslim youth. But the continued focus on cultivating moderate imams remains pretty irrelevant. In fact, very few people ever become terrorists in mosques. They may gather and plan outside some mosques, as did the 9/11 plotters from Hamburg and the Madrid train bombers, but even they did most of their plotting hanging out together in neighborhood restaurants and barbershops, playing sports, and in their friends' homes.

These young people self-mobilize to the tune of a simple, superficial, but broadly appealing *takfiri* message of withdrawal from impure mainstream society and of a need for violent action to cleanse it. It is a surprisingly flat but fluid message preadapted to any new event in the world, and it is readily shared by young people I have interviewed across Eurasia and North Africa.

One telltale sign of radicalization in the move to Takfirism is when members of a neighborhood mosque or cultural center (or just an informal discussion group that meets at a bookstore or at picnics) gel into a militant faction. This is what happened, for example, when the soccer-playing Salafi imam at the M-30 mosque in Madrid expelled Serhane Fakhet, the Tunisian, and friends (who continued to self-radicalize, playing soccer and picnicking together in the lead-up to the Madrid train bombings) or when Ali al-Timimi and his group of paintball buddies were ejected from the Dar al-Arqam Cultural Center in Falls Church, Virginia, after praising the 9/11 attack (twelve members were later convicted of aiding the Pakistani jihadi group Lashkar-e-Taiba).

Western politicians, pundits, and publics generally do not understand that the strict Salafi schools in Indonesia, Egypt, Saudi Arabia, Yemen, and elsewhere are the most vociferous and effective opponents of violent jihad. Salafi Islam is the host on which this viral Takfiri movement rides, not unlike the relationship between Christian fundamentalism and white supremacism. The host itself is not the cause of the virus and is, indeed, a primary victim. As one senior Saudi intelligence officer recently told me, "Often the first signs of someone becoming a Takfiri is that he stops praying where his family and tribe pray. He leaves the mosque and turns against his family, tribe, and our Salafi way." Most present-day Takfiris are "born again" in their late teens and early twenties and have little knowledge of religion beyond the fact that they consider themselves true Muslims who must fight enemies near and far to defend their friends and the faith that makes their friendship meaningful and enduring. Enlistment into training and actions can come via any number of routes: most often through friends or relatives or fellow travelers one happens to meet looking for ways to join the jihad.

Many academic and counterterrorism experts refer to predictive factors in "recruitment." In its heyday, Al Qaeda operated more like a funding agency than a military organization. People would come to Al Qaeda with proposals for plots. Al Qaeda would accept some 10 percent to 20 percent.[6] As we've seen, even the 9/11 suicide pilots were not "recruited" into Al Qaeda. There's no clear evidence that Al Qaeda ever had a recruiting or training infrastructure in Europe, although there is evidence that Al Qaeda and Qaeda-related groups in Pakistan's tribal areas maintain some communication with Europeans after they train in Pakistan, especially those implicated in post-9/11 plots involving the United Kingdom and United States.

Generally, however, people go looking for Al Qaeda, not the other way around. Because there's very little of the old Al Qaeda left, many who go seeking Al Qaeda are caught. Those who seek out Al Qaeda usually do so in small groups of friends and occasionally through kin. Most are schoolmates or workmates via camp or soccer or paintball, or friends who share some other study or sports activity. Some have steady jobs and family, some have only intermittent jobs and no families of their own. All have self-radicalized to some degree before they go for Al Qaeda, although an encounter with someone who has been to a Qaeda-friendly training camp in Afghanistan is occasionally an added stimulant. The overwhelming majority have not had sustained prior religious education but have become "born again" into radical Islam in their late teens and early twenties. A small percentage are Christian converts.[7]

For example, in the wake of the Iraq invasion in April 2003, a disciple of the radical Islamist preacher Sheikh Omar Bakri organized a barbecue in a London suburb for about a hundred people, most from the immigrant Pakistani community. Guests were asked for donations to help send a few volunteers to Pakistan to train for jihad. Among those who used some of the 3,500 pounds collected to pay their way to Pakistan were Mohammed Sidique Khan, one of the four suicide bombers in the July 2005 London Underground attack, and Omar Khyam, one of the conspirators convicted in the 2005 "Crevice" plot to plant fertilizer bombs around London. Their original intention was to do jihad in Kashmir, but after a quick course in bomb making, they were told to "go home" and do something there. Each joined up with a few friends to concoct a plot. Interviews by journalist Jason Burke with friends of the Crevice conspirators suggest that ten days of arduous hiking, camping, and training in Pakistan cemented commitment among buddies.[8] White-water rafting seems to have played a role in bonding the London Underground plotters (although training in a Qaeda-affiliated camp also played a role in this case). One of the four London suicide bombers was a Jamaican Christian convert and pinball buddy of others in the plot.

The boundaries of the newer-wave networks are very loose, and the Internet now allows anyone who wishes to become a terrorist to become one, anywhere, anytime. For example, the "Al Ansar" chat-room network involved plotting in half a dozen countries (United States, Britain, Canada, Sweden, Denmark, Bosnia) by young men, many of whom had never physically met. They would hack into media sites in the American Midwest to post jihadi videos, like Zarqawi's beheading of Nick Berg, and post recipes for making car bombs and suicide vests. From a basement apartment in Britain, a self-styled Irhabi 007 (Terrorist 007) helped in his spare time to coordinate plots with some high school chums in Toronto to blow up the Canadian parliament, and with others to attack the U.S. embassy in Bosnia (three conspirators who did meet physically in Bosnia were arrested with AK-47 rifles, suicide belts, and thousands of rounds of ammunition).

PUBLICITY IS THE OXYGEN OF TERRORISM

"The media are coming to the Taj!"
—PHONE CALL FROM ALLEGED LASHKAR-E-TAYIBAH
HANDLER "BROTHER WASI" IN PAKISTAN TO THE SUICIDE
SQUAD AT THE MUMBAI TAJ HOTEL SUGGESTING THAT NOW
WAS THE TIME TO KILL AS MANY GUESTS AS POSSIBLE,
THEN DIE.

Because terrorists thrive in small groups and among networks of family and friends, their threat is fueled way beyond their actual strength by publicity.

In the past, spectacular killings were common both to small tribes and great empires. Nearly three millennia ago, Moses commanded the Israelites after defeating the Midianites to "Kill all the boys, and kill every woman who has slept with a man. But save for yourselves every girl who has never slept with a man" (Numbers 31:17–18). Genghis Khan, the legendary Mongol conqueror, reportedly said: "The greatest pleasure is to vanquish your enemies, to chase them before you, to rob them of their wealth, to see their near and dear bathed in tears, to ride their horses and sleep on the bellies of their wives and daughters."[9]

Today, whereas most nations tend to avoid publicizing their more wanton killings—including most killings that might be labeled state terrorism—publicity is the oxygen that fires modern terrorism.

Witness, for example, the reaction to the failed "Christmas Day Plot" in 2009. Umar Farouk Abdulmutallab, a baby-faced twenty-three-year-old British-educated engineering student and son of a prominent Nigerian banker, attempted to blow up Northwest Flight 253 out of Amsterdam as it was about to land in Detroit. Although Abdulmutallab's father had warned the American embassy in Nigeria that his son was spouting dangerous ideas, and his name was placed on a list of people to watch for, the young man managed to board the plane with a pack of explosives and a detonating syringe strapped to his body. His case has two antecedents. The obvious one is that of Richard Reid, who eight years before had tried to bring down American Airlines Flight 63 from Paris to Miami with a shoe bomb containing the same plastic explosive that Umar had packed in his underwear; execution of the plot was clumsy and amateurish, and it failed. The other is the case of five Virginia men, ages nineteen to twenty-five, who were arrested in Pakistan in December 2009 at the home of an activist from Jaish-e-Mohammed, the group that had helped to kidnap and kill *Wall Street Journal* reporter Daniel Pearl. According to Pakistani interrogators, the American buddies—two of Pakistani ancestry, one of Egyptian, one of Yemeni, and one of Eritrean—had used Internet sites to try to contact militants in Pakistan before traveling there from the United States in late November. After making a "farewell video" with the message that Muslims must be defended, they went overseas without telling their families. Like Abdulmutallab's father, the young men's concerned families notified American authorities, who in that instance warned their Pakistani counterparts. E-mails and maps found in the band's possession indicate that they planned to travel to the Chashma Nuclear Plant in northwest Pakistan and on to a Qaeda-linked Taliban training facility.[10]

Umar's path to radicalization started out a bit lonelier, but the trajectory is pretty familiar. Like "the Tunisian," Serhane Fakhet, a key player in the Madrid train bombings, Umar was a gifted student from a well-off family who felt constantly lonely and out of place in foreign schools. He went to an English boarding school in Togo, studied Arabic in Yemen, and attended mechanical engineering classes at the elite University College, London, where he became president of the Student Islamic Society and said he found contentment and companionship. But he seems to have mainly sought friendship and solutions to personal conflicts through Internet contacts. On Facebook, he frequently mused about loneliness and love, his sexual frustrations, and his need to marry soon because "the hair of a woman can easily arouse a man." "My name is Umar but you can call me Farouk," he wrote on the Islamic Forum Web site. "May Allah reward you for reading and reward you more for helping."[11]

The Islamic Society brought him into the counterculture against "the war on terror": "I imagine how the great jihad will take place, how the muslims will win, *insha Allah* [God willing], and rule the whole world, and establish the greatest empire once again!!!" reads one post from 2005. But only after leaving London did he become truly radicalized away from merely belonging to a counterculture that includes millions of young Muslims, and into a universe of violent extremism that draws forth few. Returning to Yemen, he connected with the so-called Al Qaeda in the Arabian Peninsula, and its American-born imam, Anwar al-Awlaki, may have blessed Umar's suicide mission.[12] Awlaki, a former preacher at a Northern Virginia mosque, gained notoriety for Facebook communications with Major Malik Nadal Hasan, an American-born Muslim psychiatrist who killed thirteen fellow soldiers at Fort Hood, Texas, and for "inspiring" would-be Times Square bomber Faisal Shahzad.

Like the Tunisian and others who plotted attacks—9/11, Madrid, London—Umar cut ties with his former companions who he felt were too timid to act and cemented bonds with those who would be willing to strike. Like these others, Umar entered a seemingly privileged and parallel universe framed by the Takfiri vision of how the Prophet and his companions withdrew from Mecca to Medina to gain the spiritual and physical force to conquer the world.

Although many leap to the conclusion that Awlaki helped to "brainwash" and "indoctrinate" Major Hasan, Umar, and Shahzad, it was much more likely that they sought out the popular Internet preacher because they were already radicalized to the point of wanting further guidance to act. "The movement is from the bottom up," notes Marc Sageman, "just like you saw Major Hasan send twenty-one e-mails to al-Awlaki, who sends him back two, you have people seeking these guys and asking them for advice."[13] The influence of media-savvy imams had steadily risen since about 1997, with the birth of the interactive IslamOnline Web site by Egyptian Muslim Brotherhood leader Yusef al-Qaradawi, who also has his own Al Jazeera TV show, *Sharia and Life*. That year also saw the creation of the more radical media company Islamic Conflict Studies Bureau, by the Syrian Qaeda activist Mustafa Setmarian Nasar. It was Setmarian who arranged CNN's first Bin Laden interview and who would go on to become the Internet guru of "leaderless jihad" by individuals connected to small autonomous groups.

Like American television evangelicals, popular Internet imams interpret the complex political and social issues of the day as moral crises defined by simple binary choices that require action: for good versus evil, justice versus injustice, civilization versus barbarism, true religion versus false prophets. The Internet imams offer clear goals and courses of action for those who are already seeking the means to a glorious end where, in the words of Web celebrity Sheikh Khalid bin Abdul Rahman al-Husainan of Kuwait, "Happiness is the day of my Martyrdom."

It is not by arraying "every element of U.S. power" (as President Obama proclaimed) against would-be jihadis and those who inspire them that violent extremism will be stopped. It is by paying attention to what makes these young men want to die to kill, through listening to their families and friends, and by trying to bind with them on the Internet. "On the Internet, nobody knows you're a dog," said the cunning canine in a 1993 *New Yorker* cartoon.[14] And what goes for dogs can certainly work for police. Good investigative reporting and police intelligence, like that at the NYPD, does this sort of tracking and outreach well. Even if every airline passenger were to be scanned naked or patted down, it would not stop young men from joining the jihad or concocting new ways of killing civilians. (On August 28, 2009, Prince Nayef of Saudi Arabia survived a gruesome suicide attack by a man armed with an explosive suppository.)[15]

Truth be told, the physical threat to our population is extremely low, if fairly constant, and by no means poses any serious threat to our nation's existence or infrastructure. But each near-success breeds a monstrously outsize reaction, given the actual damage that could be done to society. (There was a report written back in the early days of car touring, on the "jerk effect": When you hit an unexpected pothole, your emotions rapidly rachet up, and you jump at the expectation of potholes at every turn for some time after.) A good risk analyst, like Carnegie Mellon's Baruch Fischhoff, would say that we exaggerate the numerator of risk, by extending it to near-misses (knowing someone who knew someone who has flown on a similar route), and we underestimate the denominator (the total number of flights). In fact, between October 1999 and September 2009 there were nearly 100 million commercial flights (99,320,309, to be exact). Six flights suffered a terrorist attack and four were successful, with 647 passengers losing their lives. That's out of seven billion (7,015,630,000) passengers. You're more likely to die while mowing your lawn than while on a flight that suffers a terrorist attack. The odds are about 10 million to 1.

Terrorists are directly responsible for violent acts, but only indirectly for the reaction that follows. To terrorize and destabilize, terrorists need publicity and our complicity. With publicity, even failed terrorist acts succeed in terrorizing; without publicity, terrorism would fade away.[16] The irony is that press and publicity are also the oxygen of an open society. But this does not require that our leaders equate what is most scary and spectacular with what is really most threatening and politically important. By amplifying and connecting relatively sporadic terrorist acts into a generalized "war," the somewhat marginal phenomenon of terrorism has become a primary preoccupation of our government and people. This transformation puts the lie to the constant refrain by our same leaders that "terrorists will gain nothing."

Terrorism remains at the top of the behavioral agendas of our political parties. This means that no matter what the outcome of our democratic elections, terrorists will continue to hold sway over our society in ways only the most audacious and outrageous among them ever imagined, at least in their thinking about the short-term product of their actions. In this sense, Bin Laden has been victorious beyond his wildest dreams—not because of anything he's done, but because of how we have reacted to the episodic near-misses and rare successes he inspires.

"THE GOLDEN AGE FOR DRUG DEALERS, WHITE-COLLAR CRIME, AND THE MOB"

A good example of the hype and hysteria is the wild concern with prison radicalization in the United States. Western Europe has a population roughly the size of the United States. In France, Muslims represent less than 10 percent of the country's population (5 million to 6 million out of 62 million), but about two thirds of the prison population (40,000 out of 60,000 total).[17] In Spain, Muslims represent about 2.5 percent of the total population (1 million out of 40 million), but 16 percent of the prison population (8,000 out of 52,000). Many draw the wrong inference from these figures, namely that Islam encourages criminal behavior.

In the United States, Muslims represent less than 1 percent of the population (2.3 million or so). The predictive factors for Muslims entering European prisons are pretty much the same as for African Americans entering U.S. prisons, namely lack of employment, schooling, political representation, and so forth. But nearly two thirds of Muslims in the United States are foreign-born, and nearly three quarters of them buy into the American Dream and believe they "can get ahead with hard work."[18] Overall, foreign-born Muslims in the United States have about the same education and economic levels as the general population, whereas foreign-born Muslims are five to seven times more likely to be poor than non-Muslims in Britain, France, and Germany and nearly ten times more likely to be poor in Spain.

Even in Europe, though, religious education is a *negative* predictor of Muslims entering prisons. Authorities consider only 2 percent of Muslim prisoners in Spain (160) to be jihadis or would-be jihadis.[19] In France, only 1 percent of Muslim prisoners (400) are considered to be jihadis. In the United States, very few Muslim inmates are known to have jihadi sympathies, and only a small handful, less than one-thousandth of a percent of the total U.S. Muslim population, have been convicted in the single plot uncovered so far. But this is apparently enough to warrant the speculation that "Al Qaeda recruits in prisons. . . . Prisons are a prime, prime target for terrorist recruiting. It is a ripe population."[20]

In fact, this one prison plot had nothing to do with Al Qaeda recruitment.[21] The man who concocted the plot was Kevin Lamar James, the native-born son of a former Black Panther who was serving ten years for robbery in New Folsom State Prison, a maximum-security prison outside Sacramento, California. He founded what he called the "Jami'yyat al-Islam al-Sakeej" ("the Authentic Islamic Group,") in prison in 1997. According to court documents, his goal was to recruit recent prisoners in the California State prison system to jihad, focusing on those about to be released or paroled so that they could go on to establish "JIS cells" on the outside.

In prison, James recruited his cellmate, Levar Haney Washington, an African-American convert to Islam who had a criminal history as a gang member. James told Washington, due for release a year before James, to "go out and do something." In a handwritten "Blueprint 2005," James laid out what he expected Washington to do on the outside, such as: learning Arabic, recruiting people with no history of felonies and teaching them to recruit others, acquiring bomb expertise, producing and distributing propaganda, and taking measures to "blend into society." It was styled a bit on the so-called Al Qaeda manual, which was publicly available on the Internet, but there is no evidence of any direct connection between JIS and any other group.

After Washington's release, James made his new cellmate, Peter Martinez, his deputy. Together James, Martinez, and Washington began scheming to attack more than a dozen military and Jewish sites in the Los Angeles area on September 11, 2005. Washington recruited two others on the outside, Gregory Vernon Patterson and Hammad Riaz Samara. Washington found Patterson and Samara in a local mosque, where they began talking about the invasion of Iraq. The conversation moved to a nearby apartment, where they psyched themselves up with images of inmates at Abu Ghraib prison being humiliated by their American captors. Patterson, an African-American convert to Islam with no criminal record, was from an upper-middle-class family, the son of a university professor. Samara, a Pakistani immigrant, was a naturalized U.S. citizen who also had no criminal background.

Their idea was a two-pronged attack using firearms, not a suicide mission. Samara authored a target list, including the Israeli "Consulate of Zion" in Los Angeles, the ticket office of the Israeli airline El Al at the L.A. airport, and Jewish synagogues. The group even debated the idea of going to Saudi Arabia to carry out an attack, figuring that it might call more attention to their group than action in the United States. They had big plans, some of them really screwy. But the plotters were resourceful, able to access and case the airfield at the L.A. airport through a duty-free store. "They were knuckleheads," one law enforcement agent said to me, "but dangerous knuckleheads only two months away from killing big-time."

The plot unraveled following a string of gas-station robberies, when police in Torrance, California, traced the number of a dropped cell phone to Patterson. At first, interrogators focused on Patterson, who they felt sure would break because of his upbringing and no criminal history. But he refused to fold, telling interrogators to "drop dead" and "if this is my martyrdom, so be it." Patterson turned out to be the most ideologically committed of the four conspirators.

It was Washington, a hardened criminal, who "sang like a bird," as one interrogator put it, and ratted out the others because he already had two prior convictions and didn't want to be put away for life under California's "three-strike" rule. Washington confessed that the robberies were to get money to buy ammunition and guns to prepare "jihad." He complained that James constantly bugged him to take off his tattoos and to find a wife in order to better "blend into society."

All were charged with conspiracy to levy war against the U.S. government through terrorism. All but James were charged with conspiracy to kill members of government. James, Martinez, and Washington identified about forty inmates they had been trying to enlist, as well as a few others from the outside, including African Americans, Hispanics, Middle Easterners, and whites. Six were deported, others remained in custody or were later paroled.

Well over four hundred FBI agents were assigned to the case (out of about twelve thousand agents in the country). Agents from as far as St. Louis were taken off other cases to cover the night shift of the FBI's Los Angeles contingent. If it were not for claims by three losers that they were jihadis, it's doubtful that anyone would have paid much attention. As one law enforcement agent told me, "The political leadership has to change their song about 'zero tolerance' for anything that smacks of jihad before we can get back to business."

One source at the White House wryly commented, "It's the Golden Age for drug dealers, white-collar crime, and the Mob." Of course, this is something of an overstatement: The FBI's success, or lack of success, in these areas has not changed all that much since the rise of terrorism as a major concern. But the gist of the White House staffer's remark is that zero tolerance for terrorism has translated into less political concern for other severe ills of society, including blindness to the shenanigans of licensed thieves on Wall Street. Indeed, when the October 2008 financial melt-down occurred—the worst economic crisis since 1929—the *New York Times* headlined a story "F.B.I. Struggles to Handle Wave of Financial Fraud Cases," which reported:

> So depleted are the ranks of the F.B.I.'s white-collar investiga-tors that executives in the private sector say they have had dif-ficulty attracting the bureau's attention in cases involving pos-sible frauds of millions of dollars. . . . "The administration's top priority since the 9/11 attacks has been counterterrorism," Peter Carr, a Justice Department spokesman, said. "In part, that's reflected by a significant investment of resources at the F.B.I. to answer the call from Congress and the American public to become a domestic intelligence agency."[22]

There have been similar assessments by U.S. officials that massive shifts of law enforcement resources to terrorism have contributed to the escalating drug crisis with Mexico.[23] Shortly after President Obama took office, FBI director Robert Muel-ler conceded that "the logical consequence of cannibalizing our criminal program to augment our national security efforts is that we have reduced the ability to surge resources within our crimi-nal branch."[24]

This isn't to say that problems of domestic radicalization should be ignored, only that serious studies should be encouraged to deter-mine what the likely threat really is. According to law enforcement officials I have interviewed, most prisoners who opt for militant forms of Islam in U.S. prisons do so to protect themselves for other militant groups, especially white supremacists. The NYPD intel-ligence unit refers to militant Islam in prison as Prislam, because when prison converts get out of jail, very few continue with militant Muslim activities. The reason, as many social-science studies of repeating offenders suggest, is that released prisoners, like most everyone else, usually adopt the mores of the surrounding social community. Because there is little popular support for militant Islam in U.S. communities anywhere, converts to radical Islam rapidly become fish out of water.

WIDGETRY AND WATERWITCHING

Antiterrorism efforts are fixated on technology and technological success, and there is no sustained or systematic approach to field-based social understanding of our adversaries' motivation, intent, will, and the dreams that drive their strategic vision, however strange those dreams and vision may seem to us. The 2009 Christmas Day airline bombing attempt, for example, was a failing caused, in part, by overreliance on technology to the detriment of social intelligence. Computers and their algorithms aren't well suited to pick up the significance of the anguish and effort it took for one of the most respected men in a nation to swallow pride and love of family and walk into an American embassy to say that his son was being dangerously radicalized. Widgets—for which there are billions of dollars—can't do the job of socially sensitive thinkers—for whom there is scant concrete support—in reading intentions, creating alliances, leveraging nonmilitary advantages, building trust, changing opinions, managing perceptions, and empathizing (though not necessarily sympathizing) with others to see what makes them tick.[25]

At countless workshops and meetings I've attended, proposals were discussed or solicited for modeling terrorist networks. Why does the U.S government prefer to give its money for widgets: elaborate models that use elegant sound and light shows to give the "client" (usually another government agency) the illusion that it all makes perfect sense? Right after 9/11 the intelligence community was frantic over how to explain that a team of terrorists (rather than a government) could cause such harm. So the intelligence community turned to computers and modelers for a fix. But the results were disappointing because the models weren't dynamic enough to accommodate the change and happenstance that characterize the evolution of terror networks. Continued reliance on widgets is favored by the fact that they tend to be expensive: The way some government contracting works, the more expensive the project that can be pushed out the door, the better the chances of promotion for the pusher. Another reason to go to widgets is that they are concrete and "deliverable," something to behold at a glance and sink the taxpayer's teeth into. But unless the field data are sound, all you get is garbage in and garbage out. To date, billions have been spent in the airy realm of widgetry, but next to nothing has been spent on field research.

Waterwitching is the illusion of predicting the location of underground water with a divining rod. Much of the lucrative industry of "modeling terrorism" resembles waterwitching. There's great hunger for "predictability" and "parameterization" and the mathematics to back it up.[26] These are fine for trying to figure out precise sets of conditions when an airplane engine might break up. But such notions are meaningless when applied to the evolutionary development of most natural phenomena, including how jihadi groups form and develop. At best, we may be able to model a set of path-dependent futures for development, possible ways that things might turn out. But the real-world triggers that move things along one path rather than another are often inherently unpredictable, like the meteor that may have wiped out the dinosaurs and let mammals come out of the closet and become us. As we've seen again and again in our case studies, random events and marginal connections can be key to how a terrorist group or plot develops.

For morally misplaced reasons, government seems to want science to be as diverse and democratic as society. Don't get me wrong, I think democracy is the best political system humans have come up with so far and that diversity is the best bet for social creativity and peace. But democracy in science spells disaster unless the science is subordinated to the highest standards of quality and excellence. For example, government often wants models to incorporate data from many different sources in order to capture maximum diversity. Now, using a diverse sample is critically important to making correct scientific generalizations. Thus, it's more likely that some biological trait is a property of all animals if examined and found in mammals, fish, and insects rather than examined only in mammals. There's also a lot of evidence coming in from people working on "complexity theory" out of the Santa Fe Institute and some top universities that a diverse bunch of people usually outperforms a homogeneous group in solving a problem—whether in business, science, or math—no matter how expert the group is.[27] So what's wrong with drawing data willy-nilly from the following kinds of sources?

- "random" selections of newspapers and other media outlets (where the need to tell a story often creates fictitious coherence, and where enormous "echo" effects propagate and amplify the initial errors from well-known outlets, like the *New York Times* or *Washington Times*, or CNN or Fox, to innumerable other information sources);

- a hodge-podge of interviews carried out by investigators who have varying agendas and points to prove (they may want to show the effects of trauma on terrorism, or humiliation, or low esteem, or deprivation, or whatever, without weighing in or weeding out other competing factors);

- unsupervised field "reports" (with no set standards of reference or reliability across investigators and settings);

- and psychological experiments (done mostly among undergraduates at big research universities, or on our own personnel, but rarely with people who really do the things we want to find out about).

Well, it's a bit like trying to build an adequate theory of physics by sampling some Ptolemy, some Kepler, and some Maharishi Mahesh Yogi. Even with bits of Einstein thrown into the pot, all you get is a tangle of spaghetti.

The development of terrorist networks, plots, and attacks resembles more the development of a complex system, with inherently chaotic and unpredictable characteristics. Much like water that becomes heated to boiling, or even more like a soup with locally different densities and viscosities, it may be impossible in principle to precisely predict where the rising cones and bubbles will first appear. But social science can help discern the space of probable pathways to and from violence in ways that even gadgetry can turn to our advantage.

LOOSEN UP AND TRY LISTENING

As I mentioned at the end of chapter 8, I've often tried, unsuccessfully, to get people in our own government to at least listen and talk to terrorists and wannabes instead of just trying to capture and kill them—or "model" them. There's precious little effort by the U.S government to push field-based research. Remarkable, really. After all, if someone wants to kill you, it's better to know why they want to kill so as to improve your chances of stopping them. In the first years after 9/11, the "human factors" research units of the Department of Defense weren't talking to terrorists at all. In the last couple of years, they've become scared that field studies in a foreign country might be viewed as a covert U.S. operation. So new government guidelines require that research partners in host nations must have their own national Institutional Review Boards (IRBs) to make sure that any study meets American university standards for "protection of human subjects."

Now, this makes little sense for two simple reasons: There are no uniform U.S. standards at the national level, and institutions in other countries (except dictatorships) generally don't want their own governments micromanaging which research should or shouldn't be allowed. Even when there are proposals for field-based research, the hurdles of the IRBs at American universities can make execution difficult, if not impossible.[28] IRBs were initially set up to protect human subjects from Nazi doctor–type experiments. They're now mostly preoccupied with preventing studies that might upset students, and seem to assume that all human subjects should be handled according to the sensibilities of American coeds. Robert Lifton, a psychiatrist who studies the psychological causes and effects of war, had a helluva time getting permission to even interview Nazi doctors for fear of upsetting the old dears.[29]

I was told by one university IRB that I would never be given permission to interview potential or convicted mass murderers overseas because I could never absolutely guarantee that what they told me wouldn't compromise them: For example, if I inadvertently found out that a suicide bombing plot was in the works and reported it, then I would be denying the suicide bomber his or her "human subjects rights."[30] For the life of me, I don't understand how stopping a person from blowing up himself and others denies anyone's human rights. Members of the IRB, none of whom need have any expertise on the subject being researched, also told me flatly that the potential legal fallout from disgruntled terrorists (lawsuits) outweighs possible benefits to the university, though I pointed out that preventing people and cities and the like from being blown up was perhaps of some benefit to the society that supports the university.

Ever since the Vietnam War, there has been mutual antipathy and antagonism between most academic social science—at least at the outstanding universities—and U.S. military operations and military-related policymaking. But for the safety of all, including keeping allied servicemen and women out of harm's way, and also preventing others from being harmed by ill-informed actions, a dialogue really should get going. There will be tensions and deep disagreements, but if social science does not engage power, then social science helps itself and all others to become unwitting slaves of power.

Nevertheless, social scientists should not be directly embedded with military units. In testimony at a March 2010 Senate hearing, I argued against efforts such as the Human Terrain System experiment in Afghanistan, which involves temporarily embedding "combat ethnographers" in infantry units for nonlethal ("non-kinetic") actions, such as helping villagers with medical care. The military and cultural reality of the terrain may favor embedded social scientists being uniformed and armed (in part, because unarmed Western civilians would more likely draw fire as high-value targets). But the possibility that social scientists would have to fire their weapons and perhaps kill local people—indeed, the mere sight of armed and uniformed American social scientists in a foreign theater—guarantees academia's profound hostility. Rather, independent, publicly transparent, science-based field research in conflict zones can help policymakers, the military, and potential adversaries avoid mistakes that lead to conflict and violence.

SIZING DOWN THE FIELD

A main problem in terrorism studies is that most "experts" have little field experience and otherwise lack the required level of detail that statistical and trend analyses could properly mine. There are many millions of people who express sympathy with Al Qaeda or other forms of violent political expression that support terrorism. There are, however, only some thousands who show willingness to actually commit violence. They almost invariably go on to violence in small groups of volunteers consisting mostly of friends and some kin within specific "scenes": neighborhoods, schools (classes, dorms), workplaces, common leisure activities (soccer, mosque, barbershop, café), and, increasingly, online chat rooms.

The process of self-selection into violence within these scenes is stimulated by a massive, media-driven political awakening in which jihad is represented as the only the way to permanently resolve glaring problems of global injustice. As Saudi Arabia's General Khaled Alhumaidan said to me in Riyadh, "The front is in our neighborhoods but the battle is the silver screen. If it doesn't make it to the six o'clock news, then Al Qaeda is not interested." These young people constantly see and discuss among themselves images of war and injustice against "our people," become morally outraged (especially if injustice resonates personally, more a problem with immigrants in Europe than America), and dream of a war for justice that gives their friendship a cause.

Most human violence is committed by young people seeking adventure, dreams of glory, and esteem in the eyes of their peers. Omar Nasiri's tale of his time with Al Qaeda, *Inside Jihad*,[31] rings true in its picture of the highs the militants get from the sense of brotherhood and sense of purpose. They want to be more than morning mist, to turn their personal passion into great acts of great magnitude. They kill and die for faith and friendship, which is the foundation of all social and political union, that is, all enduring human associations of non-kin. The most heroic cause in the world today is jihad, where anyone from anywhere can hope to make a mark against the most powerful country and army in the history of the world.

In the long run, perhaps the most important counterterrorism measure of all is to provide alternative heroes and hopes that are more enticing and empowering than any moderating lessons or material offerings (jobs that help to relieve the terrible boredom and inactivity of immigrant youth in Europe and the underemployed throughout much of the Muslim world, will not alone offset the alluring stimulation of playing at war). It is also important to provide alternate local networks and chat rooms that speak to the inherent idealism, sense of risk and adventure, and need for peer approval that young people everywhere tend toward. It even could be a twenty-first-century version of what the Boy Scouts and high school football teams did for immigrants and potentially troublesome youth as America urbanized a century ago. Ask any cop on the beat: Those things work. It has to be done with the input and insight of local communities, and chiefly peer-to-peer, or it won't work: deradicalization, like radicalization itself, engages mainly from the bottom up, not from the top down. This, of course, is not how you stop terrorism today, but how you do it for tomorrow.

Part V

WAR PARTIES— GROUPS, GODS, AND GLORY

At all times throughout the world, tribes have supplanted other tribes; and as morality is the important element of their success, the standard of morality and the number of well-endowed men will thus everywhere tend to rise and increase. . . . There can be no doubt that a tribe including many members who, from possessing in a high degree the spirit of patriotism, fidelity, obedience, courage, and sympathy, were always ready to give aid to each other and to sacrifice themselves for the common good, would be victorious over other tribes.

—CHARLES DARWIN, *THE DESCENT OF MAN*, 1871

others whom they interact and exchange with. It's pretty universal in adversarial relationships to clump and split all potential allies and enemies into a binary opposition, such as good versus evil, where each side's hidden essence is characterized as "good" by one's own side and "evil" by the other side. Human minds simply adore binary oppositions, whatever the domain of thought.[2]

Try this experiment: Gather a bunch of students or even perfect strangers and, by a flip of the coin, arbitrarily provide tags identifying some as belonging to an "A" group and a "B" group, or a "Green" group and an "Orange" group; you'll soon find members of each group spontaneously forming emotional bonds with one another.[3] You'll also see the A's and Greens systematically discriminating against the B's and Oranges while showing generosity to their own group in matters both trivial (sharing candy) and consequential (fighting).[4] Typical binary oppositions today include "us" versus "them," "civilization" versus "barbarism," "believers" versus "nonbelievers," and so on. "Al Qaeda" functions today mainly as a characterization of hidden essence: "evil" for those who oppose the label, "good" for those who adopt it.

In Los Angeles, a stranger with a blue hat risks being shot if he happens onto the turf of the gang called Bloods, whose color is red; sporting a red scarf is enough to get you killed if you chance into the territory of the rival Crips gang, whose color is blue. Bloods will not pronounce the letter C nor Crips the letter B. But many Reds will readily risk their lives to save a Red, and Blues to save a Blue.[5] There's little place for compromise in such environs; either you're with one side or against it, or you'd better stay away.

If you're a staunch Republican during a presidential campaign, your candidate is likely as honest and forthright as a person can be, but the Democratic candidate is an appalling cynic and liar. Democrats, of course, tend to think the reverse is true. Show a film clip of an Ohio State–Michigan football game to students at each university and ask them to objectively record every foul committed. If the game was held at Michigan, then Ohio students are sure to say the referees intentionally overlooked foul play. If held in Ohio, the Michigan students will bet the bank that the refs ignored rampant cheating. The same goes for the soccer fans of Manchester United and Arsenal, or Barcelona and Real Madrid. But when Britain faces Spain, playing for Britain or Spain is all that counts.[6]

The basic psychology of "us versus them" is much the same when ethnic, national, or religious groups compete for territory, vital resources, or membership. But the stakes are usually much higher (than candy, street turf, or a football or election victory) and can lead to war. Human warfare is vastly more lethal than intergroup conflict in other primate species.[7] Genocide, the extermination of one group by another, is a frequent method of "conflict resolution" that humans have practiced since prehistoric times.[8] We don't know how frequent genocide was in human prehistory, but even its occasional occurrence would have favored the emergence of bravery—fighting at personal risk on behalf of one's group. If losing the war results in genocide, you're dead anyway; so better to fight with your all to the end to give yourself and your group a chance.

What isn't clear is whether bravery was naturally selected as a genetic propensity in only some individuals, or to varying degrees in most or all individuals. Or perhaps bravery was culturally selected in the course of intergroup competition and warfare, emerging at some stage in prehistory, not as a biological adaptation of certain individuals to groups, but as a normative aspect of human societies. Culturally transmitted norms for bravery and heroic sacrifice, such as honor and esteem, might attract a variety of individuals. The wider the range of individuals attracted to bravery, the less the costs of sacrifice to each brave individual; thus, the more brave and united the society as a whole, the better able the society to wage war and compete against other societies.

What gives outnumbered insurgents and resource-poor revolutionaries the ability to resist and defeat police and armies that have vastly more material means? Moral commitment to sacrifice for their group without regard for their own material reward. As long as jihadis show such moral commitment, as martyrdom missions attest to, then even overwhelming material efforts to destroy the jihadi movement may not be enough.

But what gets group commitment going in the first place?

BRAVERY AND HEROISM (PAROCHIAL ALTRUISM)

Altruism is the sacrifice of one's own interests for the sake of others, as in giving to charity, lending a helping hand, or just taking time to offer directions to a stranger. Parochial altruism, especially bravery and heroism in war, involves sacrifice for one's own group to the detriment of rival groups.[9] Parochial altruism is a basic aspect of the evolutionary imperative of human populations to "cooperate to compete." In all cultures, parochially altruistic acts are considered noble and good. Though what is good and noble in one culture and time can be evil and ignoble for another. Individuals within a society may also differ widely in their appreciation of the value of an altruistic act, such as suicide bombing or the struggle for civil human rights.

Charles Darwin, gathering an astounding amount of data from his voyage around the world as a naturalist aboard the HMS *Beagle*,[10] and from other people's observations, tried to show that all living kinds are basically competitive and selfish. The different forms of life, including humans and their cultural shells, develop through a process of natural selection that favors survival of the best competitors for resources. This, he argued in *On the Origin of Species*, promotes adaptations only for the individual's own use in its struggle to gain resources to produce offspring: "good for itself," but "never . . . for the exclusive good of others."[11]

Under Darwin's theory, if we give to charity or help children, strangers, and the infirm, it's because we seek enhanced social status, or a heightened sense of self-worth, or affirmation of our belief that as we do for others in need so we expect others to do unto us should we become needy, or whatever else may serve our interests in the short or long run. "In the first place," Darwin later wrote, "each man would soon learn from experience that if he aided his fellow-men, he would commonly receive aid in the end." Charles Moskos, a former draftee who became one of America's most respected military sociologists, observed: "In ground warfare an individual's survival is directly related to the support—moral, physical, and technical—he can expect from his fellow soldiers. He gets such support largely to the degree that he reciprocates to others."[12]

Heroism and martyrdom, however, go way beyond the principles of reciprocity, such as quid pro quo or even the Golden Rule. Darwin puzzled mightily over what would motivate "the bravest men, who were always willing to come to the front in war, and who freely risked their lives for others?" Since the brave were off risking death—or dying—more than others, they would have fewer offspring on average. "Therefore, it hardly seems probable, that the number of men gifted with such virtues . . . could be increased through natural selection, that is, by survival of the fittest."[13] Of course, Darwin acknowledged that the brave warrior who survives the fight will often gain more power or wealth or social worth or mates, and so improve his chances for reproducing healthy and successful offspring in greater numbers. But if the risk of death is very high, then it is very doubtful that gain would outweigh loss.

How, then, could self-interest alone account for man's aptitude for self-sacrifice to the point of giving his life—the totality of his self-interests—for his extended family, tribe, nation, religion, or for humanity? The puzzle led Darwin to modify his view that natural selection only produces selfish individuals. In *The Descent of Man*, he suggests that we humans have a naturally selected propensity to moral virtue, that is, a willingness to sacrifice self-interest in the cause of group interest. Humans are above all moral animals because they are creatures who love their group as they love themselves. "It must not be forgotten that although a high standard of morality gives but a slight or no advantage to each individual man and his children over the other men of the same tribe, yet that an increase in the number of well-endowed men and an advancement in the standard of morality will certainly give an immense advantage to one tribe over another."[14]

For Alfred Russel Wallace, co-originator of the theory of evolution by natural selection, moral behavior (along with mathematics, music, and art) was evidence that humans, as opposed to all other animals, had not evolved through natural selection alone: "The special faculties we have been discussing clearly point to the existence in man of something which has not derived from his animal progenitors—something which we may best refer to as being of a spiritual essence . . . beyond all explanation by matter, its laws and forces."[15]

Needless to say, Wallace's account of altruism as a spiritual creation beyond all material explanation did not sit well with Darwin's empirical mind-bent. "I hope you have not murdered too completely your own and my child,"[16] lamented Darwin in a letter to Wallace. But Darwin himself produced no causal account of how group love might have emerged, nor did he give any good reason why natural selection should have produced truly selfless devotion only in humans, other than to say that because our ancestors were so physically weak, only group strength could get them through.

KINSHIP, AND THE POWER OF IMAGINED KIN

For nearly a century after Darwin, evolutionary thinkers struggled unsuccessfully to reconcile the seemingly antagonistic concepts of "self love" versus "group love" in biological terms. The first real progress was made in the early 1960s by William Hamilton, a graduate student who happened to be fascinated by Hymenoptera, social insects that live in colonies, such as ants, bees, wasps, and sawflies.

Each colony of Hymenoptera consists of chambers connected to one another and to the surface by small tunnels. Colonies function around one or a few queens who can usually live for years. The queen's task is to produce offspring. Males mate with the queen to produce daughters, then die. Sons have no fathers; all of their genes come from the queen mother. Most of the eggs laid by queens grow up to be infertile daughters called workers, who are specialized to maintain the colony's chambers as "rooms" for nurseries, food storage, and mating. Workers usually do double duty as soldiers who defend the colony against attack—at the cost of their lives if needed. Sometimes there's also a more specialized soldier caste whose behavior and anatomy is modified for group defense, including self-sacrifice.

Hamilton reasoned that because the daughters share most of their genes, it makes evolutionary sense for them to devote and sacrifice their lives for the group. The evolutionary task of these highly cooperative sisterhoods of workers and soldiers is to help the queen mother produce more members of the sisterhood—that is, more genetic near-copies of themselves. This insight led Hamilton to a broader theory of altruism in terms of "kin selection" and "inclusive fitness."[17] In a nutshell, genes for altruistic behaviors should tend to increase in a population when:

$$Kin\ B > C$$

Here, the fitness "cost" to survival, C, is less than the benefit to the survival of others, B, multiplied by their coefficient of kin-relatedness, Kin. By this logic, it "pays" for an individual to die if this action saves 2 siblings, 4 nieces or nephews, or 8 first cousins.

Biologist Richard Dawkins best expressed Hamilton's fundamental insight from "the gene's point of view":[18] A gene that increases the inclination to help siblings, for example, will foster its own spread by promoting individuals who are likely to bear copies of it. The important thing about genes is the information they encode, not the particular bodies they inhabit. A gene codes instructions for making bodies that can make more copies of the gene, but the information encoded hardly varies from one copy of a gene to another. Darwin didn't know about genes and so focused on individuals. From a gene's-eye view, individuals are merely "vessels" for the propagation of genes in quest of serial immortality.

Genes form coalitions with other genes to produce an individual who will likely propagate members of the coalition. An intermediate step in the process is the teaming up of gene coalitions into cells. Because cells in the individual possess identical genes (except for sperm and eggs), they are "close kin" and therefore naturally disposed to cooperate. Although genetically identical, cells are specialized for different body-building labors. The more kinds of specialization, the greater the complexity and flexibility of the body (including the brain) being built; just as the greater the division of labor in an economy, the greater the complexity and flexibility of the emerging market. Once an individual is no longer set to fulfill the function of passing on copies of its genes, the coalition starts to unravel, the cells begin to decay and malfunction, and the individual eventually dies.

Viewed from the gene's point of view, Hamilton's theory of altruism is not so much about group love as about a surreptitious form of self-love. It's as much about nepotism as altruism. Even from the individual's vantage, the theory of kin selection and inclusive fitness hardly does away with self-love and competition. For example, the theory predicts sibling rivalry when the benefits of sharing a resource are less than twice the costs because siblings only share half their genes.

Hamilton's theory goes some way toward explaining cooperation in human tribes—not as a case of morally pure self-sacrifice,
but as a particular variant of a broader evolutionary principle:
"Cooperate to compete." Take the Arab dictum "Me against my
brother, brothers against cousins, cousins against the tribe, the
tribe against the world." Yet even blood feuds between kin groups
rarely, if ever, follow strict Hamiltonian logic. Human reckoning of
kinship obligations almost never follows a purely genetic reckoning
of biological relationships: Among Arab tribes of the Middle East
and North Africa, which are organized exclusively through descent
in the father's line, which anthropologists call a *patrilineage*, parallel
cousins (father's brother's son and daughter) are considered first-
degree "blood" relatives whereas cross-cousins (mother's brother's
son and daughter)[19] are not. This bit of Arab cultural logic, which
arbitrarily gives preference to parallel over cross-cousins, has no
real basis in biological logic.

Kinship, then, is not enough to explain levels of cooperative
behavior within human societies, or the differences in collective
behavior across societies. Cooperative mechanisms or algorithms
that are based on genetic kinship should be designed to focus benefits only on close relatives. So biological kinship could not directly
explain how large groups of individuals who are distantly related or
unrelated can cooperate.

One possibility is that our psychology for picking out kin easily
"misfires"[20] or is "tricked" into overextending kin benefits to others. Because humans evolved in small groups whose members were
closely related, evolution favored a kin psychology designed to help
out members of their groups. By "overextending" the idiom and
sentiments of kinship to non-kin, large-scale cooperation may be
facilitated for trade or war. As "imagined kin,"[21] members of large
groups perform and profit from many tasks that they could not do
alone, one by one, or only within the family.

Even casual study of anthropology and history indicates that the sentiment and idiom of kinship were critical to the formation of political communities and alliances. Among Native Americans of the Northwest Coast, war between chiefdoms would end, and trade begin, when their leaders ("Big Men") exchanged gifts and became ceremonial "brothers."[22] For the ancient Hebrews and Phoenicians, "the worshipper is called brother (that is, kinsman or sister of the god)."[23] "Brotherhood" is also the common term applied today among the Christian faithful and to the fraternity (*ikhwan*) of Islam. The rhetoric of family and kinship has also been a critical mobilizer in the formation of the "imagined community" of the modern nation,[24] and a potent motivator in modern warfare, as in patriotism.[25]

The language of kinship and the emotions it evokes are also sustaining features of durable social movements as diverse as civil rights and jihad. Consider the "Oath to Jihad" quoted at the beginning of this chapter. The oath affirms that by their sacrifice, members help secure the future of their family of imagined kin.[26] As U.S. House Speaker Nancy Pelosi put it in reference to justifiable war, "I'm a mother of five. I have five grandchildren. And I always say, Think of a lioness. Think of a mother bear. You come anywhere near our cubs, you're dead."[27]

From an evolutionary standpoint, imagined kinship isn't all that different from pornography or advertising sex to sell cars or yogurt or almost anything at all. Our psychology evolved to respond to certain stimuli indicating fecundity, virility, or good health: like men to full breasts, women to well-formed muscles, and both sexes to white teeth. This happened to help us find mates who propagate our genes. But evolution only produces what's better than worse, not what's best. It was better to be sexually stimulated by features signaling reproductive potential than not. The fact that pornographers and advertisers can "trick" and "tweak" our evolutionary proclivities for all sorts of other ends was not a concern in the ancestral environment that selected for human sexual psychology.

At least since the Venus of Dolní Věstonice, a thirty-thousand-year-old ceramic nude with exaggerated hips and breasts, human cultures have learned to manipulate our species' biological endowment to make us think and act in ways that go way beyond what was necessary or relevant to survive and reproduce in ancestral evolutionary environments. Indeed, "trick" and "tweak" is basically what human culture is all about.

THE ESSENCE OF US AGAINST THEM

The notion of imagined kinship helps us to understand how group feelings can be extended beyond family and genetics. By itself, though, imagined kinship still can't explain why we consider all members of an imagined kin group to be of a kind. Imagined kin differ from real kin not only by the lack of genetic ties, but also by the lack of distinction between near kin and distant kin. In general, all members of a brotherhood or motherland have equal status, at least in terms of group membership, whereas real kin have different degrees of relatedness and no fixed or firm way of defining group membership or boundaries.

Having said all this, humans still more or less do know the difference between imagined kin and real kin, between sex objects and real people (although cultural manipulation of biology can get pretty good at blurring the line). The mere evocation of good sex is usually not enough to make you go out and buy a new car. The mere evocation of imagined kinship generally doesn't suffice to create the greater bond. As a Babylonian king once wrote, "Between kings there is brotherhood, friendship, alliance and good relations—if there is an abundance of silver and an abundance of gold."[28] The fiction of kinship works well only if it has something more to work with.

That something more may be treasure, territory, or some other common good; but it is often underpinned by a universal psychological bias known as "essentialism."[29] Studies of childhood development across cultures indicate that people everywhere tend to attribute hidden essences to human social categories, such as race, ethnicity, and personality.[30] A common and potent form of essentialism bias is to think of different groups as akin to different biological species. Throughout history, and likely through human prehistory, people have routinely mobilized their own to fight or dominate others by seeing them as belonging to a different species.

To some extent, essentialism seems to be programmed into our brains by natural selection to apply to our understanding of biological species.[31] Human beings universally and automatically divide the world of readily visible biological organisms into mutually exclusive categories that roughly correspond to the scientist's notion of biological species or genus: dog, robin, shark, oak, holly, clover, and so on. In addition, humans are innately disposed by virtue of their own brain evolution to believe that each species has an underlying causal nature, or essence, which is uniquely responsible for the typical appearance, behavior, and ecological preferences of the kind.[32] "Folk biology" is the term that anthropologists and psychologists use to label this universal and innate propensity of human beings to partition the world's readily visible biodiversity into mutually exclusive essences. As Darwin noted, this natural tendency to classify organisms into species-like biological kinds has existed "from the remotest period in history" and "is not arbitrary like the grouping of stars in constellations."[33]

There are tremendous evolutionary advantages to folk biology in terms of economy of information and ability to generate rich inferences from single instances to large classes of properties and types. When you see a lion, it really doesn't matter which lion it is, because any lion can kill you; nor does it matter much which pineapple you eat because any (ripe) pineapple can feed you. But people also universally tend to attribute hidden essences to human social categories. For the most part, this psychological ploy is used to generate notions of "in-group" versus "out-group" based on readily identifiable characteristics, whether physical features (skin color, place of residence, dress) or social and ideational attributes (language, nationality, religion).[34]

Humans, as already noted, are their own worst predators, far more deadly than lions or sharks. And in the spiraling competition between human groups, it is often prudent to make "fast and dirty" inferences about who is a potential friend or foe. A ready-made stereotype brings causal coherence to a group where initially there was none. The initially false or arbitrary presumption of a group essence makes culturally adaptive sense. A self-reinforcing inter-actional bias would foster in-group convergence and cooperation. The more you interact with some people rather than others in one domain, the greater the likelihood that you will interact with them even more in the future and in other domains as well: mating, war, economic cooperation, and so on. This reduces the energy, time, and risk involved in interacting with out-groups, which are more likely to contain potential enemies.

But essentializing has a historical downside: It biases interac-tion with out-groups toward enmity, increasing risk of conflict and injury. On balance, benefits may have outweighed costs in ances-tral environments, when humans were all probably organized in competing but relatively small and isolated bands of nomadic hunt-ers and gatherers. But in today's rapidly interconnecting world, the survival value of exclusive social groups—armed with more destructive power than any Pleistocene relative could imagine—is not apparent.

I tend to think that the extension of essentialism to social cat-egories is another case of "tricking" or "misfiring" our universal and innate knowledge systems—this time by culturally tweaking our innate beliefs in biological essentialism. This cultural play translates into significant variation in how people essentialize their own group and other groups. As an example of this variation, consider our comparative study of Indonesian madrassahs.[35] We found that 74 percent of the students in a school affiliated with Jemaah Islamiyah (compared to 7 percent of the students at other schools) believed that all people "were born evil but some learn to become good." Students who believed people are "born evil" were about eleven times more likely to believe it was their duty to kill non-Muslims. Students were also asked to imagine what would happen if a child born of Jewish parents were adopted by a religious Muslim couple. While 83 percent of students from other schools thought that the child would grow up to be a Muslim, only 48 percent of students at the JI school shared that belief. This essentialist belief that a child born of another religion could never fully become a Muslim correlated strongly with support for violence. Students with this belief were about ten times more likely than other students to believe it their duty to kill non-Muslims.

Mere belief in the group's essential unity creates a looping effect,[36] whereby people strive (or force others) to conform to group norms and stereotypes. For example, the categories Negro, black, and African-American have no sound biological basis. In the last century, many southern U.S. states adopted a "one-drop" rule, which held that a person with any trace of sub-Saharan ancestry (however small or invisible) could not be considered white. This was often informally extended to include dark-skinned Arabs from North Africa and the Middle East (as Sayyid Qutb witnessed during his sojourn in America), Hindus from India, Polynesians, Australian aborigines, and other genetically and historically unrelated "people of color."

Over time, the people who are categorized and discriminated against in this way are compelled to behave as a group, whether they want to or not. This group behavior, in turn, makes the originally imagined group "real" in a social, economic, and political sense. To rectify past patterns of discrimination, members of discriminated groups seek to "empower" themselves and

proudly claim group membership for their own (sometimes altering the group name to signal this shift). This only further reifies
the group's existence and channels its behaviors, though in often
unintended and unforeseen ways.

Human kinds are constantly being constructed and essential-
ized. For example, the categories "alcoholic" and "homosexual"
did not exist as well-defined or coherent social categories before
modern times, although diverse behaviors in past times can be
retroactively described under these labels. Now, however, we find
psychological and medical research seeking the hidden "nature"
and "gene" underlying alcoholism or homosexuality, and a looping effect in organizations such as Alcoholics Anonymous and in
movements such as the one for gay rights. Instigated by Al Qaeda
and reaction to it, the social categories "Arab" and "Muslim" are
now going through some strange loops in our society and imagination.

FRIENDSHIP

When men are friends they have no need of justice, while when they are just
they need friendship as well, and the truest form of justice is thought to be
a friendly quality.

—ARISTOTLE, *NICOMACHEAN ETHICS*, C. 350 B.C.

Friendship has always been critical to human survival, ever
since our big-brain but weak-body ancestors became human by
forming strongly coordinated teams to forage and fight. "For all
we know the bond of personal friendship was evolved," speculated
Nobel Prize–winning ethologist Konrad Lorenz, "by the necessity
for certain individuals to cease from fighting each other in order
to more effectively combat other fellow-members of the species."[37]
Friendship is often a privileged candidate for imagined kinship,

and friends often readily share essentialism bias. In today's era of globalization and cultural fragmentation, friendship has come to the fore as traditional families and cultures disintegrate. As every parent in a family on the move learns hard, the dearest thing for young people who need to make their way in the world is to make and keep friends.

People are becoming more mobile and distant from their origins, and their relevant knowledge about the world is acquired horizontally through media and peers, rather than vertically from generation to generation. Larger social movements, with their greater moral causes, are not enough to prevent young people on the move from drowning in a sea of anonymity or motivating them to kill and die for others. For that you need smaller groups of friends.

In the case studies on terrorism, we've seen how friendships form for jihad in terms of imagined kin. But what's the broader evolutionary appeal and logic of friendship that makes it such a robust strategy for sustaining larger groups and mass movements? And especially so in today's world, where the larger movements transcend traditional ethnic and territorial affinities and aspirations? Friendship is a workhorse of innovation in Silicon Valley,[38] a springboard to power in democratic politics, and the strongest base, or *al-qaeda*, for jihad.[39]

One problem with quid pro quo, the Golden Rule, and other reciprocity strategies for cooperation, is how they can spread in a population of strangers who may initially be suspicious of one another. Spatial constraints, like living or working in the same neighborhood, can increase the probability of encounters between would-be cooperators. So can social constraints on interactions, like belonging to the same linguistic group, profession, or academic discipline. When spatial and social constraints coincide or strongly overlap, as with a village or tribal lineage, and the number of people is small enough so that everyone knows everyone else either directly or through someone they know, then defection becomes relatively easy to spot and weed out. But as the world becomes more cosmopolitan, fakers, shirkers, and spies can rove into neighborhoods and mimic the prevailing linguistic dialects and cultural signals. With friendship, where the focus is on specific partners who are well known rather than on randomly encountered individuals, fairness and justice are taken for granted, and deception is much less likely to succeed.

Another problem for simple reciprocating strategies is how to deal with error and misperception related to other people's acts and intentions. Especially if your prospective partner is a stranger and you're unfamiliar with his customary ways of doing things, you may wrongly think he's trying to cheat when he's actually trying to cooperate. If you retaliate, then you're forced into an endless and destructive cycle of retribution by accident and for no good reason. You might make a mistake in implementing your own strategy and defect when you meant to cooperate. Nobody's perfect.

Especially when it concerns friends, people aren't easily provoked into defection even if a friend cheats from time to time.[40] Others may say to you, "With friends like that, who needs enemies?" And ignore them you may. Not because you're irrational, but because you may have very different criteria for weighting interactions with your friends than with strangers or mere acquaintances. I have a couple of Mexican friends who over the years have taken more material advantage of me than you can imagine: They've hocked my guitar (when that really meant something to me), "borrowed" my car and left it a wreck to rot in a ditch, seduced my sweethearts (in younger years), and robbed me blind. But they've also put their lives on the line to save mine and even risked their skin to help me arrange the escape from prison in Guatemala of someone whom I knew to be innocent but who meant nothing to them (other than that the person they were helping was someone I cared to help). I wouldn't trade that friendship for all the money in China.

Humans can't remember, integrate, and update all past interactions with everyone else in a group beyond about five to ten individuals,[41] more or less the number in a group of close friends, or clique.[42] But even friends usually don't closely monitor past dealings with one another, weighting and scrutinizing each transaction? Friends, however, do tend to concentrate their memories and interactions on one another and to be relatively uninterested in learning about or interacting with strangers once a sufficient number of friends is found.

Anthropologists Daniel Hruschka and Joe Henrich have developed a mathematical simulation of friendship as a stable and robust evolutionary strategy, which is forgiving toward preferred partners but tends to defect in interactions with strangers.[43] The model's assumptions are intuitive. People are sensitive to early interactions in a quest for reliable partners. If they encounter repeated defectors, they don't continue to play with them, as in tit-for-tat and other iterated versions of the prisoner's dilemma, but go off somewhere else to look for them. Once people build up a sufficiently strong group of preferred cooperators, they cultivate and maintain this small set of local relationships. They begin to stop looking for new partners and become slow to break with old ones.

This makes friendship a particularly useful and stable strategy in a large and noisy world. Friendship maximizes cooperation and trust among a happy few, while minimizing the menace of defection and deception from the multitude. But there's also a potential downside to overreliance on friendship: By sticking only to friends, new opportunities to hook up with even better cooperators and to achieve greater benefits may be lost. Getting through from the outside to cliques of youthful friends is a hard thing to do, especially those on an adventurous moral mission, like jihad.

TEAMWORK

Groups usually best other groups because they function better as teams. Imagined kinship and friendship may benefit group survival and success by helping to foster teams, but teamwork itself is something even more basic. There are lots of nonhuman social animals, from wasps to wolves and sparrows to spider monkeys. But none manage anything close to the subtle complexity and innovation of human teamwork. Something is missing in them, something that only humans have. And that's an awareness of what they have, an ability to represent how they are and what they believe and thus to imagine how to use what they have to make things different.

To think of a world different from the world, including heaven and hell, humans needed language and a few other mental tools. One of these other special human mental tools is "folk psychology," the mental ability to take the perspectives of others and to "read" their minds. Language and mind reading function recursively, enabling people to think thoughts about the thoughts of others, and thoughts about their own thoughts, like Russian dolls nesting one inside the other. Other species may represent what's around and have beliefs about the world. Only humans have beliefs about beliefs. Having beliefs about beliefs enables humans to be aware of "I" and "Other" and of the commonalities and differences between them, to imagine a world that is not the world, to distinguish fiction from fact, or to attribute a human state of mind to an animal, a group, or God. Folk psychology not only involves the ability to read minds, to take another person's perspective, and have beliefs about beliefs, but also to empathize, to share something of another's emotions, and so bind people together affectively for more effective action.

Teamwork, language, and mind reading perhaps co-evolved as a solution to the problem of relatively weak hominid bodies rivaling stronger predators to hunt big game. But whatever the evolutionary story, no other species has anything remotely resembling the linguistic and mind-reading skills of humans. This enables people to conjure up imaginary worlds from which they can create new realities, to go beyond the here and now into the distant past and far future. But to imagine and bring into being new worlds, people also had to better learn to survive and thrive together. And that meant teamwork that went way beyond the coordinated hunting efforts of other social animals like lions and hyenas or baboons and chimps, including complicated forms of information exchange and care for one another.

Teamwork is not merely cooperative. It's highly coordinated, and it both demands and favors special kinds of communication and cognitive skills. Members of a hunting group, war party, sports team, or space-shuttle crew have to be intimately acquainted with one another's knowledge, motivations, physical capabilities, and actions. They must be ready to respond in an instant and as a unit, recalculating everything on the fly, in the face of sudden changes in a situation, unexpected threats, and each other's unforeseen failings or successes. Teammates must be able to clearly signal to one another what course of action to take, at any moment, in whatever situation. Or they risk failure, losing the game, or death.

But what really did the trick, to produce behaviorally modern humans like us, was a team "spirit": individual bravery for a common cause that could expand the group and make it fit to beat other teams.

MACHIAVELLI OR GOOD PRINCE HARRY?

Niccolò Machiavelli was a Renaissance philosopher, diplomat, and military adviser who counseled the rulers of Florence how to play "realist" politics and use power to advantage:

> And it must be understood that a prince . . . cannot observe
> all those things which are considered good in men, being often

obliged, in order to maintain the state, to act against faith, against charity, against humanity, and against religion. And, therefore, he must have a mind disposed to adapt itself according to the wind, and as the variation of fortune dictate, and . . . not deviate from what is good if possible, but be able to do evil if constrained.[44]

Machiavelli's name has since passed into common language to refer to political or social moves that are astutely cunning or devious. There's an influential school of evolutionary psychology that holds that our ancestors only became truly human when they mastered a form of social chess that involved Machiavellian mental acrobatics.[45]

The social Machiavellian must not only constantly weigh the benefit of a cooperative association against the cost of sacrificing individual opportunity. He also has to add in the expense of constantly policing the association. He must be able to monitor signals of honesty and deception, assess the reliability of those signals, and evaluate what damage might be done by others if they lie, cheat, or defect. He also must be ever ready to revise his own strategies, contemplate potentially more lucrative alliances that have their own drawbacks, and decide whether to defect himself. He must be adept at learning to feint moves and deceive when necessary, and to develop clear reasoning to avoid deception. Indeed, one argument for the natural selection of logical inference in human cognition is the need to see through the dangers of alliances, any and all of which are fraught with personal costs and perhaps mortal peril.

Philosopher Kim Sterelny argues, rightly I think, that modern society can make the Machiavellian game seem more basic to human life than it really is.[46] The problems of deception and defection are much more serious where mass anonymity, impersonal communication media, mobility, and money facilitate defection. Mass anonymity means many one-shot interactions with people you don't care about and who don't care about you. Impersonal communication media convey little of the texture and tone of social life that gives meaning to cooperation, like a dried and pressed water lily uprooted from its pod in the pond, or e-mail spam. Mobility makes getting away with defection easy, especially after one-off interactions with strangers. And money makes defection attractive, because large amounts of portable gains can be whisked off from single interactions. But humans first evolved in far smaller social worlds where anonymity was unavailable, a shift to other groups was not a viable option, and defection from one's kith and kin almost invariably soon led to a lonely death. The need and cost of policing people to pull their full weight were likely distributed over the whole collective and were fairly minimal.

"All warfare is based on deception," declared Chinese military theorist Sun Tzu. The declaration was made some 2,500 years ago in *The Art of War*,[47] the oldest and perhaps most influential book ever written on military strategy. But this refers to warfare *between* groups, especially large groups of the kind Sun Tzu worried about during the Era of the Warring States. The sentiment provoked by war within a small fighting group is a far thing from a Machiavellian attitude. We might call it the Good Prince Harry sentiment, after Britain's Prince Harry of Wales. Harry, a second lieutenant in the Household Cavalry, was redeployed out of Afghanistan when the news media found out about his presence there. He grudgingly left his army buddies, and the thrill of the team in action:

> At least in operations then you are kept on your toes the whole time, that's what the guys join up for, I guess, that adrenaline. . . . Once you are out in the middle of the desert and all you depend on is one another, to look out for each other, then it comes down to the fact that you are all mates, all ranks aside, you are mates and look out for one another. . . . You do what you have to do, what's necessary to save your own guys. If you need to drop a

bomb . . . to save lives, that's what happens.[48] [Though Good Prince Harry's unconditional love of his buddies may not quite extend to all members of his military unit, including Muslims he dubbed Pakis and ragheads.][49]

In a large army, each soldier is rationally motivated to stay as much out of the fight as he can to avoid injury and stay alive. The dilemma is that if all the soldiers on a side behave rationally in this way, they won't fight, the battle surely will be lost, and all may die. Armies have developed various ways of dealing with this problem in the course of human history. Two repeatedly stand out: Find and execute slackers and deserters, and keep the basic fighting units small and intimate to maximize team spirit. But in a small world that's already cooperative, losing esteem in the eyes of one's peers, and status in the community, is punishment enough when esteem and status are just about the only things that socially distinguish one person's worth from another's. And snubbing or shows of disdain cost the community little to execute in terms of time and energy lost from other activities. Keeping up team fighting spirit also comes with the territory at almost no extra cost.

To kill and die with friends, as in the jihad, almost invariably involves deep love of one's group. Hatred of others may not even be necessary, only a fathomless lack of empathy and concern is. Being imbued with a righteous cause is usually not sufficient to die and kill for the group, but as we'll see in the next chapters, it's usually necessary to sustain war, especially against all odds.

CHAPTER 18
BLOOD SPORT: WAR MAKES MEN MEN

Homo homini lupus est.
[Man is the wolf of mankind.]

—THOMAS HOBBES, *LEVIATHAN*, C. 1650

The noble man's soul has two goals
To die or to achieve its dreams
What is life if I don't live
Feared and what I have is forbidden to others
When I speak, all the world listens
And my voice echoes among people
I see my death, but I rush to it
This is the death of men. . . .
I will throw my heart at my enemies' faces
And my heart is iron and fire!
I will protect my land with the edge of the sword
So my people will know that I am the man.

—ABDELRAHIM MAHMUD, *THE MARTYR*, 1937

Only the dead have seen the end of war.

—GEORGE SANTAYANA, *THE LIFE OF REASON*, 1953

THE NOBLE BEAST

There were two broad and overlapping epochs in human prehistory:
one in which men primarily hunted animals, and another in which

men primarily hunted men. The passage from one to the other may be the most important advance in human social evolution.

Humans cooperate to compete first against the elements of nature, and then against each other. Our ancestors lived in a world inhabited by rivals far more numerous, stronger, and more savage than themselves. It was a competition humans very nearly lost. Human salvation lay in persistent reliance on a social band of kin and kith for collective strength, and a special form of primate wit that made it work as a winning team.

The flip side of human teamwork is group competition. Our first major competitors were the prey we hunted and the rival animal predators that also preyed on us. Then other groups of people became humans' most feared predators and choicest prey. No other species primarily preys on itself to such an extent. The senses of all hunting animals are most stimulated in the hunt, and humans are no exception.

Human history advances fitfully, in alternating intervals of war and peace. But wars accelerate history more than peace and the commerce that peace allows. War makes for better storytelling, is much better reading, and certainly plays better on television and the Internet. War is the most stimulating path to gain and glory our species has known. It's exciting even when only imagined and lived vicariously, as in the always popular clamor for war, at least before the casualties come home. In the lead-up to the 2003 Iraq war, Fox News had a text line running on the screen: "Give War a Chance." When war came, commentary was breathless on all the channels. That's a pretty normal way societies react to the prospect of wars they think they can win.

Robert E. Lee said, "It is well that war is so terrible: We would grow too fond of it." Israeli war hero Moshe Dayan remarked, "I know of nothing more exciting than war."[1] Among the Freikorps, or "Free Militia," forerunners of the early Nazi storm troopers (SA) and SS, militia members didn't much know what they were fighting for, just what they were fighting against. Freikorps volunteer Ernst von Salomon described their mood:

> There, on the other side of the divide, they wanted property and security in life. . . . They ask us what we believe in. We do not believe at all, in anything except action itself. Action for the sake of action. Nothing, only the ability to act. We were a group of warriors, drunk from the desires of the world. Full of the impulsiveness and the joy of action. We did not know what we wanted and what we knew we did not want. War and adventures, stormy emotions, and destruction. Our job was to attack, to rule.[2]

Warfare, the class commentator and author Barbara Ehrenreich argues,[3] may be a continuation of the evolutionary drive to hunt and to avoid being hunted, but where human groups alone are predators and prey. The rituals of war, of blood sacrifice and savaging of flesh, credit this view. Ancient Greeks and Carthaginians would ritually sacrifice their own and offer burnt offerings of animals (hecatombs) to ensure good outcomes in war. The ancient Semites substituted animal for human sacrifice when they found the one true God.[4] But like the pagan gods of the Celts,[5] the Hebrew God demanded that his Chosen People slaughter every man, woman, and child of His people's enemies, as well as all their pigs, chickens, goats, and cows. "Thou shalt not kill," commands God, but that's only for His Chosen People. Against rivals mere killing isn't enough:

> But of the cities of these people, which the Lord thy God doth give thee for an inheritance, thou shalt save alive nothing that breatheth. But thou shalt utterly destroy them; namely, the Hittites, and the Amorites, the Canaanites, and the Perizzites, the Hivites, and the Jebusites. . . . I will make mine arrows drunk with blood, and my sword shall devour flesh; and that with the

blood of the slain and of the captives, from the beginning of revenges upon the enemy.

—DEUTERONOMY 20:16–17, 32:42

Hundreds of years ago, in the American Southwest, the Anasazi of Chaco Canyon killed, butchered, and ate other human beings against whom they warred. Then they ritually defecated the remains in the hearths of their victims' dwellings, probably to signal dominance and disdain.[6] The nineteenth-century Native American tribes of the lower Colorado River did much the same, carrying off the heads of their victims to their village, where "they built a fire in a hole, and when it had burned to coals, placed the heads around the fire, as one bakes pumpkins, as an insult."[7]

The sixteenth-century Aztecs of Mexico[8] and the nineteenth-century Dahomey of West Africa[9] conducted wars for the primary purpose of capturing sacrificial victims, whom they ritually ripped apart and ate. The early Spanish conquistadors would slaughter Indian idolaters whenever they pleased, and savage the women to make them love Christ. Twentieth-century German Nazi doctors would decapitate healthy but "subhuman" patients, especially those with good teeth, bake their heads for hours in crematoria until the flesh flaked off, and then give the skulls as office gifts.[10] Still in this twenty-first century, in the Ituri forest district of the Democratic Republic of the Congo, rebel forces of the Uganda-backed Movement for the Liberation of the Congo (MLC) have been repeatedly denounced by the UN Security Council[11] for grilling people on spits, boiling young girls alive, and cutting open the chests of Pygmies and other noncombatants and ritually "ripping out their hearts, livers and lungs, which they ate while still warm."[12]

At the trial of eight men accused of planning to bomb transatlantic airliners in the summer of 2006 with homemade liquid explosives, the "martyrdom video" of one of the men, Abdullah

Ahmed Ali, was played. There was relish in the prospect of shredding flesh:

> I'm doing this . . . to punish and to humiliate the *kuffar* [nonbelievers], to teach them a lesson that they will never forget. . . . Leave us alone. Stop meddling in our affairs and we will leave you alone. Otherwise expect floods of martyr operations against you and we will take our revenge and anger, ripping amongst your people and scattering the people and your body parts and your people's body parts responsible for these wars and oppression, decorating the streets.[13]

In all societies, moral norms strongly constrain and punish murder, rape, torture, desecrating the body, pillage, and plunder. But in war, all may be allowed, even encouraged. A man who kills many in our own society is a mass murderer. In war, mass killing may rate the Medal of Honor: Sergeant Alvin York, America's best-known World War I war hero, religiously rejected all forms of violence at home but got a ticker tape parade for attacking a German machine gun nest and killing twenty-eight. Torture "is basically subject to perception," said CIA lawyer Jonathan Friedman, according to meeting minutes released at a Senate hearing in June 2008. "If the detainee dies, you're doing it wrong."[14] Arguably, this may be some sort of an advance over cannibalizing an enemy, but it's doubtful the victims appreciate the difference.

War has been a supremely moral act for most societies throughout history. Hatred and dehumanization of the enemy as animals, or at least barbarians, is almost a constant of war that is fought in defense of the group. "Barbarian" is one way the United States government designates Al Qaeda, as Al Qaeda does the United States.

"The art of war," Adam Smith wrote in *The Wealth of Nations*, "is certainly the noblest of all arts."[15] The reason, he argues, is that it has allowed the progressive advance of commerce and civilization, bringing the greatest benefits of peace and prosperity to the most people for the longest time. People are most cooperative and creative when they fight others in war. "War alone brings up to their highest tension all human energies and imposes the stamp of nobility upon the peoples who have the courage to make it," exulted Benito Mussolini, the Italian dictator and founder of modern fascism.[16] This sentiment has been felt and proclaimed throughout history, regardless of whether war was to conquer or set people free.

War between human groups is as much or more a constant part of the evolution of society and civilization as peace. War is better at defining who the group is, what its boundaries are, and what it stands for. War is also more compelling and effective in generating solidarity with something larger and more lasting than ourselves. War compresses history and dramatically changes its course.

There is urgency, excitement, ecstasy, and altruistic exaltation in war, a mystic feeling of solidarity with something greater than oneself: a tribe, a nation, a movement—the Group. Following a successful attack during the American Civil War, a Union officer in the Twelfth New York expressed this common sentiment:

> It is impossible to describe the feelings one experiences in such a moment. God, Country, Love, home, pride, conscious strength & power, all crowd your swelling breast . . . proud, proud as a man can feel over this victory to our arms—if it were a man's privilege to die when he finished, he should die at such a moment.[17]

Nobel laureate William Faukner poignantly describes how these feelings so acutely linger in society well after war is done:[18]

> For every Southern boy fourteen years old, not once but whenever he wants it, there is the instant when it's still not yet two

o'clock on that July afternoon in 1863, the brigades are in position behind the rail fence, the guns are laid and ready in the
woods and the furled flags are already loosened to break out
and Pickett himself with his long oiled ringlets and his hat in
one hand probably and his sword in the other looking up the hill
waiting for Longstreet to give the word and it's all in the balance, it hasn't happened yet, it hasn't even begun yet . . . we have
come too far with too much at stake and that moment doesn't
need even a fourteen-year-old boy to think This time. Maybe
this time . . . the world, the golden dome of Washington itself to
crown with desperate and unbelievable victory.

In peace, there is calm and, ultimately, boredom. I suspect that
boredom's role in generating war over the ages is considerable. It's
a big part of today's story of why young men with few other lifeway
channels or challenges join the jihad.

WAR MAKES MEN MEN, AND WOMEN SOMEWHAT DIFFERENT

Until very recently, hunting and warfare have been occupations of
men. Indeed, in most cultures, initiation into manhood has required
proof of skill in hunting savage beasts or men. Among the Maasai
of Kenya, a boy would become a man by killing a lion and then
going to war. Frontiersmen of British and French North America
got manly reputations from hunting bear and scalping Indians. For
many Native American tribes,[19] a man had to fight in war before he
could be called a man.[20] Among the Dorzé of Ethiopia, to become
a man meant taking as a trophy an enemy's testicles—the larger
the testicles, the greater a man he would become. For the Naga of
Assam (India), the Iatmul of New Guinea, and the Shuar of Peru,
to become a man was to take off the head of another.[21] And, of
course, warfare is often linked to male sexuality, from the strategic
planning and vocabulary of invasions, to the ecstasy of conquest,

and down to the thrusting and penetrating motions of much weaponry. Not to mention modern "missile envy."

In *The Descent of Man*, Darwin noted that most human violence is committed by young men. About 80 percent to 90 percent of all human killing is committed by males, most of them aged fourteen to thirty-five.[22] In the United States, for example, men were responsible for 88 percent of all homicides between 1976 and 2004, and nearly three-fourths of these involved men killing other men. The peak years for murder in recent U.S. history were 1990 to 1994, when the homicide rate exceeded 9 killed per 100,000 people (it's been between 5 and 6 for the last few years).[23] In those years, the number of killers ranged from 23 to 30 per 100,000 for male teens aged fourteen to seventeen, from 34 to 41 per 100,000 for young men aged eighteen to twenty-four, and 15 to 18 per 100,000 for men aged twenty-five to thirty-five.[24] These trends closely follow statistics for killing in war, except that in war nearly 100 percent of killing is by men. Only in the last few decades of human history have women played any appreciable killing role in war, a dubious advance for women's rights.

Controlled experiments by the Dutch team of Mark Van Vugt, David De Cremer, and Dirk Janseen show that men sacrifice more for their group when it is competing against other groups (as in war) than if there were no intergroup rivalry.[25] Women generally scored higher than men on measures of cooperation within the group, and their levels of cooperation were not significantly affected by intergroup competition. Men scored higher than women on cooperation only when competition with other groups was in the offing. Men kill much more than women do in competitive situations and with and for small bands of buddies. And men often celebrate their conquests between the legs of women, whereas evolutionary psychology and history suggest that women who win are less likely to mirror that sort of behavior.

The data on suicide bombing bear out these general trends.

Among groups that allow female suicide bombers, fewer than 15 percent of suicide bombers are women. Overall, the rate of female suicide bombing corresponds to the general rate of female homicide and participation in war. Only among the Chechens and Tamil Tigers have female suicide bombers been represented in significant numbers. About a third of Tamil Tigers suicide bombers were young women and girls, carefully selected, cultivated, and trained for their missions because females could pass more easily through security and their dress could better hide bombs. Once enrolled, these living dead couldn't opt out lest they be executed or their families punished.

Revenge for close family members seems to be a highly significant motivator for female suicide bombers. At least this appears to be so where data are available: in Chechnya, Iraq, and Palestine. There are cases of male suicide bombers out for revenge, but studies by Ariel Merari for Palestine indicate it is not significant overall, nor can it be so for the several hundred foreign volunteers in the "Sinjar" group for jihad and martyrdom in Iraq.[26] A recent study of captured Al Qaeda volunteers by the Saudi Ministry of the Interior also fails to indicate revenge or death of a close relative as a relevant factor.[27]

Lindsay O'Rourke, a political science student at the University of Chicago who has studied female suicide attacks across the world since 1981, surmised in the *New York Times* that "surprisingly similar motives" drive men and women to blow themselves up: "The primary motivation of male and female suicide bombers is a deep loyalty to their communities combined with a variety of personal grievances . . . it is simply impossible to say one sex cares more about the others."[28] She argues that "95 percent of female suicide attacks occurred within the context of a military campaign against occupying forces," that is, in a situation of intergroup conflict.

But the issue is not who cares more about the group; it's how they care. Cross-cultural research on killing by women undertaken by psychologists Margo Wilson, Martin Daley, and David Buss indicates that women kill most often in self-defense and in defense of family, especially children.[29] Between June 2000 and April 2010, more than one-third of the sixty or so Chechen suicide bombers were women. Known as "Black Widows," they mostly volunteered to revenge the deaths of family members. For example, on November 29, 2001, Elza Gazueva volunteered for a bombing mission after her husband and brother were tortured and killed by Russian forces. She went to the Russian military headquarters and managed to get close enough to the commandant who was responsible for taking her husband and brother from her home and who had ordered their torture and death. Gazueva approached the commandant asking, "Do you remember me?" before exploding herself and killing him. Most of the other cases are quite similar, from the first Chechen suicide bombers, Khava Baraeva and Luiza Magomadova in June 2000, to Roza Nogaeva and Mariam Tuburova in September 2004.[30] Chechen suicide bombings fell off in the wake of popular revulsion to the Beslan massacre in September 2004, when Islamists seized a school in North Ossetia (Russian Federation), demanding an end to the Russian occupation of Chechnya. (In the ensuing gun battle between the hostage takers and Russian security forces, more than 300 hostages were killed, including nearly 200 children.) But bombing resumed in 2007, when the pro-Russian Chechen government moved to crush remaining militants in coordination with Russia's newly picked president of neighboring Dagestan. Dzhanet Abdullayeva, the seventeen-year-old widow of a Dagestani rebel she had met through the Internet and who was killed in 2009, was one of two "Black Widows" responsible for the March 2010 Moscow subway bombings, in which forty people died.[31]

As O'Rourke notes, women, although occasionally involved in mass bombings, are five times more likely than men to target specific individuals for assassination. Male suicide bombers rarely act against singled-out individuals, and even more rarely act alone. In almost all cases, males form part of a small group of friends that becomes a "band of brothers" whose members die for one another as much or more than for any cause. The Saudi study finds that 64 percent join through friends and 24 percent through family, a result that accords with Marc Sageman's research on how volunteers across the world join the Al Qaeda–inspired movement.[32] We've already seen some detailed examples of how these bands of buddies form. There are a few examples of two, three, or four Chechen, Uzbek, and Iraqi women striking in a coordinated suicide bombing, but scant evidence that these operations involved close friends.

Although the jihad discriminates against frontline participation by women (as most military organizations and groups still do) their occasional participation does little to lessen the general lesson that jihad is a team and blood sport for morally outraged and glory-seeking young men.

THE RISING RISK FROM ASYMMETRIC CONFLICTS AND VERY BIG WARS

The rise of large-scale, cooperative civilization has reduced death from individual violence and natural hazard. In modern times, the frequency and lethality of "small wars" have also progressively declined among nations increasingly intertwined within global trade networks. But large, catastrophic intercontinental wars that markedly change the course of history have only increased in severity.

Evidence from the archaeological study of prehistoric societies and from the ethnographic record of modern hunters and gatherers indicates that warfare was probably a frequent cause of death, averaging 13 percent to 15 percent of total deaths in small-scale tribal societies. By comparison, war was responsible for less than 1 percent of male deaths in the United States and Europe during the very bloody twentieth century.[33] Archaeologist Lawrence Keeley reasons that if industrialized countries were still organized into small bands, tribes, and chiefdoms, then there would have been 2 billion war-related deaths in the twentieth century rather than the estimated 100 million or so.[34] Harvard University psychologist Steven Pinker also charts the decline of violence from biblical times to the present and argues that, though it may seem illogical and even obscene, given the recent history of genocides around the world, we are living in the most peaceful time of our species' existence.[35]

But this may be something of an illusion.

Adam Smith's sentiment about warfare being so noble stemmed in part from the belief that powerful nations had a monopoly on weapons of mass destruction and dissuasion and thus had finally put an end to the threat against civilization from barbarians. This sentiment was justified at the end of the eighteenth century, but not today. Work by Boston University historian Ivan Arreguín-Toft reveals a steady increase since that time in the ability of "weak actors" to win wars with at least ten times less destructive means available to them than to "strong actors."[36] Indeed, since 1950, weak actors have won a majority of their "asymmetric" conflicts with strong actors, thus making future "small wars" more inviting for the less powerful.

While it's apparently true that the overall percentage of deaths from violence among humankind has generally declined, especially in homicide rates, it is also the case that large-scale wars have become increasingly catastrophic, world-changing events. A mathematical trend known as a "power-law distribution" seems to capture the progress of wars over the last couple of centuries: for each tenfold increase in the magnitude of wars there is roughly a threefold decrease in the number of wars. There were some 20 millions deaths in World War I, slightly less than half of them civilian. This compares to 72 million fatalities in World War II, about two-thirds of them civilian. Following the trends, one might expect hundreds of millions of deaths in a future war, nearly all civilian.[37] The collective implications of such violence would probably reverberate across the world to orders of magnitude greater than if those fatality figures were the accumulated results of individual homicides or small wars.[38]

Ever since World War II, deterrence—based on a credible threat of nuclear annihilation, and the rational expectation that fear of annihilation will compel people to avoid war—has maintained peace among major powers, however cold. Deterrence has worked so far, but maybe just barely. The world came perilously close to nuclear war during the Cuban missile crisis, and as more and more countries acquire nuclear weapons, the chances of miscalculation increase. Not to mention nuclear terrorism, where calculations may be skewed out of whack by divinely inspired preferences and prejudices. Without global institutions to limit reaction to any initial nuclear attack, a rapid chain of events could readily lead to the meltdown of society—not from any terrorist blast but from reaction to it.[39]

LIVING WITH NO END TO WAR

Politicians easily make war popular, even after recent catastrophic defeat: "Naturally, the common people don't want war," reasoned Nazi leader Hermann Goering, so "all you have to do is tell them they are being attacked, and denounce the pacifists for lack of patriotism and exposing the country to danger. It works the same in every country." In the United States, such jingoist calls by politicians and pundits to unprovoked or unnecessary wars have been quite successful, from the Spanish-American War to the Iraq War. Of course, if you actually *are* being attacked, then pacifism can be suicidal, as Winston Churchill rightly surmised.

"War isn't an adventure; it's a disease, like typhus," opined Antoine de Saint-Exupéry, who authored the marvelous French childhood fantasy *The Little Prince* and died piloting a plane for the Free French in World War II. If only it were so. War is not a malfunction of human nature, a flaw of history, or a failure of politics. War is no more a disease or a parasite on society, consuming resources and people, than it is a creator of cultures, generating innovation and expansion of resources, populations, and ideas. In war, or under the threat of it, people use their worst, and no small amount of self-justification, to do their best.

Only in the twentieth century, in the wake of two world wars and under threat of nuclear annihilation, have large numbers of people and their leaders begun to question if war is necessary and unavoidable. But this antiwar sentiment hardly extends to everyone. Antiwar movements over the last century have been well meaning but only marginally successful in efforts to stop killing. It's usually when the waste of lives and treasure becomes apparent to those who previously supported a war, or when defeat looms large, that pacifism gains purchase in the public.

Peace in the life of our species, like good health in the life of a person, may just be "a transitional state that presages nothing good"[40] in the end. Of course, that doesn't mean we shouldn't work as hard as we can for peace or good health. But our biology and our history say that permanent peace is about as improbable on earth as unending day. There may always be jihads of one sort or another. We may not be able to end them, but we can find ways to lessen their impact.

CHAPTER 19
BEYOND ALL REASON: THE CLAUSEWITZ DELUSION

The Moral Law causes the people to be . . . undismayed by any danger.

—SUN TZU, *THE ART OF WAR*, C. 540 B.C.

Don't ask me what the political solution is to be. . . . Our sacred duty is to fight, to resist occupation of our sacred land and change the conditions of our people. That is our duty, our sacred duty. . . . I will not accept the existence of Israel. I will never accept the existence of a state of Israel. Never, ever.

—AUTHOR'S MEETING WITH RAMADAN SHALLAH, GENERAL
SECRETARY, PALESTINIAN ISLAMIC JIHAD, DAMASCUS,
DECEMBER 15, 2009

THE CLAUSEWITZ DELUSION ("WAR IS POLITICS BY OTHER MEANS")

War is never wholly a product of reason and rational calculation,[1] never just "politics by other means," despite what von Clausewitz famously stated in his classic study, *On War.*[2] This, the sentiment of a Prussian regimental officer in the post-Napoleonic era of state interests and strategies to rearrange "the balance of power," disastrously misguided European elites into believing that wars could be started and pursued to a desired end by careful planning (although he did grant that in the fog of war events can sometimes spin out of control). Many of our political and military leaders still believe in this Clausewitz delusion: It's a mainstay in the curricula of U.S. war colleges and the international-relations departments of top U.S. universities. Yet war is almost always an emotional matter of status and pride, of shedding blood and tearing the flesh of others held dear, of dread and awe, and of the instinctual needs to escape from fear, to dominate, and to avenge.

Even the First World War—actually the first and only war whose leaders almost uniformly believed that they were following Clausewitz's dictum—is remembered in the end not so much for destroying the old monarchical world order and forcing in the modern age, for preserving democracy or bringing on communism and fascism. In France, as in most other places in Europe, "the Great War" is still today ritually remembered as it was mostly lived then: in countless village and family memorials of sorrow and pride, and collective confusion over what purpose the mass slaughter served except as a costly show of commitment to *La Patrie*, the Fatherland. But once in the battle, the French *poilus*, the German *Landsers*, and our doughboys mostly continued the fight unto death out of solidarity and for the esteem of their comrades and community.

FOR COMRADES

Among American military psychologists and historians, the conventional wisdom on why soldiers fight is that ideology is not important. Most of the studies focus on measures of "fighter spirit" among American soldiers in World War II, Korea, and Vietnam.[3] Only leadership and group loyalty seem critical. In World War II, for example, solidarity and loyalty to the group helped mightily to sustain combat soldiers, while personal commitment to the war and ideology were much less meaningful. American soldiers "ain't fighting for patriotism," and the British soldier "never gave democracy a thought."[4] Soldiers' belief in the legitimacy of a cause worth fighting for steadily increased during World War II and steadily decreased during the Korean War, yet fighting spirit remained fairly constant.[5]

In *The Deadly Brotherhood*,[6] John McManus argues that the American combat soldier in World War II did not fight and die for abstract concepts, such as democracy or love of country, but for his "devoted fraternity" or band of brothers with whom he shared dangers and hardship on the front line. A rifleman in the Thirty-second Infantry Division wrote: "Survival for one's self was the first priority by far. The second priority was survival for the man next to you and the man next to him. So, right or wrong, love of country and pride . . . was a good bit behind."

William Manchester described the importance of camaraderie in his memoirs of U.S. Marine Corps service in World War II: "Those men on the line were my family, my home. They were closer to me than . . . friends had ever been or would ever be. They never let me down, and I couldn't do it to them."[7]

A Confederate corporal in the Ninth Alabama, returning to his regiment after recovering from a battle wound, identifies this sentiment of friendship as love: "A soldier is always near crazy to get away from the army on furloughs, but as a general thing they are more anxious to get back. There is a feeling of love—a strong attachment for those with whom one has shared common dangers, that is never felt for any one else, or under any other circumstances."[8]

Ideology is only as strong as the ties of friendship and camaraderie in war. Like initiation into other legendary groups of warriors, such as ancient Sparta's hoplites or the French Foreign Legion, candidates would be stripped naked, bodily and mentally, as they trained and bonded in a common cause. To abandon a friend on the field was the greatest sin imaginable. According to Nazi SS member Johannes Hassebroeack, each in a unit "devoted himself to all of the others":

Even the ties of love between a man and a woman are not stronger than the friendship there was among us. This friendship was all. It both gave us strength and held us together, in a covenant of blood. It was worth living for; it was worth dying for. This is what gave us the physical strength and courage to do what others did not dare to do. . . . What we did—we did, of course, for Germany, for the Führer, for the future. But every one of us did what he did for every one of the others.[9]

When there is an undeniable esprit de corps, there can be great courage and sacrifice, whatever the ideology.

AND FOR CAUSE

But it is not camaraderie alone that made the Germans the best fighting soldiers of World War II or the Confederate armies persevere when much larger and better-equipped Union armies flagged. In *Frontsoldaten: The German Soldier in World War II*, Stephen Fritz argues that strong unit cohesion and ideological commitment infused the German ranks:

The Germans consistently outfought the far more numerous Allied armies that eventually defeated them. . . . On a man for man basis the German ground soldiers consistently inflicted casualties at about a 50 percent higher rate than they incurred from the opposing British and American troops under all circumstances. This was true when they were attacking and when they were defending, when they had a local numerical superiority and when, as was usually the case, they were outnumbered.[10]

By D-day (June 6, 1944), 35 percent of German soldiers had been wounded at least once and 21 percent twice or more. The impressive unit cohesion and fighting spirit of the *Landser*, the ordinary German infantryman, was most remarkable on the Russian front, where 80 percent of Germans fought. German soldiers, it seems, were far more committed to the war aims of National Socialism than previously thought, though especially among the SS. In December 1944, at Budapest, overwhelming Soviet forces were advancing into the city, and remaining German troops were faced with retreat, surrender, or death. Allied reports from the city indicated that "General [Johannes] Friessner [commanding German regular forces] can count for defense of the [Hungarian] capital on SS units that operate under the name 'Death Volunteers.'"[11] Among the 400,000 or so German soldiers in the Waffen SS, losses—killed and missing—were about one-third, versus about 10 percent for U.S. troops, and German troops fought on with massive casualty rates that typically destroyed the fighting ability of combat units in other armies, including America's. Most important were the bonds of military friendship inherited from Prussian tradition, which raised comradeship to the level of ideological and strategic doctrine.

Hitler promised a "social revolution" that would merge the all-for-one values of the combat soldier with the whole civilian population, thus creating the *Volksgemeinschaft*. The Hitler Youth was not a brainwashing factory but a place where children were encouraged to ignore social status and think about the group before the individual. The ideological movement was emotionally rewarding for children and for the soldiers the children would become. The German rank and file would readily quote philosophers and details of European history in their letters back home. These young men were well trained, deeply bonded to their peers, and highly motivated by the cause of National Socialism to take the fight to Germany's enemies.

In *Kameradschaft*, Thomas Kühne[12] traces *Volksgemeinschaft* back to medieval notions of chivalry, and then on through the French Revolution and Napoleonic era, when the Romantic idea of "general war" to save Humanity emerged, reinforced by training and military service in defense of the nation and national honor (allied to masculinity). In World War I, soldiers also saw themselves engaged in a general war for humanity's soul, but they enlisted and organized on a strongly regional basis, as in the American Civil War, bonding on the front lines into "trench families—frontline groups united by regional affinity, proximity and shared experience."

This ethos carried into World War II despite the high casualty rates on the Russian front that eviscerated fighting groups. Hitler's social revolution turned longing for community, or *Gemeinschaft*, into a national passion. "Good" was anything that strengthened the community. The highest prestige accrued to those who rejected norms—doubts, scruples, inhibitions—that impeded the fight against so-called enemies and threats to the community. The emotions generated in mutual caring, commitment, and sacrifice for others made it possible for soldiers to come to terms with war's inhuman face: destruction and killing. Even in the later stages of the war, there was a sense of group empowerment "strong enough in the group's later stages to approximate group immortality and the will to fight on against desperate odds." It explains how "never have men fought better for a worse cause" than the men who marched to the tune of "total war" under the swastika.[13]

Nazi soldiers were mostly ordinary men whom an ideological brotherhood had made extraordinarily brave. And though American leaders have repeatedly claimed that suicide bombers are "cowardly," from the 9/11 hijackers to the killers of former Pakistani prime minister Benazir Bhutto, in fact they are anything but that.

CAUSE VERSUS CALCULUS

American military historians and analysts tend to chalk up camaraderie to rational self-interest and to dismiss the notion of sacrifice for a cause as a critical factor in war:

[T]he intense primary-group ties so often reported in combat groups are best viewed as mandatory necessities arising from immediate life-and-death exigencies. Much like the Hobbesian description of primitive life, the combat situation can be nasty, brutish and short . . . one can view primary-group processes in the combat situation as a kind of rudimentary social contract which is entered into because of advantages to individual self-interest. Rather than viewing soldiers' primary groups as some kind of semi-mystical bond of comradeship, they can better be understood as pragmatic and situational responses.[14]

In Vietnam, falling morale, desertion, and fragging (killing officers) increased long after popular support for the war collapsed, and only after soldiers began feeling that "Vietnamization" (handing over security to South Vietnamese forces) was a lost cause that no soldier wanted to be the last to die for.

American soldiers said that the cause of democracy was "crap" and "a joke" in Vietnam. And yet they described the selfless bravery of the North Vietnamese "because they believed in something" and "knew what they were fighting for."[15] So, maybe *others* would die for a cause and not only for comrades.

James McPherson in *For Cause and Comrades* notes that, unlike later American armies of mostly draftees and professional soldiers, Civil War armies on both sides were composed mainly of volunteers who often joined up and fought with family, friends, and neighbors from the same communities. Unlike World War II or Vietnam vets, they wrote letters back to the same affinity groups they had fought with.

A large number of the men in blue and gray were intensely aware of the issues at stake and passionately concerned about them. How could it be otherwise? This was, after all, a *civil war*. Its outcome would determine the fate of the nation . . . the

future of American society and of every person in that society. Civil War soldiers lived in the world's most politicized and
democratic country in the mid-nineteenth century. A majority
of them had voted in the election of 1860, the most heated and
momentous election in American history. When they enlisted,
many of them did so for patriotic and ideological reasons—to
shoot as they had voted, so to speak. These convictions did not
disappear after they signed up. . . . They needed no indoctrina-
tion lectures to explain what they were fighting for, no films like
Frank Capra's *Why We Fight* series in World War II.[16]

During the Civil War, ideology was given a particularly religious cast: "Civil War armies were, arguably, the most religious in
American history. Wars usually intensify religious convictions. . . .
Many men who were at best nominal Christians before they enlisted
experienced conversion to the genuine article by their baptism of
fire."[17]

In *Fear in Battle*, John Dollard interviewed veterans from the
Abraham Lincoln Brigade, Americans who fought in the Spanish
Civil War against Franco and fascism. In response to the question:
"What would you say are the most important things that help a
man overcome fear in battle?" 77 percent cited belief in their ideology and "the aims of war" versus: leadership (49 percent), esprit
de corps (28 percent), hatred of enemy (21 percent), distraction
and keeping busy (17 percent).[18] The Lincoln Brigade was not religious, far from it; but it was motivated by a transcendental cause of
socialism as a historical necessity opposed by the evil of fascism.

During the Battle of Britain, Reginald Jones, head of Britain's
World War II "scientific intelligence" effort, put the sentiment for
comrades and cause this way:

I used to look at my wall map every morning and wonder how
we could possibly survive. Anyone in his right sense would do

the best deal he could with Hitler—but we had no thought of it. Even though we were tired by the Blitz, there was that white glow overpowering, sublime that ran through our island from end to end. It can hardly be described to those who did not experience it; it must lie very deep down among human emotions, giving the individual a strange, subdued elation at facing dangers in which he may easily perish as an individual but also a subconscious knowledge that any society which has a high enough proportion of similar individuals is all the more likely to survive because of their sacrifice.[19]

It appears, then, that, despite U.S. patriotic propaganda and the studies that discount it, American warfare from World War II to today may be the exception to the heartfelt sense of war as a noble cause. To die and kill for jihad more nearly follows the general rule, at least to judge from that "white glow overpowering" which seems to illuminate so many I talk to.

MATTERS OF PRINCIPLE

How do people decide whether or not to join violent movements, vote to support a war, or to say "yes" when asked if they support suicide attacks in public opinion surveys? A common assumption of policy makers and analysts[20] and of researchers on war[21] and terrorism[22] is that decisions to support or oppose warfare are made in an instrumentally rational manner, driven by cost-benefit calculations. But war, which arouses humans' most noble sentiments and worst fears, is rarely, if ever, simply a product of reason and rational calculation.

Research with my colleague Jeremy Ginges, a social psychologist, challenges the notion that war, or at least commitment to terrorism and political violence as a moral call to war, is basically "policy by other means." If decisions about political

violence are based more on moral than on instrumental calculations, then factors that are materially irrelevant should influence decision making. What follows is a brief summary of three
studies carried out with Palestinians and Israelis that tested this
prediction.[23]

STUDY 1: MORAL DUTY OVERRIDES RESPONSIBILITY TO FAMILY AND HOMETOWN

Seven hundred twenty Palestinian adults were recruited at fourteen university campuses across 120 locales in the West Bank and
Gaza to participate in a survey. Half of these participants were
women, and half were members of Hamas or Palestinian Islamic
Jihad. Participants were asked the extent to which the scenarios
were "certainly acceptable," "somewhat acceptable," "somewhat
unacceptable," or "certainly unacceptable." For example:

1. What is the position of Islam in your opinion regarding the bomber
   who carries out the bombing attack (which some call martyrdom
   attacks while others call suicide attacks), killing himself with the
   aim of killing his enemies as some Palestinians do. Does Islam allow
   or not allow such action?

2. What if a person wanted to carry out a bombing (which some . . .
   call suicide attacks) against the enemies of Palestine but his father
   becomes ill, and his family begs the chosen martyr to take care of
   his father, would it be acceptable to delay the attack indefinitely?

3. What if a person wanted to carry out a bombing (which some . . .
   call suicide attacks) against the enemies of Palestine but his family
   begs him to delay martyrdom indefinitely because there was a significantly high chance the chosen martyr's family would be killed in
   retaliation, would it be acceptable to delay the attack indefinitely?

4. What if the bombing attack led to the destruction of olive trees and the bombing of his hometown and school and the death of the students, would it be acceptable to delay the attack indefinitely?

Eighty-one percent of Palestinian students believe that Islam allows the actions of the suicide bomber (+SB), including nearly 100 percent of supporters of Hamas and Palestinian Islamic Jihad; 19 percent of the students did not believe Islam supports suicide bombing (–SB).

There were no differences between participants who did and did not believe that Islam supports suicide bombing and willingness to delay a martyrdom operation to help a sick father. But those who did believe that Islam supports suicide attacks were inclined to believe that an indefinite delay of a suicide attack to save one's hometown or the entire family from probable death was more unacceptable than an indefinite delay of a suicide attack to look after an ill father. Similarly, a one-month delay of a suicide attack to save the entire family from probable death was rated as more unacceptable than a one-month delay to look after an ill father. What these results show is that when people are reasoning between duty to war or to family, they aren't always making instrumental decisions that make material sense, but also decisions based on perceptions of obligations that can change as a function of which moral frame the context brings into focus.

STUDY 2: MORAL DUTY REVERSES NORMAL SENSITIVITY TO QUANTITY

Our second study was integrated in a survey of a representative sample of 1,266 Palestinian Muslim adults, half men and half women. To measure whether it was permissible or taboo in Palestinian society to think about material gains of involvement in acts of violence against the Israeli occupation, we asked:

In your view, would it be acceptable for the family of a martyr to request compensation in the amount of JD (Jordanian dinars) _____ after their son carried out a martyrdom operation? Would it be certainly acceptable, acceptable, unacceptable, or certainly unacceptable?

We randomly varied between participants the amount of money requested in this scenario: JD1,000 (about $1,500), JD10,000 ($15,000), or JD1,000,000 ($1,500,000). More than 90 percent of the participants regarded any request for financial compensation in exchange for the sacrifice of a martyr's life as unacceptable, taboo. Moreover, as the monetary amount requested increased, so did disapproval ratings.

STUDY 3: PAROCHIAL ALTRUISM

Although many Jewish residents of the Israeli-occupied West Bank moved there from Israel for reasons of finance or "quality of life," the community as a whole, typically referred to as "settlers," is politically active in supporting the Jewish state's right to permanently rule occupied Palestinian territories.[24] Our sample of 656 settlers was representative of the Jewish population of the West Bank in terms of religious and political identities. We tested willingness to violently attack Palestinians or other Israelis who were attempting to force evacuation of settlements.

More than 10 percent of the settlers reported a willingness to participate in violent attacks against Palestinians, and 6.4 percent were willing to participate in violent attacks against Israelis. While only a minority was willing to participate in violent attacks, extrapolating the findings to a total population of some 250,000 settlers indicates the seriousness of the issue. For, if we assume an adult population of 100,000, more than 10,000 may be willing to engage in violent attacks against Palestinians in the event of forced evacuation, and more than 6,000 to attack other Israelis under the same conditions. Every unit increase in a person's score on a scale of "conservative values" (loyalty to community, sanctity of values, purity of purpose) doubled the odds of participating in violent action.

These findings paint the picture of parochially altruistic political actors rebelling to advance a cause. It appears that choices people make in violent intergroup conflicts, from whether to accept a compromise to whether individuals commit themselves to violent collective action, are bound by moral duty to collective interests: to the belligerent defense of the "sacred values" of a cause against all odds.

SACRED VALUES

Sacred values often have their basis in religion, but such transcendent core secular values as a belief in the importance of individual morality, fairness, reciprocity, and collective identity ("justice for my people") can also be sacred values. These values will often trump the economic thinking of the marketplace or considerations of realpolitik. Rational choice involves selecting and ordering the best means for achieving given goals in the future. The further down the line a goal is, the less its real value here and now, and the less committed a person is to implement the means to realize it. But sacred values upset these calculations.

In many cases, sacred values are concerned with sustaining tradition for posterity. In other cases, the future takes on a transcendent value, the dream of what ought to be rather than what is, as in the fight for liberty or justice. Sometimes sacred values take on aspects of both tendencies: say, to regain the freedom that should have been or the dream of a righteous caliphate. In all of these cases, there's no discounting of the future. In fact the opposite: On the basis of sacred values, people may purposely choose to live and act now for a remote end and to value the traditions of a distant past more than the trappings of the present or probable future.

Devotion to some core values may represent universal responses to long-term evolutionary strategies that go beyond short-term individual calculations of self-interest but that advance individual interests in the aggregate and long run.[25] This may include devotion to children,[26] to community,[27] or even to a sense of fairness.[28] Other such values are clearly specific to particular societies and historical contingencies, such as the sacred status of cows in Hindu culture or the sacred status of Jerusalem in Judaism, Christianity, and Islam. Sometimes, as with sacred cows[29] or sacred forests,[30] what is seen as inherently sacred in the present may have a more instrumental origin, representing the accumulated material wisdom of generations who resisted individual urges to gain an immediate advantage of meat or firewood for the long-term benefits of renewable sources of energy and sustenance.

Matters of principle, or "sacred honor," are enforced to a degree far out of proportion to any individual or immediate material payoff when they are seen as defining "who we are." Revenge, "even if it kills me," between whole communities that mobilize to redress insult or shame to a single member go far beyond individual tit-for-tat,[31] and may become the most important duties in life. This is because such behavior defines and defends what it means to be, say, a Southern gentleman,[32] a Solomon Islander,[33] or an Arab tribesman.[34] The Israeli army has risked the lives of many soldiers to save one as a matter of "sacred duty," as have certain elite U.S. military units.[35]

Of course, sincere displays of willingness to avenge at all costs can have the long-term payoff of thwarting aggressive actions by stronger but less committed foes. Likewise, a willingness to sacrifice for buddies can help create greater esprit de corps that may lead to a more formidable fighting force. But these acts far exceed the effort required for any short-term payoff and offer no immediate guarantee for long-term success.

Seemingly intractable political conflicts—in the Middle East, Central and South Asia, Kashmir, and beyond—and the extreme behaviors often associated with these conflicts, such as suicide bombings, are often motivated by sacred values. Nevertheless, there are also significant historical instances in which sacred values have motivated peacemaking, a theme that Egypt's Anwar Sadat expressed in his autobiography, *In Search of Identity*. He recounted that the October 1973 war allowed Egypt to recover "pride and self-confidence," which freed him to think about the "psychological barrier" that was a "huge wall of suspicion, fear, hate and misunderstanding that has for so long existed between Israel and the Arabs." Based on his own experience in jail, he felt that "change should take place first at the deeper and perhaps more subtle level than the conscious level. . . . We had been accustomed . . . to regard Israel as 'taboo,' an entity whose emotional associations simply prevented anyone from approaching it." He ultimately decided on a personal visit to the Al Aqsa Mosque in Jerusalem and to the Israeli Knesset "in fulfillment of my claim that I would be willing to go anywhere in search of peace. . . . I regarded my mission in Israel as truly sacred."[36]

Appeals to sacred values, then, can be powerful motivation for making both war and peace. The issue for conflict resolvers is to determine how sacred values appeal to war and how they can be reframed to appeal to peace, which is discussed in the next part of the book.

While overwhelming military production and technological superiority is America's preferred path to victory in frontal wars fought in Clausewitzian terms of advancing policy through power, others fight against greater odds inspired by their cause, including revolutionary and guerrilla movements and jihadis. One reason resource-deficient revolutionary movements can compete with much larger armies and police is willingness to delay gratification and accept material sacrifice for a greater cause. Consider the founding of the United States. Without calculating the probability of success, a few poorly equipped rebels knowingly took on the world's mightiest empire. The Declaration of Independence concluded with the words: "And for the support of this Declaration, with a firm reliance on the protection of divine Providence, we mutually pledge to each other our Lives, our Fortunes and our sacred Honor." Now that is hardly just an expression of politics by other means.

As Osama Hamdan, the ranking Hamas politburo member for external affairs, put it to me in Damascus: "George Washington was fighting the strongest military in the world, beyond all reason. That's what we're doing. Exactly."[37]

At least, that's what he thinks. But thinking it can be enough to make it a real force.

Part VI

"THE MOTHER OF ALL PROBLEMS"—PALESTINE, THE WORLD'S SYMBOLIC KNOT

A man once jumped from the top floor of a burning house in which many members of his family had already perished. He managed to save his life; but as he was falling to the ground, he hit a person standing down below and broke that person's legs and arms. The jumping man had no choice; yet to the man with the broken limbs he was the cause of his misfortune.

If both behaved rationally, they would not become enemies. The man who escaped from the blazing house, having recovered, would have tried to help and console the other sufferer; and the latter might have realized that he was the victim of circumstances over which neither of them had control.

But look what happens when these people behave irrationally. The injured man blames the other for his misery and swears to make him pay for it. The other one, afraid of the crippled man's revenge, insults him, kicks him and beats him up whenever they meet. The kicked man again swears revenge and is again punched and punished. The bitter enmity, so whimsical at first, hardens and comes to overshadow the whole existence of both men and to poison their minds.

—ISAAC DEUTSCHER, "ON THE ARAB-ISRAELI WAR,"
NEW LEFT REVIEW, JULY–AUGUST 1967

CHAPTER 20
MARTYRDOM 101

QUESTION: WHAT IS THE MEANING OF JIHAD?

Jihad is one of Islam's dignified principles. These principles value reciprocal treatment: Who kills you, kill him. We fight for dignity [*karáma*], nation [*watan*], religion [*din*], and Al Aqsa. In the Koran, the book of Al-Tauba, verse 111, tells us that Allah brings souls to Paradise killing the enemy and getting killed—that is the high principle of jihad [*mabada samia fil jihad*].

Allah asks that we be good with everyone who does not raise a hand against us, especially the People of the Book [*ahl kitab*], Christians and Jews, we can live side by side with them, share our food with them, marry their women [if they convert to Islam], and keep their holy places safe.

But others are not as tolerant. France will not allow our women to wear their veils in school. There are commands from the Prophet and the Muslim leaders to not kill women and children, and to not uproot trees. But the Israelis kill our children and uproot our trees.

QUESTION: CAN THERE EVER BE PEACE WITH ISRAEL?

There could be a provisional truce [*hudna*, after the ten-year cease-fire between the Prophet and the Quraish tribe, which allowed Mohammed and his followers to regroup and eventually conquer the Quraish]. But never real peace [*salaam*]. Israel's withdrawal to the borders of 1967 is the minimum we can accept, along with the return of the refugees; then leave the matter to history. But I don't think they will withdraw from our land, or pull back the settlements.

We will live and see: If they withdraw to the 1967 borders and bring back the refugees, that would be good; otherwise we will continue fighting them. Israel is like the Crusaders or the Mongols and other invaders who came here and were expelled. In the end, Israel also will be expelled.

—SHEIKH HAMED AL-BETAWI, HAMAS SPIRITUAL GUIDE,

JUDGE OF THE PALESTINE SHARIA COURT, PREACHER AT

JERUSALEM'S AL AQSA MOSQUE (AUTHOR INTERVIEW,

NABLUS, SEPTEMBER 2004)

Jabaliyah Refugee Camp, Gaza Strip, September 2004.

I had an appointment with some families and friends of suicide bombers in Jabaliyah refugee camp, a dusty maze of low concrete structures that is home to more than 100,000 Palestinians. Jabaliyah is the most densely populated part of the Gaza Strip, and the Gaza Strip, with nearly 1.5 million people piled up in an area the size of, say, Gilpin County, Colorado (population less than 5,000), is one of the most densely populated dives on earth. The strip's name has the same origin as the English word "gauze." But nothing here ever seems to stop the hope from hemorrhaging. In Jabaliyah talk of pushing Jews into the sea has staged a comeback.

There was an awful heaviness and quiet in Jabaliyah, especially in the afternoons, still balmy at summer's end. Suddenly, like a battering ram that has breached the dungeon's walls, the children burst from the school. They brought, for a moment, life and a lightness of heart to the still and silent square, as they flew in every direction, chirping in search of play.

A senior Hamas organizer in Jabaliyah frowned when I smiled at the children running home from school across the plaza. "Why do you smile?" he asked in accusation, confirming his own seriousness. "We can't smile until we take back our life from the Israelis. When you see our children you should weep because the best hope for them now is to become martyrs." His suffering soul demanded that I find shame in joy.

"So all should become martyrs?" I asked.

He shook his head. "Not all our people are heroes, but our youth are running to martyrdom. With so many we must carefully select, case by case, who has courage and purity of heart."

I wanted to know if he would accept a two-state solution.

"Never," he snapped. "All of Palestine must be Muslim."

"And the Jews?"

Erez Crossing, from Israel into the Gaza Strip.

"Let them go back to New York and Russia." He snorted. "Those born in Palestine may stay as long as they submit to Muslim rule and law."

Gray and mirthless men will select a target for the martyrdom-seeking youth and find others. They cajole the youths and stroke their minds but do not brainwash them any more than our leaders do those of our soldiers.

An earnest young man of twenty cleared a seat for me from the rubble and garbage. "I choose to be a martyr because my life is dear to me, my family, and my people. We must show Israelis that Palestinian lives aren't cheap."

The humorless graybeard told the youth to go along to the mosque to pray.

"No," the youth said, politely but firmly, "I must explain something to the foreigner."

The graybeard shook his head—and walked across the plaza of children as if through a graveyard.

The youth was as compassionate in manner as anyone I'd interviewed in my anthropological sojourns. He wanted to be an electrical engineer. He so reminded me of my own son that I just lost it and had to turn away for a moment. He was tall and lean, and so he seemed taller, with wide shoulders and lips that women would one day appreciate if he gave them a chance, but he probably wouldn't. He had an intelligent, ascetic face. Except not quite. It was a look lifted by a twisted purpose that so many here take for nobility.

The young man obviously saw the turmoil in my own countenance and tried in his own way to console me with the resigned certainty of someone already within earshot of eternity:

"*Ma' leish*—never mind—I won't just give up my life. Our leaders don't think once or twice, but ten, even a hundred times if it's worth it. If they can do a roadside bombing, they won't use me. I'll be saved for a big operation."

This young man could contemplate the costs and benefits of a roadside versus suicide bombing within the group's moral frame, though it was beyond doubt that sometime soon he must die to kill.

"And what would make you and others stop thinking about becoming martyrs?" I asked him.

He smiled ruefully and said, "When Palestine is again Muslim."

Although only a few kilometers from the First World nation of Israel, Gaza has degenerated from its place in the developing Second World, as I knew it back in the 1960s and 1970s, to Third World now. You can tell Third World countries by the fact that there are no signs of buildings or roads ever being fixed. There is garbage, especially mounds of plastic, everywhere save in the many empty public garbage cans. In such places, the adverse effects of global warming on the human landscape may never match those produced by plastic. And garbage prefers company: Just toss some anywhere and it soon attracts more. This seems to happen most when people are hungry or out of hope: The gold heirlooms that are a Palestinian woman's most precious possession are being sold off here at the price of their melted bulk weight, more each year, as the garbage piles up.

Yet not far from the border crossing, at Bayt Lahiyah, there was a new spic-and-span apartment complex being built with money from the Arab Emirates, rising out of the filth and waste. Israeli bulldozers and tanks had flattened all of the homes just in front of the complex, and people just sat by their makeshift tents, some bent over with their heads in their hands or just swaying back and forth. A little boy kicking a frayed and deflated soccer ball showed me where a bullet had scarred his back as he bent over to throw a stone at a tank (it would have gone through his skull had he been standing up). I asked if he was looking forward to living in the new apartments. He didn't seem to know what I was talking about until I pointed; then his father said *"bukrah fil mishmish"*—tomorrow's apricots (something like "when pigs fly and chickens grow teeth"). "We will go on living in filth and dirt."

I wasn't sure if he was referring to the likelihood that the Palestinian Authority and their wealthy backers in the Emirates had already allotted the apartments to their own cronies (a standard practice) or whether this man was referring to prospects for peace. In any event, the little boy said he wanted to die a *shaheed*, killing Israelis. The father, closing his eyes and with a deep sigh, waved his boy away. "If only they would leave us in peace," he said.

JERUSALEM, NOVEMBER 30, 2004

I was watching an Israeli television talk show. The host was interviewing a soldier who shot and killed a thirteen-year-old Palestinian girl.

"She was a *mehabelet* [terrorist]," the soldier said.

He played to the audience: "Anyone who helps a terrorist is a terrorist."

"But maybe she wasn't helping terrorists," the show's host suggested. "She had schoolbooks, maybe she was just on her way to school. Maybe you're telling us this to justify to us and to yourself what happened."

"No, there's no way she was going to school." The soldier's tone was self-assured and castigating. "The school was more than five hundred meters away."

The talk-show audience apparently applauded. I asked an Israeli woman who was watching the show—someone I know as a generous, loving, and kind woman with teenage children of her own—what she made of this.

"I blame their parents," she replied. "They let their children risk their lives. Sometimes our soldiers have no choice."

"No choice except to blow the brains out of a kid who has no weapons on her but books?"

"You never know. Suicide bombers will try everything. It's terrible. But what can you do?"

"And your daughter . . . can't you even imagine your own daughter making a mistake? Would she deserve to die?"

She didn't answer directly, I sensed, because too much empathy might fatally weaken her resistance to the enemy. But I saw that she was struggling not to have to struggle with it.

"If only they would leave us in peace," she moaned.

AT THE ENTRY TO NABLUS, WEST BANK

I was standing with my driver from Jerusalem as we waited for the guards at the Hawara checkpoint to verify my permission from the West Bank Military Coordinator, General Mishlev, to let us through. It was hot and everything seemed to move sluggishly in between the soldiers' irregular commands to stop or go. Two young men were walking up a long passage of concrete and barbed wire toward the guard post, supporting an old woman between them. She was shriveled and bent and shrouded in black. The crowd at the checkpoint made way for the trio to reach the guard post, where machine guns were readied behind thick concrete emplacements on either side.

"Go back," the Israeli soldier ordered. "No males allowed through."

"But our mother is sick," one of the men replied. "How can she get home?"

Taxis from Nablus cannot leave Nablus, and taxis from the outside cannot get in.

"Identity papers," the soldier said to the two young men. "Papers."

He examined the documents, very slowly: *"Beseder."* Okay, he nodded. "Now go back to where you came from," and waved the three away.

The young men saw me watching, and they probably overheard the guards talking about what to do with the American. They turned themselves and their mother toward me.

"Why do they treat us like animals?" she asked, her sons careful not to show any signs that the guards, who looked on with tense boredom, might have taken as threatening.

I related the incident to a friend who serves on an interservices committee that advises Israeli defense and government. Some weeks later, he told me, "I raised the issue of behavior at the checkpoints and [Israeli Prime Minister Ariel] Sharon said, 'Don't you understand? I want them to feel humiliated, and we'll keep doing that until they stop trying to kill us.'"

But the angry eyes of the old lady, her boys, and the crowd showed me they were far from cowed.

In fact, the relationship between humiliation and violence is not so simple. My studies with psychologist Jeremy Ginges suggest that humiliation in situations of political strife, like the Israel-Palestine conflict, does reduce feelings and propensity for violence, at least among people who feel humiliated. People who feel humiliated are generally more passive and demoralized than bristling for action. But the moral outrage and violence among those who are witness to the humiliation of others they care for may actually increase. Hamas militants nearly all stress that vengeance is for national—not personal—humiliation.

SOME FACTS AND FIGURES ABOUT SUICIDE ATTACKS

Almost every major Palestinian town is ringed by Israeli settlements, and every major passage in or out of town is blocked by guns, barbed wire, and concrete. Palestinians are convinced that Israeli Army checkpoints—where people often wait hours to no avail in shadeless no-man's-lands or long tunnels—are meant to break their will and drive them from the land. The economy is practically lifeless, except for Ramallah, seat of the Palestinian Authority's patronage and above all the NGOs, which bring some activity.

The average time it takes to get by road from Hebron or Jenin to Palestine's provisional capital, Ramallah (about forty miles), is four to six hours when roads are open (instead of the one hour it used to take), but roads are also often closed. What's the damage? The West Bank, which had been agriculturally self-sufficient and a net exporter, can no longer get people to the fields and produce to the towns. Hundreds of thousands of people have now been jobless for several years. Bir Zeit University, located on the outskirts of Ramallah, was once Palestine's premier national institution of learning. Now, having lost most of its commuting students and much of its faculty, it has basically been reduced to a community college. No Palestinian students are allowed to study in Israel, few have the means to study abroad and, if they do, there is no guarantee that they will be allowed back by Israel, which continues to control all entry points into Palestine.[1]

Khalil Shikaki, a Columbia University–trained political scientist and director of the Palestinian Center for Policy and Survey Research in Ramallah, has data suggesting that popular support for suicide actions is positively correlated with the number of Israeli checkpoints that Palestinians have to regularly pass through to go about their daily business and the time needed to pass through them (this can involve spending hours at each of several checkpoints, any of which can be arbitrarily closed down at any time).

In 2005, our research group teamed up with Shikaki's to conduct a random survey of 1,250 Palestinians from 120 locales in the West Bank and Gaza. We found that around 80 percent of Palestinians support suicide bombings and believe that "Islam allows a bombing attack (which some call martyrdom attacks while others call suicide attacks) where the bomber kills himself with the aim of killing his enemies." Fifty percent of the Palestinian population reported "joy" as their primary emotion upon hearing an announcement of a suicide bombing against Israelis, versus 12 percent who mentioned "pride" and 7 percent who cited revenge as their main reaction (though brain scans suggest that getting even gives pleasure).[2] Nine percent said they felt "sadness" and 4 percent experienced "fear."

I asked a Palestinian woman, a very generous, loving, and kind person who has worked with Israelis for years, what she thinks of this: "I know it is not a good thing to feel this way, but it's human. I can't help myself, either. When I hear of it, I think, 'Is there no better way?' But when I see the images on television I feel, 'Good for them! Let them feel pain too.'"

But our research also clearly demonstrated that Palestinian support for suicide bombing is unrelated to a belief in the immutability of the conflict between Jews and Muslims, or some essential or inherent quality of Jews or Israelis. Ninety-one percent of those who said that Islam supported the actions of the suicide bomber believed that a Jewish child switched at birth and brought up by Muslims would grow up to be fully Muslim. And of those who believed that Islam sanctioned the suicide bomber, only 4 percent believed that it was the duty of Muslims to fight and kill non-Muslims.

What does predict a belief that Islam sanctions martyrs is a perceived sense of injustice. For example, we asked participants to choose between two reasons why it's socially and religiously permissible to kill other people: because of what other people have done, or because of the contrary beliefs and religion of other people. Participants overwhelmingly believed the former, but this was slightly stronger for those who believed that Islam sanctioned suicide bombers than for those who did not.

In a previous survey, however, Shikaki's Palestinian Center for Policy and Survey Research found that the Palestinian population also expressed no hatred of liberty, freedom, or democracy, and could well embrace these if they had them.

Most Israelis who see surveys showing that most Palestinians don't have Nazi-like attitudes toward Jews and express support for the values of an "open society" simply refuse to believe the surveys. And most Palestinians who see surveys that show most Israelis want peace, even if it means dismantling the settlements, also refuse to believe that this is true. That's so even if both sets of surveys are from the same pollster (whether Israeli, Palestinian, or joint Israeli-Palestinian). This unremitting loop of mutual mistrust only helps to stoke the seemingly endless killing.

Even Israelis who oppose the evident abuse and humiliation of the checkpoints countered that the checkpoints would stop on average at least one suicide bomber a day, and that Palestinians confuse cause (suicide bombing) with effect (extreme vigilance to stop it). On one level, the iron-fist policy seemed to work. In June 2004, I co-organized a NATO conference in Lisbon on suicide terrorism with Israeli psychologist and former chief hostage negotiator Ariel Merari. Isaac Ben Israel presented data showing suicide terrorism to be the deadliest form of attack during the Second Intifada, which began following Sharon's September 2000 promenade on the Haram al-Sharif (the esplanade where the Al Aqsa Mosque is located, and also ancient Israel's presumed holiest site) and the riots and killings that occurred as a result. Ben Israel is a retired Air Force general and top-notch physicist who runs a program in the history and philosophy of science at Tel Aviv University as well as his country's space agency. (He would later take over Shimon Peres's seat in Parliament, when that Nobel Peace Prize winner became president of Israel.) He found that up to mid-2004, some 527 suicide attacks were attempted; 132 of them were successful, killing 859 noncombatant civilians. But by mid-2004, the rate of terrorist attacks against civilians had dropped back to its pre-Intifada levels.

In April 2002, after Israel suffered 140 fatalities in one month (March) from suicide attacks, it launched a full-scale campaign against Hamas, including massive arrests of supporters and assassinations of leaders. Israeli troops entered the occupied areas given to the Palestinian Authority to expand intelligence coverage, tightened the chokehold on these areas through checkpoints, and began construction of the massive "fence" to separate these areas from Israel proper and some of the major Israeli settlements in the West Bank. The result was that, a year later, the number of "aborted" suicide missions had doubled, and the success rate of attacks had dropped precipitously.

Ben Israel explained to me that if one fourth to one third of any system is cut away or destroyed—molecules, information, army divisions, terrorist networks—the entire system either collapses (disintegrates toward "entropy," or randomness) or is forced to become a different sort of system altogether (by "mutating"): "In a year, Hamas will stop suicide bombing or there will be no more Hamas," he asserted. (Hamas called for a provisional halt to suicide attacks in December 2004 and did not claim another until February 2008, although initial denials from various leadership circles of Hamas indicated that there was no centrally organized planning to it, and the halt in bombings persisted into 2010.)

"I AM READY TO PAY THE PRICE"

The Nablus office complex where Sheikh Hamed al-Betawi directed various types of "community welfare" was plastered with posters of martyrs and packed with earnest young Hamas volunteers. Betawi is a spiritual leader of Hamas in the West Bank, judge of the Sharia Court of Palestine, head of the Palestine Ulema (Scholar's League) and preacher at Al Aqsa Mosque (the Jerusalem mosque that is the third-holiest site in Islam). He is classic fire-and-brimstone: "Our people do not own airplanes and tanks, only human bombs. Those who undertake martyrdom actions are not hopeless or poor, but are the best of our people, educated, successful. They are intelligent, advanced in combat techniques for fighting enemy occupation." Indeed, independent doctoral research by Basel Saleh[3] at

Kansas State University and Claude Berrebi[4] at Princeton indicate that most Hamas bombers had some college education and were economically better off than the surrounding population.

These are the prize souls that Hamas was striving to attract. Movements like Hamas look for signals of such character, such as a candidate's investment in education. Groups that sponsor suicide terror go a step further: Through spectacular displays involving the sacrifice of their precious "human capital" (educated youth with better-than-average prospects), they also signal a costly commitment to their community, which the community honors by providing new volunteers and added funding.

"I say to you what I said to Israeli intelligence and to 400,000 people at the Haram al-Sharif [Jerusalem Temple Mount]," al-Betawi raged. "I am ready to pay the price. I was deported to Lebanon with al-Rantisi [cofounder of Hamas, assassinated by Israelis in 2004], and, God willing, I will be a martyr, too. I know Israeli prisons and so do five of my children, but they know from me that Muslims and their culture fear no privation or death."

"And why," I asked, "do you say you and others are willing to make such sacrifices?"

"Because this is sacred land (*'ard al-muqadasah*), the holiest land in the world. That is why Palestine is the 'Mother of the World's Problems.'"

"Who wants to be a martyr?" I asked him.

"Our martyrs are the purest of the pure," Betawi said. "Learned often in mathematics or engineering, even the arts, they are not hopeless. They are full of personal possibilities. But they have even greater hope for their people.

"Yehia Ayash was an engineer when he led the Izz al-Din al-Qassam Brigades [Hamas military wing]. Qais Adwan was president of the Student Council at Al-Najah University, which has twelve thousand students.

"Mohamed Al-Hanbali was a student at the College of

Engineering, and his father is a millionaire. His father said to him, 'I will marry you to the most beautiful girls in Nablus.' And his son replied, 'No, Father, I will marry in heaven, my mission is to defend my people and my religion.' His father was a friend of mine.

"Do you think that the person who leads the Student Council, responsible for twelve thousand students at Al-Najah University, is a stupid person? Of course not, he was very intelligent, for that reason he chose this path. The educated person has a greater motivation for carrying out the operations and for becoming a martyr."

The one place in Nablus where young people easily express optimism in the future is Al-Najah University. More than half of the students belong to the Hamas Student Block, which had produced more suicide bombers than any other group in the country. They are not poor, uneducated, socially estranged, or psychologically deranged. Nor do most captured would-be suicide bombers have a criminal past, according to Ariel Merari. (Marc Sageman found a similar pattern among Al Qaeda operatives through 2003.[5] In America, by contrast, two thirds of criminals never finished high school and are functionally illiterate, a majority come from socially depressed areas, and 10 percent to 15 percent are mentally ill.)[6]

In the arts department at Al-Najah I was led through an exhibit whose title was Martyrs Give Us Dignity to Free Ourselves. The blazing eyes in two paintings of covered faces resembled the intense gazes of the two artists nearby. "Who are these martyrs?" I asked. "Soon to be, if God wishes," one of them replied. Their yearning for paradise was conveyed through images of another longing, incarnated in the black-eyed maidens of martyrs' heaven. But this was clearly about a more knightly, chivalrous love than a lust for heavenly virgins. "If a youth knocks saying he wants to be a martyr to get sex in paradise or money for his family, we slam the door," huffed one senior Hamas leader, expressing a common sentiment, which our research bears out.

The mock-up of paradise at the Al-Najah Martyrs' exhibit

included a small pool of water, covered with plastic flowers and leaves and surrounded by paintings of red and white roses and recently slain Hamas leaders Sheikh Ahmed Yassin and Abdul Azziz Rantisi. Little teddy bear key chains were offered, and books sold—most prominently the so-called Islamic Manifesto, *Milestones*, written in prison by the Muslim Brotherhood's Sayyid Qutb just before he was hanged in 1966. The anti-Semitic czarist-era forgery, *Protocols of the Elders of Zion*, was also on sale.

So I took the opportunity to ask one of my standard questions: "What if you take a child from a Zionist family at birth and raise him in a good Muslim family, would the child grow up to be a good Muslim, a bad Muslim, or a Zionist?" "A good Muslim," was the answer all around.

"A person is what his surroundings make him," said the Hamas student leader.

"Then why do you kill Israeli children?" I shot back.

"We do not target the children," he calmly explained. "But we do not mourn them if they are killed on an Israeli bus or if the children happen to be in the way, because Israeli society will turn them into soldiers who will try to kill us. Would we do an operation like the one that Sheikh Bin Laden did to America or our Chechen brothers did in Beslan? No, that is not our way, although what happened in Beslan is understandable and even justifiable because the Russians have killed so many Chechen children."

I posed the same question that I had posed to al-Betawi: "You say 'An eye for an eye,' but then won't the whole world become blind?"

He answered much as did al-Betawi: "Should we turn the other cheek or offer flowers? Do the Jews or Christians? We fight with any means. They have tanks, planes, and atom bombs. We have 'human bombs' (*qanabil bi sharia*). When they stop killing us, we will stop killing them."

In June 2006, Dr. Ghazi Hamad, then-spokesman of the

Hamas-led Palestinian national government, told me that Hamas's base (about 15 percent of the Palestinian electorate) would rise up in arms if Hamas immediately agreed to recognize Israel and stop violence against the occupation (the two chief demands in the "road map" for peace proposed by the "Quartet" of the United States, the European Union, Russia, and the United Nations).

"There might no longer be a Hamas," he said, "but a lot of little Al Qaedas."

Another 20 percent of the Palestinian electorate votes for Hamas, but this support can move to others (as it has previously from Fateh to Hamas), and while this group might go along with Hamas in accepting some of the Quartet proposals as they stand, the base would collapse and so would Hamas. (It would be as if the Republican or Democratic party in the United States abandoned its base to secure the support of independents.) In addition to committing political suicide by unconditionally accepting Quartet conditions, "Hamas would be left naked and in the cold," Ghazi said, "without any cards left to negotiate, as Arafat was in the end. We can only gradually bring the base along, but not now or all at once." (Ghazi clearly belongs to Hamas's "moderate" wing. He has publicly declared that the Palestinian plight is partly its own fault, and not entirely Israel's, and he was temporarily "suspended" from Hamas for opposing Hamas's takeover of Gaza in the summer of 2007.)

Hamas's talk of justice against oppression is "a big lie," insisted Ben Israel. "So, what's their target if not the children?" He answered his own question with unforgiving logic:

"The bus by itself? Who were the other persons in the bus or in a restaurant? Soldiers? No, they were all either children or women or male civilians, and I think this is the main moral difference between guerrilla fighters—freedom fighters—and the terrorists. When an Israeli army unit is attacked in the occupied territories, it is not terrorism. But bombing children in a bus with the excuse that one day they will be soldiers is a morally wrong attitude. What will prevent us from dropping some doomsday weapon on Gaza and end the conflict with the Palestinians in a few seconds? Or, not to be so extreme, to send our air force to daily bomb refugee camps, with conventional weapons: We can kill more than ten thousand people a day with this 'method.' The only 'obstacle' is ethical."

"But isn't Hamas's forgoing any help from Al Qaeda also an 'ethical' choice on their part?" I asked.

"It's true Al Qaeda isn't our problem, and Hamas doesn't have their [Qaeda's] ambition. But if they tried to bring in Al Qaeda, that would be their end. We would annihilate them."

"And annihilating Hamas, what would that accomplish in the end?" I asked.

"That they would never have a chance to annihilate us. Look, don't you think we want peace, that I want peace? Just as one of my sons leaves the army, another has to go in; my wife hasn't slept for three years, and she won't sleep for at least another three. I won't let my children ride a public bus. You know, to tell you the truth, if we had peace and open borders, and Palestinians settled here and became the majority, I would be sad that we no longer had a Jewish homeland. I would regret it. But I wouldn't go to war to stop it, provided we could all live in an open society. But Hamas doesn't want that, and I don't think the Palestinians want it enough to do something seriously about it, or they would have. They have the leaders they choose, or allow."

At Khalil Shikaki's home I met Hashim Abdul Raziq, the minister of prisons for the Palestinian Authority, who spent seventeen years in Israeli jails. His young son was with him on the couch. "Do you think that I don't want peace?" he said, and pulled his son near him in an embrace. "Do you think I want my son to suffer what I have suffered? Do you think we are really that crazy?"

Later I recalled Betawi telling me how glad he would be to sacrifice himself and his sons for the cause, if need be. Betawi is many things, but he is not crazy.

THE TWO FACES OF HAMAS

"We have no problem with a sovereign Palestinian state over all our lands within the '67 borders, living in calm," Palestinian prime minister Ismail Haniya told me in his Gaza City office in late June 2006, shortly before it was blasted in an Israeli missile attack, "but we need the West as a partner to help us through, to have a dialogue of civilizations, not a clash of civilizations."[7] Haniya's pitch to Western governments comes down to "We need you, as you need us." He has asked that Americans and Europeans end their sanctions against his government and recognize that the Arab and Muslim world sees Hamas's election to power as a genuine exercise in democracy. Engaging his government, Haniya says, would be the best opportunity for the American administration to reverse the steep decline of the United States in the esteem of Arabs and Muslims everywhere. If Palestine were the Mother of All Problems, Haniya argued, so could it also be the key to the solution.

Afterward I was invited by the Hamas leadership in Damascus for further talks, and I asked Israeli leaders if they thought this line worth pursuing. "Ask them one question," a confidant of Israeli prime minister Ehud Olmert advised me. "Would Hamas, not now but in the future, somewhere down the line, recognize the right of Israel to exist as an independent Jewish state in the area, under any conditions, any borders?"

The most forthcoming answer I got at the time was from Hamas deputy chairman Abu Musa Marzook, which fell far short of what the Israelis said they needed to hear: "You don't need conditions or recognition. There are examples. The Irish negotiations began without conditions, and East and West Germany coexisted in peace living side by side without mutual recognition, and the two Chinas."

But Marzook went on to suggest that by showing respect for Palestinians' core values, a dialogue could open. "For us, for the

Palestinians, it is not about the amount of money or the material compensation; for us, you see, there are values, and one value is *karama*, dignity, and an apology. An apology would be important to us, but words alone are not enough."

Then a former U.S. government official who had accompanied me to Damascus asked, "In your heart of hearts, not as Hamas officials, do you want peace with Israel? Do you want to live side by side as two states?"

Osama Hamdan, Hamas's political liaison with the outside, who had come to the meeting from his headquarters in Beirut, answered, "How can you live with people you cannot trust? A snake is a snake and you know what to do if you see it coming. Arafat came to the UN in 1974 with a gun and an olive branch. He said, "Don't let the olive branch fall from my hand." The Israelis did nothing. In 1984 in Morocco, the Arab countries accepted a two-state solution and peace as a strategic choice. Israel did nothing. At Madrid, there was a chance after the Gulf War; the Arabs were weak, the Israelis did nothing. When have the Israelis made any moves toward peace? They will always want to kill Arabs and drink their children's blood."

Marzook was clearly uncomfortable with his colleague's reply, because he added, "When we have two states, then we will see. Let Israel withdraw from our homeland to the 1967 borders, and let there be a Palestinian state, because there already is an Israeli state. And then there will be no resistance."

But Hamdan was not about to compromise. "Yes," he chortled, "it will not be called violence, because between two states it is war."

Marzook enjoined him that Hamas did not want war, and it seemed that there was a profound disagreement between the two leaders being played out before us. I have witnessed too many subsequent disagreements among the personalities and factions of Hamas to think it not genuinely torn about what to do with Israel.

In March 2009, Sheikh Hamed al-Betawi was in hiding after the Israelis began re-arresting any Hamas or Hamas-leaning leader they could lay their hands on due to frustration over the collapse of the Cairo negotiations earlier that month. After Israel's January 2009 incursion into Gaza, the strongest attack on Gaza since the 1967 Six-Day War, Israeli leaders seemed to assume that they had softened Hamas's resolve enough to make trade-offs, such as exchanging Corporal Gilad Shalit, an Israeli soldier captured in June 2006, for a thousand Hamas prisoners. But the Gaza attack only stiffened Hamas's resolve, at least in the short term. Although Israel, for the first time ever, offered to release prisoners who had been involved in suicide attacks and had "Jewish blood on their hands," Hamas insisted that all prisoners under discussion be released, including Marwan Barghouti, the leader of Fateh's "Young Guard" and Hamas's most popular political rival.

At his safe house, I asked Betawi again why he thought Palestine was the Mother of All Problems, and again he said, "Because this is sacred land." But when I reminded him of our previous conversation and his pledge to fight Israel until its destruction on the basis of his interpretation of a Koranic injunction, Al-Tauba 111, I was surprised that he had to look up the passage to remind himself. And then he gave it a very different take:

"The problems cannot be solved with muscles," he said, "but only with the mind. When Israel learns to use mind over muscle, then we can have a *hudna* [provisional armistice]."

"But can the *hudna* ever become a permanent peace?" I asked.

"That is for future generations to work out, and only for the good, if minds are used instead of muscles."

I related the conversation to Ben Israel, who remarked, "The world community thinks that our strike into Gaza was a mistake, as was our strike against Hizbollah [in Lebanon in 2006]. But we haven't had a peep out of Hizbollah since then, and I predict much less trouble from Hamas, at least for a while. They may still think time is on their side, but they now know that they'll lose in any muscle match. But what do they offer us? Nothing, not even a conditional something, as you well know."

A few days later, I went to see Israel's foreign minister, Tzipi Livni, as her ruling party was about to cede power and go into the opposition. Israel's centrist Kadima Party, led by Livni, had beaten Netanyahu's right-leaning Likud Party by one parliamentary seat in the recent election, but a coalition of right-wing and religious parties gave Netanyahu a majority. Then the old stalwart of the left, the Labor Party, led by Ehud Barak, who had been defense minister in the previous Kadima-led government, jumped ship and also joined Netanyahu.

"As long as Hamas remains an ideological group, they will never declare their acceptance of Israel," Livni said. "An ideological group finds it very difficult to compromise on anything that goes against their core beliefs and values."

"So is there any hope of some way of living with Hamas?" I prodded.

She noted that she herself had made the move away from rigid ideology, as had perhaps some in Hamas: "If the Palestinian nationalist camp (the Fateh-led Palestinian Authority of President Mahmoud Abbas) makes peace with us," she replied, "Hamas can say, 'It's not our fault' and then accept the status quo as the will of the people without compromising itself. But time is working against the moderates because they see that the world is doing very little to stop the extremists, who believe that all they have to do to win in the end is wait."

The next day, I asked Ghazi Hamad what he now thought about the prospect of a permanent peace with Israel.

"We believe in democracy and will respect the choice and will of the Palestinian people," he said. "We are not like the Taliban or Al Qaeda. We believe in human rights, women's rights, and international law. We do not believe in using violence to impose Islam, but support the moderate method of [Turkey's current leader Recep Tayyip] Erdogan that allows both Islamic and Western traditions to live side by side, and lets democratic elections decide policy by the ballot box instead of bullets."

I mentioned that Khalil Shikaki's polls show that Israelis and Palestinians both prefer a permanent peace, but that each side believes the other is lying about it and can't be trusted.

"People in conflict cannot think clearly," opined Hamad. "We need a symbolic breakthrough. I think Obama can make that breakthrough happen. But time is working against us because the intolerable status quo is radicalizing our young people."

And I was reminded of Longfellow's lines about "Ships that pass in the night and speak each other in passing; / Only a signal shown and a distant voice in the darkness."

CHAPTER 21
WORDS TO END WARS: THE SCIENCE OF THE SACRED

Words are like eggs: When they are hatched, they have wings.

—A PROVERB FROM MADAGASCAR

THE NEWS FROM GAZA, MID-JANUARY 2009

More than a thousand Palestinians were dead, and thousands more wounded. Perhaps hundreds of Hamas fighters were dead, but also hundreds of civilians, including women and children[1] whose only culpability was to have been born in the wrong place. Israelis couldn't stand being rocketed (imagine what America would do if rockets started hitting Texas from Mexico), but they will gain no peace this way. No nation that conquered another in the twentieth century and subsequently sought to control its territory (whether by direct occupation or not) has ultimately succeeded.[2]

As diplomats stitched together yet another cease-fire between Hamas and Israel, the most bewildering and depressing feature of this conflict was the sense that future fighting was inevitable. Rational calculation suggested that neither side could win these wars, but that both would win with peace. The thousands of lives and billions of dollars sacrificed in fighting demonstrate the advantages of peace and coexistence; still, both sides opt for war.

(By 2009, rocket fire from Gaza into Israel had dropped by 90 percent, making it the quietest year on that front in a decade. "It can last for months or years," noted Yoav Galant, the general in charge of Israel's southern command, "but ultimately it is going to

The Wall at Kalandiya checkpoint separating the West Bank from Jerusalem and Israel, and the spirit of Mahatma Gandhi, for whom "Values become your destiny."

be broken." Ismail Haniya, a leader of the current Hamas regime in Gaza, defiantly reclaimed the whole of historic Palestine, including Israel, "from [the Mediterranean] sea to [the Jordan] river.")[3]

This small territory is the world's great symbolic knot. "Palestine is the mother of all problems" is a common refrain heard from people I've interviewed across the Muslim world: from Middle East leaders to fighters in the remote island jungles of Indonesia; from Islamist senators and secular nuclear physicists in Islamabad to volunteers for martyrdom on the move from Morocco to Iraq and Afghanistan. And in the Western world, too: from the U.S. National Security Council to governments in Britain, France, Germany, Italy, and Spain.

Some observers see this as a testament to the essentially religious nature of the conflict—even to the toxic nature of religion itself. But our research suggests a way to go beyond that. For there is a moral logic to seemingly intractable religious and cultural disputes that cannot be reduced to secular calculations of interest but must be dealt with on its own terms. As I noted at the end of chapter 19, it is a logic very different from the marketplace or realpolitik.

Across the world, people believe that devotion to sacred or cultural values that incorporate moral beliefs—such as the welfare of their family and country or commitment to religion, honor, and justice—is, or ought to be, absolute and inviolable. Research with colleagues, supported by the National Science Foundation and the Department of Defense, suggests that people will reject any type of material compensation for dropping their commitment to their sacred values and will defend their sacred values regardless of the costs.[4]

In our research in the Middle East, we surveyed nearly four thousand Palestinians and Israelis between 2004 and 2008, questioning citizens from across the political spectrum, including refugees, supporters of Hamas, and Israeli settlers. We asked them to react to hypothetical but realistic compromises in which their side would be required to give away something it valued in return for lasting peace.

In one cycle of studies designed by psychologist Jeremy Ginges,[5] we used a "between-subjects" experimental design, in which we randomly chose some subjects to respond to a deal with an added material incentive, such as financial compensation, while a third group responded to a deal in which the other side made a symbolic sacrifice of one of their own sacred values. In another cycle, we used a "within-subjects" design, in which all subjects would be exposed to the same set of deals. First they would be given a straight-up offer in which each side would make difficult concessions in exchange for peace. Next they were given a scenario in which their side was granted an additional material incentive. And last came a proposal in which the other side agreed to a symbolic sacrifice of one of its sacred values. Results were similar for the between-subjects and within-subjects designs, indicating that the order in which deals were presented didn't matter and that people responded the same way to deals given singly or as part of a set.

Each set of trade-offs included an original offer we pretested as likely to be rejected ("taboo"), the same trade-off with an added material incentive ("taboo plus"), and the original trade-off with an added symbolic gesture from the other side (a separate test showed that the "tragic" trade-off held no material value for participants).

For example, a typical set of trade-offs offered to Palestinians might begin with this (taboo) premise: "Suppose the United Nations organized a peace treaty between Israel and the Palestinians; Palestinians would be required to give up their right to return to their homes in Israel; and there would be two states, a Jewish state of Israel and a Palestinian state in the West Bank and Gaza." Second, we would sweeten the pot (with the taboo plus): "In return, the USA and the European Union would give Palestine one billion dollars a year for one hundred years." Then the symbolic (tragic) concession: "For its part, Israel would apologize for suffering caused by the displacement and dispossession of civilians in the 1948 war."

Many of the respondents insisted that the values involved were sacred to them. For example, nearly half the Israeli settlers we surveyed said they would not consider trading any land in the West Bank—territory they believe was granted them by God—in exchange for peace. More than half the Palestinians considered full sovereignty over Jerusalem in the same light, and more than four-fifths felt that the "right of return" was a sacred value, too. Among Palestinians, the greater the material incentive offered, the greater the disgust registered, and the more joyful the reaction to the idea of suicide bombing. In one scenario, Israeli settlers were offered a deal to give up the West Bank to Palestinians in return for an American subsidy to Israel of $1 billion a year for one hundred years. For those among them who had chosen to live in the Occupied Territories for reasons of economy or quality of life, the offer led to increased willingness to accept land for peace, a decrease in disgust and anger at the deal, and a corresponding reduction in willingness to use violence to oppose it. But for those settlers who believe the Occupied Territories to be God's ancient trust to them, expressions of anger and disgust and willingness to use violence rose markedly.

This sort of "moral absolutist" sentiment runs directly counter to prevailing economic theories of rational choice and also counter to political-science theories of rational play in negotiation. Our results imply that using the standard approaches of business-style negotiations in such seemingly intractable conflicts will only backfire, with material offers and sweeteners interpreted as morally taboo and insulting (like accepting money to sell your child or sell out your country). Given the closeness of elections in Palestine and Israel, even a small group of absolutists can thwart any peace.

So far, the findings we've described make prospects for peace seem very dark. Many on the outside looking in on these clearly expressed "irrational" preferences simply ignore them because in a sensible world they ought not exist. Seemingly, the only realistic alternative is to fall back on material aspects of a business-style approach and leave "value issues" for last. The hope, in the meantime, is that concrete moves on material matters (electricity, water, agriculture, and so on), however small at first, will eventually accumulate enough force to dissolve the harder and more heartfelt value issues. But in reality, this is only a recipe for another Hundred Years' War, as progress on everyday material matters only heightens attention to heavy, value-laden issues of who we are and who we want to be.

Fortunately, our work also suggests another, more optimistic course. Absolutists who violently rejected profane offers of money or peace for sacred land were much more inclined to accept deals that involved their enemies making the symbolic but difficult gesture of conceding respect for the other side's sacred values. For example, Palestinian hard-liners were more willing to consider recognizing the right of Israel to exist, if the Israelis apologized for suffering caused to Palestinian civilians in the 1948 war (which Palestinians call *Naqba'*, the Catastrophe).

Elliot Abrams, senior member of the National Security Council staff responsible for Middle East affairs during George W. Bush's presidency, responded to our briefing on these results this way: "Seems right. On the settlers [being removed from Gaza, Israeli prime minister Ariel] Sharon realized too late that he shouldn't have berated them about wasting Israel's money and endangering soldiers' lives. Sharon told me that he realized only afterward that he should have made a symbolic concession and called them Zionist heroes making yet another sacrifice." Here, the settlers' enemy was their own government.[6]

Remarkably, our survey results were mirrored by our discussions with political leaders from both sides. Musa Abu Marzook, former chairman and currently deputy chairman of Hamas, said no when we proposed a trade-off for peace without granting a right of return. He became angry when we added in the idea of substantial American aid for rebuilding: "No, we do not sell ourselves for any amount." But when a potential Israeli apology for 1948 was brought up, he brightened: "Yes, an apology is important, as a beginning. It's not enough, because our houses and land were taken away from us and something has to be done about that." This suggested that progress on sacred values might open up negotiations on material issues, rather than the reverse.

We got a similar reaction from Benjamin Netanyahu, then the hard-line leader of the Israeli opposition and now prime minister again. We asked him if he would seriously consider accepting a

two-state solution following the 1967 borders if all major Palestinian factions, including Hamas, were to recognize the right of the
Jewish people to an independent state in the region. He answered,
"Okay, but the Palestinians would have to show that they sincerely
mean it, change their textbooks and anti-Semitic characterizations
and then allow some border adjustments so that Ben-Gurion [Air-
port] would be out of range of shoulder-fired missiles."

Of course, there are leaders on both sides who currently refuse
any notion of compromise, and there may be some posturing on
willingness to compromise from both Marzook and Netanyahu,
although neither has publicly brought up these ideas before or
since, and both responded to our questioning in a deeply personal
way. Making these sorts of wholly intangible "symbolic" concessions, like an apology or recognition of a right to exist or a simple
but sincere show of respect, simply doesn't compute on any utili-
tarian calculus. Words—of an apology, recognition, or respect—
aren't enough on their own, but they are the beginning; they are
the things that just might make the other side willing to listen and
calm the heat in their anger. Words have the extreme power to
change emotions. They can express the abstract and the factual,
but they can also change and inspire. And the science says they
may be the best bet to start cutting the knot.[7]

SACRED VALUES IN INDONESIA, INDIA, AND IRAN

In studies in Indonesia, we found that support for violence among
moderate as well as radical madrassah students was significantly
greater in response to a deal that involved a large material incentive to give up the struggle to have the country "ruled strictly
according to Sharia" (Muslim law).[8] From India, Sonya Sachdeva
and Doug Medin show that the sacred and secular don't mix in
the conflict over Kashmir, although the issue appears to be more
symbolically charged for Muslims than for Hindus. Hindus and

Muslims are equally likely to disapprove of a material compromise over Kashmir (taboo trade-off: "Instead of the current two-to-one split of Kashmir, it would be evenly divided between Pakistan and India") and to envisage rioting over the issue. Muslims, however, are much more likely than Hindus are to approve a deal and to downplay rioting were the other side to make a symbolic concession (symbolic [tragic] trade-off: "India would recognize the sacred and historic right that Muslims have to Kashmir and apologize for all the wrongs done over the years").[9]

In an Internet experiment designed by Morteza Dehghani and Rumen Illiev, our research team asked Iranians from inside and outside Iran to imagine these hypothetical situations:

Iran will give up its nuclear program; Israel in return will give up its nuclear program and destroy any existing nuclear weapons.

Iran will give up its nuclear program; Israel in return will give up its nuclear program and destroy any existing nuclear weapons. In addition, the EU will pay $40 billion to Iran.

There was a clear difference between the first hypothesis (taboo) and the second (taboo plus): Iranian subjects were generally approving of added material incentives, whereas a minority of 11 percent were strongly disapproving. For at least some Iranians, acquiring a nuclear capability had perhaps become something of a "sacred value" that cannot simply be bought off with material incentives.[10] Is 11 percent too few Iranians to matter? Perhaps not: even a minority, if it is committed enough, can carry the day if it is associated with a power structure that is willing to do almost anything to stay in power, like the Alawites in Syria who number between 10 and 20 percent of the population yet have ruled for decades.

In a much larger follow-up study conducted in 2010, we found that the more strongly religious people were, and the more closely they identified with Iran's rulers, the greater their anger toward material offers. But we also found that while acquiring a nuclear capability for energy and medicine had reliably become a sacred value for a significant minority of Iranians both inside and outside the country, *acquiring nuclear weapons was not reliably a sacred value.*

It appears, then, that sacred values can emerge for issues with relatively little historical background and significance when they become bound up with conflicts over collective identity. Specifically, achieving nuclear capability seems to have the capacity for assuming sacredness among at least some Iranians.[11] One political analyst cautioned the U.S. administration, "You don't bring down a quasi-holy symbol—nuclear power—by cutting off gasoline sales."[12] Indeed, Iranian officials claim that "we cannot have any compromise with respect to the Iranian nation's inalienable right" to acquire a nuclear capability.[13] In fact, our results suggest that a "carrots (or sticks) approach," which is favored by the United States, European Union, and the U.N., may actually backfire for those who identify most closely with the Iranian regime.

One obvious problem is that while people often recognize their own side's sacred values, they often ignore or downplay the importance of the other side's values. In chapter 15, we saw that Pashtun tribesmen will defend to the death the ancient code of honor known as Pashtunwali, which requires protecting valued guests at the risk of one's own life.[14] We also found that in many Middle Eastern, Central Asian, and North African societies, political, economic, and social structure is organized according to patrilineal descent (exclusively through the father's line), so the patriline's "honor" depends on "respect" and on the enforced modesty and protection of women. Thus even a small gesture that impugns the esteem of a senior male or the modesty of a postpubescent woman can rouse a whole patriline to implacable hostility, along with people from the entire community who feel their culture's most sacred values have been threatened. But even small gestures of respect toward elders and obvious attempts to maintain social distance toward women can broadcast intent to cooperate with a community in a surprisingly effective way. Here, an almost no-cost act becomes amplified through the local value system to great benefit.

REFRAMING SACRED VALUES

People hold sacred values to be absolute and inviolable. So any symbolic "concession" must not appear to violate or weaken one's own sacred values. Doing so would likely be seen as tantamount to abandoning or altering core social identity. What often makes values incompatible is the way they are applied to the here and now. While values can be held firmly, their application depends a good deal on how they are understood and what they are taken to imply, and these interpretations and applications of sacred values are not always fixed and inflexible.

The opportunities for reframing issues that involve sacred values arise from the fact that their content is generally open-textured, especially if they involve religious values, which survive in time and spread in space because they are readily reinterpretable in ways that are sensitive to changing contexts. Indeed, sacred values that seem incompatible within certain frames may actually become compatible when reframed.

What follows are some ideas for reframing sacred values in order to overcome barriers to conflict resolution, based on my with work political scientist Robert Axelrod.

EXPLOIT THE INEVITABLE AMBIGUITY OF SACRED

People often apply the "same" sacred values in different ways, which facilitates creative use of ambiguity. Many Americans consider "equality" to be a core value, a self-evident truth as stated in the Declaration of Independence and codified under the law in the

Fourteenth Amendment to the U.S. Constitution or before God. Historically, though, popular and legal notions of equality have varied considerably and continue to do so: from voting privileges only for property-holding white males to "universal suffrage," and from "separate but equal" education for whites and blacks to "equal opportunity" for all men and women.

Religious values are particularly open-textured in this way, however much people believe their own interpretation to be the only literal or right one.[15] In Judaism, the religious commandment to "keep the Sabbath holy," whose violation in biblical times was punishable by death, continues to undergo radical reinterpretation: In today's Jerusalem, a chief dispute between Orthodox and Reform Jews entails whether Sabbath observance allows for driving on Saturdays. Or take the biblical commandment "Thou shalt not kill." Many U.S. conservatives believe it warrants both an anti-abortion agenda and capital punishment, whereas many U.S. liberals consider this commandment to warrant abolition of capital punishment and a pro-choice agenda. American leaders who seek election or to govern from the center must learn to finesse seemingly contrary interpretations of sacred values in creative ways.

For both Israelis and Palestinians, "the Land" is sacred, with Jerusalem at its center. Israelis simply refer to their country as "the Land" (*ha-aretz*), whereas for Palestinians "Land and Honor" (*'ard wal ard*) are one. Israeli political leaders creatively reinterpreted the historical scope of "the Land," first to justify claims on Gaza and then to justify leaving it. If Palestinians, who simply refer to Jerusalem as "the Holy" (Al Quds), can reframe their idea of the city to include only its Arab neighborhoods and part of the Temple Mount (Haram Al-Sharif), then Israel might be willing to accept the Palestinian capital there. Reframing the issue in this way need not call into question "the strength of attachment" to the sacred value of Jerusalem.

For Muslims, the meaning of jihad, or holy war, can be interpreted in radically different ways, whether as an inner mental struggle for the preservation of faith or as physical combat against external enemies who threaten Islam. For supporters of militant Islamist groups whom we have surveyed, including members of Hamas, jihad is the "Sixth Pillar" of Islam, which trumps four of the five traditional pillars (almsgiving, pilgrimage, fasting, and prayer); only the pillar expressing faith in God stands up to jihad. For many other Muslims, there is no such Sixth Pillar, and professed belief in it may be heretical and blasphemous. Given the popular and political division of Palestinian society today, Palestinian leaders must carefully navigate meanings of jihad without alienating major segments of Palestinian society or the outside world.

This issue of reframing jihad is currently an important consideration in Saudi Arabia's counterterrorism efforts. As one senior Saudi official recently said to me:

> During the Afghanistan war [with the Soviets] we daily praised the mujahedin and Bin Laden in our newspapers. He was the leader of the Arab heroes. Mujahedin entered our vocabulary in a positive frame. Then we said he was bad. The people were confused. Before a hero and overnight a bad man. We had to reframe jihad to distinguish "moral jihad" from the Takfiri ideology. The mujahedin had been heroes for us, and for you [America] in Afghanistan, and now they were terrorists . . . and we had to have a way of reframing jihad in order to show that the Takfiri way of jihad was different, their training, ideology, tactics.[16]

SHIFT THE CONTEXT

One way leaders can navigate through the muddle of meanings that attend sacred values is to shift the context so that one sacred value becomes more relevant than others in a specific context. At West Point, for example, cadets acculturate to two competing "honor codes." There is a formal one, which requires telling the truth and obeying the orders of superiors, and an informal one, which entails loyalty to peers. Army leaders understand that at times they must carefully balance vertical loyalty to commanders with horizontal loyalties to comrades, for example, by not punishing cadets who refuse to snitch on their buddies.

When I spoke about suicide bombers with Sheikh Hassan Yusef, a West Bank Hamas leader detained in Israel's Ketziot Prison, he told me, "God created people to live, not to die. . . . We have to find an exit." In a similar vein, then–Palestinian prime minister Ismail Haniya said, "We need a dialogue of civilizations, not a clash of civilizations."[17] These Hamas leaders clearly mean here to appeal to our common understanding of humanity as being equal to, or greater than, Islamist calls for martyrdom. Of course, on other occasions and in other circumstances these same leaders may reverse priorities, for example, when they feel that possible windows of opportunity for a breakthrough to the outside, such as international recognition or aid, are closed to them. Such changing appeals do not necessarily represent either flip-flops in thinking or hypocrisy, but a fluid appreciation of values according to how circumstances can be framed in terms of them. That is part of the paradoxical nature of sacred values, "eternal" and morally absolute, yet widely open to interpretation.

One way to shift context is to change a value's scope from the here and now to an indefinite time in the future. In the 1920s, for example, the Soviet leader Joseph Stalin moved the goal of a world victory for communism to an indefinite future when he declared communism in one country to have priority, contradicting Lenin's views that the world's imperial powers were imminently about to destroy themselves.

Ami Ayalon, former head of Shin Bet, Israel's counterterrorism and internal security agency, expressed to us his view that Hamas's proposals for a *hudna*, or provisional armistice, could be moving in this direction.[18] Consider that the first *hudna* was the eighth-century Treaty of Hudaibiyyah, a nonaggression pact between Mohammed and the Quraish tribe. The founder of Hamas, Sheikh Ahmed Yassin, originally offered a ten-year *hudna* in return for complete withdrawal from all territories captured in the Six-Day War and the establishment of a Palestinian state in the West Bank and Gaza. At various times, Yasin offered terms for *hudnas* that were potentially renewable for thirty, forty, or one hundred years, although it would never signal recognition of Israel.

Ahmed Yusef, political adviser to the Hamas government in Gaza, told us that there is no limit in principle to how many times a *hudna* might be renewed. He compared Hamas's practical willingness to live alongside Israel to the willingness of the Irish Republican Army (IRA) to accept a permanent armistice with Great Britain while still refusing to recognize British sovereignty over Northern Ireland. Of course, the IRA never refused to recognize Britain's existence, and many Israelis believe that Hamas's refusal of recognition and permanent peace indicates that any *hudna* will just be a smoke screen to allow military preparation for an eventual attack on Israel.

PROVISIONALLY PRIORITIZE VALUES

Fulfilling one sacred value may require the delay of achieving others. At the start of the Civil War, President Abraham Lincoln was willing to postpone emancipation to save the Union. Similarly, Israeli leader David Ben-Gurion was willing to accept a partition of Palestine that left Israel without control over historical Judea or Jerusalem in order to attain statehood.[19] Lincoln and Ben-Gurion both wanted the delay to be only provisional. Nevertheless, later in life Ben-Gurion argued against settlement in the West Bank and Gaza. This example suggests that prioritization of current values may allow for a change in the scope of values over time.

Yasser Arafat, who headed the Palestine Liberation Organization (PLO), steered that organization to officially recognize Israel. But Fateh, the PLO's largest contingent and also headed by Arafat, has never renounced its guiding principles and goals, which include, in Article 12 of Fateh's constitution, the "complete liberation of Palestine, and eradication of Zionist economic, political, military and cultural existence."[20] Israeli governments were never entirely convinced that Arafat's commitment to the PLO position on recognition of Israel trumped the Fateh constitution's prohibition of recognition. Successive Israeli governments have rejected the idea that any Palestinian government that included Hamas would possibly "allow" recognition of Israel, considering this idea a Hamas ploy to mask its real intentions to destroy Israel. But several senior members of the present Israeli government and opposition to whom we spoke consider Arafat's successor, Mahmoud Abbas, to be sincere in recognizing Israel's right to exist and in wanting peace, despite the persistence of nonrecognition clauses in Fateh's constitution. This suggests, again, that pragmatic prioritization of one value over another, however provisional to begin with, may facilitate a more permanent realignment of values.

REFINE SACRED VALUES TO EXCLUDE OUTMODED CLAIMS

Article 32 of the Hamas Covenant (1988) highlights "Zionist scheming . . . laid out in *The Protocols of the Elders of Zion*." This is a notorious anti-Semitic tract forged by Russian tsarist police. In private, Hamas leaders grant that it may not be a statement of fact. By explicitly renouncing its endorsement of the *Protocols*, Hamas could demonstrate that it no longer wants others to see it as anti-Semitic. Likewise, Israel could distance itself from the old Zionist slogan that Palestine was "A land without people for a people without land."[21]

Our talks with leaders on both sides indicate awareness that their current positions involve outmoded and historically inaccurate claims. They also acknowledge that, were the other side to renounce such blatant falsehoods, this could lead to a psychological breakthrough. Overcoming historical precedents and emotional barriers to renouncing even patently false claims, however, may require neutral mediation by those who understand both sides. Even then, it takes time. According to Lord John Alderdice, a principal mediator in the Northern Ireland conflict, it took nine years of back-and-forth for this to happen in Northern Ireland.[22]

USE ONE SIDE'S SACRED VALUES TO AMPLIFY THE IMPORTANCE OF THE OTHER SIDE'S CONCESSIONS

Another relatively low-cost way to show respect for others' values is to find things that mean much to the other side but little to one's own. Consider the case of "Ping-Pong diplomacy" between the United States and China. As expected, the Chinese won match after match against the visiting American table-tennis team in 1971. In the United States Ping-Pong is considered a "basement sport," so there was little at stake. In contrast, table tennis is a sport of national prestige to China.[23] At little cost to itself, the United States was able to provide something of great symbolic value for the other side. America demonstrated respect for Chinese sensitivity about receiving equal treatment on the world stage. This was done by demonstrating that America does not always have to better China in matters that the Chinese care for.

An example of a relatively small symbolic step that may have big implications is the recent approval by the Israeli education ministry of a textbook for Arab third-graders in Israel that for the first time describes Israel's 1948 War of Independence as a "catastrophe" for many Palestinians and their society. Rami Khouri, director of the Issam Fares Institute at the American University of Beirut and editor at large of the Beirut-based *Daily Star*, opined, "This may be the first tangible sign that the Zionist Israeli establishment is prepared to move in the direction of acknowledging what happened to Palestinians in 1948, which is a vital Palestinian demand for any serious peace-making effort to succeed. Israelis in turn would expect a reciprocal Palestinian acknowledgment of Israel's core narrative."[24]

It is noteworthy that the revised textbooks are only for Arab children, not Jewish children, which is why, above, we characterized this symbolic step as "relatively small." Exposing Jewish children to a more balanced history carries increased risk for undermining part of Zionism's moral narrative among the next generation. Undertaking the added risk may require an offsetting symbolic gesture from the other side. As Netanyahu said, a change in Palestinian textbooks that omitted reference to Jewish perfidy since the time of Mohammed could reciprocally signal a sincere change of heart. (Unfortunately, when Mr. Netanyahu became prime minister again in 2009, his minister of education reversed course and expunged all references to the so-called Palestinian catastrophe, or *Naqba'*, from Israeli textbooks for Arab children.)

THE ART OF APOLOGY

A closer look at apologies in political conflicts indicates that they may not be so much deal makers in themselves as means of facilitating political compromise that may also involve significant material transactions. This was the gist of Abu Marzook's remarks about a sincere apology being only "the beginning" of negotiations over land and compensation.

A telling example concerns the Federal Government of Germany's apology to the Jewish people.[25] In 1948, the newly established State of Israel was in dire economic straits. But Israel and the World Jewish Congress refused compensation from Germany for the property of murdered European Jews. Israel insisted that before any amount of money could be considered, Germany must publicly declare contrition for the murder and suffering of Jews at German hands.

On September 27, 1951, German chancellor Konrad Adenauer delivered a much anticipated speech at the Bundestag, the German national parliament, acknowledging that "the Federal Republic and with it the great majority of the German people are aware of the immeasurable suffering that was brought upon the Jews of Germany and the occupied territories during the time of National Socialism. The overwhelming majority of the German people abominated the crimes committed against the Jews and did not participate in them." Although this symbolic concession to Jewish sensibilities was only halfhearted—because, in fact, the majority of wartime Germans at least acquiesced to Nazi actions—it was enough to start the reconciliation process between Israel and Germany.

Symbolic gestures don't always stand alone, unhinged from all material considerations. Rather, they often help to recast a moral frame that determines the scope and limits of possible material transactions and negotiations.[26]

Consider, in this regard, attempts by Israeli and Palestinian negotiators to reach agreement following the 2000 Camp David summit. Israeli prime minister Ehud Barak had expressed readiness to state regret for the suffering of Palestinian refugees who fled or were expelled during what Israel calls its War of Independence and what Palestinians call the Catastrophe (*al-Naqba'*) and to perhaps accept shared responsibility but not primary responsibility (as Palestinian leaders insisted). Bill Clinton was further prepared to declare publicly the need to compensate and resettle refugees, without requiring Israel to accept refugees into its own territory or to acknowledge responsibility for their sorrow.[27]

At Taba, in January 2001, the Palestinian delegation responded positively,[28] but the timing was wrong. Clinton was ceding power to George W. Bush, and Ehud Barak was about to be replaced by Ariel Sharon. The new leaders wanted to revise the decisions of their political rivals.

Another important lesson from this case is that without the acceptance of responsibility, apologies don't work. For Palestinians, Israel's continued settlement activity has been inconsistent with steps made toward realization of Palestinian rights, including acknowledging some responsibility for the 1948 "Catastrophe" and recognition of the plight of Palestinian refugees. For Israelis, in turn, the Palestinian Authority's failure to prevent armed attacks on Israeli civilians had been inconsistent with Palestinian overtures of recognition of the right of the Jewish people to an independent state in the region. This resulted in distrust of the other's sincerity by both sides. Symbolic gestures provide openings only if consistent actions follow.

An apology should be consistent with one's own core values while simultaneously demonstrating sensitivity to the values of others. A good example why this is necessary is Japan's repeated apologies for atrocities committed in World War II. China dismissed Japan's apologies and practically froze relations between the two countries when Japanese prime minister Junichiro Koizumi visited the Yasukuni Shrine, a shrine that honors Japan's 2.5 million war dead but also includes fourteen convicted top war criminals.[29]

In 1995, Japan set up the Asian Women's Fund to pay out money to former "comfort women," victims of its sexual slavery practices in countries occupied in World War II. But the Japanese government stressed that the money came from "citizens," and not from the government itself, arguing that postwar treaties absolve it from all individual claims related to World War II. The governments of Taiwan and South Korea rejected payments from the fund, accusing Japan of failing to take clear moral responsibility in "atoning" for its treatment of the women.[30]

Likewise, a qualified apology can be seen as worse than none at all. Take, for example, the U.S. administration's apology for the abuse of detainees at Abu Ghraib Prison in Iraq. In May 2004, Secretary of Defense Donald Rumsfeld offered his "deepest apology" to "those Iraqis who were mistreated."[31] He then went on to claim that mistreatment was not the fault of U.S. policy, purpose, or principle, but of a few wayward soldiers whose behavior was "inconsistent with the values of our nation, inconsistent with the teachings of the military, and it was fundamentally un-American." The qualifier—a few wayward soldiers—resulted in an angry dismissal of the apology by many in the Arab and Muslim world,[32] a dismissal amply justified by subsequent revelations about U.S. policy permitting water-boarding[33] and other forms of torture.[34]

THE DIFFICULTY OF RESPECTING THE OTHER

Understanding sacred values abroad requires some empathy, even with enemies, with the "who we are" identity aspect that is often hard for members of opposing cultures to understand. Consider America's pacification of postwar Japan. Many in the wartime U.S. administration believed the Japanese emperor to be a war criminal who should be executed. But wartime advisers, such as anthropologists Ruth Benedict and Margaret Mead, as well as psychological-warfare specialists in General Douglas MacArthur's command,[35] argued that preserving, and even signaling respect for, the emperor might lessen the likelihood that the Japanese, who held him in religious awe, would fight to the death to save him. Moreover, his symbolic weight could be leveraged by the occupation government to bolster pro-American factions in postwar Japan.

Sometimes the symbolic value of a gesture that is weighty to the parties directly involved may seem trivial to an outside party. If France allowed Muslim women to wear headscarves in public schools, which is now prohibited, beneficial effects might reverberate across the Muslim world. For most Americans, it's a no-brainer. The problem is that in France, unlike in the United States, signs of physical and religious distinction in school are viewed as affronts to the defining value of French political culture ever since the French Revolution, namely, a universal and uniform sense of social equality (however lacking in practice). "The only community is the nation," declared former French prime minister Dominique de Villepin[36]—an uninterrupted national sentiment that dates to 1762 and Jean-Jacques Rousseau's *Social Contract*. The only two moral entities widely recognized in France are the individual and the state.[37]

This example shows that recognizing one another's sacred values isn't transparent, even for allies and for members of societies that seem similar in so many other ways. More important, it illustrates that recognizing and showing respect for another's core values is really possible only if doing so doesn't entail compromising one's own core values.

RATIONAL VERSUS DEVOTED ACTORS

Ever since the end of World War II, "rational-actor" models have dominated strategic thinking at all levels of government policy[38] and military planning.[39] Rational-actor models have always had serious deficiencies as general models of human reasoning and decision making because human behavior cannot be reduced purely to rational calculation. But in a confrontation between states, and especially during the Cold War, these models proved useful in anticipating an array of challenges and in formulating policies to prevent nuclear war. Now, however, we are witnessing the rise of "devoted actors," such as suicide terrorists,[40] who are willing to make extreme sacrifices that use a logic of appropriateness[41] (I choose something because I think it is appropriate for perceived rules or to what I consider to be my identity)[42] rather than the logic of consequences (I choose something for its anticipated consequences).[43] This is also evident for the most tenacious conflicts that are grounded in cultural and religious opposition, rather than those based primarily on political competition for resources.

The assumption that adversaries act according to cost-benefit logic is standard in risk assessment and modeling by American diplomatic, military, and intelligence services. "Look at the National Security Council's composition, which determines the direction of U.S. foreign policy," said Richard Davis, a former director of terrorism prevention at the White House Homeland Security Council.[44] "It is institutionally structured within a narrow intellectual frame weighted to consideration of practical costs and benefits in terms of our national economy, law enforcement, intelligence, and military. There is only limited provision for missions of health, education, or human services that represent our values." Indeed, the U.S. National Security Strategy document explicitly states a commitment to "results-oriented planning" that focuses on "actions and results rather than legislation or rule-making." It embodies a clear focus on practical consequences rather than on moral principles whose consequences may be indeterminate.

Political leaders often appeal to sacred values as a least-cost method of mobilizing their constituents to action,[45] of enforcing policy goals,[46] and of discrediting adversaries (for example, when U.S. politicians accuse one another of disregard for "the sanctity of marriage" or of usurping "God's gift of life"). What works as sacred in one society is often entirely ineffective and mundane in another. When Iranian president Mahmoud Ahmadinejad publicly embraced and kissed on the hand an elderly woman who used to be his schoolteacher, Iran's ultraconservative *Hizbollah* newspaper intoned: "This type of indecency progressively has grave consequences, like violating religious and sacred values."[47] Contrast the Iranian example with the kissing expected of American candidates on campaign tours. A gesture that calls forth a rallying cry to protect sacred values in one culture is utterly innocuous in another.

Many policymakers, however, argue that all so-called sacred values are only "pseudo-sacred," because in a world of scarce resources, there is always room for trade-offs:[48] People cannot really devote all of their time, energy, and life to upholding any one such value. Even apparently irrational behaviors arguably reflect rational calculations of the holdout's long-term interests, however incomprehensible those interests appear to others.[49] Consider the angry resistance of the impoverished Lakota Sioux to offers of hundreds of millions of dollars in compensation for the Black Hills, of which the U.S. government has claimed ownership since 1877.[50] The Sioux say that claims on their land are claims to their identity as a people.

In these and other examples, the actors may be described as "holding out" for greater benefits, such as eternal glory over worldly greed, whereas, for them, glory is a more rewarding and hence more rational outcome. But we only obscure the issue by giving post hoc interpretations of any seemingly irrational behavior (in the sense of immunity to material trade-offs) so as to fit a rational-actor model. No explanatory power is thereby gained.

Recently a group of Holocaust survivors traveled to Majdanek death camp in Poland on what they considered a sacred mission to search for mementos of those killed by the Nazis. "We've spent a million dollars so far to find rings worth maybe a hundred dollars retail," said an organizer of the expedition. "But the objects tell a powerful story. There is no way that a modern person can understand the experience, but looking at an object . . . its rescue gives us all an opportunity to connect with the people here and their sacrifice."[51] Again, one might rationally construe these actions as calculated for securing a sense of collective identity or mitigating emotionally costly guilt or grief, or whatever. You can always interpret behavior as a rational choice after the fact. That may describe, but won't explain, anything.[52]

It's true that sacred values are sometimes used as self-serving "posturing" or part of some strategy for economic or psychological benefits.[53] Politicians will exploit sacred values for their own material interests or some greater future gain, such as enhanced personal prestige and votes. Nevertheless, the seeming intractability of certain political conflicts and the reality of violence associated with these conflicts, such as suicide bombings, compels scholars and policy makers to pay greater attention to the nature and depth of people's commitment to sacred values. Our leaders seem to understand the importance of such values at home, but not abroad.

DAMASCUS, DECEMBER 2009

In December 2009, a delegation of the World Federation of Scientists, led by Lord John Alderdice, went to Damascus to meet leaders of Syria and Hamas. The objective was to gain insight from our interviews to create new theoretical and practical frames for negotiation and cooperation. I asked the Israeli leadership what questions they might have for our delegation, and my colleague Bob Axelrod and I delivered their answers back to Israel's prime minister.

We also attended meetings with other Palestinian factions, including Palestinian Islamic Jihad (PIJ), although we hadn't been informed they were in the offing before our arrival in Damascus. I checked on the Internet after our surprise meeting with Ramadan Shallah, general secretary of the PIJ, and found him on the FBI's most-wanted terrorist list, with a $5 million reward for information leading to his arrest or conviction, and so I related our discussions to U.S. authorities. No doubt those we met in Damascus assumed we would be reporting back.

The WFS delegation was also tasked with probing the plausibility and potential significance of material cooperation on "economic" projects—such as solutions to regional problems of water, energy, and the environment—in seeking novel and productive pathways to resolving long-standing conflicts. All Syrian and Palestinian leaders we talked to rejected any economic cooperation before a peace settlement was reached. No support emerged for the idea that economic cooperation could help resolve the region's deep-seated conflicts without first addressing perceived threats to core values. As Syria's Foreign Minister Walid Muaellem said:

"Mr. Netanyahu says to us and the Palestinians: 'Let's concentrate on economic relations but not on who has sovereignty over the land.' But sovereignty over land is the key to this region, because it is for Arabs a question of honor and dignity, *'Ard wal ard'* [Land is honor]."

In regard to Hamas, the principal question that interested Israel was:

"Is there any possibility that Hamas could ever recognize Israel, not necessarily now but in the future, under whatever conditions? And if so, what would Hamas want for it?"

In a previous visit to Damascus, Israeli leaders told me beforehand that a positive response would, in their minds, represent a "strategic shift" in Hamas's attitude and hence justify engaging Hamas as a potential partner in peace. Some in Hamas had answered "perhaps" and others "no." But this time Khaled Meshaal, chairman of the Hamas Politburo, pointedly rejected the question about the future possibility of Hamas recognizing Israel as being inappropriate because it ignores basic asymmetries in: (1) existing rights between Israelis and Palestinians (which violates the core value of "dignity"), and (2) the current balance of forces and power:

Why is this question always the first question being asked? It is a question that requires that the Palestinians make the first concession. It does not speak to Palestinian rights at all. The basic rights of Palestinian people must first be recognized: to live without violence, without killing, without siege or arrest, to have hope without occupation. There is not much discussion from the other side about this. Nobody asks Israel if they will first recognize us. . . . The Israelis have rights, but we also have rights; no one can have the exclusive right to basic rights.

Meshaal then went on to outline Hamas's conditions for the proper time and context to pose the question of recognition:

> After Israel withdraws to the 1967 borders, and there is a Palestinian state with full and complete sovereignty with its capital in East Jerusalem, and the issue of the refugees is settled, then you can ask your question again and we will have a different answer. If a sovereign Palestinian state chooses to recognize Israel, Hamas would accept that choice.
>
> Only a sovereign Palestinian could recognize Israel. Why? Because you must have complete freedom to make the decision. You can't ask a person in prison, of his own free will, to recognize the rights of his jailers, when the prisoner's rights are ignored and not guaranteed. You can't expect the prisoner under torture to be satisfied talking about financial arrangements with the jailer. To achieve normal relations, there has to be a referendum to make the decision. It has to be the choice of the people.

Khaled Meshaal comes off as a natural leader, with more authority and charisma than any other Palestinian leader I've met. He could be humorous and self-deprecating. Unlike less commanding leaders, he made no attempt to show how important he was by taking calls, or allowing aides to interrupt him with other business, and his pontifications were kept short. He did not seem to personally begrudge Israeli prime minister Netanyahu an earlier assassination attempt by poisoning, which had almost killed him. Meshaal was straightforward without being arrogant and did not appear on the surface to be a schemer or duplicitous, although his intelligence and physical control are nuanced enough to be able to craft deception. He projected confidence in ultimate victory, although as Bob Axelrod surmised, "even a cursory analysis of his strategy would suggest it will take a long war of attrition to have a chance to work."

Meshaal made it clear that he had no interest in global jihad: "I'm not affiliated with a global movement, but I can understand the anger that has led others to it. The response of others who are oppressed and who created Al Qaeda is sometimes exaggerated and irrational. We are a resistance movement against an occupation. We haven't made any operation outside Palestine. We have never sought to kill a Jew because he was a Jew. We don't fight America."

But perhaps the most interesting question I posed to Meshaal was: "In your heart, do feel that peace—*salaam*—with Israel is possible? . . . Be as sincere as you can, personally." According to his own aides, Meshaal was surprised by the question, which he supposedly had never heard before, and they were surprised by his answer:

"The heart is different from the mind, and the mind resists by all logic, but the heart says yes. In my heart, I feel peace—*salaam*—with Israel is possible. But when we have a balance of power . . . to force Israel to keep to its commitments."

The word *salaam* (peace) was used in the question, and *salaam* was used in the answer. The Hamas watchword *hudna* (armistice) never came up. By contrast, PIJ's Ramadan, who believes Hamas shares his goal of repossessing Israel but is too "tactically conciliatory in proposing a long-term *hudna*," responded: "Never, ever."

I also asked Meshaal: "Suppose Israel were to make a unilateral no-cost concession, like apologizing for part of the suffering caused by the dislocation and dispossession of the Palestinian people in 1948. Would that mean something to you?"

His answer, like Marzook's, was that such words would "mean something, but aren't enough:"

They are important, even if they are only words, if they are sincere. . . . Our religions say "the world began with the word" and wars start with words. . . . In my heart, I can understand the search for signals to exchange and keenness to see lights on the horizon. But for eighteen years since [the] Madrid [Conference] we've tried every medicine, every surgery. Now, words would not be enough to keep the patient alive. I wish it were that simple. The key is the balance of forces that creates conditions for peace. . . . We will not be second-class citizens.

Understanding sacred values isn't about a group hug. It's about understanding human nature—what it is to be human. With sacred values, cost-benefit calculus is turned on its head, and business-style negotiations can backfire. Asking the other side to compromise a sacred value by offering material concessions can be interpreted as an insult and make matters worse, not better. Surprisingly, however, our studies and discussions with political leaders indicate that even materially intangible symbolic gestures that show respect for the other side and its core values may open the door to dialogue and negotiation in the worst of conflicts.

Apologies and shows of respect acknowledge the dignity of others and can speak to other people's sacred values. But it's often terribly painful to make these and other symbolic gestures and then, having made them, to have them accepted as sincere by your adversary without risking a serious backlash at home. That's why it generally takes someone with sufficient power or reputation, like Anwar Sadat or Nelson Mandela, to make such moves.

Finding ways to reframe cultural core values so as to overcome psychological barriers to symbolic offerings that show respect for the other side's sacred values is a daunting challenge. But meeting this challenge may offer greater opportunities for breakthroughs to peace than hitherto realized. "Mere" words and symbols may prove more powerful than billions of dollars in aid or bombs and bullets—at least in opening up opportunities for practical solutions. Though difficult, creatively reframing sacred values may provide a key to unlocking the most deep-seated conflicts. That's the kind of insight that the anthropology and psychology of religion and sacred values could bring about. There may be few more urgent fields of study in the world today than "the science of the sacred."

Part VII

THE DIVINE DREAM AND THE COLLAPSE OF CULTURES

Le XXIème siècle sera religieux ou ne sera pas—
The 21st century will be religious or will not be.

The greatest mystery is not that we have been flung at random among the profusion of the earth and the galaxies, but that in this prison we can fashion images sufficiently powerful to deny our nothingness.

—ANDRÉ MALRAUX, ANTIFASCIST, ANTICOMMUNIST SECULAR
FRENCH ELITIST, 1901–1976

Soccer buddies in Hebron's Wad Abu Katila neighborhood.

CHAPTER 22
BAD FAITH: THE NEW ATHEIST SALVATION

Greater love hath no man than this: that he lay down his life for
his friends.

—JOHN 15:13

HEBRON, WEST BANK, FEBRUARY 2008

At five A.M. on February 4, 2008, twenty-year-old Mohammed
Herbawi and his close friend and soccer buddy Shadi Zghayer
silently left their homes in the West Bank city of Hebron on a suicide bombing mission across the Green Line to Israel. As always
with this sort of thing, parents were left completely in the dark.
At ten A.M., one of the young men managed to detonate his vest
near a toy store in a shopping center in Dimona, a small town that
houses Israel's secret nuclear program, killing seventy-three-year-
old Lyubov Razdolskaya and wounding forty others. Lyubov had
been on her way to the bank along with her husband, Edward Ged-
alin, who was critically wounded. The couple immigrated to Israel
from Russia in 1990, and worked in the physics department of Ben-
Gurion University until they retired in 2002. They were shortly to
have celebrated their fiftieth wedding anniversary.

Hamas took responsibility for the Dimona attack—the first
suicide attack claimed by Hamas since it suspended "martyrdom
actions" in December 2004—after Fateh's Al Aqsa Martyrs Brigades had first claimed it for their own. But the Hamas politburo
in Damascus clearly didn't order it or even know about it. Osama

Hamdan, the de facto Hamas foreign minister headquartered in Beirut, initially said he had no idea who was responsible. When I asked senior Hamas leaders in the West Bank if this meant that the political leadership in exile didn't know about the attack, they said, "Yes, you can conclude that; we certainly didn't."

I went to Hebron on February 9, 2008, to interview friends and families of the two young men who carried out the Dimona attack. These two friends were members of the same Hamas neighborhood soccer team as a number of others who died in suicide attacks: the Masjad (mosque) Al Jihad soccer team located in the neighborhood of Wad Abu Katila, with participation also from members of the Masjad al-Rabat team. Wad Abu Katila is a residential quarter of 7,000 to 8,000 people, neither rich nor poor but with lots of unfinished construction because of the collapse of the Palestinian economy during the Second Intifada. Several on the team also attended, or had planned to attend, the local Palestine Polytechnic University.

Basma Hamori was waiting for me at the top of the stairs with her son Ahmed, Mohammed Herbawi's younger brother. She was divorced from her sons' father and worked in a child-care center. I came with the Associated Press stringer who had sent in his dispatch reporting that Basma and Shadi's mother, Ayiza, were proud of their sons, who would go to heaven. Almost all mothers of suicide bombers will say this to reporters on a first account. But when I ask the mothers and fathers, "Would you want any of your other children to do it?" almost all say, as did Basma, "Not for all the world," or other words of that sort.

I questioned the reporter just before entering Basma's apartment: "Have you ever met a mother who is happy about something like this?"

"No," the reporter answered, "but our society respects martyrs."

"Do you think it's because of the religion?" I asked.

"I'm not religious and I respect them. It's a terrible thing for a right cause, recognition of our rights. At least it gets the Israelis to recognize we exist."

Basma asked Ahmed to bring cookies and coffee. "I don't understand, I don't believe he died." Basma's eyes, you could see, were shot from days of crying. She quietly insisted with a weary voice: "If only I would have known, I am against it, against it."

"You see," she held up a picture of her cell phone with Mohammed's picture. "He's still with me." Her face resembled a frightened doe's. "He's always with me. I can't believe he's not alive. I would have looked at him, talked to him, pleaded with him, cried and begged him not to do it. And he would have listened to me. That's why he didn't tell me, because he knew he couldn't resist a mother's influence, which is the strongest influence in a boy's life. That's why they never tell their mothers."

Ahmed suddenly left the room. He was fifteen, in the tenth grade, the same age as when his brother was arrested (another brother, nineteen-year-old Muntaz, was serving a one-year prison sentence for belonging to Hamas). Ahmed soon returned with two stacks of posters, wall-size and smaller folio-size. He offered them with resignation and pride.

"This is my brother," as if to show me, and himself, that there was still something alive and substantial left of his brother.

I took a small one.

"He was a star for the team." Ahmed's eyes, strained beyond their years, sparkled for a second. "Sometimes he would be the goalie, sometimes a striker."

I nodded.

"*Ana hazin*" [I am sad]. He plopped back down on the couch, deflated.

The poster with the seal of Hamas's Qassam Brigades read: "You took your rifle and went. You blew up your belt and burned. So as the son that they killed would rise up again."

Hamas poster of martyrs Mohammed Herbawi (left) and Shadi Zghayer.

Basma looked at the smiling image of her son (on the left) and she, too, smiled ever so faintly. "The Israelis kept him in prison for two and a half years. When he came out, he still loved soccer. He still loved those boys. And then there was the divorce. He worked hard and gave me most of the money. My job at the day-care center doesn't give enough. Maybe it was too hard on him, all of it."

"And all those boys played soccer?" I asked.

"Yes, and the others who became martyrs before, some boys

on the senior team. He [Mohammed] was only fifteen then, in the tenth grade, but he was arrested just after Muhsein Qawasmeh and some of the other boys he played soccer with became martyrs. The Americans and Israelis want us to leave our land. The boys are telling them we don't want to leave. But theirs is not the way. That way is crazy [*majnun*]. God, let them leave us alone."

Across town, the backyard of Fellah Nasser ed-Din, former imam of the Hamas-affiliated Al Jihad mosque for fifteen years and the sometime coach of its soccer team, is blessed with a magnificent view of the Hebron hills and littered with the carcasses of cell phones (about 125,000,000 cell phones are discarded worldwide every year, a piddling part of globalization's garbage, but particularly evident in the developing world, where waste is out in the open).

"Muhsein was the brightest of the bunch," Nasser ed-Din told me. "He was an outstanding student, 99 percent, always first in school. The young boys in the mosque would gather around him. He taught them religion and soccer. He was beloved. He was energetic, even charismatic, but no extremist. I never saw any hint of violence in him."

"Why, then, do you think he went out to kill?" I asked.

"In his last year in high school—I talked to him about his studies and knew him well—he changed. His family also came to me and said he wasn't focusing on his lessons."

"And the other boys who went out to kill and died?"

"Muhsein, Hazem, Fadi, and Fuad were close friends from Wad Abu Katila [a once middle-class neighborhood in increasingly impoverished Hebron]." Soft-spoken, they were all good students, good looking, and from good families. Basma also lived close by.

"They all loved soccer. I love soccer." The coach beamed. "Let me show you something."

Fellah Nasser ed-Din rushed into his house and was out in a flash with two stacks of photo albums under his arms.

"Here I am as a boy on my school team," he said, clearly proud and happy with his memories. "And here I was a coach. See. Yes, those boys were all good players, but Muhsein was their natural leader. He was a good organizer, small like [the Argentinean soccer star Diego] Maradona. His mother is a schoolteacher and raised him well. His family had a bookstore. He was the smartest of all."

"Did he organize the team or the attacks?" I asked.

"No, no. It's not like that. There's no team captain or coach. They organized themselves. They even organized matches with fifteen other local teams in honor of fallen martyrs. Sports means cooperation, caring, and tolerance for other players, and in this spirit they also organized themselves in prayer and in discussions about religion, and in thinking of ways to help their community overcome the restrictions, the suffering, the blood. They found their own way."

And then he added: "People don't have much trouble finding one another for actions like this. We've been fighting the Jews for a century and we'll go on fighting until we win our dignity and land back. All of it. As long as we're one team (*ma domna fariq wahid*)."

THE END OF FAITH AND OTHER PULP FICTION

In the best-seller *The End of Faith: Religion, Terrorism and the Future of Reason*,[1] Sam Harris, a graduate student in neuroscience with remarkable polemical skills, pulls no punches in deference to the tender religious sensibilities of others. (God help us, now that academic pundits have suddenly discovered we are all faced with the end of faith, end of history, end of evil, end of poverty, end of the nation-state, end of life, and so on.) Harris bemoans the destructive nature of religion and implores all people with any modicum of reason to fight against it. In the spirit of philosopher Dan Dennett's *Breaking the Spell*,[2] *Vanity Fair* contributor Christopher Hitchens's *God Is Not Great*,[3] and biologist Richard Dawkins's blockbuster *The God Delusion*,[4] Harris insists that secular moderation toward religion and ecumenical tolerance only enable bizarre and belligerent beliefs to thrive and extremists to flourish, with cruel and savage consequences for the world. It is stated almost as a law of nature. Later, I'll discuss the science, or rather lack of science, behind this missionary call. Here I only want to introduce some common misconceptions about suicide bombers and Muslims that have reached hysterical proportions.

Harris begins his book with a vivid anecdote that he presents to the reader as commonsense fact:

> The young man takes his seat beside a middle-aged couple. . . . The young man smiles. With the press of a button he destroys himself, the couple at his side, and twenty others on the bus. The nails, ball bearings, and rat poison ensure further casualties on the street and in the surrounding cars. All has gone according to plan.
>
> The young man's parents soon learn of his fate. Although saddened to have lost a son, they feel tremendous pride at his accomplishment. They know that he has gone to heaven and prepared the way for them to follow. He has also sent his victims to hell for eternity. It is a double victory.
>
> These are the facts. This is all we know for certain about the young man. . . . Why is it so easy, then, so trivially easy—you-could-almost-bet-your-life-on-it easy—to guess the young man's religion?

The lesson drawn from juxtaposing this observation with the suicide attacks of September 11 is that "we can no longer ignore the fact that billions of our neighbors believe in the metaphysics of martyrdom, [and] are now armed with chemical, biological, and nuclear weapons. . . . We are at war with Islam. It may not serve our immediate foreign policy objectives for our political leaders to openly acknowledge this fact, but it is unambiguously so." Harris and others in the fellowship that Christopher Hitchens calls the Four Horsemen of the Apocalypse (Harris, Hitchens, Dawkins, and Dennett) see science at the front line of this necessary and inevitable struggle against Islam in particular, and religion in general. No joke.

First some contrary facts: Suicide bombers are not only Islamic or religiously motivated. In fact, until 2001 the single most prolific group of suicide attackers had been the Tamil Tigers of Sri Lanka, an avowedly secular movement of national liberation whose supporters are nominally Hindu. In the Middle East before 2001, most suicide bombings occurred in Lebanon, and about half were by secular nationalists (Syrian Nationalist Party, Lebanese Communist Party, Lebanese Ba'ath Party).[5] True, since 2001 the overwhelming majority of suicide attacks have been sponsored by militant Muslim groups, but there isn't much precedent in Islamic tradition for suicide terrorism. Modern suicide terrorism became a political force with the atheist anarchist movement that began at the end of the nineteenth century, which resembles the jihadi movement in many other ways.

As for the "tremendous pride" that invariably trumps parental love, I have yet to meet parents who would not have done anything in their power to stop their child from such an act, though none of the dozens I've talked to ever knew, and few ever imagined, that their child could do such a thing. In history, psychology, and political-science classes, one regularly hears that Spartan and samurai mothers smiled when told their sons had died in battle. As Harvard psychologist Steven Pinker once wryly noted, of course there's no record of a Spartan or samurai mother ever writing such a thing; we just have to take the leaders' words for it. I've gone to homes where the press has reported that the parents were happy and proud of their son. I've heard the interviewing journalists ask, with the crowd and officials around, "Were you proud and happy?" Sometimes the parents say they are. What are they going to say when first informed of their child's death? That it was senseless and stupid? That goes against people's innate inclinations to give a sense to any heart-wrenching loss. Never have I heard a *shaheed*'s parent say, *in private*, "I am happy" or even "I am proud."

In *Letter to a Christian Nation*, Harris goes on to lambaste believers of all faiths, though he still has an itch in his craw for Islam: "Seventy percent of the inmates of France's jails, for instance, are Muslims. The Muslims of Western Europe are not atheists. . . . An atheist is a person who believes that the murder of a single little girl—even once in a million years—casts doubt upon the idea of a benevolent God."[6] The implied logic—that religious people in general, and Muslims in particular, tend to do more terrible things than do atheists—is hollow.

As we saw in chapter 16, immigrant Muslims in America tend to be slightly more religious than non-Muslims, but are underrepresented in U.S. prisons relative to their numbers in the general population. The predictive factors for Muslims entering European prisons are pretty much the same as for African Americans (religious or atheist) entering U.S. prisons: underemployment, poor schooling, and political marginalization. Controlling for population sizes, Muslims are about six times more likely to be arrested for jihadi activity in Europe than in America,[7] although the political pressure on law enforcement to get more arrests is greater in America (given "zero tolerance" in U.S. law enforcement for anything related to jihadi activity). But even in Europe, the more someone is exposed to Muslim religious education, the less likely he or she is to enter prison.

Atheists, to be sure, may well believe that the killing of a little girl is evidence against the existence of God. The proposition is true but trivial. Atheists, who have also killed tens of millions of people, among them millions of little girls, can equally take the murders they themselves have committed as evidence against God's power to intervene.[8] In the *Encyclopedia of Wars*,[9] Charles Phillips and Alexander Axelrod survey 1,763 violent conflicts throughout history, of which only 123 (7 percent) were religious. Nearly all major conflicts in recent times, which have been far more murderous than in the past, have been decidedly nonreligious (the two world wars, the Korean and Vietnam wars, and the Cambodian and Rwanda genocides, among others).

As to the call for science and scientists to do battle against religion in order to reduce violence and increase happiness in the world, I see no evidence that with religion banished, science will reduce violence and increase happiness. Nor do I see evidence that religion necessarily contributes more to unhappiness than to happiness. Religions throughout history have tended to lessen social distance within a group as they have increased distance and occasions for misunderstanding and conflict with other groups. But so do other determinants of cultural identity, such as language, ethnicity, and nationalism.

There is also a historically robust correlation between war and religious rituals, including costly ceremonial labors to build and maintain monumental works, and various forms of bodily deprivation and mutilation.[10] But costly ritual commitment, even in a religious group convinced of its own singular rightness and truth, does not necessarily translate into intolerance or bellicosity. On the contrary, analysis of data from the U.S. National Election Study by researchers at the University of Notre Dame indicates that for Pentecostals who are most strongly engaged in religious activity, and who most strongly profess faith in divine guidance for their daily lives, there is greater trust of fellow citizens even outside the group than exhibited by less committed Pentecostals, atheists, or mainline Protestants, Catholics, and Jews.[11]

Recent surveys across the world[12] show that the less educated and poorer a society is, the more religious it tends to be. (The

United States is a glaring exception to the tendency.) For atheists, this confirms that religion is an immature form of human understanding born of ignorance that will disappear with the elevation of human life by science. For theists, this confirms that materialism is a monumental barrier to spirituality and that greed and moral relativity lead to a decadent self-indulgence and social alienation that religion disallows.

The actual causal relations between religion, war, poverty, and lack of knowledge about the outside world are not well studied or understood. Jamaica, for example, is a poor nation with one of the highest murder rates in the Western Hemisphere, and also the highest per capita membership in religious institutions and cults. Yet religious groups there are much more involved in trying to reduce violence between rival street gangs and political factions than in inciting violence.

At particular times in history, religions are strongly associated with intellectual creativity and the expansion of human freedoms and opportunities. At other times, the opposite is true. There's no evidence I'm aware of to suggest today that belief in Islam or any other religion necessarily or probably leads to violence or that belief in science and devotion to atheism leads to tolerance and peace. To illustrate, consider a few examples.

Islam also stops violence. The only organizations I've found that have actually enticed significant numbers of voluntary defections from the ranks of would-be martyrs and jihadis—in Indonesia, Saudi Arabia, Pakistan, Egypt, and elsewhere—are Muslim religious organizations. Recall, also, that during the massacres in Rwanda, many Muslims saw it as their religious duty to save, at their own peril, thousands of non-Muslims, both Tutsi and Hutu, when churches, governments (including the United States and France), and secular NGOs turned away.[13]

According to the Four Horsemen—Harris, Hitchens, Dawkins, and Dennett—science education is a natural antidote to sacred terror. But there's no evidence that science education stops terrorism. Indeed, independent studies by Oxford sociologist Diego Gambetta,[14] forensic psychiatrist Marc Sageman,[15] and journalist and political scientist Peter Bergen[16] indicate that a majority of Al Qaeda members and associates went to college, that the college education was mostly science oriented, and that engineer and medical doctor are the professions most represented in Al Qaeda. Much the same has been true for Hamas.

Atheism doesn't stop intolerance: Analyzing British Broadcasting Corporation interviews of 10,069 people in ten nations on four continents, (atheist) psychologists Ara Norenzayan and Ian Hansen find that atheists are just as likely as religious believers to be intolerant of other people's beliefs and to scapegoat others for the world's troubles.[17]

Harris has taken me to task for doubting his assertions. In 2006, he wrote on his Web site:

> Scott Atran rebukes Richard Dawkins, Steven Weinberg and me for the various ways we each criticized religion at a recent conference at the Salk Institute. . . . Atran makes insupportable claims about religion as though they were self-evident: like "religious beliefs are not false in the usual sense of failing to meet truth conditions"; they are, rather, like "poetic metaphors" which are "literally senseless." How many devout Christians or Muslims would recognize their own faith in this neutered creed?[18]

Steven Weinberg, a Nobel Prize–winning physicist and a humanist I admire, said that "religion is an insult to human dignity. With or without it, you'd have good people doing good things and evil people doing evil things. But for good people to do evil things, it takes religion." This is a classic argument made in bad faith. For, as any social worker, judge, or law-enforcement officer in a violent neighborhood or prison also can tell you, "With or without religion, you'd have bad people doing bad things and good people doing good things. But for evil people to do good things, it takes religion."

As for Harris's contention that I make insupportable claims about how people actually process religious concepts (as opposed to what Harris and even religious believers say they think), there is substantial evidence that people do not cognitively process religious beliefs as they do facts; indeed, the findings of a small industry of experiments on the issue have been published in some of the world's most reputable scientific journals.

Well, damn the facts; world salvation is on the march here.

DAWKINS'S DELUSION: THE SLAVISH MIND

In their haste to redeem humanity by saving it from religion, many of the new atheist scientists whom Dan Dennett dubs the Brights (as opposed to the Dims?) often studiously avoid science in their apparently willful ignorance of the facts. In one of the world's best-selling works of so-called nonfiction, *The God Delusion*, Richard Dawkins, who is justly famous for his pioneering work in evolutionary biology, writes as fact his fantasy of the slavish gullibility of jihadis, which he also finds in children and Bible believers, though not in exceptional scientists:

> Suicide bombers do what they do because they really believe what they were taught in their religious schools; that duty to God exceeds all other priorities, and that martyrdom in his service will be rewarded in the gardens of Paradise. And they were taught that lesson not necessarily by extremist fanatics but by decent, gentle, mainstream religious instructors, who lined them up in their madrasahs, sitting in rows, rhythmically nodding their innocent little heads up and down while they learned every word of the holy book like demented parrots.

In fact, none of the nineteen 9/11 hijackers or thirty-odd Madrid train-bomb conspirators attended a madrassah, and the one July 2005 London Underground suicide bomber, Shehzad Tanweer, who did attend a madrassah in Pakistan, did so very briefly. Only a relatively small minority even had a boyhood religious education, including the 9/11 plotters. "Decent, gentle" mainstream religious instructors generally do not teach the duty to suicide bomb, and even the overwhelming majority of Salafi (Muslim "fundamentalist") instructors vehemently oppose it, as do most Wahabis, who generally profess loyalty to the state.

Certainly madrassahs exist that do shun secular education and encourage rote learning of the sort that Dawkins describes. But terrorist groups rarely draw from their students because these lack the needed social, linguistic, and technical skills to successfully carry out operations in hostile territory. In Pakistan and Indonesia, the two countries with the greatest number of madrassahs as well as jihadi groups, we've seen that less than 1 percent of the madrassahs can be associated with jihadis. Even those that are associated with important terrorist organizations, like Pakistan's Lashkar-e-Tayibah and Indonesia's Jemaah Islamiyah, not only encourage science, or at least technical education, but usually offer only to the top of the class the opportunities for advanced education and training in activities useful for terrorism. As people who have gone through these schools have made clear to me, just parroting the Koran is not the kind of linguistic skill that gets you a top role in the jihad.

Dawkins cites and even praises a number of serious scientific works on the cognitive and evolutionary origins of religious belief, but simply chucks their main findings when he claims, for reasons only Freud would know, that grown people seek religion because they miss their fathers. Earlier in life, children allegedly believe because "natural selection builds child brains with a tendency to believe whatever their parents and tribal leaders tell them." Children, like "computers, do what they are told: they slavishly obey any instructions given in their own programming language."[19]

What's the scientific evidence presented for Dawkins's own science fiction that children or jihadis are robotic learners? None. Now, it's almost the sworn duty of any scientist to cite any serious counterevidence to one's own claims. In this case, counterevidence is overwhelming.[20]

Not content to banish all religion, and what he calls its bedfellows, "myth" and "falsehood," Dawkins also doubts whether any "anti-scientific fiction" is healthy for children, such as *Harry Potter* (which he hasn't read), if it involves "bringing up children to believe in spells and wizards." But here at least he is willing to let science decide what fantasy should be nixed or get the nod: "Whether that has a sort of insidious affect on rationality, I'm not sure. Perhaps it's something for research." (Though the fact of his own earlier readings about frogs turning into princes appears not to have had the effect in the predicted direction.)[21] Now, I'm all for research, but the aim of it here seems ridiculous and dull.

"About once every hundred years some wiseacre gets up and tries to banish the fairy tale," wrote C. S. Lewis (who was wrong about a lot of things but not this). Why? "It is accused of giving children a false impression of the world they live in. But I think that no literature that children could read gives them less of a false impression. I think what profess to be realistic stories for children are far more likely to deceive them. I never expected the real world to be like fairy tales. I think that I did expect school to be like the school stories. The fantasies did not deceive me; the school stories did."[22] Not to mention that, as almost every parent and psychologist knows, fairy tales, myths, religious lore and the like grab attention and teach consequences in quite compelling ways.

RELIGION ISN'T CHILDISH SCIENCE

The scientific revolution began in earnest when a Polish cleric, Nicolaus Copernicus, bucked his faith and theorized that the earth orbited the sun. The Church did not pay much mind as long as the theory remained in the realm of speculation. But when Italian philosopher Galileo Galilei empirically confirmed the theory with a telescope, the Church banned Copernicus's teachings as "false and altogether opposed to the Holy Scripture." In 1633, Galileo himself was brought to trial by the Holy Inquisition and compelled to recant.

Given the supposed risk of society's moral degradation in the face of the free choice to make up one's own mind ("I think, therefore I am"), the Church violently insisted that faith in absolute authority ("In the beginning, God created the heavens and the earth") always trumps the more tentative teaching that goes with clear reasoning and experimental observation. When the Enlightenment unshackled scientific thinking from lingering religious control, religion opted for a separate realm where science would not operate. Science, for the sake of its peace and independence, generally accepted this division into separate *magisteria*.

Today, increasingly many on the science side argue that this separation was at best a temporary armistice, at worse an act of cowardice and capitulation, and that science should now usurp the religious realm in order to conquer it and make people less superstitious, more knowledgeable, and happier. I'm skeptical, in part because a main justification for the move stems from a false premise: that religion is a childish attempt at explaining phenomena, to be replaced by science since we now know better.

A common refrain among new-atheist missionaries is that a main aim of religion, other than getting people to join to kill, has been to provide a unified theory of the world of the sort that science now seeks in more cautious and measured ways.[23] As Christopher Hitchens (who is often right, but not about this) puts it:

Religion comes from the period of human prehistory where nobody . . . had the smallest idea of what was going on. It comes from the bawling and fearful infancy of our species, and is a babyish attempt to meet our inescapable demand for knowledge (as well as for comfort, reassurance, and other infantile needs). Today the least educated of my children knows much more about the natural order than any of the founders of religion.[24]

Bravo for Hitchens's kids, but their knowledge is irrelevant to what religion is about. Religion survives science, as it does secular ideology, not because it is prior to or more primitive than science or secular reasoning, but because of what it affectively and collectively secures for people, however "infantile" such reassurance may seem to some. Religious adults are not childish or weak-minded: Studies show that, at least in our societies, religious adults have very different mind-sets from those of children, concentrating more on the moral dimensions of their faith and less on its supernatural attributes.

Science is the attempt to associate the flux of our perceptible experiences into a logically thorough structure of thought, in which each event is uniquely and convincingly correlated with that structure in ways that are collectively identifiable and replicable. Science aims to reveal how facts are reliably coordinated with, and conditioned by, one another. This open yet systematic curiosity about nature is a neutral vessel as far as morality is concerned: It plies the skies of reason and can cause great evil, when targeted to war and domination, or great good, when carrying out the aims of healing the sick, reducing poverty, or promoting civil and human rights.

Religion, by contrast, is less interested in how the universe has always been than in how our tiny piece of it ought to be, however that flies in the face of logical or empirical consistency. It isn't concerned with the rational foundation of material existence, but with the moral worth of human values and goals that don't necessarily lend themselves to logical justification or empirical confirmation. But it is a moral vessel that can be steered across the sea of our tragic comedy in practically any direction: toward great evil or great good, or it may confound its moral bearings and be cast adrift in cults going nowhere.

From a scientific perspective, human beings are accidental and incidental products of the material development of the physical universe, almost wholly irrelevant and readily ignored in any general description of its functioning. Beyond Earth, there is no intelligence—however alien or like our own—that is watching out for us or cares. We are alone. But when we focus on the "incidental" case of human existence, human intelligence and reason searches for the hidden traps and causes in our surroundings, for intelligence evolved with and will always remain leashed to our animal passions—in the struggle for survival, the quest for love, the yearning for social standing and belonging. This intelligence does not easily suffer loneliness, any more than it abides the looming prospect of death, whether individual or collective.

But doesn't religion impede science, and vice versa? Not necessarily. Leaving aside the sociopolitical stakes in the opposition between science and religion, a crucial difference between science and religion is that factual knowledge as such is not a principal aim of religious devotion, but plays only a supporting role.

Only in the last decade has the Catholic Church acknowledged the factual plausibility of Copernicus, Galileo, and Darwin. In 1992 the Catholic Church cleared Galileo's name, and in 2000 Pope John Paul II apologized to God (not to Galileo) for the trial. The earlier religious rejection of their theories stemmed from challenges posed to a cosmic order unifying the moral and material worlds. A long lag time was necessary to refurbish and remake the moral and material connections in such a way that would permit faith in a unified cosmology to survive. But many believers today shun the orthodoxy of such totalizing religious views of the world, and are happy to give science its due. As Al Gore quipped to White House reporters, "People have known for years that you can have the Earth circle around the sun and still believe in God."[25]

THE REALIST ILLUSION

To avoid misunderstanding, let me say right away that I consider as bunk most of the claims by postmodernists and by many in cultural studies that scientific knowledge is merely a local (Western elite) worldview and is no more or less "socially constructed" than discourse about race or the manifest destiny of empires and nations. Science is guided by a faith in reason that always flies ahead of the facts (for example, in the use of mathematical prediction), but is "conformable to nature"[26] (in part, I think, because the world contains countable things—like stars, stones, and seasons—that can be put into increasingly precise correspondence with one another by a mind equipped by mathematics and evolved with other means to do so).

There are deep and unresolved debates about what exactly gives science its privileged path to empirical truth and knowledge of a reality that transcends our own existence. Yet I have no doubt that it produces knowledge, the validity of which is independent of human observation. What I do doubt—because I find it factually false—is the claim by Sam Harris and others "that in ethics, as in physics, there are truths waiting to be discovered, and thus we can be right or wrong in our beliefs about them"[27] as we can be right or wrong about beliefs in atomic structures or $E = mc^2$. For example, the founding principles of human rights—liberty, equality, fraternity, or even sovereignty over one's own body and the pursuit of happiness—were anything but "natural" and "self-evident." Human rights weren't discovered, but invented for social engineering of a kind unprecedented in human history.

The political and social movement for recognition of human rights began in earnest in the second half of the eighteenth century, particularly with the Jean Calas affair in France (1760s): he was broken on the wheel and water-boarded. The Italian politician Cesare Marquis de Beccaria, commenting on the case, proposed making such "torments" of an individual human being a measure of the "contempt of all mankind." In *Inventing Human Rights*,[28] Lynn Hunt chronicles how the right to protect the body from torment became the first human right accorded to individuals.

Through the emotional reaction to their violation, "human rights" became "self-evident." This helped to define the concepts of "individual" and "humanity" for Enlightenment thinkers, including Voltaire, Adam Smith, and Thomas Jefferson. These concepts became cornerstones of our moral culture, first inscribed in the Declaration of Independence, then in the U.S. Bill of Rights and the French Declaration of the Rights of Man, and more recently in the United Nations Universal Declaration of Human Rights.

Monotheism created the concept of a single humanity, worthy of improvement and salvation. However, belonging to humanity guaranteed "equal rights" before God only in paradise, not on earth. For the religious orders of the day, individual bodies could be butchered, burned at the stake, disemboweled, drawn and quartered, and mutilated and tortured in public spectacles. England only banned burning at the stake in 1790, a year after France abolished all forms of judicial torture. These spectacles were sacrificial displays of individual suffering that were meant to repair the body politic that had been sinned against. The individual sinner would not be reformed or rehabilitated but given over to the crowd as an offering for the greater good. In countries that still publicly administer beheadings, stoning to death, amputation of limbs, flogging and other insults to the body and person, these practices do not generate moral outrage but represent redemption. Hidden torture in detention centers lacks even this redemptive quality.

Ideas of "self-evident," "natural," and "human" rights are anything but inherently self-evident or natural in the history of our species. For example, the culturally widespread and age-old practice of slavery flourished in Europe and America into the nineteenth century, lingering in lynchings through America's Jim Crow South into the 1960s. It was only banned in Saudi Arabia and Muscat in 1970 and in Niger in 2003, and still is practiced along the fringes of the Sahara. Racism and subordination of women remain, of course, very much a part of the modern world, although in many places they have become less noxious than in the Stone Age.

The American and French republics began to render real the fictions of individual and equal rights through new mores, laws, and wars, and not through independent scientific discoveries.

The belief that true knowledge and discovery of facts about morality and (nonhuman) nature is a philosophical conceit common both to religious dogmatists and new-atheist "realists." But whereas religious dogmatists see all facts as products of some divine fantasy, new-atheist realists imply that fact and fantasy have no common ground in the brave new world of scientific realism applied to human affairs. In both cases, dogma can be dangerous.

OVERBLOWING IDEOLOGY

The scientific ignorance and tomfoolery of many of the new atheists with regard to religion, and history, makes me almost embarrassed to be an atheist.[29] But when foolishness is promoted as a course of political action, then it becomes potentially dangerous to everyone's health. A sentiment that only feeds into the current wave of violence is Harris's suggestion in *The End of Faith* that a total war on Islam may be unavoidable.

Islam and religious ideology per se aren't the principal causes of suicide bombing and terror in today's world—at least no more than are soccer, friendship, or faith for a better future. What is the cause of the current global wave of terrorism, then? Nothing so abstract or broad as any of these things, but bits of all of them, embedded and acting together in the peculiar sorts of small- and large-scale social networks that are emerging in this time in history.

Throughout human history, it is commitment to a religious or transcendental dream that ultimately sustains cooperation and competition between large groups, including the motivation for people to kill and die for others who aren't genetic kin. We've also seen that the connection of the jihadi nightmare with Islam across the world and the centuries is only fragmentary and diffuse. Even a superficial examination of studies and experiments in human cognition and reasoning demonstrates unequivocally that ideas do not "invade" and occupy minds, or spread from mind to mind like self-replicating viruses or genes, as Dawkins and company maintain.[30] However simple and appealing may be the notion of an ideology as a self-replicating high-fidelity "meme," psychologically that's pretty baseless and unrelated to how the mind actually works[31]—almost as distant from reality as the claim that religion itself is the greater cause of human group violence.

Over the course of human history, and across the world today, religion has helped to promote tyranny and rebellion against oppression, to inspire monumental works of creativity and of stunning stupidity, to keep people in fear and to diminish their fears, to deliver justice and to excuse injustice, to help and to harm children and other living things.[32] The scientific study of religion and irrationality suggests that neither is likely to go away or even be greatly diminished by science and rational debate.[33] Reason's greatest challenge—in politics, ethics, or everyday life—is to gain knowledge and leverage over unreason: to cope with it, compete with it, and perhaps channel it; not to fruitlessly try to annihilate it by reasoning it away.

I certainly don't criticize the Four Horsemen and other scientifically minded new atheists for wanting to rid the world of dogmatically held beliefs that are vapid, barbarous, anachronistic, and wrong. I object to their manner of combat, which is often shrill, scientifically baseless, psychologically uninformed, politically naive, and counterproductive for goals we share.

CHAPTER 23

HUMAN RITES: NATURAL ORIGINS AND EVOLUTION OF RELIGION

The anxious concern for happiness, the dread of future misery, the terror of death, the thirst for revenge, the appetite for food and other necessities. Agitated by fears and hopes of this nature . . . men scrutinize, with a trembling curiosity, the course of future causes, and examine the various and contrary events of human life. And in this disordered scene, with eyes still more disordered and astonished, they see the first obscure traces of divinity.

—DAVID HUME, *THE NATURAL HISTORY OF RELIGION*, 1757

We—with God's help—call on every Muslim who believes in God and wishes to be rewarded to comply with God's order to kill the Americans and plunder their money wherever and whenever they find it. . . . Almighty God says: "Do ye prefer the life of this world to the hereafter?" But little is the comfort of this life, as compared with the hereafter. Unless ye go forth, He will punish you with a grievous penalty, and put others in your place . . . for God hath power over all things.

—OSAMA BIN LADEN, "FATWA URGING JIHAD AGAINST
AMERICANS," 1998

E ver since Edward Gibbon's *Decline and Fall of the Roman Empire*,[1] written in Britain as the American Republic was born, scientists and secularly minded scholars have been predicting the ultimate demise of religion. But in many places around the globe, religious fervor is increasing. At the beginning of the twenty-first century, new religious movements (NRMs) continued to arise at a furious pace—perhaps at the rate of two or three per day.[2] There are now more than 2 billion self-proclaimed Christians (about one third of humanity), a quarter of whom are Pentecostals or Charismatics (people who stay in mainstream Protestant and Catholic churches but have adopted Pentecostal practices like healings, speaking in tongues, casting out demons, and laying hands upon the sick). The Winner's Chapel, a Pentecostal church that celebrates newfound market wealth and success, is less than twenty years old but already has tens of thousands of members in thirty-two African countries. During the same period, the Falun Gong, a Buddhist offshoot, has grown to over 100 million adherents in East Asia, and Islamic revivalist movements have spread across the Muslim world.

The United States—the world's most economically powerful and scientifically advanced society—is also one of the world's most professedly religious societies. Evangelical Christians and fundamentalists include about 25 percent of Americans, and together with charismatics constitute about 40 percent of the American population. According to a June 2008 Pew poll, more than 90 percent believe in God or a universal spirit, including one in five of those who call themselves atheists. More than half of Americans surveyed pray at least once a day, but about three quarters of religious believers in America think that there is more than one way to interpret religious teachings and that other religions can also lead to eternal salvation.[3] Even in France, the most secular of societies, two thirds of the population believe in "a spirit, god or life force."[4]

An underlying reason for religion's endurance is that science treats humans and intentions only as incidental elements in the universe, whereas for religion they are central. Science is not particularly well suited to deal with people's existential anxieties—death, deception, sudden catastrophe, loneliness, or longing for love or justice. Religion thrives because it addresses people's yearnings and society's moral needs.

Although science may never replace religion, science can help us understand how religions are structured in individual minds (brains) and across societies (cultures) and also, in a strictly material sense, why religious belief endures. Religion is neither a naturally selected adaptation of our species nor innate in us. All of its cognitive and social components are universally found in various mundane thoughts and activities. Nevertheless, since the Upper Paleolithic, several naturally selected elements of human cognition have tended to converge in the normal course of social interaction to produce a near-universal family of phenomena that most people recognize as religion. Roughly, religion exploits ordinary cognitive processes to passionately display costly commitment to supernatural agents that are invoked to deal with otherwise unsolvable existential problems, such as death and deception.

EVOLUTIONARY ENIGMAS

The origin of large-scale cooperative societies is an evolutionary problem because people frequently cooperate with genetic strangers of unknown reputation whom they will never meet again, and whose cheating, spying, lying, and defection cannot be monitored and controlled.[5] Kinship cannot drive cooperation among genetic strangers, although "imagined kinship"—a cultural manipulation of kin psychology and terminology ("brotherhood," "motherland," etc.)—can be a potent psychological mobilizer of groups formed through other means.[6] Difficulty in maintaining trust based on accurate information about reputation is progressively less reliable the larger the group (reliability of information and mutual trust for an n-person group tends to decline as a function of $1/n$).[7] Moreover, "Watch my back and I'll watch yours," and other sensible reciprocity strategies in politics and economics fail to account for cooperation with people you only meet once:[8] like aiding a stranger who asks for directions or a dollar for food, taking the hand of a lost child or a disabled person to cross the street, leaving a tip at a roadside restaurant you'll never visit again, or risking life and limb to save someone you don't know.

Studies show that people are usually quite suspicious of strangers who belong to an entirely different social milieu or cultural group and don't even bother to find out about their reputation or the history of their past transactions. The default assumption is usually zero-sum: anything I do for the other person is likely to be bad for me.[9] But other studies show that invoking God or other supernatural concepts leads to reduced cheating and greater generosity between anonymous strangers.[10] The key to the difference in behavior seems to be belief that there's a God watching over to make sure everyone stays honest.[11]

Thus, as societies grow, it can be harder to enforce moral and altruistic norms, and to punish free-riders on the public good. This in turn can make such societies less cohesive and less able to compete with other expanding societies. Moral deities define the sacred boundaries of societies and the taboos you can't transgress. If you really believe in these moral gods, then the problem of punishment becomes easier, as you punish yourself for misbehavior. Consider the power of taking an oath before God among the Pashtun as a way of ensuring that a potential liar or thief would think twice before acting for fear that Big Brother would always know what went on and exact retribution, even if no other person on earth could possibly spot the transgression:

[B]ecause the role of honor is so serious . . . particularly because oaths required of men who are accused of dishonorable acts (such as theft) come from potentially dubious sources, there are a host of supernatural consequences that will rain down upon the perjurer should a man lie. These include becoming poor, having your opinions disregarded, having your body become pale and ugly, seeing your land and livestock lose their productivity, as well as endangering the life of your children.[12]

But the natural origin of gods and religious traditions is itself an evolutionary puzzle because all religions require costly commitment to beliefs that violate basic tenets of rational inference and empirical knowledge necessary for navigating the world: like the belief in sentient but bodiless beings or beings with bodies that defy gravity and can pass through solid walls.[13] In all religions, there are bodiless but sentient souls and spirits that act intentionally though not in ways empirically verifiable or logically understandable. For the Christian philosopher Søren Kierkegaard, true faith can only be motivated by "a gigantic passion" to commit to the "absurd." Abraham's willingness to sacrifice more than his own life—that of his only and beloved son—is exemplary: "For love of God is . . . incommensurable with the whole of reality . . . there could be no question of human calculation."[14] Hundreds of millions of people across the planet celebrate Abraham's actions as noble and heroic, rather than murderous, evil, or insane.

Imagine creatures who consistently believed that the dead live on and the weak are advantaged over the strong, or that you can arbitrarily suspend the known physical and biological laws of the universe with a prayer. If people literally applied such prescriptions to factual navigation of everyday life they likely would be either dead or in the hereafter in short order—too short for most individuals to reproduce and the species to survive. The trick is in knowing how and when to suspend factual belief without countermanding the facts and compromising survival. But why take the risk of neglecting the facts at all, even in exceptional circumstances?

Religious practice is costly in terms of cognitive effort (maintaining both rational and nonrational networks of beliefs) as well as material sacrifice (ranging from human sacrifice to prayer time) and emotional expenditure (inciting fears and hopes). A review of anthropological literature on religious offerings concludes: "Sacrifice is giving something up at a cost. . . . 'Afford it or not,' the attitude seems to be."[15] Indeed, what could be the calculated gain from:

> Years of toil to build gigantic structures that house only dead bones (Egyptian, Mesoamerican, and Cambodian pyramids).
>
> Giving up one's sheep (Hebrews) or camels (Bedouin) or cows (Nuer of Sudan) or chickens (Highland Maya) or pigs (Melanesian tribes, Ancient Greeks), or buffaloes (South Indian tribes).
>
> Dispatching wives when their husbands die (Hindus, Inca, Solomon Islanders).
>
> Slaying one's own healthy and desired offspring (the first-born of Phoenicia and Carthage, Inca and postclassical Maya boys and girls, children of South India's tribal Lambadi).
>
> Chopping off a finger for dead warriors or relatives (Dani of New Guinea, Crow and other American Plains Indians).
>
> Burning your house and all other possessions for a family member drowned, crushed by a tree, or killed by a tiger (Nâga tribes of Assam).
>
> Knocking out one's own teeth (Australian aboriginals).
>
> Making elaborate but evanescent sand designs (Navajo, tribes of Central Australia).
>
> Be willing to sacrifice one's life to keep Fridays (Muslims) or Saturdays (Jews) or Sundays (Christians) holy.

As billionaire Bill Gates pithily put it, "Just in terms of alloca-
tion of time resources, religion is not very efficient. There's a lot
more I could be doing on a Sunday morning."[16]

Evolution can't account for religion simply as a biological
adaptation, naturally selected for some ancestral task that is
"hard-wired" into us. Try to come up with an adaptive logic that
generates a unitary explanation for all of the strange thoughts
and practices above, or for just stopping whatever you're doing to
murmur often incomprehensible words while gesticulating several times a day. And individual devotion to religion is quite variable, much wider than for other behaviors that likely did evolve
as adaptations: the ability to walk, to see, to think about other
people thinking, or to imagine imaginary worlds that may or may
not come to be. There's no gene for the complex of beliefs and
behaviors that make up religion any more than there's a gene for
science; nor is there likely any genetic complex with lawlike or
systematic qualities that is responsible for most religious belief
or behavior.[17]

Research with my colleague Joe Henrich, an anthropologist
and behavioral economist, suggests that the two evolutionary enig-
mas, large-scale cooperation and costly religion, have resolved one
another through a process of cultural coevolution.[18] This coevolution centers on the concept of costly communal commitment to
absurd, counterintuitive ideas that have no consistent logical or
empirical connection to everyday reality.

BORN TO BELIEVE: THE STORYTELLING ANIMAL

Humans are cause-seeking, purpose-forming, storytelling animals. As the eighteenth-century Scottish philosopher David Hume
famously noted, we find patterns in nature and look for the "hidden springs and principles" that bring those patterns to life and let
us navigate them.[19] We can't help doing this. Nature made us so.

Our mental facility for confabulation is strikingly evident in experiments with split-brain patients, where the left hemisphere (which controls language and the right hand) is physically cut off from the right hemisphere (which controls the left hand).[20] In one classic study, images were selectively presented to each hemisphere: The left was shown a chicken claw, the right a snow scene. Patients were presented with an array of objects and asked to choose an object "associated" with the image they were shown. A representative answer was that of a patient who chose a snow shovel with his left hand and a chicken with the right. Asked why he chose these items, "he" (that is, the left hemisphere story spinner) said: "Oh, that's simple. The chicken claw goes with the chicken and you need the shovel to clean out the chicken shed." Michael Gazzaniga, who carried out the experiment, observes, "The left brain weaves its story in order to convince itself and you that it is in full control."

For the most part, our penchant for storytelling is a beneficial thing. Because the world we live in does have lots of recurring and sequential patterns, like sunsets and seasons and birth and death, knowing these regularities helps us to better survive and reproduce. Hunters and gatherers were able to systematically track game and store the resources of good times in anticipation of bad times. Agriculturalists were capable of subsisting on the land they settled because they could understand and manage the seasonal flooding of a river, the water needs and life cycles of plants, and the motivations of enemies to plunder the crops. We moderns can enjoy machines that work for us because we can represent the patterns we find in nature, manipulate their causes in our imagination, and create new applications that help us function in the world.

But we humans also expect to find patterns and underlying principles where there are none. Flip a coin that comes up ten heads in a row and most people believe there's a better than even chance that the next flip will be tails. "There's a sucker born every minute," quipped P. T. Barnum, who might have been talking about people in a casino who rush into the seat of any player who has had a long string of bad luck at the slot machine. Even apparent lack of regularity tends to be overgeneralized into a causal pattern: "Lightning never strikes twice in the same place," goes the age-old untruth.

This built-in "flaw" of our causal understanding is rarely catastrophic, and is usually far outweighed by the benefits. That's pretty standard for most of our evolutionary endowments. For example, we humans are also prone to bad backs and to choking when we eat and speak. Thank goodness, though, for upright posture, which frees our hands and widens the horizon of sight. Good, too, that we have speech, which vastly expands our field of communication and the sharing of thoughts. The creations of evolution resemble more the works of an amateur tinkerer than a trained engineer. Perfect may be better than good in an ideal world. But in the real world, good only has to beat out less good by a little to get to the top of the heap.

And so we tell ourselves stories. We look for and impose purpose on the events of our life by weaving them into a meaningful narrative with the hand of intentional design. Our constantly cause-seeking brain makes it hard to believe that "stuff just happens," especially if the stuff happens to us. This view is backed up by a recent experiment in which people were asked what patterns they could see in arrangements of dots or stock market information.[21] Before asking, the experimenters made half their participants feel a lack of control, either by giving them feedback unrelated to their performance or by having them recall experiences where they had lost control of a situation. The results were remarkable. When people felt a lack of control they would fall back on preternatural and supernatural explanations. That would also suggest why religions enjoy a revival during hard times.[22]

The greater the impact of events on our lives, the greater the drive to impose meaning on those events. Terrible, senseless accidents can never just be senseless accidents, our mind's voice tells us. When psychologist Jesse Bering and his students carried out interviews with atheists, it became clear that they often tacitly attribute purpose to significant or traumatic moments in their lives, as if some agency were intervening to make it happen.[23] It seems that's just the way our brains are wired: Atheists can muzzle some if its expression, but even they can't seem to completely stop it in themselves.

A parent may spend years trying to find some significance in his child's untimely death. An earthquake victim is likely to want a story to explain why she survived and those around her didn't. And there are those ready to help find a story: After a massive earthquake in Pakistan's Azad Kashmir, jihadi groups riding Pakistani military vehicles blasted over loudspeakers what their banners read: "This happened because you have turned from God's path. We can help you find the true path." In early 2010, the Rev. Pat Robertson similarly declared that the massive Haitian earthquake happened because Haitians had long ago sworn "a pact with the devil."[24]

SUPERNATURAL AGENTS

Religions invariably center on supernatural agent concepts, such as gods, angels, ancestor spirits, demons, and jinns. Granted, nondeistic "theologies," such as Buddhism and Taoism, doctrinally eschew personifying the supernatural or animating nature with supernatural causes.[25] Nevertheless, people who espouse these faiths routinely entertain belief in an array of minor "buddhas" that behave "counterintuitively" in ways that are inscrutable to factual or logical reasoning. Buddhist Tibetan monks and Japanese samurai warriors ritually ward off malevolent deities by invoking benevolent spirits and conceive altered states of nature as awe inspiring.

Mundane concepts of *agent* (intentional, goal-directed actors) are central players in what psychologists refer to as "folk psychology," specifically the "theory-of-mind module" (or ToM). ToM is a species-specific cognitive system devoted to "mind reading," that is, making inferences about the knowledge, beliefs, desires, and intentions of other people. Recent brain-imaging (fMRI) studies show that people's statements about God's level of involvement in social events, as well as the deity's purported emotional states, reliably engage ToM-related prefrontal and posterior regions of the brain that appeared latest in human evolution.[26]

One plausible hypothesis is that notions of *agent* evolved hair-triggered in humans to respond "automatically" under conditions of uncertainty to potential threats (and opportunities) by intelligent predators (and protectors).[27]

From this evolutionary vantage, the proper evolutionary domain of *agent* encompasses animate objects, but its actual domain inadvertently extends to moving dots on computer screens, voices in the wind, faces in clouds, eyes in the shadows, and virtually any complex design or uncertain circumstance of unknown origin.[28] For example, in Miami many people claim to have spotted the Holy Virgin in windows, curtains, and television afterimages as long as there was hope of keeping young Elián González from returning to godless Cuba. On the day of the World Trade Center attacks, newspapers showed photos of smoke billowing from one of the towers that "seems to bring into focus the face of the Evil One, complete with beard and horns and malignant expression, symbolizing to many the hideous nature of the deed that wreaked horror and terror upon an unsuspecting city."[29]

A number of studies reveal that children and adults spontaneously interpret the contingent movements of dots and geometric forms on a screen as interacting agents, whether as individuals or groups, with distinct goals and internal goal-directed motivations.[30] In the 1940s, Heider and Simmel made a silent cartoon animation in which two triangles and a circle move against and around each other and a diagram of a house. People who watched almost always made up a social plot in which the big triangle was seen as an aggressor.[31] Young children spontaneously overattribute agency to all sorts of entities (clocks, clouds), and may thus be predisposed to construct agent-based representations of many phenomena.[32]

Why? Because, from an evolutionary perspective, it's better to be safe than sorry regarding the presence of agents under conditions of uncertainty. Such reliably developing programs provide efficient reactions to a wide—but not unlimited—range of stimuli that would have been statistically associated with a presence of dangerous agents in ancestral environments. Mistakes, or "false positives," would usually carry little cost, whereas a true response could provide the margin of survival. This was true at least until these supernatural agents were selected by cultural evolution to begin demanding costly actions, under threat of divine punishment, or offers of sublime rewards, or until they evoked hostility in the followers of another god.

This cognitive proclivity would favor emergence of malevolent deities in all cultures, just as a countervailing Darwinian propensity to attach to protective caregivers would favor conjuring up benevolent deities. Thus, for the Carajá Indians of Central Brazil, intimidating or unsure regions of the local ecology are religiously avoided: "The earth and underworld are inhabited by supernaturals. . . . There are two kinds. Many are amiable and beautiful beings who have friendly relations with humans . . . others are ugly and dangerous monsters who cannot be placated. Their woods are avoided and nobody fishes in their pools."[33] Similar descriptions of supernaturals appear in ethnographic reports throughout the Americas, Africa, Eurasia, and Oceania.

Our brains may be trip-wired to spot lurkers (and to seek protectors) where conditions of uncertainty prevail—when startled, at night, in unfamiliar places, during sudden catastrophe, in the face of solitude, illness, prospects of death, et cetera. Given the constant menace of enemies within and without, concealment, deception, and the ability to generate and recognize false beliefs in others would favor survival. In potentially dangerous or uncertain circumstances, it would be best to anticipate and fear the worst of all likely possibilities: The unseen presence of a deviously intelligent agent that might just want your head as a trophy. Unfortunately, a worst-case analysis fosters unnecessary wars.

As we saw in chapter 17, humans habitually "trick and tweak" their own innate releasing programs, as when people become sexually aroused by makeup (which artificially highlights sexually appealing attributes), fabricated perfumes, or undulating lines drawn on paper or dots arranged on a computer screen, that is, pornographic pictures.[34] Horror movies, for example, play off hair-trigger agency detection to catch our attention and build suspense. Much of human culture—for better or worse—can be arguably attributed to focused stimulations and manipulations of our species' innate proclivities.[35] Such manipulations can serve cultural ends far removed from the ancestral adaptive tasks that originally gave rise to them, although manipulations for religion often centrally involve the collective engagement of existential needs (wanting security) and anxieties (fearing death).

THE APPEAL OF THE ABSURD (COUNTERINTUITIVE BELIEFS)

How do our minds make an *agent* concept into a god? And why do people work so hard against their preference for logical explanations to maintain two views of the world, the real and the unreal, the intuitive and the counterintuitive?

Whatever the specifics, certain beliefs can be found in all religions that fit most comfortably with our mental architecture. Thus, anthropologists and psychologists have shown that people attend to, and remember, things that are unfamiliar and strange, but not so strange as to be impossible to assimilate. Ideas about God or other supernatural agents tend to fit these criteria. They are "minimally counterintuitive," as anthropologist Pascal Boyer calls them:[36] weird enough to get your attention and lodge in memory but not so weird as to be rejected altogether, like a burning bush that speaks, a frog that transforms into a prince, or a woman who turns into a block of salt.

Psychologist Ara Norenzayan, along with me and other colleagues, studied the idea of minimally counterintuitive agents.[37] We presented college students as well as Maya Indians with lists of fantastical creatures and asked them to choose the ones that seemed most "religious." The convincingly religious agents, the students said, were not the most outlandish—not the turtle that chatters and climbs or the squealing, flowering marble—but those that were just outlandish enough: giggling seaweed, a sobbing oak, a talking horse. Giggling seaweed meets the requirement of being minimally counterintuitive. So does a God who has a human personality except that he knows everything or a Spirit with a mind but no body.

What goes for single or simple religious beliefs and utterances goes also for more complex collections of religious beliefs.[38] The Bible, for example, is a succession of mundane events—walking, eating, sleeping, dreaming, copulating, dying, marrying, fighting, suffering storms and drought—interspersed with just a few counterintuitive occurrences, such as miracles and appearances of supernatural agents. The same is true of the Koran, the Hindu Veda, the Maya Popul Vuh, or any other cultural corpus of religious beliefs and narratives.

Religious beliefs are counterintuitive because they purposely violate what studies in cognitive anthropology and developmental psychology indicate are universal expectations about the world's everyday structure, including such basic categories of "intuitive ontology"—the ordinary ontology of the everyday world that is built into the language learner's semantic system—as *person, animal, plant,* and *substance*.[39] Studies reveal that children across cultures do not violate such categorical constraints in learning the meaning of words. But in many religions, though never in reality, animals can conceive of the distant past and far future, plants can walk or talk, and mountains and lakes can have feelings, wishes, beliefs, and desires.

All the world's cultures have religious myths that are attention-arresting because they are counterintuitive in the technical sense of violating intuitive ontology. Still, people in all cultures also *recognize* these beliefs to be counterintuitive, whether or not they are religious believers. In our society, Catholics and non-Catholics alike are undoubtedly aware of the difference between Christ's body and ordinary wafers, or between Christ's blood and ordinary wine. Catholics are no more crazed cannibals for their religious beliefs than are Muslims sick with sex when they invoke the pretty girls floating in paradise.

Reasoning and inference in the communication of many religious beliefs is cognitively designed never to come to closure, but to remain open-textured. To claim that one knows what Judaism or Christianity is truly about because one has read the Bible, or what Islam is about because one has read the Koran, is to believe there is an essence to religion and religious beliefs. But psychological science (and the history of exegesis) demonstrates that this claim is false.

Polls suggest that 30 to 40 percent of all religious Christians say they believe that the Bible is the literal word of God[40] and about 50 percent of religious Muslims say they believe this of the Koran.[41] But deeper study shows that evangelicals and other self-styled "fundamentalists" who espouse belief in a stable text as literal words of God do not ascribe fixed meanings to them. Indeed, it is literally impossible for normal human minds to do so. As for "one infinite, omnipotent, and eternal God," observed Thomas Hobbes, even the religiously enlightened "choose rather to confess He is incomprehensible and above their understanding than to define His nature by 'spirit incorporeal,' and then confess their definition to be unintelligible."[42]

Instead of fixing meaning, studies show that people use the words to evoke many different ideas to give sense and significance to various everyday contexts.[43] Consider a telling example of how religious beliefs are actually processed by human minds. Many argue that the Ten Commandments mean exactly the same thing today as they did when Moses received them on Mount Sinai.[44] That's hardly likely, given changes in social conditions and expectations over the last two and half millennia. Thus, failure to heed the commandments to honor the Sabbath or forswear blasphemy merited capital punishment in ancient Israel, but no one in our time and in our society is condemned to death for frolicking on the Sabbath or cursing their Maker.

One study by students in my class on evolutionary psychology compared how people interpret the Ten Commandments. The study found that only autistics—who take social cues, including what is said, strictly at face value—produced consistently recognizable paraphrases: for example, "Honor the Sabbath" might be rendered as "Honor Sunday (or Saturday)." In contrast, university students and members of Jewish and Christian Bible study groups produced highly variable interpretations that third parties from those groups could not consistently identify with the original commandments: "Honor the Sabbath" might be interpreted as "Don't Work So Hard" or "Take Time for Your Family."[45] Despite people's own expectations of consensus, interpretations of the commandments showed wide ranges of variation, with little evidence of consensus. (Unlike religious utterances, control phrases such as "two plus two equals four" or "the grass is green" do pass intact from mind to mind.)

Rather, religion is psychologically "catchy"—cognitively contagious—because its miraculous and supernatural elements grab attention, stick in memory, readily survive transmission from mind to mind, and so often win out in the cultural competition for ideas that the collectivity can use. Like other human productions that are easy to think and good to use, religious beliefs spontaneously reoccur across cultures in highly similar forms despite the fact that these forms are not evolved by natural selection or innate in our minds. Religion is no more an evolutionary adaptation as such than are other near universals like calendars, maps, or boats.

THE TRAGEDY OF COGNITION

Core religious beliefs minimally violate ordinary notions about how the world is, with all of its inescapable problems, to produce surprising but easy-to-remember supernatural worlds that treat existential problems, like fear of death and worry about deception and defection: for example, a world with beings that resemble us emotionally, intellectually, and physically except they can move through solid objects and be immortal, such as angels, ancestral spirits, and souls.

It's not enough for an agent to be minimally counterintuitive for it to earn a spot in people's belief systems. Mickey Mouse and the talking teapot are minimally counterintuitive, but people don't truly believe in them. An emotional component is needed for belief to take hold. If your emotions are involved, then that's the time when you're most likely to believe whatever the religion tells you should be believed. Religions stir up emotions through their rituals—swaying, singing, bowing in unison during group prayer and other ceremonial rituals, sometimes working people up to a state of physical arousal that can border on frenzy. And religions gain strength during the natural heightening of emotions that occurs in times of personal crisis, when the faithful often turn to shamans or priests. The most intense emotional crisis, for which religion can offer powerfully comforting answers, is when people face mortality.

"I simply can't build up my hopes on a foundation consisting of confusion, misery and death," wrote Anne Frank, a Jewish teenager doomed to die in a Nazi concentration camp. "I hear the ever approaching thunder, which will destroy us too; I can feel the sufferings of millions; and yet, if I look up into the heavens, I think that it will all come right, that this cruelty will end, and that peace and tranquility will return again. . . . I want to be useful or give pleasure to people around me who yet don't really know me. I want to go on living after my death!"[46]

There's no rational or empirically evident way to escape our eventual death. The tragedy of human cognition—of our ability to imagine the future—is that there is always before us the looming reality of our own demise, whereas the prospect of death for other creatures only arises in actual circumstances, in the here and now. Evolution has endowed all its sentient creatures with the mental and physical means to try to do everything in their power to avoid death, yet practically all humans soon come to understand through everyday reason and evidence that they can do nothing about it in the long run. Cross-cultural experiments and surveys indicate that people more readily accept the truth of narratives containing counterintuitive elements, including miracles, when they are reminded of death through images or descriptions,[47] or when facing danger or insecurity, as with pleas of hope for God's intervention during wartime.[48]

Fear of death, then, is an undercurrent of belief. The spirits of dead ancestors, ghosts, immortal deities, heaven and hell, the everlasting soul: The notion of spiritual existence after death is at the heart of almost every religion. Believing in God and the afterlife is a way to make sense of the brevity of our time on earth, to give meaning to this short existence.

COSTLY COMMITMENT

We are a cultural species, evolved to have faith in culture. Unlike other animals, humans rely heavily on acquiring behavior, beliefs, motivations, and strategies from others in their group. These psychological processes have been shaped by natural selection to focus our attention on those domains and those individuals most likely to possess fitness-enhancing information.[49]

Like our own distant ancestors, contemporary foragers routinely process plant foods to remove toxins, often with little or no conscious knowledge of what happens if you don't process the food.[50] Such foods often contain low dosages of toxins that cause little harm for months or even years, and don't badly damage the food's flavor. But these toxins can accumulate and eventually cause severe health problems and death. A naive learner who favors her own experience of eating the foods without performing the arduous and time-consuming processing will do less work in the short run but possibly die earlier in the long run. *Placing faith in traditional practices, without understanding why, can be adaptive.* Similarly, manufacturing complex technologies or medicines often involves a sequence of important steps, most of which cannot be skipped without producing something shoddy. We also have faith that any electronics we buy won't blow up in our faces, and that the buildings we go in won't collapse.

But here's the rub: Because of language, it's simple for people to lie. You just have to say one thing and do another. Politicians do it often enough; so do shysters and fraudsters like Bernie Madoff. With evolution of language, faith in culturally transmitted information became vulnerable to exploitation, particularly by successful and prestigious individuals who could now transmit practices or beliefs they themselves may not hold. Language makes deception easy and cheap. Before language, learners observed and inferred people's underlying beliefs or desires by their behavior. Those wishing to deceive would have to actually perform an action to transmit it.

Suckers, though, really aren't born every minute—at least when it comes to most things that are important. It usually takes a lot of work, like cozying up to a victim, or special circumstances, like a distraction, to lure people into a con. That's because humans are universally endowed with a couple of important ways of deciding whether or not to trust what others say and do.

The first way of figuring out who to trust is by *rational reasoning*: Consider if a person's expressed beliefs, and the actions they imply, are logically in line with their other beliefs and empirically consistent with prior actions.[51] If the political candidate who expresses belief in the sanctity of the family also expresses belief in free love or turns out to be an adulterer, then you might conclude that the candidate's belief in family sanctity is suspect. (There are various psychological "biases and heuristics" that impinge on academic notions of "pure rationality,"[52] but these are orthogonal to the basic distinction between rational and religious beliefs.)

The second way to spot deception is by looking for *costly commitment*: See if the person expressing a belief is willing to commit himself to act on those beliefs. Studies show that young children usually refuse to taste a new food offered by a stranger unless the stranger eats it first.[53] If the food were really bad or dangerous, then it would have been too costly to the stranger to eat it. Developmental studies of the cultural transmission of altruistic giving show that neither preaching nor exhortation to charitable giving are effective without opportunities to observe costly giving by the models.[54] Similarly, studies of beliefs about the existence of entities like intangible germs and angels show that children only subscribe to those agents whom adults seem to endorse through their daily actions, and seem rather skeptical of unseen and supernatural agents that are unendorsed in our culture, like demons and mermaids.[55] Interviews with a racially diverse sample of parents from highly religious Christian, Jewish, Mormon, and Muslim families reveal that parents see religion holding their families together on a virtuous life course primarily because of costly investments in "practicing (and parenting) what you preach."[56]

A person who is being courted usually knows that a suitor is really in love if the suitor courts with extravagant disregard for expense and time, and struggles against all comers and through thick and thin. That kind of "irrational" and costly display is hard to fake.[57] It makes little sense unless the suitor is sincerely in love beyond reason, at least during courtship, because it's unreasonable for anyone to believe that his current honey is the most attractive and understanding person in the world and that no other will ever come along to compare.

Preposterous beliefs fail the test of rational reasoning, which puts them at a disadvantage relative to mundane beliefs in terms of the learner's own commitment to figuring out the social relevance and implications of a belief. But religious beliefs overcome this disadvantage through ritual acts of costly commitment. These extravagant acts are designed to convince learners to pay attention to what socially successful actors say and do, to try to understand the underlying meanings and motivations for that success, and if possible to emulate it.

Mundane beliefs can be undermined by reasoned argument and empirical evidence. Not so religious beliefs, which are rationally inscrutable and immune to falsification: You can't possibly disprove that God is all-seeing or show why he's not more likely to see just 537 things at once. Experiments suggest that once people sincerely commit to religious belief, attempts to undermine those beliefs through reason and evidence can stimulate believers to actually strengthen their beliefs.[58] For the believer, a failed prophecy may just mean there is more learning to do and commitment to make.

Preposterous beliefs involve more costly displays of commitment, and require more costly commitments from believers, than do mundane beliefs. Devotion to supernatural agents tends to spread in a population to the extent they elicit costly commitments, usually in the form of ritual ceremonies, offerings, and sacrifices.[59] When participants in costly rituals demonstrate commitment to supernatural beliefs, then observers who witness these commitments are more inclined to trust and follow the participants and so enhance group solidarity and survival. Consider, again, taking an oath before God among the Pashtun in terms of the ritual that underscores its seriousness, which involves time and labor and intense scrutiny by others:

> Because swearing a false oath within village or farmstead is believed to bring illness or reduce the productivity of the land, the ritual must be held away from human habitation. Because the surface of the land is presumed to be polluted by contact with thieves, adulterers, and criminals, a half-meter deep hole is dug and a copy of the Quran laid in it. After undergoing ritual ablutions, the accused places his right arm on the Quran and swears by Allah that what he is saying is true and fair. Since at least some of the evil consequences that can befall a false swearer apply equally to a false accuser, demanding an oath unfairly also has serious consequences and may impugn the honor of the accuser.[60]

An examination of eighty-three utopian communes of the nineteenth century indicates that religious groups with more costly rituals were more likely to survive over time than religious groups with fewer rituals. Members and leaders often explicitly acknowledged that costly demands increased their religious engagement.[61] Among Israeli kibbutzim (socialist agricultural settlements operating on the principle of labor according to ability with benefits according to need), groups with more religious rituals showed higher levels of cooperation than other religious and secular groups with fewer rituals.[62] Religious kibbutzim also economically outperform secular kibbutzim.[63]

Religious beliefs, then, are more likely to spread in a population and promote cooperation through mutual commitment than secular beliefs alone. Religious trust generally carries over to other beliefs and actions that the participants may affiliate with their ritualized religious beliefs, including cooperative works, charity, economic exchange, and warfare. As cooperating groups increase in size and expand, they come into conflict, competing with other groups for territory and other resources. The growing scope and cost of religious beliefs is both cause and consequence of this increasing group cooperation, expansion, and competition.

RELIGIOUS RITUALS AND THE RISE OF CIVILIZATIONS
Collective commitment to the absurd is the greatest demonstration of group love that humans have devised.

It is in religious rituals that supernatural agents, through their surrogates and instruments, manifest themselves in people's affections. The ceremonies repetitively occur to make highly improbable, and therefore socially unmistakable, displays of mutual commitment. Within the congregation's coordinated bodily rhythms (chanting, swaying) and submission displays (bowing, prostrating) individuals commune with, and signal giving over part of their being to, the intensely felt existential yearnings of others. This demonstration, in turn, conveys the intention or promise of self-sacrifice by and toward others (charity, care, defense, support) without any specific person or situation necessarily in mind. Profession of religious belief and adherence to its costly rituals is a convincing statement of open-ended social commitment.

Archaeological research that focuses on the co-evolution of ritual and society reveals that religious rituals became much more

formal, elaborate, and costly as societies developed from foraging bands to chiefdoms to states.[64] In ancient Mexico, for example, the nomadic egalitarian way of hunter-gatherer bands (before
4000 B.P., or before the present) selected for informal, unsched-
uled rituals from which no one was excluded. Much the same goes
for contemporary hunter-gatherers, such as the !Kung of Africa's
Kalahari Desert, whose primary religious rituals, such as trance
dancing, include everyone in the camp and are organized in an ad
hoc manner depending on the contingencies of rainfall, hunting
prospects, illnesses, and so forth.[65]

With the establishment of permanent villages and multivil-
lage chiefdoms (4000–3000 B.P.), main rituals were scheduled by
solar and astral events and managed by social achievers (Big Men
and chiefs). This also appears to be the case for predynastic Egypt
(6000–5000 B.P.) and China (4500–3500 B.P.), as well as for nineteenth-century chiefdoms of Native North Americans. After the
state formed in Mexico (2500 B.P.), most important rituals were
performed by a class of trained full-time priests, materially subsi-
dized by society, using religious calendars and occupying temples
built at enormous costs in labor and lives. This is also true for the
state-level societies of ancient Mesopotamia (after 5500 B.P.) and
India (after 4500 B.P.), which, like their Mesoamerican counterparts, also practiced costly and fearsome human sacrifice.

Consider also what is arguably the first comparative study
of society over time. The great fourteenth-century historian Ibn
Khaldûn examined different waves of Islamic invasion of the
North African Maghreb and the ensuing fate of their dynasties.
He found that "dynasties of wide power and large royal authority
have their origin in religion based on . . . truthful propaganda [that
is, with demonstrated commitment]. . . . Superiority results from
group feeling . . . individual desires come together in agreement,
and hearts become united. . . . Mutual cooperation and support
flourish. As a result, the extent of the state widens, and the dynasty

grows."[66] Contemporary studies indicate that Islam's spread into Kenya and other parts of Sub-Saharan Africa is associated with Muslim rituals (fasting, abstention from alcohol, from adultery, and from eating pork, etc.) drawing people into tighter networks of trust that facilitate trade and economic success.[67] Similar considerations apply to the current growth of the Protestant evangelical movement in Africa, Asia, and Latin America.[68]

Religious beliefs and obligations mitigate self-interest and reinforce trust in cultural norms, like the Ten Commandments or the Golden Rule, by conferring on them supernatural authorship, or "sacredness," and by enforcing them through supernatural punishment, or "divine retribution." Sacred beliefs and values are invariably associated with taboos: nonnegotiable prohibitions on beliefs and behaviors that transgress the sacred. Punishment for transgressing taboos provides concrete markers and proof of the meaning and importance of what is sacred for society. Together, sacred values and taboos bound moral behavior at the most basic level of conduct in society (sex, diet, dress, greeting) and at the most general level (warfare, rule, work, trade). Along with religious rituals and insignia, these bounds strongly identify one cultural group as different from another, reinforcing interactions with one's "own kind" while distancing the group from others.

The ancient Hebrew kingdom of Judah, to take an example, used circumcision, dietary laws, prohibition against Sabbath work, and other ritual rules and commandments to mark off their belief in the ineffable one true God with no name. This enabled the alliance of Hebrew hill tribes to set themselves apart from coastal peoples (Philistines, Canaanites) and to pull themselves together to withstand conquest and fragmentation by stronger invaders (Egyptians, Babylonians).[69] Violating the Sabbath along with idolatry were considered the gravest of norm violations and punishable by death. These were the most arbitrary markers of collective identity relative to the concrete needs of social life shared with other groups (in contrast to taboos against stealing, adultery, murder, and the like). Willful disregard of them was considered a strong signal of personal sin and rebellion. If left unchecked, rebellion could spread to the whole body politic and spell chaos and ruin, especially in a competitive situation of constant warfare against other groups: "For rebellion is as the sin of witchcraft, and stubbornness is as iniquity and idolatry" (Samuel 15:23).

For the Hebrews, as for the Catholic Church and its Holy Inquisition in their fight for survival against the Protestant Reformation, intolerance for religious deceivers "who fake miraculous signs" or who secretly entice defection "to serve other gods" was extreme: "the dreamers of dreams shall be put to death," and it is incumbent on those who find them out to assist in their execution, whether "your brother . . . your son or daughter . . . the wife . . . your friend" (Deuteronomy 13:6, 15). This religious prescription expresses the primacy of large-scale corporate society over kin and tribal loyalties and is a hallmark of state-level and trans-state societies. Recall that "Islam" means "submission" of family and tribe to the larger community under God.

Thus, in the course of human history, moral religions requiring costly commitments made large-scale cooperation possible between genetic strangers, people who weren't kin and kith, especially cooperation to compete in war. A quantitative cross-cultural analysis of 186 societies found that the larger the group, the more likely it culturally sanctioned deities who are directly concerned about human morality.[70] Another survey of 60 societies reveals that males in warring societies endure the costliest religious rites (genital mutilation, scarification, etc.) that "ritually signal commitment and promote solidarity among males who must organize for warfare."[71]

Recent surveys and experiments by my colleagues Jeremy Ginges, Ian Hansen, and Ara Norenzayan with Palestinians and Israeli settlers in the West Bank and Gaza show that frequency of involvement in religious rituals predicts support for martyrdom missions (for Palestinians, suicide attacks; for settlers, support for the 1993 Hebron mosque massacre by a religious immigrant). This relation is independent of mere expressions of religious devotion (amount of prayer). Similar findings were obtained for representative samples of Indian Hindus, Russian Orthodox, Mexican Catholics, British Protestants, and Indonesian Muslims. Greater ritual participation predicts both declared willingness to die for one's god or gods and belief that other religions are responsible for problems in the world.[72]

To the extent that oppression of religious minorities and leaders results in broadcasting their costly commitments, then such oppression can help rather than hinder the growth of their message and following. Historical studies suggest that early Christianity spread to become the majority religion in the Roman Empire through displays of costly commitment, such as martyrdom and charity: for example, risking death by caring for non-Christians infected with plague.[73] In the case of the civil rights movement, the mediatization of police brutality ultimately worked to the good, by sensitizing America's political establishment and mainstream population to the oppressive plight of minorities.

So publicizing martyrdom actions is a good idea if you want the attraction of martyrdom to increase, but a bad idea if you want it to end.

ABRAHAM'S CHILDREN

The Takfiri call to spectacular acts of killing and self-sacrifice is a media-wise act of zealotry. Its proximate goal is to gain publicity and support for a global cause of God-given "justice." It is but one extreme variant of what billions of people who follow the Abrahamic religions consider to be one of the most moral acts in all of human existence: Abraham's willingness to slit the throat of his most beloved son for a voice no one else could hear. For Christians, only God's bloody sacrifice of *His* only son for the sake of some unrealized and perhaps unrealizable notion of "humanity" rivals Abraham's willingness to sacrifice.

Almost two thousand years ago, the last of the Jewish Zealots fighting Rome pledged to kill one another rather than submit to Roman rule. Their young leader, Eleazer, reportedly rallied them with these words:

> My loyal followers, long ago we resolved to serve neither the Romans nor anyone else but only God . . . now the time has come that bids us prove our determination by our deeds. . . . One thing only let us spare our store of food: it will bear witness when we are dead to the fact that we perished, not through want but because . . . we chose death rather than slavery. . . .
>
> Ever since primitive man began to think, the words of our ancestors and of the gods . . . have constantly impressed on us that life is the calamity for man, not death. Death gives freedom to our souls and lets them depart to their own pure home where they will know nothing of any calamity; but while they are confined within a mortal body and share its miseries, in strict truth they are dead. . . . And isn't it absurd to run after the freedom of this life and grudge ourselves the freedom of eternity? . . . So let us deny our enemy their hoped-for pleasure at our expense, and without more ado leave them dumbfounded by our death and awed by our courage.[74]

The Zealots' hope was that by their extreme sacrifice and the renown that they hoped to gain from it, the idea of Israel would survive. Two millennia later, this is how the government and people of modern Israel interpret their deed. Through glorious sacrifice in costly commitment to a cause that is based upon the absurd, cultural groups can aspire to survive much stronger competition and triumph in the end. Let's try not to oblige the jihadis through our own intemperate reaction to their ploy.

Humans often use religion to cooperate to compete. (For example, in the 1950s, at the height of the Cold War, the Pledge of Allegiance was altered to include God.) As Darwin noted, in competition between groups with similar levels of technology and population size, those groups will tend to win out that favor and transmit willingness to sacrifice some self-interest for group interests (which also promote individual interests in the long run). Most cultures celebrate costly personal commitments as morally good and glorious. Many such celebrations are timeworn collective rituals—including quasi-religious national celebrations—with proven success in fostering cooperation within the group and making it more competitive with other groups. That basic dynamic is still with us and is unlikely to go away. As we'll see in the next chapter, it is especially palpable in traditional mainstream America, even more so than in other modern societies. But new globalized forms of religion, unhinged from traditional cultures and territories, now vie through the media for the mass of humanity. The jihad is one. Beliefs in the salvational power of human rights or evangelical atheism are also derivative forms. They all have common historical roots in monotheism, although they have very different moral priorities, so that the gods of one people become the devils of another.

CHAPTER 24
OUR RELIGIOUS WORLD

He that is not with me is against me; and he that gathereth not
with me scattereth abroad.

—JESUS OF NAZARETH, MATTHEW 12:30

And the Lord said unto the servant, Go out into the highways and
hedges and compel them to come in.

—LUKE 14:23

Religion is associated with large-scale cooperation within
groups and enduring conflict between groups. Religious
devotion is both universal and variable across cultures. Religion has been ordained both a weapon of oppression and of the
oppressed: "The opium of the people," wrote communism's sire,
Karl Marx; "Rebellion to tyrants is obedience to God," proclaimed
Ben Franklin as his motto for the new American Republic—a
sentiment echoed by Poland's Solidarity movement in mobilizing
religion against the Marxist state.[1] Religious inspiration has fired
creative imagination to raise many of humankind's greatest monuments, and religious conformity has shot innovation down.

So what is religion, heaven or hell? The answer, I think, is both,
and everything in between.

And the jihadis' dream? As clearly hell to us as it is heaven to them.

The moral differences between different dreams for humanity are clear, even if many elements of those dreams are the same.

WHAT'S UNIVERSAL ABOUT MORALITY AND WHAT'S NOT?

Belief in moral "rightness" or "truth" is a matter of faith. There is blind, closed, reactionary, and dogmatic faith, like the Holy Inquisition's faith in the existence of witches and the power of torture to reveal the truth about the Devil. And there is open faith with reason and insight and the belief that cruel punishment demeans everybody's life. Such faith motivated a small band of American colonists to oppose the mightiest empire in the world. It was faith in the good sense, the will of men of reason—a will bolstered by "firm reliance on the protection of divine Providence," however personified or disincarnate that Providence might be.

Recent studies suggest that there is a universal stock of moral intuitions that become part of any society's moral faith. But the relative importance of each element of the stock can vary from one cultural group to another and help to foment conflict between them. The combination of moral intuitions into a moral culture is not a natural or logical determination, but an undetermined product of historical contingency and willful choice. Faith in the American Dream is one such product; faith in violent jihad is another.

Studies by social psychologists Richard Nisbett and colleagues suggest that human cultures fall into two broad categories, individualist (mainly the United States and Western Europe) and collectivist (much of the rest of the world).[2] Anthropologist Richard Shweder and his colleagues argue that for so-called collectivist societies, there is also a strong "ethics of community" (authority, respect, duty, loyalty); often there is an "ethics of divinity" (purity, sanctity) as well.[3] Here, too, there is evidence of universal cognitions.

Experiments by Jonathan Haidt and Craig Joseph involving thousands of subjects suggest that all of these elements may be part of every culture, but each element varies to a different degree from culture to culture,[4] so that even within a single broad cultural faith, like the American Dream, there can be marked cultural differences. American liberals tend to insist on individual rights and are uncomfortable with pronouncements and institutions built on the foundations of "the ethics of community" and the "ethics of divinity" because they can lead to patriotic jingoism (overblown loyalty), inequality (subordination of the weak or disadvantaged), and exclusion (racism, proscriptive nationalism, and other forms of purification). Conservatives, however, want a more circumscribed, more interdependent social life, which requires a regulation of relationships that goes beyond addressing harm and promoting fairness to individuals. This includes limits to sexual relations, management of obligations and authority, and the control of group boundaries and borders.

Haidt and Joseph's Internet Study of the Five Foundations of Morality in America

When you decide whether something is right or wrong, to what extent are the following considerations relevant to your thinking?

Whether or not . . . someone was harmed [harm]

someone acted unfairly [reciprocity]

someone did something to betray his or her group [group loyalty]

the people involved were of the same rank or status [authority]

someone did something disgusting [purity]

Using Jon Haidt's questionnaire, psychologists Nadine Obeid and Jeremy Ginges found that, at least on some hot-button issues, conservatives clearly incline more than liberals to believe that others share their values. For example, pro–gay marriage activists are predictably "liberal" in that they consider addressing harm and promoting fairness to be high moral values (above 2.5 on a scale from 1 to 5), but not in-group cohesion, authority, or purity (all valued below 2.5). Anti-gay activists are predictably "conservative" in that they score high on all five moral values. But whereas conservative activists tend to underpredict how liberal activists respond, liberal activists strongly overpredict how conservative activists respond. Conservatives, it seems, are markedly less biased in their beliefs about the attitudes of the other side than liberals are on the issue, and they may feel that they have less far to go in reaching out to others.

Despite these moral differences inside America, and even despite the "culture wars" that sometimes seem to erupt from them, there is still a broad consensus about the "proper" mix of moral elements within a fairly narrow range compared to other societies around the world. The original American revolutionaries mixed the universal elements of morality in a very particular way. As I noted in chapter 22, the "self-evident" aspects of "human nature" that the Creator supposedly endowed us with—including "inalienable rights of life, liberty and the pursuit of happiness"—are anything but inherently self-evident and natural in the life of our species. The social engineering of individual liberty required upgrading the element of individuality, that is, our innate awareness of individuals as self-motivated agents who can act on their own to achieve goals.

The focus of empathy shifted to people as individuals and voluntary participants in civic communities. The Americans also downgraded elements of authority, loyalty, and purity then current in European politics. The French revolutionaries who followed lowered the importance of the individual while raising that of one group, the nation. That's why whole classes of counterrevolutionaries, rather than individuals alone, could be collectively condemned and punished regardless of any individual crimes they may have committed. Most modern revolutions and regimes follow the French example more than the American.

RELIGION IN AMERICA

I find it unsettling how uncurious so many of my colleagues and intellectual soul mates are to the historical underpinnings of American political culture and the genuine appeal of religious conservatism for so many of our fellow citizens. Like most of my French colleagues as well, who are generally not religious, they appear to think that people who insist on expressing their religiosity in public are peculiarly backward. For who—besides jihadis perhaps—would want to show such loony mental laundry to the world?

Recent economic studies (most notably *Unequal Democracy* by Princeton political scientist Larry Bartels)[5] show that when Democrats have been in the White House, lower-income American families experienced slightly faster income growth than higher-income families and that the reverse was true when Republicans were in control. If people voted rationally for their economic interests, one would expect Democrats to be perennial favorites among the working poor and the middle class. Conservative whites who vote Republican generally cite "group values" of patriotism and national security as the most important issues in deciding who should be president. Over the last few generations, it's only when these voters perceive the economy to be in truly dire straits, or when a previous Democratic administration has been successful in palpably increasing their prosperity, do patriotism and national security take on slightly less value than usual (though enough to tip elections).

Why is such apparently irrational behavior—at least irrational from the point of enlightened self-interest—so widespread in America?

American political conservatism is often allied with religious conservatism, although many Americans also believe in one without the other. Consider the expression of religious devotion in the United States, as indicated by belief in the Bible and by church attendance (averaged over three successive Gallup polls from 2005 to 2007). The classic division between the Blue states of the East and West versus the Red states of the South and Middle America is apparent: in the East and West, one in four people believe that the Bible is fable; in the South and Midwest, only one in seven believe that.

In his book *The Conscience of a Conservative*,[6] Arizona's Barry Goldwater, the Republican presidential candidate in the 1964 election, wrote:

> Every man, for his individual good and for the good of his society, is responsible for his own development. The choices that govern his life are choices that he must make; they cannot be made by any other human being. . . . Conservatism's first concern will always be: Are we maximizing [individual] freedom?

For Goldwater, "Politics [is] the art of achieving the maximum amount of freedom for individuals that is consistent with the maintenance of social order." The political implication of this rugged cowboy conservatism is to minimize government intervention in personal life. While religious conservatives generally agree that government should leave people alone, they also believe that churches and communities should take an active role in people's social and even political life. As Francis Fukuyama notes in his book *Trust*, sectarian religious communities like the Quakers, Baptists, and Methodists "created small, tight-knit groups whose members were bound to each other through common commitments to values like honesty and service."[7] Herein lies the original power that created America.

NEITHER INDIVIDUAL NOR NATION: SARAH PALIN AND THE SECTAR-IAN COMMUNITY IN AMERICA

Unlike the centralized European and Canadian churches, whether Catholic or Protestant, American congregations were, and still are, concretely rooted in local communities with strong personal ties. Americans voluntarily chose and supported their community church, internalizing and shaping the community's egalitarian moral values, instead of being compelled to belong to a state-subsidized, hierarchical institution. Where American churches have emphasized the God-given individual impulse to "life, liberty and the pursuit of happiness," the Roman Catholic Church and the Church of England in Canada have stressed the social virtues of that country's first constitution: "peace, order and good government."[8]

American churches have been more risk-prone, preaching practical working values over humanistic doctrines. "American denominations had to compete like business for customers, for support, for income," noted political sociologist Seymour Lipset. Unlike in other countries, Americans often opt to go to different churches depending on changing personal, social, economic, or political preferences. It's as acceptable to change churches as to change homes or shopping brands, provided that your choice is also motivated by moral conscience rather than mere personal opportunity and benefit.

Sarah Palin grew up as a member of the Assemblies of God, the largest Christian Pentecostal movement (about 66 million members worldwide). The movement consists of a self-described "cooperative fellowship" of self-propagating, self-supporting, and self-governing churches. All profess faith in the deity of Christ, the original fall and final salvation of man through belief in Christ's blood sacrifice and his Second Coming, and the evangelical mission to spread this belief in order to save as many other souls as possible. The movement also acknowledges loyalty to the national government, but allows every church and believer to take the stance each feels is most appropriate and to support or not support national wars as conscience dictates.

Although Palin grew up a Pentecostalist, in her adult life she attended a number of different churches. She is now part of the evangelical movement of Christian Charismatics, the fastest-growing religious movement in the world (over 450 million adherents). The Charismatic movement as a whole is more loosely structured and defined than the Pentecostal movement, more "postconfessional" than denominational, and opinioned somewhere between Pentecostals and other Christians (including Catholics) on a wide range of social and political issues. For example, a 2006 survey by the Pew Research Foundation[9] found that one-third of U.S. Charismatics (33 percent) agreed that "God fulfills politics and elections," versus nearly half (46 percent) of Pentecostals and about a quarter (24 percent) of all Christians surveyed who agreed with the idea.

Charismatics tend to be more wary of institutional authority than classic Pentecostalists, more casual in their attire, and more innovative and modern in their forms of outreach. Sports, the media, advertisement, and public education are all useful means for bringing morally lost and scattered souls into the flock. But toward those who consciously *choose* to remain outside and reject salvation, like many secular liberal Democrats, there can be little room for concession or compromise.

Charismatics also tend to believe that religious experience shouldn't be restricted to church-related activities but ought to morally motivate and infuse as much of a person's social, economic, and political life as possible, even as Church and State remain separate: in the Pew survey, 71 percent believe that religious groups should express social and political views, and nearly as many (67 percent) believe that religion is more important to them than nationality. When Sarah Palin said that the Iraq war was "a task that is from God," other religious conservatives may have thought she was wrong, but they honored her sentiment as fundamentally moral.

"Action," "challenge," and "change" are watchwords of the Charismatic movement, which encourages people to "leave the comfort zone" to wage "spiritual combat" in any realm of life where the forces of good and evil, God and Satan, may battle. In this sense, the Charismatic movement is arguably both revivalist and "conservative" in the traditional sense of seeking to be consistent with the founding organizational principles and moral ethos of the republic. "Change" is not a politically expedient notion for Charismatics, but a guiding principle of life and renewal.

America's vigorous religious ethic not only allows novelty and surprise, but encourages them as long as they give profit and competitive advantage to sectarian interests. A Gallup poll in 1973 asked: "Some people are attracted to new things and new ideas, while others are more cautious about things. What's your own attitude?" Nearly half the Americans (49 percent) said they were attracted to novelty; only 13 percent favored caution. Canadians preferred caution (35 percent) over newness (30 percent). As *New York Times* columnist David Brooks put it, "From voters, the demand is: Surprise Me Most."[10] That's something that makes a Frenchman cringe.

During the 2008 U.S. presidential campaign, there was a spate of pundit and academic analysis of religion in America on the heels of Sarah Palin's nomination for the vice presidency under the banner of the Republican Party. What was remarkable was how well the analysts described the trees but missed the forest. In one article in the leading French newspaper *Le Monde*, titled "Sarah Palin, A Funny Kind of Parishioner" (*Sarah Palin, une drôle de paroisienne*) sociologist Yannick Fer described the Charismatic movement to which Palin belongs insightfully and accurately. But his conclusion, which would make sense if it were about France, was widely off the mark:

> The [political] positions inspired by this religious conviction are conservative, to the point of opposing the autonomy of the individual in the quest to impose "the values of the Bible" on all of society; for, it is a matter of "saving" the nation as much as individuals. The Charismatic creed [in America] reaches the point of contradiction: Everyone is free and responsible for their choice, but there is only one path—a fundamental ambiguity that makes for a political object that is poorly defined, unstable, and problematic.[11]

In fact, the Pew survey found that a majority of U.S. Charismatics believe that the Bible and the right path for doing good and fighting evil in life are open to interpretation, though a majority believes that both abortion and homosexual behavior are never justified.

As we saw in chapter 21, in France, successive French leaders from the French revolution to the present have repeated the mantra that, beyond the individual, "the only community is the nation." That's why notions of multiculturalism and religious sectarianism have little place in French political philosophy. Although European Enlightenment values of individual freedom and choice also entered strongly into the American Republic's political constitution (especially via Thomas Jefferson and friends), the fundamental social constituent of economic and political culture in the United States was neither the individual nor the state, but the sectarian community. The religious community in the United States was a civic as well as moral community, a combination that infused American economic and political culture with particular dynamism.

Ironically, it was a French nobleman who first noted this novel historical condition. Alexis de Tocqueville stressed in *Democracy in America*, his masterful analysis of the young republic, written in 1835, that religious conservatism in America does *not* mean sacrifice of individual interest for group interest, or subservience of the individual to the State or any other ruling collectivity. Rather, religion mitigates the selfishness of unbridled individualism and "private animosities," while shoring up free institutions that engage "aspiring hopes" as against "general despotism [that] gives rise to indifference."

> It must be acknowledged that equality, which brings great benefits to the world, nevertheless . . . tends to isolate them from each other, to concentrate every man's attention on himself; and it lays open the soul to an inordinate love of material gratification. . . . Religious nations are thus naturally strong on the very point on which democratic nations are weak, which shows of what importance it is for men to preserve their religion as their conditions become more equal. . . . Thus it is, that, by respecting all democratic tendencies not absolutely contrary to herself, and by making use of several of them for her own purposes, Religion sustains a successful struggle of that spirit of individual independence which is her most dangerous opponent. . . . As soon as several of the inhabitants of the United States have taken up an opinion or feeling which they wish to promote, they look out for mutual assistance; and as soon as they have found out each other they combine. From that moment they are not longer isolated men, but a power seen from afar, whose actions serve as an example, and whose language is listened to.[12]

When Sarah Palin invoked God to help Alaska get a natural-gas pipeline, she was doing exactly what de Tocqueville described: rallying people to come together to promote a project:

> I think God's will has to be done in unifying people and companies in getting that gas line built, so pray for that. But I can do my job there in developing our natural resources and doing things

like getting the roads paved and making sure our troopers have their cop cars and their uniforms and their guns, and making sure our public schools are funded, but really all of that stuff doesn't do any good if the people of Alaska's heart isn't right with God. And that is going to be your job, as I am going to be doing my job, let's strike this deal, your job is going to be going out there, reaching the people, herding people, throughout Alaska, and we can work together to make sure God's will is done here.[13]

One key to previous Democratic success in the presidency has been to inspire people to greater sacrifice and cooperative effort through belief in a providential mission. President John Kennedy, in his inaugural address, asked citizens to renew their faith and effort on behalf of the country by renewing faith in their God-given destiny. Through such cooperative spirit, the impossible could become possible, whether getting to the moon, defeating communism, or even wiping out poverty:

> The world is very different now. For man holds in his mortal hands the power to abolish all forms of human poverty and all forms of human life. And yet the same revolutionary beliefs for which our forebears fought are still at issue around the globe— the belief that the rights of man come not from the generosity of the state, but from the hand of God. . . . With a good conscience our only sure reward, with history the final judge of our deeds, let us go forth to lead the land we love, asking His blessing and His help, but knowing that here on earth God's work must truly be our own.

De Tocqueville surmised, correctly it seems, that religion in America would give its democracy greater vigor, endurance, cooperative power, and competitive force than any strictly authoritarian regime or unbridled democracy.

In 1852, communism's cofounder Friedrich Engels wrote to Karl Marx that California's sudden rise as a social and economic force "out of nothing" was "not provided for in the [*Communist*] *Manifesto.* . . . We shall have to allow for this." He puzzled over the apparent exception of "Yankee blood" to the universal rule of "historical determinism." During a brief visit to North America in 1888, Engels observed that, unlike the case in Canada or Europe, "Here one sees how necessary the feverish spirit of the Americans is for the rapid development of a new country."[14] (But Marx, though he claimed that Communist theory was exclusively grounded in the history of human practice, actually professed an idealistic faith common to German and French Romantics, to wit: "It may work in practice, but if it doesn't work in theory, ignore it.")[15]

The great German political economist Max Weber attributed this "feverish spirit" to American capitalism's peculiar "Protestant ethic." An anecdote of his illustrates the religious sentiment that seemed to pervade American business life, which depended on personal trust and long-term credit relations. In 1904, on a long railroad journey through what was then U.S. Indian territory, Weber sat next to a traveling salesman of "undertaker's hardware" (iron letters for tombstones) and casually mentioned the strong church-mindedness of Americans. The salesman responded, "Sir, for my part everybody may believe or not believe as he pleases; but if I saw a farmer or a businessman not belonging to any church at all, I wouldn't trust him with fifty cents. Why pay me, if he doesn't believe in anything?"[16] Americans have traditionally tended to build economies on credit and trust in the future and others, rather than with cash and legal contracts. (But Americans, at least policy makers and negotiators, also tend to treat members of other cultures, such as political rival Russia[17] or economic rival Japan,[18] with greater distrust and self-serving bias—"our side is inherently fairer than yours"—than some other cultures treat one another.)

RELIGIOUS ORIGINS OF CIVIL RIGHTS

The role of religion in America, as in world history generally, has always been both reactionary and progressive. Benjamin Franklin believed religion could be harnessed to fight tyranny. But then he also believed that Negroes and Indians and Germans and all other "swarthy" peoples who were not of English complexion should be excluded from what a like-minded John Adams would call America's "Commonwealth of Christian Virtue."

It was not Enlightenment views of humanity that drove the abolitionist movement in America in the first half of the nineteenth century, observes Columbia University historian Simon Schama,[19] or the civil rights movement in the second half of the twentieth. It was a religious reckoning against "the national sin," pulsating from the pulpit in thunderous throbs and answered by congregations in rapturous song, sway, and action. Not that Enlightenment views couldn't be used to advance these causes: treating people as chattel clearly violates the basic human right of the Enlightenment to sovereignty over one's own person. Thomas Jefferson and John Quincy Adams invoked this type of argument on occasion to limited effect. But it was the pious and passionate devotion and willingness to die of those like the black slave rebel Nat Turner and the white insurrectionist John Brown, whom France's Victor Hugo compared to Spartacus[20] and others saw as "the father of American terrorism,"[21] that stirred people to fight until change.

For a decade after the Civil War, civil rights blossomed in the South under Union military protection, with many Southern blacks elected to state and national office. For Southern whites, though, blacks in office were shameful symbols of defeat, economic dispossession, and degradation. Preachers in white Protestant churches railed against the loss of traditional sacred values—of honor, duty, and respect—to modern Yankee vices of crass commerce, sexual license, and drunkenness. Everything changed when Democrat Samuel Tilden won the popular vote in the disputed presidential election of 1876 and Republican Rutherford B. Hayes agreed to remove the troops to win office through the electoral college. The Ku Klux Klan and other religiously inspired groups of poor and Southern whites were now free to act, terrorizing blacks and any others who would uphold the Fifteenth Amendment of the U.S. Constitution for the next century. Only the southern black churches kept the opposing sacred hopes of freedom and dignity for all alive in the black counterculture.

Ivy League intellectuals and liberal youth no doubt helped to rouse national support for the civil rights movement, but the inspiration to sustained struggle and sacrifice came from preachers like Martin Luther King and his forebears. They saw freedom's future in One Nation Under God as the fulfillment of Saint Paul's Epistle to the Galatians (3:28): "There is no Jew or Greek, neither slave nor freeman, there is neither male or female, for you are all one in Jesus Christ." It was the black churches that began creating a color-blind America, or at least a rainbow with no hard lines. That heritage of religious outreach and fellowship is also part of Barack Obama's church conscience, cadence, and appeal and not, as some political conservatives and liberals intimate, a mere bone he's thrown to the masses.

GLOBALIZED RELIGION

Globalization has created a market of social movements, both political and religious. But these political and religious movements are very different now from those in times past. They have become dislocated from ancient roots of ethnicity and territory as well as from more recent ties to nations and cultural areas (or "civilizations").[22] Economic globalization, whatever its considerable material benefits, is erasing traditional paths to security and well-being among masses of culturally unmoored and marginalized peoples. And among their youth, the mores of society—even the very word "society"—seem contrary to the feverish hope of unbounded friendships and emancipation.

The preferred purchases in this global market are the "purist" forms of politics and "fundamentalist" religions. They are the ones that have become standardized and superficial enough so that traditional knowledge and learning, and the weight of cultural history and the social order, count for little or nothing. Christian and Islamic "revivalist" movements fit the bill, but not Eastern Orthodoxy and Hinduism, which are still too closely tied to a particular part of the world. With these new fundamentalisms, the absolute and arbitrary boundaries of "the sacred"—now almost completely divorced from their previous role in helping to establish cooperation within and competition between cultures, nations, and civilizations—become the primary markers of collective identity: the Ten Commandments, "pro-life," the justice of "an eye for an eye," the world according to the *hadith* (original sayings of the Prophet), the division of material and intellectual life (food and sex, art and literature) into *halal* (the licit) and *haram* (the illicit). Blasphemous words and actions that violate these markers, like cursing God or depicting the Prophet in cartoons, are taken as frontal assaults on these globalized forms of collective identity, more threatening even than military attacks on cultural territory.

These markers are simple to learn, readily remembered, and easy to implement in clear and concrete terms that have no particular relationship with people's personal pasts. It matters not that there's almost no causal connection between these sacred markers and their original sources, as long as people believe them to have ancient authority and can apply them in the current context. Contrary to what the current crop of new atheists claim,[23] these fundamentalisms have no historically fixed connection or shared "essence" with whatever founding texts they may use, like the Bible or Koran.[24]

French political scientist Olivier Roy perceptively observes that today's Christian Evangelical and Muslim Salafi movements are thoroughly modern and novel "reformulations of religion rather than a return to ancient practices left aside during the parentheses of secularization."[25] Across the planet, there are mass conversions moved by television and the Internet and the twenty-four-hour news cycle of world events. People are "born again" into new global religions, not born into them: As I've noted before, relatively few people who join the jihad ever grew up with religious education. These media-driven movements feed off one another, especially in their most extreme and militant forms. There's a lot in common, for example, between what Marc Sageman has dubbed "leaderless jihad"[26] and the "leaderless resistance" of the Aryan Nations, or between the jihadi movement and the Christian Identity Movement's vision of Revelation and the bloody apocalyptic fantasies of Tim LaHaye's Left Behind series (around 50 million sold, at last count).

"Leaderless jihad" most aptly refers to recent developments in the global jihadi movement, exemplified by Mustafa Setmarian Nasar (aka Abu Musa al-Suri; see chapter 11). A veteran of the Soviet-Afghan War, Setmarian had lived and married in Spain and later went to England, where he edited *Al-Ansar* for the Algerian Groupe Islamique Armée (GIA). After a falling out between the GIA and Bin Laden, in 1997 Setmarian joined Bin Laden in Afghanistan and began lecturing in mujahedin training camps on leaderless resistance. His collected works were published online in early 2005 in a 1,600-page manifesto, *Da'wah lil-Muqawamah Al-Islamiyah Al-'Alamiyah* (A Call for the Islamic Global Resistance).[27]

Setmarian's online treatise contains important elements of the tract "Leaderless Resistance," written in 1983 by Louis Beam, a former Aryan Nations "ambassador" and Texas Ku Klux Klan leader.[28] Leaderless resistance rejects traditional pyramidal organization in favor of a collectivity of self-organized groups with no apparent leader. These groups act on their own initiative, based on their own interpretation of ideology, to carry out attacks or foment violence against the American government (and also against Jews, blacks, and other nonwhite Christians, supposedly in accordance with Revelation 12:10). The aim is to protect the wider movement from destruction through decapitation, and to absolve it of responsibility for the actions of associated groups. Beam's brief tract became the new bible of the cyber-based White Pride Movement that extends across the Americas, Europe, and into South Africa, and its philosophy of plausible deniability has become the legal foundation for numerous radical and militant Internet Web sites that host extreme ideas and plans.

Another intriguing example of convergence concerns the works of white supremacist ideologue William Pierce, which inspired Timothy McVeigh's 1995 bombing of a federal office building in Oklahoma City: For example, Pierce's *The Turner Diaries*, written in 1978, ends with the hero plowing his jet into the Pentagon with an atom bomb on a successful suicide mission.[29] (See also Pierce's analysis of the 9/11 attacks being carried out for the right reasons by the wrong people.)[30]

CULTURE CRASH

The global political conflicts that today's religious reformulations inspire don't represent a *clash* of traditional territorial cultures and civilizations,[31] but rather their collapse. The jihad, for one, is much more about global youth culture than the Koran or restoring the defunct caliphate. But it's a particular kind of youth culture, one that virulently opposes the unbounded possibilities that secular society often tolerates: free love and pornography, alcohol and hard drugs, making money and caring just for oneself. The sacred values that frame secular society (including human rights) and permit such practices must then be null and void. On the other side of the looking glass, some secularists argue that the very existence of religious intolerance is so dangerous that religion should be wiped from the earth,[32] or at least kept on a choke leash.[33] Fat chance.

Over the last century, the proportion of humanity that affirms no religious affiliation has grown steadily, from about 3 million people in 1900 to nearly 1 billion today.[34] But the trend is reliable only in Europe (particularly countries of the European Union), Canada, Australia, New Zealand, and America's "blue"[35] states (particularly the Northeast and West Coast). These are places where liberal democratic values (including advocacy of global human rights and environmental awareness), a large middle class, and per capita income are comparatively strong.[36]

In France, for example, only 30 to 40 percent of the population claim to be "religious"[37] (although at least two thirds of French folk believe in "God, spirit, or a life force"),[38] and the practice of Catholicism, the dominant religion, has been steadily declining for years. But the European trend away from religion is not necessarily irreversible, as the great French secularist André Malraux surmised half a century ago. Take the case of Russia, the core of the former Soviet Union. For more than seventy years, atheists ruled the Soviet Union. Beginning in the first year of school and for each year all the way through college, Soviet students were required to take a course in atheism. But because the educators cared nothing about religion, they made little progress. The assumption was that since religion is bunk, you needn't really know anything about religion to refute it,[39] and so educational efforts to stifle religion were shallow. There was also often intense discrimination against religious believers. But oppression of religious minorities and leaders often results in broadcasting their costly commitments, which then helps rather than hinders the growth of their message and following.[40] We saw in the previous chapter that early Christianity spread to become the majority religion in the Roman Empire through costly displays such as martyrdom and charity (for example, risking death by caring for non-Christians infected with plague).[41] The payoff? In Russia today, 96 percent of the people profess some sort of faith in God, about the same number as in the United States.[42]

In fact, both Protestant Evangelicalism and Islamic Revivalism are gaining ground throughout Europe, Asia, and Africa.

Globalization is producing a growing gap between secular and religious society. Believers in the new global fundamentalist religions, which cut through and across cultures, share less and less cultural substance with secular folk. Secular folk increasingly know nothing, and couldn't care less, about what believers believe and why. This is because the traditional religions are increasingly irrelevant—to secular folk and believers alike—the more societies become globally involved, and because the new global religions have nothing organic to do with whatever traditional aspects of society secular folk might have grown up to be tolerant toward. Secularists see believers as believing in what's crazy; believers see secularists as mired in what's meaningless. Each side demands that the other come to its senses and seek unconditional surrender. Or else. That's a prescription for conflict and war, not for democracy, tolerance of diversity, or global consensus.

I'm aware that we are living on the cusp of perhaps the second great tipping point in human history, and that this is an awesome and chancy thing to experience. I can almost imagine myself in ancient Mesopotamia, following the advent of the written word, as if in a time machine, out of the cold and cyclical universe of oral memory and myth and into the spiraling torrent of history and civilizations. And then today, cruising in cyberspace among all the world's words and through all of its walls, I can see once-indispensable material technologies and territorial relationships, like books and nation-states, vanishing in a chain reaction of knowledge and technology produced by a global social brain that anybody can access but nobody can manage.

If people could soar like winged angels and demons, they wouldn't need cars or airplanes; and if they can surf for knowledge in no time and bind into communities unbound by space, then libraries and borders become irrelevant. Yet I can no more foretell the actual forms of knowledge, technology, and society that are likely to result than an ancient Bushman or Sumerian could foresee how people could split the atom, frolic on the moon, crack the genetic code, or bond unto death on the Internet. (And anyone who says they can is just blowing smoke in your face.) But I'm reasonably sure that whatever new forms arise, they will have to accommodate fundamental aspects of human nature that have barely changed since the Stone Age: love, hate, jealousy, guilt, contempt, pride, loyalty, friendship, rivalry, the thrill of risk and adventure, accomplishment and victory, the desire for esteem and glory, the search for pattern and cause in everything that touches and interests us, and the inescapable need to fashion ideas and relationships sufficiently powerful to deny our nothingness in the random profusion of the universe.

As things now stand, I see a chance that political freedom and diversity will triumph, but also a chance that a brave new world of dumbing homogeneity and deadening control by consensus will prevail. Or perhaps they will alternate in increasingly destructive cycles. For the media-driven global political awakening is the oxygen that is both opening societies and spreading spectacular violence to close them.

As it happened, around the Shiite holiday of Ashura (December 28, 2009), I received an e-mail from a friend in Tehran who said how helpless he felt to stop the merciless beating of a young woman by government thugs, but he went on to say, "We will win this thing if the West does nothing but help us keep the lines of communication open with satellite Internet." The same day, I saw the Facebook communications of "farouk 986," the 2009 Christmas Day plane-bomb plotter who bound himself into a

EPILOGUE:
ABE'S ANSWER—THE QUESTION OF POLITICS

During the American Civil War, Abraham Lincoln made a speech in which he referred sympathetically to the Southern rebels. An elderly lady, a staunch Unionist, upbraided him for speaking kindly of his enemies when he ought to be thinking of destroying them. His response was classic: "Why, madam," Lincoln answered, "do I not destroy my enemies when I make them my friends?"[1]

TETUÁN, MOROCCO, JUNE 2007

"What do you think is going on in Mezuak? Why do they want to be martyrs?" the *New York Times* reporter asked me about the young men in this neighborhood bound for glory and a grave in Iraq.

People often want an author to give a book in a sentence. What I told the *Times* reporter then will do fine for this one: "People, including terrorists, don't simply die for a cause; they die for each other, especially their friends."[2]

In that light, I should have offered Lincoln's wisdom at that White House meeting when the woman from Vice President Cheney's office told me in the sternest tough-guy voice she could muster that the way to stop young people from choosing the path to radicalization is to bomb them in their lairs. (Never mind the impracticality of this, see-

TALKING TO THE ENEMY

ing as how the places I had talked to her about were in the middle of several large European and allied cities.)

Granted, Lincoln had little political "experience" beyond a single term in Congress fifteen years before being elected president. Still, his thought is for the ages. How, precisely, to make our enemies our friends is perhaps the most difficult political challenge of all—without having to fear or fabricate a common enemy to do it (as when Reagan mused to Gorbachev that a Martian invasion might finally bring humanity together).

THE WHITE HOUSE, FEBRUARY 2008

So I got another chance, back at the White House for a briefing to staff from the National Security Council and Homeland Security. I showed some charts and graphs on terror networks and gave my spiel about the need for field-based research to understand what's happening in the communities that produce jihadis in order to offer young people a different path.

"I'm convinced," one of the senior staffers said, "but . . ." He reached down for his BlackBerry and looked at the screen in mock surprise: "I don't see any messages here in the last five minutes telling me that we have to move right away on field-based research," he said, glancing up and around like a prairie dog with a conspiratorial smile.

The guy was smart. He was teaching me, in the quickest and most pointed way, how things work here.

"You'll have a better chance with Congress on this, and we'll see how we can help."

He was right about Congress, where you can usually find some subcommittee willing to listen, and he was helpful. The problem, though, is that Congress hasn't much say on anything to do with national security, or even foreign policy. Yes, Congress has long-term control over the budget, but most foreign-policy plans and decisions run on a short-term schedule that Congress usually only

The 99—anti-jihadi Muslim superhero comic books appeal to youth.

reacts to when things go way south. The White House sets practically the entire agenda, then gives the departments of Defense and State directives for realizing that agenda, including any related "human factors" research, which is usually a very distant and paltry afterthought. At the National Security Council, there's no representation for health, education, labor, or most anything to do with social relationships and human welfare. Almost all who sit and advise are from defense, intelligence, and economic agencies.

(The State Department's Agency for International Development is an exception that only proves the rule.)

So I tried a glibber tack, though dead-serious at its core, to show that bombing doesn't come close to delivering the kind of positive messages you can find in sport or with action heroes. There's a commercial action-adventure series called *The 99*, in which young Muslim superheroes dodge bullets and bullies to aggressively "fight for peace," with "multicultural initiatives" and "worldwide relief efforts," as the first issue trumpets. (Started as a comic book in Arabic and English versions by Naif Al-Mutawa, a Columbia University graduate from Kuwait, in 2009 it was dubbed "one of the top 20 trends sweeping the globe" by *Forbes* magazine and is now moving into television and film.)[3]

I put out my comic books on the large oval table, asked the people around it to look, and argued that adventure beats "moderation through education"—the second hackneyed cure for terrorism after bombing—any day in the world of the young, who yearn for adventure in life. Besides, the data show that most young people who join the jihad had a moderate and mostly secular education to begin with, rather than a radical religious one. And where in modern society do you find young people who hang on the words of older educators and "moderates"? Youth generally favors actions, not words, and challenge, not calm. That's a big reason so many who are bored, underemployed, overqualified, and underwhelmed by hopes for the future turn on to jihad with their friends. Jihad is an egalitarian, equal-opportunity employer (well, at least for boys, but girls are Web-surfing into the act): fraternal, fast-breaking, thrilling, glorious, and cool. Anyone is welcome to try his hand at slicing off the head of Goliath with a paper cutter.

Now, I have no illusions that comic books will do the trick. In the United States and across the world, readership for comic books has declined by about an order of magnitude since my youth. And even more since my father's time, when Superman's motto of

"Truth, Justice, and the American Way" was actually an important part of popular and civic culture. (In World War II, German soldiers would taunt Americans by yelling, "Fuck Superman!") Television and especially blockbuster movies are the only real channels through which comic-book action heroes make it into the mainstream nowadays; and these newer mass commercial heroes, like the Terminator, are hardly good moral models for wayward youth.

I really like *The 99*, but my intention is not to push these particular comic-book heroes. What counts is the counter-radicalization strategy that the comics illustrate. A *Newsweek* article took up the point and put it more succinctly: "These kids dream of fighting for some meaningful cause that will make them heroes in their communities. No, '*The 99*' comic books are not going to solve that problem. But . . . attracting young people away from jihadi cool . . . might even help convince Washington that 'knowledge is the true base of power.'"[4]

When you look at young people like the ones who grew up to blow up trains in Madrid in 2004, carried out the slaughter on the London Underground in 2005, and hoped to blast airliners out of the sky en route to the United States in 2006 and 2009, when you look at whom they idolize, how they organize, what bonds them and what drives them, then you see that what inspires the most lethal terrorists in the world today is not so much the Koran or the teachings of religion as it is a thrilling cause and call to action that promises glory and esteem in the eyes of friends, and through friends, eternal respect and remembrance in the wider world that they will never live to enjoy.

Because the young, feeling immortal, do not fathom how short and fragile life and memory are—even remembrance of heroes—or how forever long are death and forgetfulness. They don't understand that their deaths are staged so that stories will be broadcast, not about them—they are as nameless as their victims—but about the Cause.

If we can discredit their vicious idols (show how these bring murder and mayhem to their own people) and give these youth new heroes who speak to *their* hopes rather than just to ours, then we've got a much better shot at slowing the spread of jihad to the next generation than we do just with bullets and bombs. And if we can desensationalize terrorist actions, like suicide bombings, and reduce their fame (don't help advertise them or broadcast our hysterical response, for publicity is the oxygen of terrorism), the thrill will die down. Then the terrorist agenda will likely extinguish itself altogether, doused by its own cold raw truth: It has no life to offer. This path to glory leads only to ashes and rot.

ERICE, SICILY, MAY 2008

Barack Obama seemed poised to wrap up the Democratic presidential nomination and I was at a gathering of the World Federation of Scientists Permanent Monitoring Panel on Terrorism. Pakistani Senator Khurshid Ahmad, an Islamic economist and leading intellectual of modern Islamic Revivalism, was speaking to Ramamurti Rajaraman, one of India's great theoretical physicists and secular humanists. Said the senator, a self-proclaimed Muslim fundamentalist: "Obama is a ray of hope in an otherwise dismal situation for three reasons: His election would be a blow to racism around the world. He embodies the aspirations of a new generation inside and outside America, which looks towards him as a harbinger of change who may respect the feelings and wishes of people. And he has been outspoken on a number of issues, which at least shows that he is open to dialogue on issues that have been ignored by the present unilateral American leadership. But I fear America's political class will keep him tied to bad policies in Pakistan and across Muslim lands."

"Why does the United States get to choose Obama?" Rajaraman retorted, directing a mock scolding toward me. "We want him, the world needs him, and we all deserve him more than you do."

"So you think he's the Messiah?" I laughed.

"He is hope," the Indian scientist was more serious now. "Hope is better than fear and despair. This War on Terror only increases the world's despair."

Good enough.

Fear may be the oldest and strongest emotion in our species. In forbidding forests, fear kept our forebears safe from predators, firing our hearts and brains at every uncertain shadow or noise. "Better safe than sorry" is a good survival strategy. Afraid for nothing, you still live; wrongly unafraid, you die.

But "in politics, what begins in fear usually ends in folly," said the English philosopher-poet Samuel Taylor Coleridge. Still, the politics of fear is a classically effective sales con, like the vacuum-cleaner vendor who throws down dirt and convinces you how much you need his product to clean up the mess.

The politics of hope plays to a less primitive emotion. "Hope is a waking dream," said Aristotle, of things that never were but could be. It is a yearning that the future will be different from what we can reasonably expect today, and that there is more to existence than what we see in the here and now. Religion and science are rooted in hope, whatever else their uses or abuses. So is political imagination: "Some men see things the way they are, and ask why?" mused Robert Kennedy. "I dream of things that never were, and ask why not?"

It is the hope that fear between peoples will lessen and that all will be freer to pursue happiness for their families and communities. Of course, many knew little about the junior senator from Illinois or even where or what Illinois was, but people—especially the young—projected their own hopes on him as well as hopes for humanity. They saw in him the face of diversity, a growing symbol that is already making it harder for Al Qaeda and associates to promote the demonization of America, which drives their viral movement. (For this alone, he may have deserved his Nobel Peace Prize).[5]

Earlier in December, people were already starting to think about Obama in the needy neighborhood of Mezuak. I was back doing fieldwork on Mamoun Street, where Rifaat "the Kid" once sold candies from his cart and listened to Kounjaa' "the Afghan" praise the heroism of Sheikh Osama and the mujahedin, just across from Rue Boujmaa, where Jamal "the Chinaman" grew up, not far from the old home of his loyal buddies, the Oulad Akcha brothers, Mohammed and Rachid—before all these young men went to Madrid and blew up trains full of people, then themselves.

"Min huwa batal 'andak?" (So, who's your hero?), I asked Muhsein Chabab, who worked with children in Mezuak.

"When I was an adolescent, it was John Travolta (an American actor) and Jacques Brel (a French singer), but now I have no heroes. 'We live in a political world,' like Bob Dylan sang, but political people are not good. Osama Bin Laden is not so good and Colin Powell is not so good. Barack Obama? *J'espère bien mais j'crois pas* [I do hope but don't believe]."

Rarely do youth today cite "political people" as heroes. In Europe, the only "political" names you'll hear repeated are the warrior Che Guevara and the peacemaker Nelson Mandela, and a few John Kennedys. But who is there today for global youth?

Barack Obama projects hope, but does he truly have the audacity of Abe Lincoln's dream to turn the next generation of enemies into friends? It won't happen by pushing policy from the top, but by attracting people to make their way toward one another, by inspiring uplifting action that can snowball through social networks and across traditional boundaries of culture, creed, and class. The novelty of Obama's presidential campaign was to inspire and mobilize youth to canvass communities, to use science to understand the patterns of their beliefs and preferences, to find ways to fit those patterns to the candidate's hopes, and to prod like-minded people to link up in neighborhoods and on the Internet to further connect and convince others. In the twenty-first century, this may be the way the future is won within that ancient frame of all human politics and social movement: "Cooperate to compete."

DOWN THE STREET FROM THE CYPRUS BARBERSHOP, MEZUAK, MID-NOVEMBER 2008

A group of boys was playing soccer on a patch of dirt between a heap of garbage and the street. I guessed their ages to range from about ten to fifteen. They pretended to ignore me until I asked, "So what do you want to be when you grow up?"

"An archaeologist," one boy said immediately, as he kicked the ball away and headed toward me. The others followed him and moved in my direction.

"Why an archaeologist?" I asked.

"To discover things," he answered.

"Like treasure?" I pressed.

The boy laughed. "Our history." I wasn't expecting this.

"I want to be a doctor, to help people get better," another boy chimed in.

Then another: "Policemen help people, too. That's what I want to be. And to stop bad people from hurting good people."

A short, roly-poly boy stuck out his chest. "I will be a player for Barça [probably the world's most admired soccer team, which refuses commercial advertising but pays the United Nations to wear the logo of its children's fund, UNICEF]."

"Who will you play like?" I asked.

"Eto'o" [Barça's Cameroonian star].

"Is he the best?"

"Yes."

"No, he's not," the archaeologist said.

"It's Zinedine [the recently retired French-Algerian star of the World Cup and Real Madrid]," said the policeman.

"Zinedine," said the doctor, too.

"Maybe Zinedine," muttered the boy who would be Eto'o, bending to peer pressure.

"Ronaldinho!" shouted a younger boy, about eight, who had just joined the commotion.

"Zinedine! Zinedine!" insisted the policeman.

The little boy puckered his mouth and nodded his head in reluctant agreement.

"He's my brother," said the victorious policeman. "He's going to be the garbage collector and clean up this mess," pointing toward the heap.

The little boy shuffled back, as I witnessed the wonder of group dynamics.

"The best is Barack Obama," said the archaeologist, flooring me.

"He doesn't count," protested Eto'o.

"He beat everyone in America, everyone in the world. A Muslim!" the archaeologist explained.

"His father is Muslim," the policeman clarified.

"That makes him a Muslim," deduced the doctor.

"Why does this matter?" I asked.

"Because," reasoned the archaeologist, "he won't want to kill Muslims."

Mustapha, a journalist for the *Maghreb News* (*Al-Ahdath Al-Maghribia*) who had been running language interference between me and the kids, interjected:

"We were watching the elections until five o'clock in the morning. We cheered when Ohio voted for Obama. Just to make sure, we waited for Virginia, and we cheered again."

Ali, the engaging owner of the Coiffure Cyprus barbershop, had been running some errands and crossed the street to greet us. We had talked just before about the young men he attended who died in Madrid, and the others bound for Iraq. He heard Mustapha, put down his bags, and explained: "Hope isn't always reality. The Middle East is a rose, a flower so sweet that no bees can resist it for their honey. Bees, you know, have to work together, and Obama must as well. That's the way of the world [*tariq al-'alam*]."

"But people can change things," I protested. "The only true law of history is the law of surprises."

The barber of boys who would kill for a cause—or become archaeologists, doctors, policemen, soccer stars, even Barack Obamas—lifted his eyebrows and then his whole face to the sky, stroked his beard, and sighed with a smile that said, *Maybe tomorrow, but not today.*

> We had the idea that Obama came with hope. . . . There is a difference between Obama's words and actions. . . . It makes us desperate. Words now can have real effect only if followed by practical actions.
>
> —KHALED MESHAAL, CHAIRMAN, HAMAS POLITICAL BUREAU, DAMASCUS, DECEMBER 16, 2009 (MEETING WITH AUTHOR)[6]

"You can't eat or pocket dreams," preach the realists and the rationally pure, though it's only they who really do. For faith in collective dreams and heroes, perhaps more than industry and hard power, gives impetus to lives and civilizations.

History says that our ancient tribal future is fired forward by faith in groups, their gods and glory, no matter how secular these may appear, as with notions of the nation and what's noble. Faith makes fellowship a potent force for great virtue or for great vice: strong enough even to make vicious enemies into virtuous friends when sacred values can be shared. The trick to the turn is to be savvy about it, and maybe scientific, but also sincere.

Force and deception may be fine for war, but that is all you'll get. Dare we dream of something more to do with our enemies? For wars are truly won when enemies become friends. Then let's go out of the house, with whatever protection we need, and talk to the stranger before we shoot, or at least before we shoot again. On some things, we'll find, we won't change minds, and on some of these things we shouldn't. But who knows what a world could be made if we listen and learn at the camps of fallen angels?[7]

Then we must act to make it.

Author in front of the Palestine Polytechnic University in the Wad Abu Katila neighborhood of Hebron, which some of the suicide attackers from Hamas's Al Jihad Mosque soccer team attended.

NOTES

CHAPTER 1: SULAWESI

1. B. Obama (2004), *Dreams of My Father: A Story of Race and Inheritance*. New York: Three Rivers Press.
2. C. Hose, W. McDougall (1912), *Pagan Tribes of Borneo*. London: Macmillan.
3. T. L. Pennell (1909), *Among the Wild Tribes of the Afghan Frontier*. London: George Bell & Sons.
4. C. Lévi-Strauss (1955), *Tristes tropiques*. Paris: Plon.
5. J. Glover (2001), *Humanity: A Moral History of the Twentieth Century*. New Haven: Yale University Press.
6. B. Anderson (1983), *Imagined Communities: Reflections on the Origin and Spread of Nationalism*. New York: Verso.
7. A. Varshney (2003), "Nationalism, Ethnic Conflict, and Rationality." *Perspectives on Politics* 1:85–99.
8. C. Darwin (1871), *The Descent of Man, and Selection in Relation to Sex*. London: John Murray, pp. 164–66.

CHAPTER 2: TO BE HUMAN

1. G. Allison and P. Zelikow (1999), *Essence of Decision: Explaining the Cuban Missile Crisis*, 2nd ed. New York: Longman.
2. M. Dobbs (2008), *One Minute to Midnight: Kennedy, Khrushchev, and Castro on the Brink of Nuclear War*. New York: Knopf.
3. A. Mozgovoi (2002), *Cuban Samba of the "Foxtrot" Quartet: Soviet Submarines During the Year 1962 Caribbean Crisis*. Moscow: Military Parade (trans. S. Savranskaya, National Security Archives).
4. M. Lloyd (2002), "Soviets Close to Using A-bomb in 1962 Missile Crisis, Forum Told." *Boston Globe*, October 13.
5. R. Axelrod and M. Cohen (2001), *Harnessing Complexity: Organizational Implications of a Scientific Frontier*. New York: Basic Books.

6.   See R. Henig (2007), "Darwin's God," *New York Times Magazine*, March 4, www.nytimes.com/2007/03/04/magazine/04evolution.t.html?_r=1&page wanted=1.

7.   N. Chomsky (2006), Comments on Edge.com, *The Reality Club*, "Beyond Belief: Science, Religion, Reason, and Surivival." Salk Institute, La Jolla, November 5–7. www.edge.org/discourse/bb.html.

8.   É. Durkheim (1912), *Les formes élémentaires de la vie religieuse: Le système totémique en Australie*. Paris: F. Alcan.

9.   The way I figure now, if these young men and women are even remotely more fated to use their bodies as barricades for our freedom, then sharing education and hopes for the future in some common destiny is decent and good for our democracy.

10. E. Wax (2002), "Islam Attracting Many Survivors of Rwanda Genocide: Jihad Is Taught as 'Struggle to Heal.'" *Washington Post*, September 23. www.washingtonpost.com/wp-dyn/articles/A53018–2002Sep22.html.

11. D. Behar et al. (2008), "The Dawn of Human Matrilineal Diversity." *American Journal of Human Genetics* 82:1130–40.

12. A. Norenzayan and A. Shariff (2008), "The Origin and Evolution of Religious Prosociality." *Science* 322:58–62.

13. S. Atran and A. Norenzayan (2004), "Religion's Evolutionary Landscape: Counterintuition, Commitment, Compassion, Communion." *Behavioral and Brain Sciences* 27:713–70.

14. R. Rappaport (1999), *Ritual and Religion in the Making of Humanity*. New York: Cambridge University Press.

15. F. Roes and M. Raymond (2003), "Belief in Moralizing Gods." *Evolution and Human Behavior* 24:126–35.

16. J. Gray (2003), *Al Qaeda and What It Means to Be Modern*. London: Faber & Faber.

17. A. Toynbee (1972), *A Study of History*. New York: Oxford University Press.

18. O. Roy (2008), *La sainte ignorance*. Paris: Seuil.

19. S. Huntington (1996), *The Clash of Civilizations and the Remaking of the World Order*. New York: Simon & Schuster.

20. Z. Brzezinski (2008), "The Global Political Awakening." *International Herald Tribune*, December 17.

CHAPTER 3: THE MOORS OF MEZUAK

1.   C. Colón [Christopher Columbus] (1493; 1982), "Este es el primer viaje y las derrotas y camino que hizo el amirante don Cristóval Colón cuando

descubrió las Indias." In C. Colón, *Textos y documentos completos*, Madrid: Alianza, p. 15.

2. Cited in: Muhammad XII of Granada, Wikipedia, http://en.wikipedia .org/wiki/Boabdil.

3. W. Irving (1871), *The Alhambra*. Philadelphia: J. P. Lippincott, pp. 174–76.

4. J.-L. Miège, M. Benaboud, N. Erizini (1996), *Tétouan: Ville andalouse marocaine*. Rabat: Kalila wa Dimna.

5. G. Goçalbes Busto (1993), *Al-Mandari el grenadine fundador de Tetuán*, 2nd ed. Granada: T. G. Arte.

6. A. Elliot (2007), "Where Boys Grow Up to Be Jihadis." *New York Times Magazine*, November 25.

7. Cited in M. Slackman (2005), "Victor in Iran Vows to Press Atom Work." *International Herald Tribune*, June 27.

8. J. Esposito, D. Mogahed (2008), *Who Speaks for Islam? What a Billion Muslims Really Think*. Gallup Press.

CHAPTER 4: CREATION OF THE WESTERN WORLD

1. C. Darwin (1871), *The Descent of Man, and Selection in Relation to Sex*. London: John Murray, pp. 136, 156–57.

2. S. Washburn, ed. (1961), *The Social Life of Early Man*. New York: Wenner-Gren Foundation for Anthropological Research.

3. D. Young (1992), *Origins of the Sacred: The Ecstasies of Love and War*. New York: HarperPerennial.

4. D. Behar et al. (2008), "The Dawn of Human Matrilineal Diversity." *American Journal of Human Genetics* 82:1130–40.

5. H. Gross (1966), "The So-called Gottweig Interstadial of the Würm Glaciation." *Current Anthropology* 7:239–43.

6. J. Diamond (1997), *Guns, Germs, and Steel: The Fate of Human Societies*. New York: W. W. Norton.

7. A. Toynbee (1972), *A Study of History*. New York: Oxford University Press.

8. As the Abbasid Caliphate weakened, Mamluks began to assert control. Mamluk dynasties ruled India during the thirteenth century. They took over Egypt from the Ayyubid Sultanate, a former patron, ruling from 1250 until their defeat by the Ottomans in 1517. It was the Mamluks who finally stopped the Mongols in Syria at the Battle of Homs in 1260. Napoleon Bonaparte was so impressed by Mamluk daring during his invasion of Egypt in 1798 that he used Mamluk cavalry in his European

campaigns. On March 1, 1811, Egypt's Ottoman governor, Mohammed Ali, invited hundreds of Mamluk leaders to his palace to celebrate a declaration of war against Arabia's Wahabis, and murdered all but one to destroy Mamluk power for good.

9. C. Lévi-Straus (1966), *The Savage Mind*. Chicago: University of Chicago Press.

10. Aeschylus (472 B.C.; 1893), "The Battle of Salamis." In *The Persians*, lines 384–432, in W. H. Appleton (ed.), *Greek Poets in English Verse*. Cambridge: Riverside Press.

11. J. Maundeville (1322; 1848). *The Book of Sir John Maundeville*. In T. Wright (ed.), *Early Travels in Palestine*. London: Henry G. Bohn, pp. 207–27.

12. R. Stark (1997), *The Rise of Christianity: How the Obscure, Marginal Jesus Movement Became the Dominant Force in the Western World in a Few Centuries*. New York: HarperCollins.

13. N. Cohn (1962), "Medieval Millenarism," in S. Thrupp (ed.), *Millenial Dreams in Action*. The Hague: Mouton.

14. Cited in J. Burns (2001), "America the Vulnerable Meets a Ruthless Enemy." *New York Times*, September 12.

15. A. Toynbee, *A Study of History*, p. 201.

CHAPTER 5: SUBMISSION

1. Al Kindi, cited in A. Hourani (2002), *A History of the Arab Peoples*. Cambridge, MA: Harvard University Press, p. 79.

2. A. I. Sabra (1976), "The Scientific Enterprise." In B. Lewis (ed.), *The World of Islam*. London: Thames & Hudson, p. 182.

3. B. Lewis (1964), *The Middle East and the West*. New York: Harper & Row, p. 12; B. Lewis (2002), *What Went Wrong? Western Impact and Middle Eastern Response*. New York: Oxford University Press, pp. 152–53.

4. S. Souček (2000), *A History of Inner Asia*. Cambridge: Cambridge University Press.

5. The Mongol conquests of the thirteenth and fourteenth centuries were among the most brutal in recorded history. But unlike the conquest of Western Europe by fractious Germanic tribes, which shattered the *Pax Romana*, the Mongols under Genghis Khan and his heirs effectively established a *Pax Mongolica* from East Asia to Eastern Europe, including the Silk Road. The Moroccan judge Ibn Battûta (1304–ca. 1370) traveled in relative safety from the Atlantic, across the entire Islamic

world and on through Mongol-held territory, to China and the Pacific, providing direct comparative knowledge of the social, cultural, and economic life of the vast African and Eurasian territories he explored (though some of what he related was fanciful). His near contemporary, the Venetian Marco Polo (1254–1324), was one of the first Europeans to journey the Silk Road's entire length. Marco became a close confidant of Kublai Khan, grandson of Genghis Khan. In Kublai's newly built capital of Beijing, Marco learned about block printing of paperback books and paper currency. He marveled at the imperial postal system, a pony express, and was intrigued by gunpowder and the art of making noodles (which Muslims in southern Italy were already thinning into spaghetti). Kublai gave Marco a letter for Pope Clement IV requesting one hundred learned men to teach his people about Christianity and Western science, though the pope wanted only a military alliance for a new crusade against the Muslims. Marco Polo's account of Far East riches inspired Columbus to try to reach those lands by a western route, and realize the waking dream of connecting the whole world.

6. A. Klieman (1970), *Foundations of British Policy in the Arab World: The Cairo Conference of 1921*. Baltimore: Johns Hopkins University Press.

7. S. Atran (1989), "The Surrogate Colonization of Palestine," *American Ethnologist* 16:716–44.

8. G. Antonius (1939; 1969), *The Arab Awakening: The Story of the Arab National Movement*. Beirut: Librairie de Liban.

9. B. Lewis (1964), *The Middle East and the West*, p. 25.

10. D. Painter (1986), *Oil and the American Century: The Political Economy of U.S. Foreign Policy, 1941–1954*. Baltimore: Johns Hopkins University Press, p. 35.

11. Ibid., p. 37.

12. K. Deffeyes (2005), *Beyond Oil: The View from Hubbert's Peak*. New York: Hill & Wang.

13. During the last year of the Bush administration, both the Republican presidential candidate, John McCain, and the former chairman of the Federal Reserve, Alan Greenspan, conceded that the Iraq war was, in large part, about control of oil. But they had to backtrack: America couldn't also go to war for something so mundane. Most of the other forty or so dictatorships around the world have no key resources we need, and the United States has ignored them.

14. S. Atran (2003). "US Off Target in Terror War." *Detroit Free Press*, March 7.

15. In an ironic turn of events, after the United States defeated the Iraqi

army in the Second Gulf War, the U.S. administration pressured the Mongolian government to send about 150 troops for the occupation. These were scheduled to enter Baghdad first, to showcase the "Coalition of the Willing," until someone realized this was a dumb move. (Conversations with U.S. Foreign Service officials stationed in Mongolia, and with former CIA analyst Mike Scheuer.)

CHAPTER 6: THE TIDES OF TERROR

1. According to the U.S. State Department Report *Patterns of Global Terrorism 2001*, no single definition of terrorism is universally accepted, though for purposes of statistical analysis and policy making, "The term 'terrorism' means premeditated, politically motivated violence perpetrated against noncombatant targets by subnational groups or clandestine agents, usually intended to influence an audience." By this definition, the Nazi occupiers of France rightly denounced the "subnational" and "clandestine" French Resistance fighters as "terrorists." Indeed, there is no principled distinction between "terror" as defined by the U.S. Congress, and "counterinsurgency" as allowed in U.S. armed forces manuals. The U.S. extends the concept of "state terrorism" only to enemy nations, never to itself or allies. In the 1980s, the International Court of Justice used the U.S. administration's own definition of terrorism to call for an end to American support for "terrorism" on the part of Nicaraguan contras.

2. Flavius Josephus Ben Matthias (1985), *The Jewish War* [66–73 A.D.]. Dorset Press, 4.206.

3. D. Rapoport (2002), *Anthropoetics* 8, Spring–Summer.

4. T. Roosevelt (1901), First Annual Message to Congress, December 3. www.geocities.com/presidentialspeeches/1901.htm.

5. Submission to 60th U.S. Congress, April 9, 1908, Doc. 426, by Ch. Bonaparte, Attorney General, on behalf of Pres. Th. Roosevelt. http://tmh.floonet.net/articles/bonaparte.html.

6. T. Roosevelt (1904), The Roosevelt Corollary to the Monroe Doctrine, May. www.theodore-roosevelt.com/trmdcorollary.html.

7. Cited in S. Schama (2009), *The American Future: A History*. New York: Ecco, p. 117.

8. Ibid., pp. 118–119.

9. A. Bacevich (1982), "Disagreeable Work: Pacifying the Moros, 1903–1906." *Military Review* 62:49–61.

10. H. Gomez Jr. (2000), *The Moro Rebellion and the Search for Peace: A Study of Christian-Muslim Relations and Its People.* Zamboanga City, Philippines: Silsilah Publications.

11. S. Winchester (2003), *Krakatoa.* New York: HarperCollins.

12. J. Ellis (1975), *The Social History of the Machine Gun.* New York: Pantheon Books.

13. L. Wright (2006), *The Looming Tower: Al-Qaeda and the Road to 9/11.* New York: Alfred A. Knopf.

14. Reuven Paz (2003), "The First Islamist *Fatwah* on the Use of Weapons of Mass Destruction." *PRISM Special Dispatches on Global Jihad* 1 (1), May. www.e-prism.org.

15. Salafi, Wahabi, and Takfiri all refer to purist forms of Sunni Islam. But acts and celebrations of martyrdom, including suicide attack and flagellation to emulate the martyrdom of others, have always been more a mainstay of Shi'a society than of Sunni. A foremost contributor to the contemporary cult of martyrdom is the Iranian revolution of 1979 and the radical Shi'a doctrine of its ayatollahs. During the Iran-Iraq War (1980–1988), tens of thousands of young Iranian soldiers followed their buddies across the minefields in sacrifice for those to come after. Car bombings by Iran's Lebanese protégés, beginning with the Islamic Dawa Party's assault on the Iraqi embassy in Beirut in 1981 and Hizbollah's bombings of the U.S. embassy and the U.S. Marine and French barracks in 1983, brought suicide attack to the international stage. In 1992, Israel sent hundreds of Hamas leaders into exile in Lebanon, where Hizbollah helped take care of them, along with exiled leaders of the Palestinian Islamic Jihad, where they learned Hizbollah terror tactics. In Sudan, Hizbollah also forged links with Al Qaeda affiliates, and Hizbollah videos were used to train Qaeda operatives. But Hizbollah, once it joined Lebanese state politics, stopped their suicide bombing campaign well before those of Hamas and Al Qaeda began.

16. S. Qutb (1951), *As-salamu al-'alamiyah wal-Islam* [World Peace and Islam]. Maktabat Wihbeh.

17. O. Bin Laden (1998), "Jihad Against Jews and Crusaders." World Islamic Front Statement, February 23. www.fas.org/irp/world/para/docs/980223-fatwa.htm.

18. S. Qutb (1964; 1981), *Milestones* [Ma'alim fi al-Tariq]. Mother Mosque Foundation.

CHAPTER 7: A PARALLEL UNIVERSE

1. "Jarrah ended up in Germany because the only other option his family left him was to marry his cousin in Canada" (Dirk Laabs, personal communication, June 13, 2007).

2. Khaled Sheikh Mohammed, mastermind of the 9/11 attack, also credited U.S. support for Israel as his main motive for wanting to kill Americans and Jews, and not his time spent at a small Baptist college and then at the North Carolina Agricultural and Technical State University.

3. National Commission on Terrorist Attacks upon the United States (2004), *Final Report*, September 22, p. 160. www.9–11commission.gov/report/index.htm (hereafter, 9/11 Commission Report).

4. T. McDermott (2005), *Perfect Soldiers*. New York: HarperCollins, p. 54.

5. 9/11 Commission Report and interrogations of Ramzi Bin al-Shibh (aka Omar), October 7, 2002, and May 20, 2003.

6. Combating Terrorism Center at West Point (2007), *Cracks in the Foundation: Leadership Schisms in Al-Qa'ida 1989–2006*, September. www.ctc.usma.edu/aq/pdf/Harmony_3_Schism.pdf.

7. M. Sageman (2008), *Leaderless Jihad: Terror Networks in the Twenty-first Century*. Philadelphia: University of Pennsylvania Press.

8. M. Sageman (2004), *Understanding Terror Networks*, Philadelphia: University of Pennsylvania Press.

9. D. Gambetta and S. Hertog (2006), "Engineers of Jihad." Paper presented at the CSCW-PRIO Workshop on the Role of First Actors in Civil Wars, Oslo, August 17–18.

10. M. Sageman, *Leaderless Jihad*.

11. K. Peraino (2008), "Destination Martyrdom: What Drove So Many Libyans to Volunteer as Suicide Bombers for the War in Iraq? A Visit to Their Hometown—the Dead-End City of Darnah." *Newsweek*, April 19.

12. Kingdom of Saudi Arabia (2007), *The Saudi Experience of Countering Terrorism*. Riyadh: Ministry of Interior, Document Processing Center.

CHAPTER 8: FARHIN'S WAY

1. S. Atran (2005), "In Indonesia, Democracy Isn't Enough." *New York Times*, October 5.

2. Agence France-Presse (2008), "Indonesia Executes Bali Bombers, Backlash Feared." November 8.

3. See interviews in S. Neighbour (2005), *In the Shadow of Swords: On the Trail of Terrorism from Afghanistan to Australia*, Sydney: Harper Perennial, pp. 18–32.

4. Ibid., p. 91.
5. Farhin never gave a loyalty oath to Sungkar, nor was he ever "officially" JI, as were other Afghan Alumni who held titled positions. Indeed, most JI operatives were not "official," namely Imam Samudra, operations chief of the Bali bombing, who stayed with Darul Islam.
6. P. Bergen (2006), *The Osama Bin Laden I Know.* New York: Free Press.
7. L. Wright (2006), *The Looming Tower: Al-Qaeda and the Road to 9/11.* New York: Knopf, p. 107.
8. P. Bergen and P. Cruickshank (2008) "Special Report: Is Al Qa'ida in Pieces?" *Independent*, June 22.
9. In 2007, Saudi scholar Sheikh Salman al-Qudah, one of Bin Laden's former favorites for having urged Muslims to fight Americans stationed in Saudi Arabia, went on MBC Middle East television to denounce "my brother Osama" for killing "many innocent people, children, elderly, and women." More than two-thirds of commentaries on the Al Jazeera Web site were favorable. Most telling is the book *Rationalization of Jihad* by Sayyid Imam al-Sharif (available in translation at www.lauramansfield.com/j/revisions.asp). In the book, Al Sharif, known as Dr. Fadl, denounces the "blemishing of *jihad*" with "grave violations of sharia in recent years [by] those who kill hundreds, including women and children, Muslims and non-Muslims, in the name of Jihad." This is an important declaration by someone with impeccable jihadi credentials: Al-Sharif is an Egyptian surgeon who tended wounded mujahedin in the Soviet-Afghan war, cofounded a branch of Al Jihad with Zawahiri in Pakistan, operated on Bin Laden in Sudan after an attempted assassination, and wrote influential treatises defending the doctrine of *takfir*, which gives theological cover to targeting even Muslim civilians in Islam's defense. This so unsettled Zawahiri that he penned his own book-size renunciation of his erstwhile mentor's "revisionism."

CHAPTER 9: THE ROAD TO BALI

1. Imam Samudra (2004), *Aku Melawan Teroris* [I Fight Terrorists]. Solo, Indonesia: Jazeera.
2. CNN (1997) Peter Arnett interviews Osama Bin Laden, March. www.anusha.com/osamaint.htm; www.robert-fisk.com/usama_interview_cnn.htm.
3. Printout in police interview with Imam Samudra, January 12, 2003, cited in S. Neighbour, *In the Shadow of Swords*, p. 316.
4. In Indonesia's first parliamentary elections in 1955, the PNI (Indonesia

National Party), the party founded by President Sukarno, the leader of the struggle for independence, garnered 22.3 percent of the vote and the Indonesian Communist Party 16.4 percent. These two parties combined fell just short of the 39.3 percent secured by the two main Muslim parties, Nahdlatul Ulama ("Revival of Islamic Scholars") and Masyumi (*Partai Majelis Syuro Muslimin*), dedicated to setting up an Islamic state. When smaller nationalist, Christian, and left-wing parties are included, however, the non-Islamic parties slightly outperformed the combined Islamic parties.

5. E. Ho (2006), *The Graves of Tarim: Genealogy and Mobility Across the Indian Ocean*, Berkeley: University of California Press.

6. Abu Bakr Ba'asyir (2000), "A System for the Caderisation of Mujahidin in Creating an Islamic Society," presented to the First Indonesian Congress of Mujahidin, Yogyakarta, August 5–7, trans. Tim Behrend. www .arts.auckland.ac.nz/FileGet.cfm?ID=1291fbbb–4eed–4eb8-bca4– 375a0d95fa63.

7. S. Neighbour, *In the Shadow of Swords*, p. 155.

8. International Crisis Group (2003), *Jemaah Islamiyah in South East Asia: Damaged but Still Dangerous*. Asia Report No. 63, August 26, p. 10. www.crisisgroup.org/home/index.cfm?l=1&id=1452.

9. International Crisis Group (2006), *Terrorism in Indonesia: Noordin's Networks*. Asia Report No. 114, May 5. www.crisisgroup.org/home/index .cfm?id=4092.

10. P. Lloyd (2003), "Imam Samudra to Face the Death Penalty," transcript from ABC Radio (Australia), September 10. www.abc.net.au/am/ content/2003/s942690.htm.

11. International Crisis Group, *Terrorism in Indonesia*, p. 19.

12. Ibid., p. 16.

13. Indonesian security forces interrogation of Parmin, alias Yasir Abdul Baar alias Aslam, April 25, 2008.

14. International Crisis Group (2010), *Indonesia: Jihadi Surprise in Aceh*. Asia Report No. 189, April 20, www.crisisgroup.org/en/regions/asia /south-east-asia/indonesia/189-indonesia-surprise-in-aceh.aspx; T. Allard (2010), "Aceh Group Planned to Kill Yudhoyono," *Sydney Morning Herald*, May 15.

15. Cited in S. Atran (2005), "The Emir: An Interview with Abu Bakr Ba'asyir, Alleged Leader of the Southeast Asian Jemaah Islamiyah Organization." *Spotlight on Terrorism* 3:9, Jamestown Foundation. http://jamestown.org/terrorism/news/article.php?articleid=2369782.

16. S. Rionaldo (2009), "Two Indonesian Churches Receive Bomb

Threats." *Compass Direct News,* October 14. www.rightsidenews
.com/200910146845/global-terrorism/two-indonesian-churches-receive-
bomb-threats-from.html.

17. P. Gelling (2009), "Radical Books Raise Fears in Indonesia of Spread of
Militants' Ideas." *New York Times,* February 9.

CHAPTER 10: THE JI SOCIAL CLUB

1. D. Sevastopulo (2007), "Al-Qaeda Operative Admits Planning 9/11."
Financial Times, March 15.

2. CNN (2004), "Praise, Caution at Hambali Arrest." CNN.com, February
26. www.cnn.com/2003/WORLD/asiapcf/southeast/08/15/hambali.reax
/index.html.

3. 9/11 Commission Report, p. 154.

4. Nasir Abas and Ken Ward, personal communications, September 9–10,
2007.

5. S. Atran (2005), "The Emir: An Interview with Abu Bakr Ba'asyir,
Alleged Leader of the Southeast Asian Jemaah Islamiyah Organization." *Spotlight on Terrorism* 3:9, Jamestown Foundation, http://james-
town.org/terrorism/news/article.php?articleid=2369782.

6. Testimony of Abu Bakr Bafana (2006), *United States v. Zacarias Moussaoui,* U.S. District Court for the Eastern District of Virginia, Alexan-
dria, Virginia, March 8. http://cryptome.org/usa-v-zm–030806–01.htm.

7. Ibid.

8. 9/11 Commission Report, p. 151.

9. Defendant's exhibit 946, *United States v. Moussaoui* (No. 01–455), substi-
tution for the testimony of Riduan Isamuddin ("Hambali").

10. Ibid.

11. Ken Ward, former Australian intelligence officer, personal communication, September 5, 2006.

12. Abu Rusdan was appointed caretaker JI emir in April 2002, when
Ba'asyir was about to be arrested, though it was Zulkarnaen who
chaired the meeting announcing the change. Abu Rusdan presided over
the Markaziyah meeting on October 17, 2002, when Nasir Abas asked
Zulkarnaen his famous question. Markaziyah secretary Abu Dujana
issued the invitations. Zulkarnaen reported on the situation in Ambon.
According to Abas, Zulkarnaen disappeared after that meeting. (Nasir
Abas and Ken Ward, personal communication, September 10, 2007.)

13. In a pretrial police interrogation, Mubarok said that Amrozi had sought
approval from Ba'asyir for an event in Bali that he wanted to carry out
with his brothers. Ba'asyir reportedly replied, "It's up to you, as you

know the situation in the field." Later, Mubarok withdrew this statement. (Interrogation of Wan Min Wan Mat in Police Report No Pol:Lp02/III/2004/DENSUS 88 Anti Terror, case of Abu Bakr Ba'asyir, Kuala Lumpur, March 30, 2004.)

14. Abu Bakr Ba'asyir (2000), "A System for the Caderisation of Mujahidin in Creating an Islamic Society." Presented to the First Indonesian Congress of Mujahidin, Yogyakarta, August 5–7. Trans. Tim Behrend; available at http://www.arts.auckland.ac.nz/FileGet.cfm?ID=1291fbbb-4eed-4eb8-bca4-375a0d95fa63.

15. There are two kinds of schools that provide explicit religious education in Indonesia. The first is an "Islamic day school" administered by the state and is called *madrassah negeri*. The second, dubbed *pesantren*, is privately funded and administered and has no explicit ties to the state and very little oversight. The term *madrassah* (pl. *madaris*) is used to refer to both Islamic day schools and to *pesantrens*.

16. J. Magouirk and S. Atran (2008), "Jemaah Islamiyah's Radical Madrassah Network." *Dynamics of Asymmetric Warfare* 1 (1).

17. Ali Imron (2004), *Ali Imron Sang Pengebom* (*Ali Imron, the Bomber*). Jakarta: Republika Press.

18. International Crisis Group (2004), "Indonesia Backgrounder: Why Salafism and Terrorism Mostly Don't Mix." Asia Report No. 83, September 13. www.crisisgroup.org/home/index.cfm?id=2967&l=1.

19. International Crisis Group (2009), "Indonesia: Radicalisation of the 'Palembang Group.'" *Asia Briefing* No. 92, May 29. www.crisisgroup.org/home/index.cfm?id=6110.

20. S. Atran, J. Magouirk, and J. Ginges (2008), "Radical Madrassas in Southeast Asia." *CTC Sentinel* (Combating Terrorism Center, West Point) 1 (3). www.ctc.usma.edu/sentinel/CTCSentinel-Vol1Iss3.pdf.

21. Interrogation of Parmin, alias Yasir Abdul Baar, alias Aslam, April 25, 2008. International Crisis Group (2010), *Indonesia: Jihadi Surprise in Aceh*. Asia Report No. 189, April 20.

22. International Crisis Group (2009), "Indonesia: Noordin Top's Support Base." Asia Briefing No. 95, August 27. www.crisisgroup.org/home/index.cfm?id=6289&l=1.

CHAPTER 11: THE GREAT TRAIN BOMBING

1. "Encuestas sobre temas de actualidad (April 2007)—Encuestas el juicio por el 11-M va despejando dudas en la ciudadanía." www.neolectum.com/tmtic/tmt8200tdt/tvsport/tmt8221.html; *El Mundo* (2004), August 10, www.elmundo.es/papel/2004/08/10/espana/1677465.html.

2. Fernando Reinares, director of research on global terrorism, Real Insti-
   tuto Elcano, Madrid, cited in *Le Monde* (2007), "A Madrid, fin du procès
   des auteurs des attentats," July 4.
3. The information, quotes, and storyline in the following sections come
   from several sources: pretrial and trial testimony, interviews with investigative reporters, police, and intelligence. Several quoted reminiscences
   are from Justin Webster's outstanding documentary *The Madrid Connection* (2007). The film independently takes much the same line that
   Marc Sageman and I developed, namely, that the Madrid plot was mostly
   a self-organized affair driven by the converging ambitions of two main
   players: Serhane Fakhet, "el Tunecino," and Jamal Ahmidan, "el Chino."
   We differ mainly on the operational role of Al Qaeda and other outside
   agents, which *The Madrid Connection* suggests may be significant but we
   see as insignificant.
4. Conversations with *El País* investigative reporters José Yoldi and Jorge
   Rodriguez (2007), Madrid trial, May 30.
5. "Atentados terroristas del día 11 de marzo de 2004 en Madrid, Juzgado
   Central de Instrucción Nº 6, Audencia Nacional, Madrid, Sumario Nº
   20/2004, April 10, 2006 [hereafter called Madrid Train Bombing Indict-
   ment], *Quicaagésimo tercero*: Contexto Islamista de las investigaciones,"
   pp. 1344–47.
6. Ministerio del Interior, Dirección General de la Policía, Brigad Provin-
   cial de Extranjera y Documentación, "Asunto: Altercaciones conviven-
   cia C.I.E." Madrid, December 2, 2004.
7. Cited in A. Elliot (2007), "Where Boys Grow Up to Be Jihadis." *New
   York Times Magazine*, November 25. www.nytimes.com/2007/11/25/
   magazine/25tetouan-t.html.
8. *El País* (2007), May 28.
9. M. Marlasca and L. Rendueles (2007), *Una historia del 11-M que no va
   gustar a nadie*. Madrid: Ediciones Temas de Hoy.
10. Information provided to the author by the Centro Nacional de Inteligen-
    cia (CNI), Madrid, March 2007.

CHAPTER 12: LOOKING FOR AL QAEDA

1. Conversation with Ernest Ekaizer, *El País* deputy editor, March 7, 2007.
2. Interview with Spanish Guardia Civil personnel, Madrid, May 28, 2007.
3. Lamari had been jailed in 1997 by Judge Baltasar Garzón along with
   ten members of the Algerian terrorist Groupe Islamique Armé (GIA),
   although there was scant evidence that Lamari ever belonged to GIA or

engaged in any terrorist activity at the time. Sentenced to fourteen years (later reduced to nine), he was released from prison in 2002 through an administrative error, went underground, and vowed revenge against Spain. A few days before he died, Lamari called a friend in Valencia to say that "we will meet in heaven and tell my friends to pray for me." Intelligence officials tell me insistently that Lamari was the "brains" behind the attack, though they say they can't reveal the evidence. Marc Sageman is more than skeptical: "You don't spend all your time picking asparagus and artichokes [as Lamari did before his arrest] if you're running a terrorist operation. He probably was picked up because he happened to know some bad guys, got pissed off in jail, and came out ready to kill someone."

4. *El País*, June 28, 2004.
5. M. Cohen and J. March (2000), "Leadership in an Organized Anarchy." In M. Brown (ed.), *Organization and Governance in Higher Education.* Boston: Pearson Custom Publishing.
6. Madrid Train Bombing Indictment, "Cuadragésimo quinto: Análisis de la financiación y otras ceustiones relacionadas," pp. 1126–49.
7. 9/11 Commission Report, pp. 169–73.
8. M. Kenney (2007), *From Pablo to Osama: Trafficking and Terrorist Networks, Government Bureaucracies, and Competitive Adaptation.* University Park: Pennsylvania State University Press.
9. B. Ivry (2003), "Black-Market Arms Dealing Still Thriving." *Record*, October 7. www.sais-jhu.edu/publicaffairs/SAISarticles03/Bond_Black-Market_100703.pdf.
10. R. Axelrod and M. Cohen (2000), *Harnessing Complexity: Organizational Implications of a Scientific Frontier.* New York: Basic Books.
11. H. Simon (1981), *Sciences of the Artificial*, Cambridge, MA: MIT.
12. Cited in Pablo Ordaz (2006), "Entrevista con la esposa de Jamal Ahmidan, 'El Chino,' jefe operativo del 'comando' del 11-M." *El País*, March 8.

CHAPTER 13: THE ORDINARINESS OF TERROR

1. G. Berns et al. (2005), "Neurobiological Correlates of Social Conformity and Independence During Mental Rotation." *Biological Psychiatry* 58:245–53.
2. M. Gardner and L. Steinberg (2005), "Peer Influence on Risk Taking, Risk Preference, and Risky Decision Making in Adolescence and Adulthood: An Experimental Study." *Developmental Psychology* 41:625–35, p. 612.
3. R. Collins (2008), *Violence: A Micro-sociological Theory.* Princeton: Princeton University Press.

4. H. Arendt (1970), *Eichmann in Jerusalem: A Report on the Banality of Evil*. New York: Viking Press.
5. S. Milgram (1974), *Obedience to Authority*. New York: Harper & Row.
6. P. Zimbardo, "The Stanford Prison Experiment." www.prisonexp.org.
7. M. Haritos-Fatouros (1988), "The Official Torturer: A Learning Model for Obedience to the Authority of Violence." *Journal of Applied Social Psychology* 18:1107–20.
8. W. Klein (2002), "Social Reality and Self-Construction: A Case of "Bounded Irrationality?" *Basic and Applied Social Psychology* 24:105–114.
9. C. McCauley (1972), "Extremity Shifts, Risk Shifts, and Attitude Shifts After Group Discussion." *European Journal of Social Psychology* 2:417–36.
10. N. Christakis and J. Fowler (2007), "The Spread of Obesity in a Large Network over 32 Years." *New England Journal of Medicine*, 357:370–79.
11. J. Cacioppo, J. Fowler, and N. Christakis (2009), "Alone in the Crowd: The Structure and Spread of Loneliness in a Large Social Network." *Journal of Personality and Social Psychology* 97 (6).

CHAPTER 14: PRYING INTO PAKISTAN

1. S. Atran (2006), "Is Hamas Ready to Deal?" *New York Times*, August 17.
2. S. Atran (2006), "Pakistan: Balancing Act." *Bulletin of the Atomic Scientists* 6 (2), November–December.
3. Al Qaeda's chief of operations, Abu Zubaydah, was captured in a LeT safehouse in Faisalabad, Pakistan, in March 2002. He was responsible for training Islamic militants in Qaeda training camps and contacting field operatives when an atttack was being planned.
4. A. Sen (2008), "Terrorists Planned 9/11 in India." *Washington Times*, November 30. www.washingtontimes.com/news/2008/nov/30/terrorists-planned-a-911-in-india/?page=2.
5. A. Sen (2008), "Shaken India Points Finger at 'Neighbors.'" *Washington Times*, November 27. www.washingtontimes.com/news/2008/nov/27/125-now-dead-indias-911.
6. A. Sen (2010), "Double Take: The U.S. Now Acknowledges Lashkar-e-Toiba's Global Gambit."*Outlook* (India), April 12. www.outlookindia.com/article.aspx?264924.
7. C. C. Fair (2007), "Militant Recruitment in Pakistan: A New Look at the Militancy-Madrassah Connection." *Asia Policy* 4:107–34. http://nbr.org/publications/asia_policy/AP4/AP4%20Fair.pdf.
8. A. Arqam Naqash (2008). Reuters, December 12.

9. According to Indian police, Ajmal Amir Kasab, sole survivor of the ten-member Mumbai attack team, was a Punjabi who trained in Muzaffarabad, the capital of Azad Kashmir, and later in other camps. Much like the Qaeda-affiliated camps along the Afghan border, LeT camps had twenty to thirty people at a time, and some of the trainers were former Pakistani army officers. There Ajmal trained in handling arms, navigating the sea and survival techniques, and how to use GPS, Google Earth maps, and video images of his targets. At some of the sessions, he told interrogators, Hafiz Saeed, the Lashkar leader, gave motivational speeches, covering a host of pan-Islamic grievances, from Kashmir and Afghanistan, to Iraq and Palestine.

10. P. Hoodbhoy, interviewed by C. Otten (2008), "Die Menschen sin blind vor Hass." *Focus-Online-Redakteurin.* www.focus.de/politik/ausland/tid–12856/pakistan-die-menschen-sind-blind-vor-hass_aid_355157.html.

11. Pervez Hoodbhoy is a courageous man of outspoken opposition to nuclear armament and all forms of fanaticism. Early on, he publicly denounced Abdul Qadeer Khan, revered father of Pakistan's atomic bomb, for corruption and warmongering. Hoodbhoy's tireless efforts to foster peace with India through dialogue and film documentaries, to challenge all forms of religious discrimination, and to defend and enable women's access to education and even simple medical care, have earned him wide reprobation in his own country as an "enemy of the State and God." But others see him as reluctantly heroic and better than most, though he thinks better than none.

12. N. Kralev and B. Slavin (2009), "Clinton Warns of Pakistan Nukes." *Washington Times*, April 24.

13. S. Gregory (2009), "The Terrorist Threat to Pakistan's Nuclear Weapons." *CTC Sentinel* (Combating Terrorism Center at West Point) 2 (7). www.ctc.usma.edu/sentinel/CTCSentinel-Vol2Iss7.pdf.

14. S. Younger (2009), *The Bomb: A New History.* New York: Ecco.

15. From S. Atran (2006), "Risk in the Wild: Reassessing Terrorist Threats from the Field." Presentation to the Risk and Society panel, annual meeting of the American Association for the Advancement of Science, St. Louis, February.

16. R. Garwin (2002), "Nuclear and Biological Megaterrorism." Report to the 27th session of the International Seminars on Planetary Emergencies, World Federation of Scientists, Erice, Italy, August 21. www.fas.org:rlg/020821-terrorism.htm; and personal communication, February 11, 2005.

17. B. Fischhoff, S. Atran, and M. Sageman (2008), "Mutually Assured

Support: A Security Doctrine for Terrorist Nuclear Weapons Threats." *Annals of the American Academy of Political and Social Science*, special issue, *Terrorism Briefing for the New President* 618:160–67.

CHAPTER 15: A QUESTION OF HONOR

1. T. L. Pennell (1909), *Among the Wild Tribes of the Afghan Frontier: A Record of Sixteen Years' Close Intercourse with the Natives of the Indian Marches*. London: George Bell & Sons, pp. 48–49, 60–61, 116, 124.

2. House of Lords debate, February 26, 1908, vol. 184, cc. 1715–32. hansard.millbanksystems.com/lords/1908/feb/26/india-north-west-frontier-policy#S4V0184P0_19080226_HOL_23.

3. H. Hussain (2004), "Waziristan—The Past." *Defence Journal*, November. www.ordersofbattle.darkscape.net/site/analysis/waziristanthe_past_overview_of.htm.

4. Madeleine Albright responds to questions by Atran and others at "The Strategic Importance, Causes, and Consequences of Terrorism: A Multidisciplinary Colloquium." University of Michigan, Ann Arbor, March 11, 2004.

5. G. Rasuly-Paleczek (2001), "The Struggle for the Afghan State: Centralization, Nationalism and Their Discontents." In W. van Schendel and E. Zürcher (eds.), *Identity Politics in Central Asia and the Muslim World*. London: I. B. Tauris.

6. R. Tapper (1988), "Ethnicity, Order, and Meaning in the Anthropology of Iran and Afghanistan." In J.-P. Digard (ed.), *Le Fait Ethnique en Iran et en Afghanistan*. Paris: Editions du CNRS.

7. A. Ahmad and L. Grau (2002), *Afghan Guerrilla Warfare: In the Words of the Mujahideen Fighters*. Osceola, WI: Zenith Press.

8. O. Roy (1994), *The Failure of Political Islam*. Cambridge, MA: Harvard University Press, pp. 158–59.

9. O. Roy (1990), *Islam and Resistance in Afghanistan*, 2nd ed. Cambridge: Cambridge University Press.

10. G. Crile (2007), *Charlie Wilson's War*. New York: Grove Press.

11. T. Barfield (2003), *Afghan Customary Law and Its Relationship to Formal Judicial Institutions*. Washington, DC: United States Institute for Peace. www.usip.org/files/barfield2.pdf.

12. A. Wardak (2002), "*Jirga*: Power and Traditional Conflict Resolution in Afghanistan." In J. Strawson (ed.), *Law After Ground Zero*. London: Cavendish.

13. S. Atran (1985), "Managing Arab Kinship and Marriage." *Social Science Information* 24: 659–96.

14. F. Barth (1954), *Political Leadership Among the Swat Pathans*. London: Athlone Press.

15. R. Pehrson (1966), *The Social Organization of the Marri Baluch*. Chicago: Aldine.

16. This same branching structure can also merge into ever more inclusive and strongly tethered groups when opportunities to expand the resource base arise. Indeed, by harnessing the structural possibilities inherent in the segmentary lineage system, and in the codes of honor and loyalty associated with it, Mohammed and his successors were able to unite the fractious Arab tribes in one poor, small corner of the world, and expand their dominion across three continents. Of course, the lineage system strongly supported tribal loyalty, and it took great skill to transfer the primary loyalty of his followers from the tribe to the community of believers.

17. T. Pennell, *Among the Wild Tribes of the Afghan Frontier*. pp. 122–23.

18. T. Barfield, *Afghan Customary Law and Its Relationship to Formal Judicial Institutions*, p. 36.

19. Combating Terrorism Center at West Point (2007), *Cracks in the Foundation: Leadership Schisms in Al-Qa'ida 1989–2006*, September, pp. 14ff. http://www.ctc.usma.edu/aq/pdf/Harmony_3_Schism.pdf.

20. N. Kralev (2000). "Clinton to Taliban: Forsake al Qaeda." *Washington Times*, July 16.

21. M. Sageman, personal communication, July 2009.

22. S. Gregory (2009), "The Terrorist Threat to Pakistan's Nuclear Weapons." *CTC Sentinel* (Combating Terrorism Center at West Point) 2 (7). www.ctc.usma.edu/sentinel/CTCSentinel-Vol2Iss7.pdf.

23. House of Lords debate, February 26, 1908, vol, 184, cc. 1715–1732.

24. J. Burke, personal communication, January 2009.

25. A January 2010 report by the Senate Foreign Relations Committee adapted part of this framework (outlined in my *New York Times* op-ed, "To Beat Al Qaeda, Look to the East," December 13, 2009) to the problem of "Al Qaeda in Yemen and Somalia" (http://foreign.senate.gov/imo/medi/doc/Yemen.pdf, p. 6). But more field research is needed to justify the extension of the framework to new contexts.

26. P. Chalk (2009), "The Philippines' Continued Success Against Extremists." *CTC Sentinel* (Combating Terrorism Center at West Point) 2 (8), www.ctc.usma.edu/sentinel/CTCSentinel-Vol2Iss8.pdf.

27. M. Sageman (2009), "Confronting al-Qaeda." Testimony to the Senate Foreign Relations Committee, October 7. http://foreign.senate.gov/testimony/2009/SagemanTestimony091007p.pdf.

28. A. Giustozzi, ed. (2009), *Decoding the New Taliban: Insights from the Afghan Field*. New York: Columbia University Press.

29. A. Rubin and M. Mazetti (2009), "Afghan Suicide Bomber Killed C.I.A. Operatives." *New York Times*, December 31.

30. R. Rahimullah (2009), "The Significance of Qari Zain's Assassination in Pakistan." *CTC Sentinel* (Combating Terrorism Center at West Point) 2 (7), www.ctc.usma.edu/sentinel/CTCSentinel-Vol2Iss7.pdf.

31. R. Pape (2009), "To Beat the Taliban, Fight from Afar." *New York Times*, October 15.

32. Gen. S. McChrystal to Sec. Defense R. Gates (2009), Commander's Initial Assessment, NATO International Security Assistance Force, Afghanistan, August 30, p. 2. http://media.washingtonpost.com/wp-srv/politics/documents/Assessment_Redacted_092109.pdf.

33. See also C. Dickey (2009), "Losing Afghanistan's Drug War." *Newsweek*, July 31. www.newsweek.com/id/209830.

34. N. Rosen (2010), "Something from Nothing: U.S. Strategy in Afghanistan." *Boston Review*, January–February, www.bostonreview.net/BR35.1/rosen.php.

35. S. Atran (2010), "Pathways to and from Political Violence: Testimony to the Senate Armed Services Subcommittee on Emerging Threats and Capabilities." March 10. http://armed-services.senate.gov/statemnt/2010/03%20March/Atran%2003-10-10.pdf.

CHAPTER 16: THE TERROR SCARE

1. S. Atran (2006), "Commentary: A Failure of Imagination (Intelligence, WMDs, and 'Virtual Jihad')." *Studies in Conflict and Terrorism* 29: 263–78.

2. *Daily Times* (2009), "Al Qaeda Still Greatest Threat to US, UK: Obama, Brown." November 17. www.dailytimes.com.pk/default.asp?page=2009%5C11%5C17%5Cstory_17-11-2009_pg1_3.

3. P. Webster (2009), "Al-Qaeda Still Biggest Threat to British Security, Says Gordon Brown." *Times* (London), November 16. www.timesonline.co.uk/tol/news/politics/article6918483.ece.

4. A. de Borchgrave (2007), "Terror Wars: The Missing Sleeper Cells." United Press International online, May 3. http://archive.newsmax.com/archives/articles/2007/5/3/150302.shtml.

5. G. Tenet (2007), *At the Center of the Storm: My Years at the CIA*. New York: HarperCollins.

6. M. Sageman (2004), *Understanding Terror Networks*. Philadelphia: University of Pennsylvania Press, 2004.

7. Ibid.

8. J. Burke (2008), "Omar Was a Normal British Teenager Who Loved His Little Brother and Man Utd: So Why at 24 Did He Plan to Blow Up a Nightclub in Central London?" *Guardian*, January 20.

9. D. Buss (2006), *The Evolution of Evil*. "What Is Your Dangerous Idea?" Edge World Question Center. www.edge.org/q2006/q06_12.html.

10. K. Haider (2009), "Taliban Planned to Use Americans in Pakistan Attacks." Reuters, December 26. www.reuters.com/article/idUS-TRE5BP0HI20091226.

11. P. Rucker and J. Tate (2009), "In Online Postings Apparently by Detroit Suspect, Religious Ideals Collide." *Washington Post*, December 29.

12. V. Morton (2009), "Awlaki Personally Blessed Detroit Attack." *Washington Times*, December 29.

13. Cited in E. Schmidt and E. Lipton (2010), "Focus on Imams as Recruiters for Al Qaeda." *New York Times*, January 1.

14. Cartoon by P. Steiner (1993), *New Yorker*, July 5, p. 61.

15. See C. Dickey (2009), *The Shadowland Journal*, October 1, christopherdickey.blogspot.com/2009/10/warning-very-graphic-video-of-bombing.html.

16. See F. Laporta (2007), "Sobre la pervivencia del terror." *El País*, July 2.

17. F. Khosrokhavar (2004), *L'Islam dans les prisons*. Paris: Balland.

18. Pew Research Center Survey (2007), *Muslims in America: Middle Class and Mostly Mainstream*, May 22. http://pewresearch.org/assets/pdf/muslim-americans.pdf.

19. Ibid.

20. ABC News (2005), "Terror Plot Hatched in California Prison: Authorities Thwart Attack Intended for Next Month," August 16. http://abcnews.go.com/WNT/Investigation/story?id=1042853.

21. Author interviews with FBI personnel, April 2007.

22. E. Lichtblau, D. Johnston, and R. Nixon (2008), "F.B.I. Struggles to Handle Wave of Financial Fraud Cases." *New York Times*, October 19.

23. CNN (2009), Discussions and interviews on *State of the Union with John King*, March 5.

24. D. Johnston and N. Lewis (2009), "President to Maintain Agencies' Terrorism Focus." *International Herald Tribune*, March 25.

25. S. Atran (2010), "Pathways to and from Violence: Testimony before the Senate Armed Services Subcommittee on Emerging Threats and Capabilities," March 10, http://armed-services.senate.gov/statement/2010/03%20March/Atran%2003-10-10.pdf.

26. For a particularly insightful critique of the foolishness of much formal-

ization in economics, see N. Nicholas Taleb (2007), *Black Swans: The Impact of the Highly Improbable*. New York: Random House.

27. S. Page (2007), *The Difference: How the Power of Diversity Creates Better Groups, Firms, Schools, and Societies*. Princeton: Princeton University Press.

28. S. Begley (2008), "Coddling Human Guinea Pigs." *Newsweek*, August 9, www.newsweek.com/id/151756.

29. R. Lifton (2000), *The Nazi Doctors: Medical Killing and the Psychology of Genocide*. New York: Basic Books.

30. S. Atran (2007), "Research Police: How a University IRB Thwarts Understanding of Terrorism." *Institutional Review Blog*, May 28. www.institutionalreviewblog.com/2007/05/scott-atran-research-police-how.html.

31. O. Nasiri (2006), *Inside Jihad: My Life with Al Qaeda*. New York: Perseus Books.

CHAPTER 17: ALL IN THE FAMILY

1. Cited in R. Wright (2000), *Nonzero: The Logic of Human Destiny*. New York: Random House, p. 208.

2. C. Lévi-Straus (1966), *The Savage Mind*. Chicago: University of Chicago Press.

3. M. Brewer (1979), "Ingroup Bias in the Minimal Situation: A Cognitive-Motivational Analysis," *Psychological Bulletin* 86:307–24; T. Ostrom and C. Sedkides (1992), "The Outgroup Homogeneity Effect in Natural and Minimal Groups." *Psychological Bulletin* 112:536–52.

4. S. Fiske (2002), "What We Know About Bias and Intergroup Conflict, the Problem of the Century." *Current Directions in Psychological Science* 11:123–28.

5. Y. Jah, Sister Shah'keyah (1995), *Uprising: Crips and Bloods Tell the Story of America's Youth in the Crossfire*. New York: Scribner.

6. F. Manjoo (2008), *True Enough: Learning to Live in a Post-fact Society*. New York: Wiley.

7. S. Bowles (2006), "Group Competition, Reproductive Leveling, and the Evolution of Human Altruism." *Science* 314:1569–72, supporting online materials.

8. L. Keeley (1996), *War Before Civilization: The Myth of the Peaceful Savage*. New York: Oxford University Press; S. LeBlanc and K. Register (2003), *Constant Battles: The Myth of the Peaceful, Noble Savage*. London: St. Martin's Press.

9. S. Bowles (2006). "Parochial Altruism." *Science* 314:1569–72.

10. C. Darwin (1958), *The Voyage of the* Beagle. New York: Bantam.

11. C. Darwin (1859), *On the Origins of Species by Means of Natural Selection.* London: John Murray, p. 210.

12. C. Moskos (1980), "Surviving the War in Vietnam." In C. Figley and S. Leventman (eds.), *Stranger at Home: Vietnam Veterans Since the War.* New York: Praeger.

13. C. Darwin (1871), *The Descent of Man, and Selection in Relation to Sex.* London: John Murray, pp. 163–65.

14. Ibid., p. 166.

15. A. R. Wallace (1899), *Darwinism.* London: Macmillan, pp. 475–76.

16. C. Darwin (1903), *More Letters of Charles Darwin.* London: John Murray, vol. 2, p. 39.

17. W. Hamilton (1964), "The Genetical Evolution of Social Behaviour." *Journal of Theoretical Biology* 7:1–52.

18. R. Dawkins (1976), *The Selfish Gene.* New York: Oxford University Press.

19. S. Atran (1985), "Managing Arab Kinship and Marriage." *Social Science Information* 24:659–96.

20. J. Tooby and L. Cosmides (1989), "Evolutionary Psychology and the Generation of Culture, part I, Theoretical Considerations." *Ethology and Sociobiology* 10:29–49.

21. R. Nesse (1999), "The Evolution of Commitment and the Origins of Religion." *Science and Spirit* 10:32–33, 46.

22. G. P. Murdock (1934), *Our Primitive Contemporaries.* New York: Macmillan.

23. W. Robertson Smith (1891; 1972), *The Religion of the Semites.* New York: Schocken, p. 44, n. 2.

24. B. Anderson (1991), *The Imagined Communities.* New York: Verso.

25. G. Johnson (1987), "In the Name of the Fatherland: An Analysis of Kin Term Usage in Patriotic Speech and Literature." *International Political Science Review* 8:165–74.

26. D. Rhode and C. J. Chivers (2002), "Qaeda's Grocery Lists and Manuals of Killing." *New York Times*, March 17.

27. U.S. Congresswoman Nancy Pelosi (2006), cited in Online NewsHour, March 30.

28. Cited in R. Wright (2000), *Nonzero: The Logic of Human Destiny*, New York: Vintage, p. 101.

29. D. Medin, A. Ortony (1989), "Psychological Essentialism." In S. Vosniadou and A. Ortony (eds.), *Similarity and Analogical Reasoning.* New York: Cambridge University Press.

30. L. Hirschfeld (1996), *Race in the Making: Cogntion, Culture, and the*

Child's Construction of Human Kinds. Cambridge, MA: MIT Press.

31. S. Atran and D. Medin (2008), *The Native Mind and the Cultural Construction of Nature.* Cambridge, MA: MIT Press.

32. S. Atran (1998), "Folk Biology and the Anthropology of Science: Cognitive Universals and Cultural Particulars." *Behavioral and Brain Sciences* 21:554–609.

33. C. Darwin, *On the Origin of Species.*

34. S. Gelman and L. Hirschfeld (2008), "How Biological Is Essentialism?" In D. Medin and S. Atran (eds.), *Folkbiology,* Cambridge, MA: MIT Press.

35. S. Atran, J. Magouirk, and J. Ginges (2008), "Radical Madrassahs in Southeast Asia." *CTC Sentinel* (Combating Terrorism Center, West Point) 1 (3).

36. I. Hacking (1995), "The Looping Effect of Human Kinds." In D. Sperber, D. Premack, A. Premack (eds.), *Causal Cognition.* New York: Oxford University Press.

37. K. Lorenz (1963), Presentation to the British Institute of Biology Symposium, The Natural History of Aggression, October.

38. B. Wong (2006), *The Chinese in Silicon Valley: Globalization, Social Networks and Ethnic Identity.* Boulder, CO: Rowman & Littlefield.

39. M. Sageman (2004), *Understanding Terror Networks.* Philadelphia: University of Pennsylvania Press.

40. I. Silk (2003), "Cooperation Without Counting: The Puzzle of Friendship." In P. Hammerstein (ed.), *Genetic and Cultural Evolution of Cooperation.* Cambridge, MA: MIT Press.

41. R. Milardo (1992), "Comparative Methods for Delineating Social Networks." *Social and Personal Relationships* 9:447–61.

42. R. Dunbar (1998), "The Social Brain Hypothesis." *Evolutionary Anthropology* 6:178–90.

43. D. Hruschka and J. Henrich (2006), "Friendship, Cliquishness, and the Emergence of Cooperation." *Journal of Theoretical Biology* 239:1–15.

44. N. Machiavelli (1531; 1950), *The Prince and the Discourses.* New York: Modern Library, ch. 18.

45. R. Byrne and A. Whiten (1998), *Machiavellian Intelligence: Social Expertise and the Evolution of Intellect in Monkeys, Apes, and Humans.* Oxford: Oxford University Press.

46. K. Sterelny (2007), "Social Intelligence, Human Intelligence, and Niche Construction." *Philosophical Transactions of the Royal Society* 362:719–30.

47. Sun Tzu (c. 500 B.C.; 1910), *The Art of War,* www.kimsoft.com/polwar.htm.

48. Prince Harry of Wales (2008), cited in BBC News, March 2.

49. M. Taylor and A. Gillan (2009), "Racist Slur or Army Banter? What the Soldiers Say." *Guardian*, January 13. www.guardian.co.uk/uk/2009/jan/13/military-prince-harry-race-issues.

CHAPTER 18: BLOOD SPORT

1. M. van Creveld (2008), *The Culture of War.* New York: Ballantine Books.
2. Freikorps leader E. von Salomon, cited in T. Segev (1987), *Soldiers of Evil: The Commandants of the Nazi Concentration Camps*, New York: McGraw-Hill, pp. 65–66.
3. B. Ehrenreich (1997), *Blood Rites: Origins and History of the Passions of War.* New York: Henry Holt.
4. W. Robertson Smith (1894), *Lectures on the Religion of the Semites.* London: A. & C. Black.
5. H. E. Davidson (1988), *Myths and Symbols in Pagan Europe: Early Scandinavian and Celtic Religions.* Syracuse, NY: Syracuse University Press.
6. C. Holden (2000), "Cannibalism: Molecule Shows Anasazi Ate Their Enemies." *Science* 289:1663.
7. Cited in L. Spier (1933), *Yuman Tribes of the Gilga River.* Chicago: University of Chicago Press, p. 175.
8. I. Clendinnen (1991), *Aztecs.* Cambridge: Cambridge University Press.
9. R. Law (1985), "Human Sacrifice in Pre-colonial West Africa." *African Affairs* 84:53–87.
10. S. Mekhenet and N. Kulish (2009), "Uncovering the Lost Path of the Most Wanted Nazi." *New York Times*, February 4.
11. BBC News (2003), "UN Condemns DR Congo Cannibalism." news.bbc.co.uk/2/hi/africa/2661365.stm; Isango, E. (2005), "Cannibalism Shock as Atrocities Revealed," theage.com, March 18.
12. R. Ngowi (2003), "Congo Rebels Accused of Cannibalism." Associated Press, May 19.
13. BBC News (2008), "'Suicide Videos': What They Said." April 4. http://news.bbc.co.uk/2/hi/uk_news/7330367.stm.
14. U.S. Senate Armed Services Committee (2008), Committee Hearing, June 17, supporting documents, *Counter Resistance Strategy Minutes* (pages 2–3 of 5) 13:40, Oct 2, 2002, p. 15. http://levin.senate.gov/newsroom/supporting/2008/Documents.SASC.061708.pdf.
15. A. Smith (1993), *An Inquiry into the Nature and Causes of the Wealth of Nations.* New York: Oxford University Press, bk. 5, pt. 1, ch. 1.
16. B. Mussolini (1932), "La dottrina del fascismo." *Enciclopedia Italiana*, vol. 14. Rome: Ardita.

17. J. McPherson (1997), *For Cause and Comrades: Why Men Fought in the Civil War*. New York: Oxford University Press, p. 85.

18. W. Faulkner (1948; 1972), *Intruder in the Dust*. New York: Vintage, pp. 194–95.

19. R. Lowie (1954), *Indians of the Plains*. New York: McGraw-Hill.

20. H. Turney-High (1949), *Primitive War: Its Practice and Its Concepts*. Columbia: University of South Carolina Press, p. 145.

21. S. Atran (2002), *In Gods We Trust: The Evolutionary Landscape of Religion*. New York: Oxford University Press.

22. M. Wilson and M. Daley (1988), *Homicide*. New York: Aldine de Gruyter; D. Buss (2005), *The Murderer Next Door: Why the Mind Is Designed to Kill*, New York: Penguin.

23. Crime in the United States, 1986–2005. www.fbi.gov/ucr/05cius/data/table_01.html.

24. L. Hellmuth (2000), "Has America's Tide of Violence Receded for Good?" *Science* 289:582–585.

25. M. Van Vugt, D. De Cremer, and D. Janssen (2007), "Gender Differences in Cooperation and Competition: The Male-Warrior Hypothesis." *Psychological Science* 18:19–23.

26. Data provided by the Combating Terrorism Center, West Point.

27. Presented at the Riyadh Meeting on Terrorism, Security Forces Officers Club, January 25–28, 2008.

28. L. O'Rourke (2008), "Behind the Woman Behind the Bomb." *New York Times*, August 2.

29. M. Wilson and M. Daley, *Homicide*; D. Buss, *The Murderer Next Door*.

30. A. Speckhard (2005), *Chechen Russian Uzbek Suicide Terrorism Study, Interim Report*, Brussels: NATO.

31. P. Pan (2010), "One Moscow Suicide Bomber Was Teenage Widow of Islamist Rebel," *Washington Post*, April 3.

32. M. Sageman, *Understanding Terror Networks*.

33. S. Bowles (2006), "Group Competition, Reproductive Leveling, and the Evolution of Human Altruism." *Science* 314:1569–72, supporting online materials.

34. L. Keeley (1996), *War Before Civilization: The Myth of the Peaceful Savage*. New York: Oxford University Press, p. 93.

35. S. Pinker (2007), "A History of Violence." *New Republic*, March 19.

36. I. Arreguín-Toft (2001), "How the Weak Win Wars: A Theory of Asymmetric Conflicts." *International Security* 26:93–128.

37. L. Richardson (1960), *Statistics of Deadly Quarrels*. Pittsburgh: Boxwood Press.

38. See R. Axelrod and M. Cohen (2001), *Harnessing Complexity*. New York: Basic Books.

39. B. Fischhoff, S. Atran, and M. Sageman (2008). "Mutually Assured Support: A Security Doctrine for Terrorist Nuclear Weapons Threats." *Annals of the American Academy of Political and Social Science*, special issue, *Terrorism Briefing for the New President* 618:160–67.

40. J. Romains (1923; 1972), *Knock, ou, le triomphe de la médecine*, Paris: Gallimard.

CHAPTER 19: BEYOND ALL REASON

1. J. Keegan (1994), *A History of Warfare*. New York: Alfred A. Knopf.

2. C. von Clausewitz (1903), *On War*. London, p. 23.

3. R. Smith (1983), "Why Soldiers Fight: Part 1, Leadership, Cohesion, and Fighter Spirit." *Quality and Quantity* 18:1–32.

4. S. Stouffer et al. (1949), *Studies in Social Psychology in World War II*, vol. 2, *The American Soldier: Combat and Its Aftermath*. Princeton: Princeton University Press (see especially the chapter titled "The General Characteristics of Ground Combat").

5. R. Smith (1983), "Why Soldiers Fight: Part 2, Alternative Theories." *Quality and Quantity* 18:33–58.

6. J. McManus (2003), *The Deadly Brotherhood: The American Combat Soldier in World War II*. New York: Presidio Press.

7. W. Manchester (1988), *Goodbye Darkness: A Memoir of the Pacific War*. New York: Random House, p. 451.

8. J. McPherson (1997), *For Cause and Comrades: Why Men Fought in the Civil War*. New York: Oxford University Press, pp. 85, 87.

9. SS member J. Hassebroeack, cited in T. Segev (1987), *Soldiers of Evil: The Commandants of the Nazi Concentration Camps*. New York: McGraw Hill, pp. 89–90.

10. S. Fritz (1995), *Frontsoldaten: The German Soldier in World War II*. Lexington: University Press of Kentucky, p. 24.

11. *Le Monde*, December 19, 1944, p. 2; see also C. Ailsby (1998), *Hell on the Eastern Front: The Waffen SS War in Russia, 1941–1945*. Osceola, WI: Zenith Press.

12. T. Kühne (2006), *Kameradschaft: Die Soldaten des nationalsozialistischen und das 20 Jahrhundert*, vol. 173 of *Kritische Studien zur Geschichtwissenschaft*. Göttingen: Vandenhoeck & Ruprecht.

13. Ibid.

14. C. Moskos (1975), "The American Combat Soldier in Vietnam." *Journal of Social Issues* 3:25–37.

15. C. Moskos (1970), *The American Enlisted Man: The Rank and File in Today's Military*. New York: Russell Sage Foundation, p. 148; R. Spector (1994), *After Tet: The Bloodiest Year in Vietnam*. New York: Vintage, p. 71.

16. J. McPherson (1997), *For Cause and Comrades*, pp. 91–92.

17. Ibid., p. 62.

18. J. Dollard (1944), *Fear in Battle*. Washington, DC: Infantry Journal, pp. 40–41.

19. R. V. Jones (1978), *The Wizard War: British Scientific Intelligence, 1939–1945*. London: Coward, McCann & Geoghegan, pp. 181–82.

20. G. Allison and P. Zelikow (1999), *Essence of Decision: Explaining the Cuban Missile Crisis*, 2nd. ed. New York: Longman.

21. J. Gaddis (1995), *Strategies of Containment: A Critical Appraisal of Postwar National Security*, rev. ed. New York: Oxford University Press.

22. J. Madsen (2004), "The Rationale of Suicide Attack." *Risq* online, September, www.risq.org/modules.php?name=News&file=print&sid=367.

23. J. Ginges and S. Atran (2009), "What Motivates Participation in Violent Political Action: Selective Incentives or Parochial Altruism?" *Annals of the New York Academy of Science* 1167:115–23.

24. D. Weisburd (1989), *Jewish Settler Violence: Deviance as Social Reaction*. University Park and London: Pennsylvania State University Press.

25. C. Lim and J. Baron (1997), "Protected Values in Malaysia, Singapore, and the United States." Department of Psychology, University of Pennsylvania. www.sas.upenn.edu/~baron/lim.htm.

26. W. Hamilton (1964), "The Genetical Evolution of Social Behavior." *Journal of Theoretical Biology* 7:1–52.

27. É. Durkheim (1912; 1995), *The Elementary Forms of Religious Life*. New York: Macmillan.

28. M. Hauser (2006), *Moral Minds: How Nature Designed Our Universal Sense of Right and Wrong*. New York: Ecco.

29. M. Harris (1966), "Cultural Ecology of India's Sacred Cattle." *Current Anthropology* 7:261–76.

30. S. Atran, D. Medin, and N. Ross (2005), "The Cultural Mind: Environmental Decision Making and Cultural Modeling Within and Across Populations." *Psychological Review* 112:744–76.

31. R. Axelrod and W. Hamilton (1981). "The Evolution of Cooperation." *Science* 211: 1390–96.

32. R. Nisbett and D. Cohen (1996), *The Culture of Honor*. Boulder, CO: Westview Press.

33. L. Havemeyer (1929), *Ethnography*. Boston: Ginn & Co.

34. E. Peters (1967), "Some Structural Aspects of the Feud Among the Camel Herding Bedouin of Cyrenaica." *Africa* 37: 261–62.

35. M. Bowden (2000), *Black Hawk Down: A Study of Modern War*. London: Penguin.

36. A. Sadat (1977), *In Search of Identity: An Autobiography*. New York: Harper & Row, p. 304.

37. Osama Hamdan (2006), Interview with S. Atran, Damascus, Syria, February 26.

CHAPTER 20: MARTYRDOM 101

1. In the second half of 2008, Israel began to lift some roadblocks, thanks in large part to the efforts of Israel's former brigadier general Dov "Fufi" Sedaka, who once administered the occupied territories. But the physical infrastructure of the main checkpoints remains, such as barbed wire fences and concrete gun emplacements, and the psychological effects of the checkpoints are still strong. In 2010, people were still wary about returning to family homes outside of the cities for fear that the roadblocks will reappear; and they tend not to go to schools or contract for goods beyond the roadblocks that remain fresh in their memory. (The overwhelming loss in trade and income still owes to the closing of the borders with Israel.)

2. J. Ginges and S. Atran (2008), "Humiliation and the Inertia Effect: Implications for Understanding Violence and Compromise in Intractable Intergroup Conflicts." *Journal of Cognition and Culture* 8:281–94.

3. B. Saleh (2004), "Economic Conditions and Resistance to Occupation in the West Bank and Gaza Strip: There Is a Causal Connection." Paper presented to the Graduate Student Forum, Kansas State University, April 4.

4. C. Berrebi (2007), "Evidence About the Link Between Education, Poverty, and Terrorism Among Palestinians." *Peace Economics, Peace Science and Public Policy* 13 (1), www.bepress.com/peps/vol13/iss1/2.

5. M. Sageman (2004), *Understanding Terror Networks*. Philadelphia: University of Pennsylvania Press.

6. Pew Center on the States (2008), "One in a Hundred: Behind Bars in America in 2008." www.pewcenteronthestates.org/uploadedFiles/One%20in%20100(3).pdf; M. Pfeiffer (2007), *Crazy in America: The Hidden Tragedy of the Criminalized Mentally Ill*. New York: Carroll & Graf.

7. S. Atran (2006), "Is Hamas Ready to Deal?" *New York Times*, August 17.

CHAPTER 21: WORDS TO END WARS

1. L. Baker (2009), "Israel Rejects Suggestions of Gaza 'War Crimes.'" Reuters news service, January 17. www.reuters.com/article/latestCrisis/idUSLH286481.

2. The Communist Chinese conquest of Tibet is half an exception, as Tibet has intermittently been part of China over the centuries. But continued resistance in Tibet, and partial world support for it, suggests the matter still isn't settled.

3. R. McCarthy (2009), "Hamas's Rhetoric of Resistance Masks New Stance After Gaza War." *Guardian*, December 28. www.guardian.co.uk/world/2009/dec/28/hamas-birthday-celebrations.

4. J. Ginges, S. Atran, D. Medin, and K. Shikaki (2007), "Sacred Bounds on Rational Resolution of Violent Political Conflict." *Proceedings of the National Academy of Sciences* 104:7357–60; S. Atran, R. Axelrod, and R. Davis (2007), "Sacred Barriers to Conflict Resolution." *Science* 317:1039–40.

5. J. Ginges and S. Atran, (2009), "Noninstrumental Reasoning over Sacred Values: An Indonesian Case Study." In D. Ross, D. Bartels, C. Bauman, L. Skitka, and D. Medin (eds.), *Psychology of Learning and Motivation,* vol. 50, *Moral Judgment and Decision Making.* San Diego: Academic Press.

6. In March 2009, I mentioned to then Israeli foreign minister Tzipi Livni that leaders in Gaza had said to me, "Sharon gave us [Hamas] Gaza by humiliating Abu Mazen [Palestinian Authority President Mahmoud Abbas] and not even giving him a fig leaf of credit for Israel leaving." Livni responded: "Yes, I told Sharon at the time that we should have made a symbolic gesture to Abbas, like giving him the keys to Gaza City when we withdrew. I don't know if Abbas would have accepted the keys to Gaza, or anything from Israel, but it was a mistake not to have made a symbolic gesture to him."

7. In March 2009, during conversations between a delegation from the World Federation of Scientists and Hamas leaders, Ahmed Yusef, political adviser to the leadership in Gaza, praised President Obama for a recent public gesture of friendship and respect to the Iranian people. Yusef stressed that similar "symbolic gestures" could break ground for talks between parties in the Middle East conflict, including Hamas—an idea that Yusef said he passed on in a letter to Obama through Senator John Kerry. When a member of the WFS delegation asked Yusef how this interest in symbolic gestures came about, Yusef referred to our work.

8. Ibid.

9. S. Sachdeva and D. Medin (2009), "Group Identity Salience in Sacred Value Based Cultural Conflicts: An Examination of Hindu-Muslim Identities in the Kashmir and Babri Mosque Issues." In *Proceedings of the 31st Annual Conference of the Cognitive Science Society (CogSci)*, Amsterdam.

10. M. Dehghani, R. Iliev, S. Sachdeva, S. Atran, J. Ginges, and D. Medin (2009), "Emerging Sacred Values: The Iranian Nuclear Program." *Judgment and Decision Making* 4:550–53.

11. R. Cohen (2009), "The U.S.-Iran Triangle." *New York Times*, September 28.

12. H. Jaseb and F. Dahl (2009), "Iran Signals No Compromise on Nuclear Issue," Reuters, September 12, www.reuters.com/article/idUSLA38110920090912.

13. S. Begley (2010), "When Nukes Become Sacred." *Newsweek*, January 8. www.newsweek.com/id/229865.

14. S. Atran (2009), "To Beat Al Qaeda, Look to the East." *New York Times*, December 13.

15. S. Atran and A. Norenzayan (2004), "Religion's Evolutionary Landscape." *Behavioral and Brain Sciences* 27: 713–70.

16. Conversation with S. Atran, Security Forces Officers Club, Riyadh, February 23, 2008.

17. S. Atran (2006), "Is Hamas Ready to Deal?" *New York Times*, August 17.

18. S. Atran, R. Axelrod, and R. Davis (2007), "Give Palestine's Unity Government a Chance." Huffington Post, March 7. www.huffingtonpost.com/scott-atran-robert-axelrod-and-richard-davis/give-palestines-unity-go_b_42882.html.

19. S. Atran (1989), "The Surrogate Colonization of Palestine, 1917–1939." *American Ethnologist* 16:716–44.

20. Fateh Constitution (1964). web.archive.org/web/20070607150221/www.fateh.net/e_public/constitution.htm.

21. The expression "a land without people for a people without land" was first popularized by Israel Zangwill a century ago. Zangwill's point was that Palestine's Arab population was not then a distinct nationality, not that there were no persons living there.

22. J. Alderdice (2007), Interview with Scott Atran at Fifth Meeting, Permanent Monitoring Panel on Terrorism, World Federation of Scientists, Erice, Italy, May 1.

23. R. Eckstein (1993), "Ping-Pong Diplomacy: A View from Behind the Scenes." *Journal of American–East Asian Relations* 2:327–40.

24. R. Khouri (2007), "A Different History Lesson." *International Herald Tribune*, August 3.

25. I. Lustick (2006), "Negotiating Truth: The Holocaust, *Lehavdil*, and *al-Nakba*." *Journal of International Affairs* 60:51–80.

26. In the mid-1990s, Isaac Ben Israel led a team that contracted with the Chinese to sell American AWACS (spy plane) technology for about half a billion dollars. But toward the end of Bill Clinton's tenure, under pressure from Congress, the United States insisted that Israel cancel the deal. The Chinese were furious. They demanded that the Israelis pay them back, plus $2.5 billion for breach of contract—five times the original value of the agreement—or China would never deal with Israel again. "You know we had offers to help the Syrians and the Iranians on their weapons systems, but we thought you were our friend," Ben Israel recalls the Chinese as saying. Ben Israel asked then–prime minister Ehud Barak what to do. Barak told him: "Do anything except pay the 2.5 billion, because we don't have it." So Ben Israel went to Singapore, which has close relations with Israel, because Singapore's leaders know the Chinese well. "It's a matter of respect," said the Singaporeans, "of not losing face. You must apologize and mean it; say it was entirely your fault and that those involved on the Chinese side were wronged. Then they may be much more willing to come to a mutually acceptable compromise." Ben Israel reported back to Barak, who called in his advisers. Lawyers from the Israeli Ministry of Justice adamantly advised against making any such apology, for fear that Israel would be setting itself up for endless lawsuits. "Well, what do you think?" Barak asked Ben Israel. Ben Israel answered that Israel should apologize, which Israel did, and the Chinese settled for $25 million from Israel as a token of contrition—1 percent of the original sum demanded.

27. A. Gresh (2001), "The Middle East: How the Peace Was Lost." *Le Monde diplomatique*, English language edition, September. http://mondediplo.com/2001/09/01middleeastleader.

28. I. Lustick, "Negotiating Truth."

29. People's Daily Online (2006), "Japan PM's Shrine Visit Sparks Anger in China." August 16.

30. N. Onishi (2007), "Japan's 'Atonement' to Former Sex Slaves Stirs Anger." *New York Times*, April 25.

31. J. Garromone (2004), "Rumsfeld Accepts Responsibility for Abu Ghraib." American Foreign Press Service, May 7.

32. E. Barkan (2006), "The Worst Is Yet to Come: Abu Ghraib and the Politics of Not Apologizing." In E. Barkan and A. Karn (eds.), *Taking Wrongs Seriously: Apologies and Reconciliation*. Stanford, CA: Stanford University Press.

33. International Committee of the Red Cross (2007), *ICRC Report on the*

Treatment of Fourteen "High Value Detainees" in CIA Custody. February, www.nybooks.com/icrc-report.pdf.

34. U.S. Senate Armed Services Committee (2008), Statement of Lt. Colonel (Ret.) Diane E. Beaver, June 17. http://armed-services.senate.gov/statemnt/2008/June/Beaver%2006-17-08.pdf.

35. J. Dower (1999), *Embracing Defeat: Japan in the Wake of World War II.* New York: W. W. Norton.

36. Interview with Dominique de Villepin (2005), "Il n'y a de communauté que nationale." *La Vie* (Paris), no. 314, February 24, p. 16.

37. O. Roy (2004), *Globalized Islam.* New York: Columbia University Press.

38. G. Allison and P. Zelikow (1999), *Essence of Decision: Explaining the Cuban Missile Crisis,* 2nd ed. New York: Longman.

39. J. Gaddis (1995), *Strategies of Containment.*

40. S. Atran (2006), "The Moral Logic of Suicide Terrorism." *Washington Quarterly* 29:127–47.

41. B. Hoffman and G. McCormick (2004), "Terrorism, Signaling, and Suicide Attack." *Studies in Conflict and Terrorism* 27:243–81.

42. T. Schelling (1960), *The Strategy of Conflict.* Cambridge, MA: Harvard University Press.

43. J. March and J. Olsen (1989), *Rediscovering Institutions: The Organizational Basis of Politics.* New York: Free Press.

44. R. Davis (2007), interview with S. Atran, Washington, DC, March 28.

45. A. Varshney (2003), "Nationalism, Ethnic Conflict and Rationality." *Perspectives on Politics* 1: 85–99.

46. R. Goodin (1980), "Making Moral Incentives Pay." *Policy Sciences* 12: 131–45.

47. ABCNewsOnline (2007), "Ahmadinejad Under Fire for Embracing His Teacher," ABC News online, May 2. www.abc.net.au/news/news-items/200705/s1912815.htm.

48. A. Hoffman, J. Gillespie, D. Moore, K. Wade-Benzoni, L. Thompson, and M. Bazerman (1999), "A Mixed-Motive Perspective on the Economics Versus Environmental Debate." *American Behavioral Scientist* 42:1254–76.

49. P. Tetlock (2003), "Thinking the Unthinkable: Sacred Values and Taboo Cognitions." *Trends in Cognitive Science* 7:320–24.

50. F. Lazarus (1999), *Black Hills, White Justice: The Sioux Nation Versus the United States, 1775 to the Present.* Lincoln: University of Nebraska Press.

51. S. Roberts (2005), "Revisiting a Killing Field in Poland." *New York Times,* November 4.

52. In an experiment, psychologist Douglas Medin asked people if they

would leave him their wedding ring so that he could have a jeweler make an exact material copy, and then they could choose either the original or the copy (without being told which is which) plus a significant cash bonus. In the experiment, which we've replicated, most people refuse the bargain. Those who trade are usually in the process of getting a divorce or are foreign spouses of Americans from cultures in which rings are not symbols of the sanctity of marriage.

53. J. Baron and M. Spranca (1997), "Protected Values." *Organizational Behavioral and Human Decision Processes* 70:1–16.

CHAPTER 22: BAD FAITH

1. S. Harris (2004), *The End of Faith: Religion, Terrorism, and the Future of Reason*. New York: W. W. Norton.

2. D. Dennett (2005), *Breaking the Spell: Religion as a Natural Phenomenon*. New York: Viking Adult.

3. C. Hitchens (2007), *God Is Not Great: How Religion Poisons Everything*. New York: Twelve.

4. R. Dawkins (2006), *The God Delusion*. New York: Houghton Mifflin.

5. S. Atran (2003), "Genesis of Suicide Terrorism." *Science* 199:1534–39, supplementary online materials.

6. S. Harris (2006), *Letter to a Christian Nation*. New York: Alfred A. Knopf, pp. 44, 52.

7. M. Sageman (2008), *Leaderless Jihad*. Philadelphia: University of Pennsylvania Press.

8. As Stalin reportedly said when warned of Catholic opposition to his power lust: "How many divisions does the Pope have?" Now, one could argue, with some reason, that communism and other forms of evangelical atheism are really religions after all: dogmatic in their belief in the transcendent forces and direction of human history, and often mercilessly cruel to sinners who refuse to see the light. One could then simply redefine "atheist" as "non-dogmatic" so as to exclude the obvious counterexamples, as the Four Horsemen do. For example, the Horsemen claim that Hitler was raised and remained Catholic. But as the diaries of his equally "Catholic" culture and propaganda minister, Josef Goebbels, indicate, Nazi leaders saw themselves as "apostates" motivated by "anti-Semitism [as] the focal point of our spiritual struggle." As for the Church, wrote Goebbels: "It is clear nonsense for a spiritual and ecclesiastical power to meddle so much in political and military questions." At the end of the war, after elimination of the Jews, "we shall see to it that . . . such attempts at interference are rendered impossible." (J. Goebbels

[1948], *The Goebbels Diaries, 1942–1943*. New York: Doubleday, pp. 8, 166, 359.)

9. C. Phillips and A. Axelrod (2004), *Encyclopedia of Wars*. New York: Facts on File.

10. F. Roes and M. Raymond (2003), "Belief in Moralizing Gods." *Evolution* and *Human Behavior* 24:126–35.

11. M. Welch, D. Sikkink, E. Sartain, and C. Bond (2004), "Trust in God and Trust in Man: The Ambivalent Role of Religion in Shaping Dimensions of Social Trust." *Journal for the Scientific Study of Religion* 43:317–43.

12. Pew Global Attitudes Project (2002), "Among Wealthy Nations . . . U.S. Stands Alone in Its Embrace of Religion." December 19. http://pewglobal. org/reports/display.php?ReportID=167.

13. M. Lacey (2004), "Ten Years After Horror, Rwandans Turn to Islam." *New York Times*, April 7.

14. D. Gambetta and S. Hertog (2007), "Engineers of Jihad." Sociology Working Papers, no. 2007-10. www.nuff.ox.ac.uk/users/gambetta/Engineers %20of%20Jihad.pdf.

15. M. Sageman (2004), *Understanding Terror Networks*. Philadelphia: University of Pennsylvania Press.

16. P. Bergen and M. Lind (2007), "A Matter of Pride: Why We Can't Buy Off Osama Bin Laden." *Democracy Journal*, no. 3, winter. www .democracyjournal.org/article.php?ID=6496.

17. A. Norenzayan and I. Hansen (2009), "Does Religion Promote Scapegoating?" Unpublished manuscript.

18. S. Harris (2006), Edge discussion, "Beyond Belief: Science, Religion, Reason and Survival." Salk Institute, La Jolla, November 5–7. www .edge.org/discourse/bb.html#harris.

19. R. Dawkins, *The God Delusion*. pp. 172–90.

20. See, for example, L. Hirschfeld (1996), *Race in the Making*.

21. M. Breckford and U. Khan (2008), "Harry Potter Fails to Cast Spell over Professor Dawkins." *Telegraph*, October 21. www.telegraph.co.uk/ news/3255972/Harry-Potter-fails-to-cast-spell-over-Professor-Richard-Dawkins.html.

22. C. S. Lewis (1952), "On Three Ways of Writing for Children." http://209.85.229.132/search?q=cache:gW4qFbT_4LQJ:campus .huntington.edu/dma/leeper/DM101/Readings/On%2520Three%2520 Ways%2520of%2520Writing%2520for%2520Children.rtf+On+three+ ways+of+writing+for+children&hl=en&ct=clnk&cd=1&lr=lang_en.

23. This is something of a rehash of the logical empiricist and positivist philosophies popular in America and Britain in the first half of the twentieth century.

24. C. Hitchens, *God Is Not Great*. p. 64.

25. A. Gore (1999), cited in the Drudge Report, May 28.

26. S. Atran (2007), Comments on P. Davies, "Taking Science on Faith." Edge.com. www.edge.org/discourse/science_faith.html.

27. S. Harris, *The End of Faith*.

28. L. Hunt (2007), *Inventing Human Rights: A History*. New York: W. W. Norton.

29. This doesn't apply to Dan Dennett, who treats the science of religion in a serious way. Dan believes that universal education should include instruction in the history of religion and a survey of contemporary religious beliefs. Once out in the open for everyone to examine, science can better beat religion in open competition. My own guess is that it won't work out that way, any more than logic winning out over passion or perfume in the competition for a mate.

30. D. Sperber (1996), *Explaining Culture: A Naturalistic Approach*. Cambridge: Cambridge University Press; S. Atran and D. Medin (2008), *The Native Mind and the Cultural Construction of Nature*. Cambridge, MA: MIT Press.

31. S. Atran (2001), "The Trouble with Memes." *Human Nature* 12:351–81.

32. Dennett seems to grant as much, but argues that defenders of religion can't only claim the good part of the cake; they must take moral responsibility of all for it, including the bad. The same, of course, could be said for how science is used, as in Zyklon-B, Hiroshima, Agent Orange, or cluster bombs. Some will say that "real" science is concerned only with knowledge, and not how it's put to use, yet also claim for science the benefits, say, of electricity or medicine or the future of technologies in improving health and the environment.

33. S. Atran (2002), *In Gods We Trust: The Evolutionary Landscape of Religion*. New York: Oxford University Press.

CHAPTER 23: HUMAN RITES

1. E. Gibbons (1776–1789; 1845), *The Decline and Fall of the Roman Empire*, 6 vols. London: International Book Co.

2. T. Lester (2002), "Supernatural Selection." *Atlantic Monthly*, February 8.

3. J. Salmon (2008), "Most Americans Believe in Higher Power, Poll Finds." *Washington Post*, June 24.

4. European Commission (2005), "Social Values, Science and Technol-

ogy." *Eurobarometer*, 225, Wave 63.1, June. ec.europa.eu/public_opinion/ archives/ebs/ebs_225_report_en.pdf.

5. E. Fehr and U. Fischbacher (2003), "The Nature of Human Altruism." *Nature* 425:785–791.

6. G. Johnson (1987), "In the Name of the Fatherland: An Analysis of Kin Term Usage in Patriotic Speech and Literature." *International Political Science Review* 8:165–74.

7. M. Nowak and K. Sigmund (1998), "Evolution of Indirect Reciprocity by Image Scoring." *Nature* 393:573–77.

8. J. Henrich et al. (2006), "Costly Punishment Across Human Societies." *Science* 312:1767–70.

9. L. Thompson and R. Hastie (1990), "Social Perception in Negotiation." *Organizational Behavior and Human Decision Processes* 47:98–123.

10. J. Bargh and T. Chartland (1999), "The Unbearable Automaticity of Being." *American Psychologist* 54:462–79.

11. A. Norenzayan and A. Shariff (2008), "The Origin and Evolution of Religious Prosociality." *Science* 322:58–62.

12. T. Barfield (2003), *Afghan Customary Law and Its Relationship to Formal Judicial Institutions*. Washington, DC: United States Institute for Peace, p. 12.

13. S. Atran and A. Norenzayan (2004), "Religion's Evolutionary Landscape: Counterintuition, Commitment, Compassion, Communion." *Behavioral and Brain Sciences* 27:713–70.

14. S. Kierkegaard (1843; 1955), *Fear and Trembling and the Sickness unto Death*. New York: Doubleday.

15. R. Firth (1963), "Offering and Sacrifice." *Journal of the Royal Anthropological Institute* 93:12–24.

16. Cited in G. Keillor (1999), "Faith at the Speed of Light," *Time*, June 14.

17. S. Atran (2002), *In Gods We Trust: The Evolutionary Landscape of Religion*. New York: Oxford University Press.

18. S. Atran and J. Henrich (2010), "The Evolution of Religion." *Biological Theory* 5(1).

19. D. Hume (1758; 1955), *An Inquiry Concerning Human Understanding*. New York: Bobbs-Merrill.

20. M. Gazzaniga, R. Ivry, and G. Mangun (1998), *Cognitive Neuroscience: The Biology of the Mind*. New York: W. W. Norton.

21. J. Whitson and A. Galinsky (2008), "Lacking Control Increases Illusory Pattern Perception." *Science* 322:115–17.

22. P. Norris and R. Inglehart (2004), *Sacred and Secular: Religion and Politics Worldwide*. New York: Cambridge University Press.

23. J. Bering (2009), "God's in Mississippi, Where the 'Getting' Is Good." *Scientific American*, October 9. www.scientificamerican.com/blog/post .cfm?id=gods-in-mississippi-where-the-getti–2009–10–09.

24. P. Robertson (2010), CBN broadcast, January 13. www.politico.com/ blogs/bensmith/0110/Robertson_Haiti_cursed_since_Satanic_pact .html?showall.

25. I. Pyysiäinen (2003), "Buddhism, Religion, and the Concept of 'God.'" *Numen* 50:147–71.

26. D. Kapoggianis et al. (2009), "Cognitive and Neural Foundations of Religious Belief." *Proceedings of the National Academy of Sciences, USA* 106:4876–81.

27. S. Guthrie (1993), *Faces in the Clouds: A New Theory of Religion*. New York: Oxford University Press.

28. D. Sperber (1996), *Explaining Culture*.

29. *Philadelphia Daily News* (2001), "Bedeviling: Did Satan Rear His Ugly Face?" September 14.

30. P. Bloom and C. Veres (1999), "The Perceived Intentionality of Groups." *Cognition* 71:B1–B9.

31. F. Heider and M. Simmel (1944), "An Experimental Study of Apparent Behavior." *American Journal of Psychology* 57:243–49.

32. D. Keleman (2004), "Are Children 'Intuitive Theists'? Reasoning About Purpose and Design in Nature." *Psychological Science* 15:295–301.

33. W. Lipkind (1940), "Carajá Cosmography." *Journal of American Folk-Lore* 53:248–51.

34. W. Hamilton and G. Orians (1965), "Evolution of Brood Parasitism in Altricial Birds." *Condor* 67:361–82.

35. D. Sperber, *Explaining Culture*.

36. P. Boyer (1994), *The Naturalness of Religious Ideas: A Cognitive Theory of Religion*. Berkeley, CA: University of California Press.

37. A. Norenzayan, S. Atran, J. Faukner, and M. Schaller (2006), "Memory and Mystery: The Cultural Selection of Minimally Counterintuitive Narratives." *Cognitive Science* 30:531–53.

38. J. Barrett and M. Nyhof (2001), "Spreading Nonnatural Concepts." *Journal of Cognition and Culture* 1:69–100.

39. S. Atran (1989), "Basic Conceptual Domains." *Mind and Language* 4:7–16.

40. F. Newport (2007), "One-Third of Americans Believe the Bible Is Literally True, High Inverse Correlation Between Education and Belief in a Literal Bible." May 25, Princeton: Gallup News Service, www.gallup .com/poll/27682/OneThird-Americans-Believe-Bible-Literally-True.aspx.

41. Pew Research Organization (2007), Pew Report, *Muslim and Mostly Mainstream*, May 22. http://pewresearch.org/assets/pdf/muslim-americans .pdf.

42. T. Hobbes (1651; 1901), *Leviathan*. New York: E. P. Dutton.

43. J. Barrett and F. Keil (1996), "Conceptualizing a Nonnatural Entity: Anthropomorphism in God Concepts." *Cognitive Psychology* 31:219–47; B. Malley (2004), *How the Bible Works*. Lanham, MD: AltaMira Press.

44. L. Schlesinger (1999), *The Ten Commandments: The Significance of God's Laws in Everyday Life*. New York: HarperCollins.

45. S. Atran and A. Norenzayan (2004), "Religion's Evolutionary Landscape." *Behavioral and Brain Sciences* 27:713–70.

46. A. Frank (1993), *Anne Frank: The Diary of a Young Girl*. New York: Bantam (originally published in Dutch as *Het Achterhuis* in 1944).

47. A. Norenzayan and I. Hansen (2006), "Belief in Supernatural Agents in the Face of Death." *Personality and Social Psychology Bulletin* 32: 174–87.

48. M. Argyle and B. Beit-Hallahmi (2000), *The Social Psychology of Religion*. New York: Routledge.

49. J. Henrich and F. Gil-White (2001), "The Evolution of Prestige: Freely Conferred Deference as a Mechanism for Enhancing the Benefits of Cultural Transmission." *Evolution and Human Behavior* 22:165–96.

50. W. Beck (1992), "Aboriginal Preparations of Cycad Seeds in Australia." *Economic Botany* 46:133–47.

51. R. Byrne and A. Whiten (1998), *Machiavellian Intelligence: Social Expertise and the Evolution of Intellect in Monkeys, Apes, and Humans*. Oxford: Oxford University Press.

52. A. Tversky and D. Kahneman (1974), "Judgment Under Uncertainty: Heuristics and Biases." *Science* 185:1124–31.

53. L. Harper and K. Sanders (1975), "The Effect of Adults' Eating on Young Children's Acceptance of Unfamiliar Foods." *Journal of Experimental Child Psychology* 20:206–14.

54. N. Henrich and J. Henrich (2003), *Why Humans Cooperate: A Cultural and Evolutionary Explanation*. New York: Oxford University Press.

55. P. Harris (2006), "Germs and Angels: The Role of Testimony in Young Children's Ontology." *Developmental Science* 9:76–96.

56. L. Marks (2004), "Sacred Practices in Highly Religious Families: Christian, Jewish, Mormon, and Muslim Perspectives." *Family Process* 43:217–31.

57. R. Frank (1988), *Passions Within Reason*. New York: W. W. Norton.

58. L. Festinger, H. Riecken, and S. Schachter (1956), *When Prophecy Fails*. Minneapolis: University of Minnesota Press.

59. T. Tremlin and E. T. Lawson (2006), *Minds and Gods: The Cognitive Foundations of Religion*. New York: Oxford University Press.

60. T. Barfield, *Afghan Customary Law*. p. 13.

61. R. Sosis and E. Bressler (2003), "Cooperation and Commune Longevity: A Test of the Costly Signaling Theory." *Cross-Cultural Research* 37:211–39.

62. R. Sosis and B. Ruffle (2003), "Religious Ritual and Cooperation: Testing for a Relationship on Israeli Religious and Secular Kibbutzim." *Current Anthropology* 44:713–22.

63. A. Fishman and Y. Goldschmidt (1990), "The Orthodox Kibbutzim and Economic Success." *Journal for the Scientific Study of Religion* 29:505–11.

64. J. Marcus and K. Flannery (2004), "The Coevolution of Ritual and Society." *Proceedings of the National Academy of Sciences USA* 101:18257–61.

65. Lee, R. (1979), *The !Kung San: Men, Women and Work in a Foraging Society*. New York: Cambridge University Press.

66. Ibn Khaldûn (1377; 2005), *The Muqaddimah: An Introduction to History*. Princeton: Princeton University Press, ch. 3, sec. 3, pp. 125ff.

67. J. Ensminger (1997), "Transaction Costs and Islam: Explaining Conversion in Africa." *Journal of Institutional and Theoretical Economics* 153:4–28.

68. P. Freston (2001), *Evangelicals and Politics in Asia, Africa, and Latin America*. New York: Cambridge University Press.

69. M. Sweeney (2001), *King Josiah of Judah*. New York: Oxford University Press.

70. F. Roes and M. Raymond (2003), "Belief in Moralizing Gods." *Evolution and Human Behavior* 24:126–35.

71. R. Sosis, H. Kress, and J. Boster (2007), "Scars for War: Evaluating Signaling Explanations for Cross-Cultural Variance in Ritual Costs." *Evolution and Human Behavior* 28:234–47.

72. J. Ginges, I. Hansen, and A. Norenzayan (2009), "Religious and Popular Support for Suicide Attacks." *Psychological Science* 20:224–30.

73. R. Stark (1997), *The Rise of Christianity: How the Obscure, Marginal Jesus Movement Became the Dominant Force in the Western World in a Few Centuries*. New York: HarperCollins.

74. Flavius Josephus Ben Mathias (first century A.D.; 1981), *The Jewish War* [A.D. 67–73], bk. 7, 315–416. New York: Dorset Press.

CHAPTER 24: OUR RELIGIOUS WORLD

1. C. Smith, ed. (1996), *Disruptive Religion: The Force of Faith in Social-Movement Activism*. New York: Routledge.

2. R. Nisbett (2003), *The Geography of Thought: How Asians and Westerners Think Differently*. New York: Free Press.

3. R. Shweder, N. Much, M. Mahapatra, and L. Park (1997), "The 'Big Three' of Morality (Autonomy, Community, and Divinity), and the 'Big Three' Explanation of Suffering." In A. Brandt and P. Rozin (eds.), *Morality and Health*. New York: Routledge.

4. J. Haidt and C. Joseph (2004), "Intuitive Ethics: How Innately Prepared Intuitions Generate Culturally Variable Virtues." *Daedalus* 133:55–66.

5. L. Bartels (2008), *Unequal Democracy: The Political Economy of the New Gilded Age*. Princeton: Princeton University Press.

6. B. Goldwater (1960; 1990), *The Conscience of a Conservative*, repr. Washington: Regnery Gateway.

7. F. Fukuyama (1995), *Trust: The Social Virtues and the Creation of Prosperity*. New York: Free Press, pp. 46–47.

8. S. Lipset (1993), "Culture and Economic Behavior: A Commentary." *Journal of Labor Economics* 11:S330–47.

9. Pew Forum on Religion and Cultural Life (2006), a Ten-Country Survey of Pentecostals, October. http://pewforum.org/surveys/pentecostal.

10. D. Brooks (2008), "Surprise Me Most." *New York Times*, September 9.

11. Y. Fer (2008), "Sarah Palin, une drôle de paroissienne." *Le Monde*, September 11.

12. A. de Tocqueville (1835; 1984), *Democracy in America*. New York: Penguin, pp. 153–55, 200–201.

13. Cited in "Palin's God Too Much for Presidency" (2008), *You Decide 2008*, September 12. www.youdecide2008.com/2008/09/12/palins-god-too-much-for-presidency.

14. R. Tucker, ed. (1978), *The Marx-Engels Reader*. New York: W. W. Norton, p. 477.

15. K. Marx and F. Engels (1953), *Letters to Americans*. New York: International Publishers, p. 204.

16. H. Gerth and C. Wright Mills, eds. (1946), *From Max Weber: Essays in Sociology*. New York: Oxford University Press, p. 303.

17. L. Ross and C. Stillinger (1991), "Barriers to Conflict Resolution." *Negotiation Journal* 8:389–404.

18. M. Gelfand et al. (2001), "Culture and Egocentric Biases of Fairness in Conflict and Negotiation." *Journal of Applied Psychology* 86:1059–74.

19. S. Schama (2009), *The American Future: A History*. New York: Ecco, p. 182.

20. V. Hugo (1859), Letter written from Hauteville-House, Guernsey, December 2, in V. Hugo (1889), *Actes et Paroles 2, Pendant l'exil: 1852–1870*.

21. K. Chowder (2000), "The Father of American Terrorism." *American Heritage* 51:81.

22. A. Toynbee (1972), *A Study of History*. New York: Oxford University Press.

23. R. Dawkins (2006), *The God Delusion*. New York: Houghton Mifflin.

24. S. Harris (2004), *The End of Faith: Religion, Terrorism, and the Future of Reason*. New York: W. W. Norton.

25. Cited in S. Le Bars and F. Supiot (2008), "Les religions à l'épreuve de la mondialisation." *Le Monde*, December 21–22, p. 14.

26. M. Sageman (2008), *Leaderless Jihad*. Philadelphia: University of Pennsylvania Press.

27. Mustafa Setmariam Nasar (2005), *Da'wah lil-Muqawamah Al-Islamiyyah Al-'Alamiyyah* [A Call for the Islamic Global Resistance]. www.fsboa .com/vw/index.php?subject=7&rec=27&tit=tit&pa=0.

28. L. Beam (1983), *Leaderless Resistance*. http://reactor-core.org/leaderless-resistance.html.

29. W. Pierce (1978), *The Turner Diaries*. Washington, DC: National Alliance (written under the pen name Andrew MacDonald).

30. W. Pierce (2001), "Free Speech." November 7. www.natvan.com/free-speech/fs0111c.html.

31. S. Huntington (1996), *The Clash of Civilizations and the Remaking of the World Order*. New York: Simon & Schuster.

32. C. Hitchens (2007), *God Is Not Great: How Religion Poisons Everything*. New York: Twelve.

33. D. Dennett (2005), *Breaking the Spell: Religion as a Cultural Phenomenon*. New York: Viking Adult.

34. G. Paul and P. Zuckerman (2007), "Why the Gods Are Not Winning." Edge.org, "The Third Culture." www.edge.org/3rd_culture/paul07/paul07_index.html.

35. D. Park, J. Bafu, and B. Shor (2007), "Statistical Modeling, Causal Inference, and Social Science: Comparing Red States and Blue States." November 4, Religiosity and Income in the U.S. www.stat.columbia .edu/~cook/movabletype/archives/2007/11/religiosity_and.html.

36. Pew Global Attitudes Project (2007), "World Publics Welcome Global Trade—but Not Immigration." April 10. http://pewglobal.org/reports/display.php?ReportID=258.

37. Ibid.

38. European Commission (2005), "Social Values, Science and Technology." Special *Eurobarometer*, 225/Wave 63.1, June, http://ec.europa.eu/public_opinion/archives/ebs/ebs_225_report_en.pdf.

39. P. Forese (2008), *The Plot to Kill God: Findings from the Soviet Experiment in Secularization*. Berkeley: University of California Press.

40. The Chinese government may be making the same mistake. In October 2007, I was invited to Beijing, along with some prominent new atheists, to give a talk on religion that was cosponsored by the Chinese government Commission on Atheism, whose goal is to eliminate religion by using science education to replace "superstition." In my talk, I said that equating religion with superstition is naive. (To my surprise, I was applauded anyway, only to realize that many in the audience, like those attending the Communist Party Congress that was going on at the same time, applauded just about anything said from a government-sanctioned pulpit.)

41. R. Stark (1997), *The Rise of Christianity: How the Obscure, Marginal Jesus Movement Became the Dominant Force in the Western World in a Few Centuries*. New York: HarperCollins.

42. R. Stark (2008), *What Americans Really Believe*. Waco, TX: Baylor University Press.

ABE'S ANSWER—THE QUESTION OF POLITICS

1. A. Lincoln, cited in W. Ury (1991), *Getting Past No: Negotiating with Difficult People*. New York: Bantam Books, p. 146.

2. A. Elliot (2007), "Where Boys Grow Up to Be Jihadis." *New York Times Magazine*, November 25.

3. The backdrop of the series is that when the Mongols sacked the imperial city of Baghdad in A.D. 1258, they "planned not only to conquer the greatest empire the world had ever known, but to eradicate its hope—its potential—thereby destroying its future. That would require more than sword and club, sinew and blood. That would require destroying the empire's true base of power . . . destroying its knowledge." But just before the last great Arab caliphate expired, and its vast library burned down, the Abbasid scholars and scientists used alchemy to invest 99 magical gems with all of the library's knowledge. These "Noor Stones" (*al-nur*, "the Light," an attribute of Allah) were scattered around the world, but when they are found by the right person, they give him or her an extraordinary power derived from one of the 99 names of God: Jabbar, a combination of Samson and the Hulk; Noora, who lords over light; Darr, the giver of terrible pain; Raqib, the far-seeing watcher; and so on. When all the gems are found, and their powers combined in the perfect community of 99 superheroes, invincible good will govern the earth.

4. C. Dickey (2008), "'Jihadi Cool.'" *Newsweek*, April 15. www.newsweek.com/id/132147.

5. S. Atran (2009), "Barack's Nobel: A Symbolic Gesture of Hope to the World's Youth." Huffington Post, October 10. www.huffingtonpost.com/scott-atran/baracks-nobel-a-symbolic_b_316442.html.

6. In December 2009, we asked a randomized sample of 1,200 Palestinians in Gaza and the West Bank to rank people according to how much they admire them. Topping the heap was Marwan Barghouti, leader of Fateh's "Young Guard," who is currently serving multiple life sentences in an Israeli jail for involvement in suicide bombings. Next was Hizbollah leader Hassan Nasrallah. Osama bin Laden and Iranian president Mahmoud Ahmadinejad ranked in the middle. Barack Obama came dead last, a telling indication of fading hopes in his promise for a new commitment to peace and justice in the Middle East, as expressed in his June 2009 Cairo speech. Words are necessary but not sufficient, and if spoken need to be followed up lest they be considered insincere and better not to have been uttered at all.

7. In June 2010, the United States Supreme Court upheld a law banning the provision of "material support" to groups listed by the State Department as terrorist organizations, including any talking to terrorists that involves communication of expert or scientific knowledge and information. The decision didn't consider as relevant the fact that not all such groups are equally bad or dangerous. Some groups that were widely considered terrorist organizations have become our partners in pursuing peace and furthering democracy.

    The African National Congress is now the democratically elected ruling party in South Africa, and of course Nelson Mandela is widely considered a great man of peace. The Provisional Irish Republican Army now preaches nonviolence, and its longtime leader, Martin McGuinness, is Northern Ireland's first deputy minister. Mahmoud Abbas and the Palestinian Liberation Organization have become central players in Middle East peace negotiations. In each case, private citizens—clergymen, academics, scientists, and others—worked behind the scenes to end the violence by exchanging reliable knowledge.

    War and group violence are ever present, and their prevention requires constant effort and innovation. Sometimes this means listening and talking with enemies and probing gray areas for ways forward to figure out who is truly a mortal foe and who just might become a friend. See S. Atran and R. Axelrod (2010), "Why We Talk to Terrorists." *New York Times*, June 30.

INDEX

Page numbers of illustrations appear in *italics*.